Frommer's®
Seattle

My Seattle
by Karl Samson

FLYING FISH, A GIANT HAMMERING MAN, AND A GROUP OF PEOPLE

waiting for a streetcar that hasn't run in decades. What do these have in common? They're among my favorite images of Seattle, and together they sum up this city's off-kilter aesthetic. Perhaps Seattle's slightly skewed sensibility is a response to the city's drop-dead gorgeous setting on Puget Sound. When you're living in Paradise, why not have a little fun? All it takes is one glance over the city at sunset to understand how Seattle seduces people. To the west, the Olympic Mountains rise on the far side of the Sound. To the southeast looms the immense bulk of Mount Rainier. On all sides of the city, the surrounding lakes and bays sparkle in the setting sun. There's no better place to take in these views than from atop the Space Needle, Seattle's retro-futuristic architectural icon.

In case you're wondering about those other Seattle icons, fish fly daily at Seattle's Public Market, Jonathon Borofsky's *Hammering Man* towers over the Seattle Art Museum's front door, and those hapless sculptured souls have been *Waiting for the Interurban,* in funky Fremont, for years. Sympathetic Seattleites often dress this latter sculpture in seasonally appropriate, if not entirely stylish, attire. That's just the way Seattle is—a little bit quirky, a whole lot of fun.

FISHMONGERS AT PIKE PLACE MARKET (left) You might not think that a whole salmon is the perfect souvenir of your summer vacation, but the fishmongers of Pike Place Market will be glad to pack your purchase on dry ice so you can take it home on the plane.

SPACE NEEDLE AND CITY SKYLINE (above) Built for the 1962 World's Fair, the Space Needle is the most immediately recognizable symbol of Seattle. On a clear day (or night) the view from the top takes in mountains, the Puget Sound, and the city. But to best see the Space Needle framed by Seattle, you need to head up to Kerry Viewpoint on the slopes of Queen Anne Hill.

© Lawrence Worcester/Lonely Planet Images

© Chuck Pefley/Alamy

WAITING FOR THE INTERURBAN (above) You'd probably look just as downcast as these folks if you were waiting for a trolley that doesn't run. This sculpture, called *Waiting for the Interurban,* is located in the Fremont neighborhood—Seattle's proletariat-turned-hipster haven—and is often dressed in seasonally appropriate clothing.

SEATTLE CENTRAL LIBRARY (right) While local libraries usually aren't on most vacation itineraries, the Seattle Central Library is one book collection that should not be missed. Before it opened, architect Rem Koolhaas's bold house of glass and steel was as controversial as *The Catcher in the Rye* in a conservative school district.

PIKE PLACE MARKET (right) Sure, Pike Place Market is touristy, but there's so much to see, do, and eat here that it's easy to spend a whole day wandering around this maze of shops. Founded in 1907 as a farmer's market, the Public Market was saved from demolition in the 1970s and is now a National Historic District.

MOUNT RAINIER AND GIG HARBOR MARINA (below) Almost everywhere you turn in the Puget Sound area, you catch glimpses of mountains across the water. Here Mount Rainier looks over Gig Harbor Marina and the waters of the south Sound.

HAMMERING MAN (left) No, it's not Paul Bunyan's shadow; it's Jonathon Borofsky's *Hammering Man,* an animated, three-story steel sculpture that stands outside the main entrance to the Seattle Art Museum. The museum specializes in both Northwest Coast Indian art and African art.

SAFECO FIELD AT SUNSET (below) Seattle may have a soggy reputation, but you don't have to worry about a Mariners game getting rained out at Safeco Field. When the weather is inclement, the retractable roof is rolled closed and the baseball game continues.

FERRY ARRIVING IN FRIDAY HARBOR
(above) In this city surrounded by water, no visit is complete without spending some time on a boat. The behemoth car ferries that ply Puget Sound and the San Juan Islands are an economical way to get out on the water. Many ferries charge passengers only in one direction, so for the price of a one-way ticket, you can do a round-trip ride.

CENTER FOR WOODEN BOATS (right)
If you're looking for something more interesting than the big-tour-boat experience, head to the Center for Wooden Boats, at the south end of Lake Union. You can sign up for a brief cruise or rent one of their handsome little boats and sail on your own.

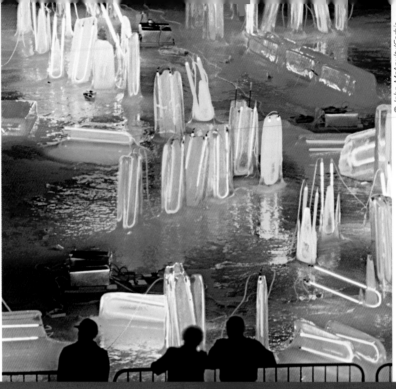

LIGHT AND WATER INSTALLATION (above) Tacoma's native son Dale Chihuly has almost single-handedly turned the Puget Sound area into one of the most important art-glass-producing regions on earth. However, Chihuly has also been known to work in ice and neon, as in this installation that he once staged at the Tacoma Dome.

A BEAUTIFULLY POURED LATTE (right) As just about everyone on the planet knows, Seattle has long been obsessed with coffee, and this obsession has raised the pouring of a latte to an art form. Sure you can grab your coffee on the run, but it's much more relaxing to savor a cup that's perfect to the last drop.

W HOTEL SEATTLE (right) Judging by the number of residents you'll see dressed in black, Seattle can claim a respectable hip quotient. So where do these hip folks hang out? Right downtown you'll find the luxurious and stylish W Seattle. Even if you don't stay here, you can lounge around in its swanky lobby, the "Living Room."

EXPERIENCE MUSIC PROJECT (below) Some people say it looks like a giant melted guitar, which is fitting for a building that houses a museum of rock 'n' roll. Designed by architect Frank Gehry, the EMP was originally planned as a memorial to Seattle native Jimi Hendrix.

© W Seattle

© Douglas Peebles/Corbis

**MOUNT SHUKSAN WITH PICTURE LAKE
(left)** A long day trip or a quick overnight from Seattle can get you into spectacular alpine scenery on Mount Rainier, Olympic National Park, or Mount Baker and the North Cascades National Park Complex. Just remember that up in the mountains, snow often lingers into July.

HYDROFOIL RACES (below) Every summer, days of thunder return to Seattle's Lake Washington as the month-long Seafair festival stages its popular hydroplane boat races. Think of it as NASCAR on water as these monster boats roar up and down the lake, kicking up huge rooster tails.

CHERRY BLOSSOMS AT THE UW (above)
Spring weather in Seattle may frequently be gray and drizzly, but all that rain brings out an explosion of color across the city as gardens burst into bloom. Cherry trees on the University of Washington campus put on one of the best spring floral displays.

ORCA WHALE OFF LIME KILN PARK (right)
Orca whales, along with salmon, are the quintessential symbols of the Northwest, and during the summer the two come together off the western shore of San Juan Island. Here, off Lime Kiln State Park, orcas gather to feed on salmon and can often be seen just offshore.

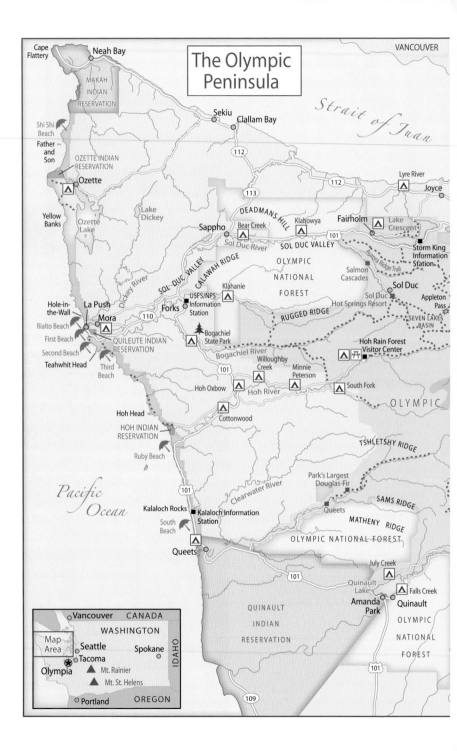

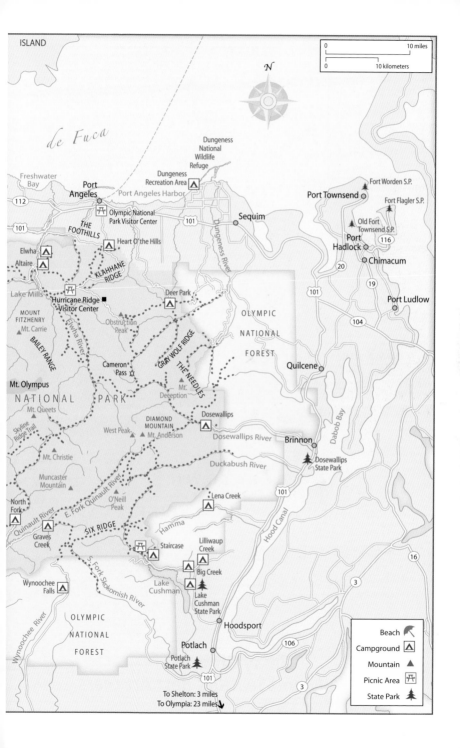

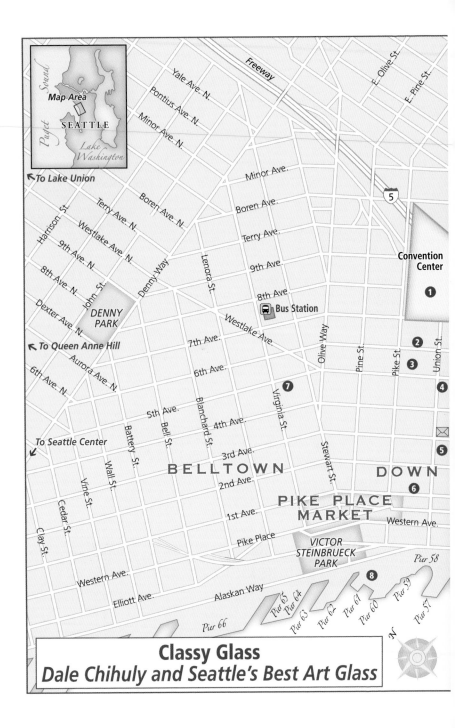

Classy Glass
Dale Chihuly and Seattle's Best Art Glass

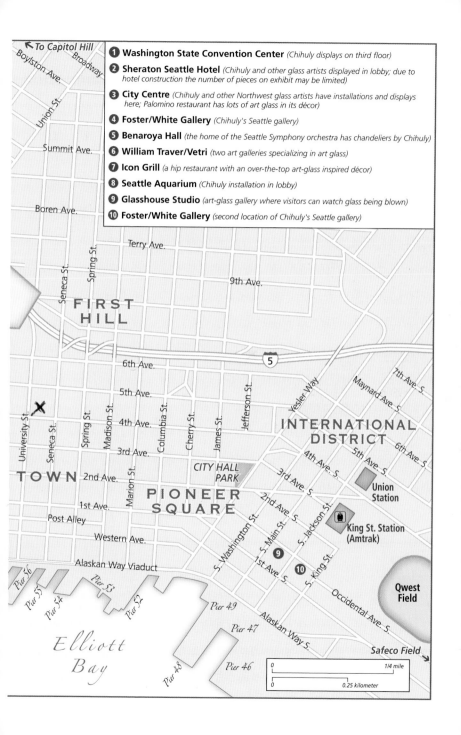

1 **Washington State Convention Center** (Chihuly displays on third floor)

2 **Sheraton Seattle Hotel** (Chihuly and other glass artists displayed in lobby; due to hotel construction the number of pieces on exhibit may be limited)

3 **City Centre** (Chihuly and other Northwest glass artists have installations and displays here; Palomino restaurant has lots of art glass in its décor)

4 **Foster/White Gallery** (Chihuly's Seattle gallery)

5 **Benaroya Hall** (the home of the Seattle Symphony orchestra has chandeliers by Chihuly)

6 **William Traver/Vetri** (two art galleries specializing in art glass)

7 **Icon Grill** (a hip restaurant with an over-the-top art-glass inspired décor)

8 **Seattle Aquarium** (Chihuly installation in lobby)

9 **Glasshouse Studio** (art-glass gallery where visitors can watch glass being blown)

10 **Foster/White Gallery** (second location of Chihuly's Seattle gallery)

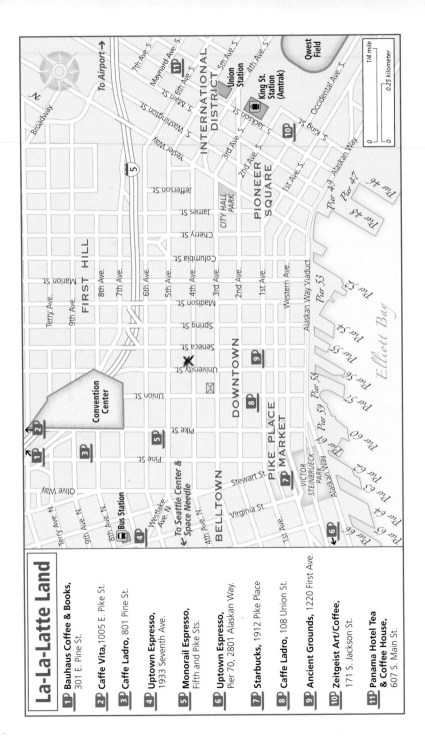

La-La-Latte Land

1. **Bauhaus Coffee & Books,** 301 E. Pine St.

2. **Caffe Vita,** 1005 E. Pine St.

3. **Caffe Ladro,** 801 Pine St.

4. **Uptown Espresso,** 1933 Seventh Ave.

5. **Monorail Espresso,** Fifth and Pike Sts.

6. **Uptown Espresso,** Pier 70, 2801 Alaskan Way.

7. **Starbucks,** 1912 Pike Place

8. **Caffe Ladro,** 108 Union St.

9. **Ancient Grounds,** 1220 First Ave.

10. **Zeitgeist Art/Coffee,** 171 S. Jackson St.

11. **Panama Hotel Tea & Coffee House,** 607 S. Main St.

Frommer's®

Seattle 2010

by Karl Samson

WILEY

Wiley Publishing, Inc.

ABOUT THE AUTHOR

Karl Samson lives in Oregon, where he spends his time juggling his obsessions with traveling, gardening, outdoor sports, and wine. Each winter, to dry out his webbed feet, he flees the soggy Northwest to update *Frommer's Arizona*. Karl is also the author of *Frommer's Washington State* and *Frommer's Oregon*.

Published by:

WILEY PUBLISHING, INC.

111 River St.
Hoboken, NJ 07030-5774

ISBN 978-0-470-49771-5

Editor: John Vorwald with Anuja Madar
Production Editor: Jana M. Stefanciosa
Cartographer: Roberta Stockwell
Production by Wiley Indianapolis Composition Services

Front cover photo: Seattle Washington, Space Needle amongst vertical pieces of public Space art work. ©Larry Trupp / Alamy Images
Back cover photo: Neon signs at night Pike's Place Market. ©D. Hurst / Alamy Images

For information on our other products and services or to obtain technical support, please contact our Customer Care Department within the U.S. at 877/762-2974, outside the U.S. at 317/572-3993 or fax 317/572-4002.

Wiley also publishes its books in a variety of electronic formats. Some content that appears in print may not be available in electronic formats.

Manufactured in the United States of America

5 4 3 2 1

CONTENTS

8 CITY STROLLS 157

9 SEATTLE SHOPPING 169

10 SEATTLE AFTER DARK 184

11 SIDE TRIPS FROM SEATTLE 198

12 FAST FACTS 258

INDEX 266

LIST OF MAPS

HOW TO CONTACT US

In researching this book, we discovered many wonderful places—hotels, restaurants, shops, and more. We're sure you'll find others. Please tell us about them, so we can share the information with your fellow travelers in upcoming editions. If you were disappointed with a recommendation, we'd love to know that, too. Please write to:

Frommer's Seattle 2010
Wiley Publishing, Inc. • 111 River St. • Hoboken, NJ 07030-5774

AN ADDITIONAL NOTE

Please be advised that travel information is subject to change at any time—and this is especially true of prices. We therefore suggest that you write or call ahead for confirmation when making your travel plans. The authors, editors, and publisher cannot be held responsible for the experiences of readers while traveling. Your safety is important to us, however, so we encourage you to stay alert and be aware of your surroundings. Keep a close eye on cameras, purses, and wallets, all favorite targets of thieves and pickpockets.

FROMMER'S STAR RATINGS, ICONS & ABBREVIATIONS

Every hotel, restaurant, and attraction listing in this guide has been ranked for quality, value, service, amenities, and special features using a **star-rating system.** In country, state, and regional guides, we also rate towns and regions to help you narrow down your choices and budget your time accordingly. Hotels and restaurants are rated on a scale of zero (recommended) to three stars (exceptional). Attractions, shopping, nightlife, towns, and regions are rated according to the following scale: zero stars (recommended), one star (highly recommended), two stars (very highly recommended), and three stars (must-see).

In addition to the star-rating system, we also use **seven feature icons** that point you to the great deals, in-the-know advice, and unique experiences that separate travelers from tourists. Throughout the book, look for:

Finds	Special finds—those places only insiders know about
Fun Facts	Fun facts—details that make travelers more informed and their trips more fun
Kids	Best bets for kids, and advice for the whole family
Moments	Special moments—those experiences that memories are made of
Overrated	Places or experiences not worth your time or money
Tips	Insider tips—great ways to save time and money
Value	Great values—where to get the best deals

The following **abbreviations** are used for credit cards:

AE	American Express	**DISC**	Discover	**V**	Visa
DC	Diners Club	**MC**	MasterCard		

TRAVEL RESOURCES AT FROMMERS.COM

Frommer's travel resources don't end with this guide. **Frommers.com** has travel information on more than 4,000 destinations. We update features regularly, giving you access to the most current trip-planning information and the best airfare, lodging, and car-rental bargains. You can also listen to podcasts, connect with other Frommers.com members through our active-reader forums, share your travel photos, read blogs from guidebook editors and fellow travelers, and much more.

The Best of Seattle

Imagine yourself sitting in a park on the Seattle waterfront, a double- tall latte and a marionberry scone close at hand. The snowy peaks of the Olympic Mountains shimmer on the far side of Puget Sound, while ferryboats come and go across Elliott Bay. It's a summer day, and the sun is shining. (Hey, as long as we're dreaming, why not dream big?) It just doesn't get much better than this, unless, of course, you swap the latte for a microbrew and catch a 9:30pm summer sunset. No wonder people love this town so much.

Okay, so the waterfront is as touristy as San Francisco's Fisherman's Wharf, but what a view! Seattle is a city of views, and for many visitors, the must-see vista is the panorama from the top of the Space Needle. With the 21st century in full swing, this 1960s-vintage image of the future may look decidedly 20th-century retro, but still, it's hard to resist an expensive elevator ride in any city. You can even take a monorail straight out of *The Jetsons* to get there (and, en route, pass right through the Frank Gehry–designed Experience Music Project).

EMP, as the Experience Music Project is known, is yet another of Seattle's architectural oddities. Its swooping, multicolored, metal-skinned bulk rises at the foot of the Space Needle, proof that real 21st-century architecture looks nothing like the vision of the future people dreamed of when the Space Needle was built for the 1962 World's Fair. EMP was the brainchild of Microsoft co-founder Paul Allen, who built this rock-'n'-roll cathedral to house his vast collection of Northwest rock memorabilia. Housed inside the bizarre building, you'll also find Allen's Science Fiction Museum (is this town a computer nerd's dream come true, or what?).

Allen's money has now changed the architectural face of both the north and south ends of downtown Seattle. At the south end, you'll find the state-of-the-art Qwest Field— home to Allen's Seattle Seahawks NFL football team. Together with the Seattle Mariners' Safeco Field, Qwest Field is part of a massive sports-arena district. At the north end of downtown, near the southern shore of Lake Union, Allen is busily creating the South Lake Union district, a neighborhood of modern condominiums, office buildings, and retail spaces that are transforming what for years was one of the city's most overlooked and underutilized close-in neighborhoods. There is even a streetcar line here that connects downtown Seattle with Lake Union.

Allen projects aside, Seattle is a vibrant city with a bustling downtown that has seen numerous big development projects in recent years. In 2007, the Seattle Art Museum opened a major expansion that turned this art repository into a world-class museum. The museum's Olympic Sculpture Park opened its doors that same year. Located at the north end of the waterfront, this hillside sculpture park, with its monumental sculptures and its breathtaking views of the Olympic Mountains, is unequaled in the Northwest, not only for its collection of sculptures, but also for its scale and landscaping. In 2009, Seattle's light-rail system began running between downtown and Tukwila (near Seattle-Tacoma International Airport). An extension all the way to the airport was expected to open in December 2009.

It's clear that Seattle has not grown complacent despite the ups and downs of the fickle high-tech industry from which the city now derives so much of its wealth. Sure, it has traffic congestion to rival that of L.A. And, yes, the weather really is lousy for most of the year.

But Seattleites manage to overcome these minor inconveniences, in large part by spilling out into the streets and parks whenever the sun shines. To visit Seattle in the summer is to witness an exodus; follow the lead of the locals and head for the great outdoors. Should you brave a visit in the rainy season, don't despair: There are compensations for such misfortune, including a roof on Pike Place Market and an espresso bar on every block.

WATER, WATER EVERYWHERE . . . & FORESTS & MOUNTAINS, TOO

Over the years, through Boeing's booms and busts, the rise and fall of grunge, the coming and going of Frasier, and the bursting of the high-tech bubble economy, one thing has stayed the same here in Seattle: the beautiful and wild landscape that surrounds the city. The sparkling waters of Elliott Bay, Lake Union, and Lake Washington wrap around this city of shimmering skyscrapers, and forests of evergreens crowd the city limits. Everywhere you look, another breathtaking vista unfolds. With endless boating opportunities, and beaches and mountains within a few hours' drive, Seattle is ideally situated for the outdoor pursuits that are so important to the fabric of life in the Northwest.

Few other cities in the United States are as immersed in the outdoors aesthetic as Seattle. The Cascade Range lies less than 50 miles to the east of downtown Seattle, and across Puget Sound stand the Olympic Mountains. In the spring, summer, and fall, the forests and mountains attract hikers, mountain bikers, anglers, and campers, while in winter, the ski areas of Snoqualmie Pass, Stephens Pass, and Crystal Mountain draw snowboarders and skiers.

Though impressive mountains line the city's eastern and western horizons, a glance to the southeast on a sunny day will reveal Seattle's most treasured sight—Mount Rainier, a 14,410-foot-tall dormant volcano that looms large, so unexpected that it demands your attention. When "the Mountain is out," as they say here in Seattle, Seattleites head for the hills.

However, as important as "the Mountain" is to Seattle, it is water that truly defines the city's character. And I don't mean the city's infamous rain. To the west lies Elliott Bay, an arm of Puget Sound; to the east is Lake Washington; and right in the middle of the city is Lake Union. With so much water, Seattle has become a city of boaters, who take to the water in everything from regally appointed yachts to slender sea kayaks. Consequently, the opening day of boating season has become one of Seattle's most popular annual festivals.

However, Seattle is perhaps best known as the coffee capital of America. To understand Seattle's coffee addiction, it is necessary to study the city's geography and climate. Seattle lies at almost 50 degrees north latitude, which means that winter days are short. The sun comes up around 7:30am, goes down as early as 4:30pm, and is frequently hidden behind leaden skies. A strong stimulant is almost a necessity to get people out of bed through the gray days of winter. Seattleites love to argue over which espresso bar or cafe in town serves the best coffee (and the answer isn't always Starbucks, despite the famous coffee company's global expansion from its humble beginnings in Seattle).

So pack your travel mug and your rain jacket, and, just for good measure, don't forget your sunglasses (who knows, you might get lucky). You can leave the suit and the Italian shoes at home; remember, this is a city that turned casual Fridays into a way of life. Now, for a few more tips on how to get the most out of your visit to Seattle, peruse these listings of some of Seattle's best.

1 THE MOST UNFORGETTABLE SEATTLE EXPERIENCES

- **Eating Your Way Through Pike Place Market:** Breakfast at Le Pichet, espresso at what was once the only Starbucks in the world, lunch at Café Campagne, a martini at The Pink Door, dinner at Matt's in the Market, Celtic music at Kells, and a nightcap at Il Bistro—that's how you could spend a day at Pike Place. Between stops on this rigorous itinerary, you can people-watch, listen to street musicians, and shop for everything from fresh salmon to tropical fruits, to magic tricks, to art glass. See chapters 6 and 10.

- **Strolling the Olympic Sculpture Park:** With views of Puget Sound and the Olympic Mountains and sculptures by Alexander Calder, Claes Oldenburg, and Richard Serra, this terraced park at the north end of the Seattle waterfront is great for a stroll any time of day, but is absolutely sublime at sunset. See p. 124.

- **Joining the Underground:** Rome has its catacombs, Paris has its sewers, and Seattle has its underground. Now, some people, including my own brother, think I'm nuts for enjoying the Seattle Underground tour, but corny sewer jokes aside, this tour is fascinating and a great introduction to the seamier side of Seattle's early history. See p. 138.

- **Spending an Afternoon in the Ballard Neighborhood:** Watch the salmon climb the fish ladders and swim past viewing windows at the Hiram M. Chittenden (Ballard) Locks. Check out the exhibits at the Nordic Heritage Museum, and then stroll the shady streets of old Ballard. Have a meal at Ray's Boathouse, keeping an eye out for bald eagles, and then finish the day on the beach at Golden Gardens Park. See chapter 7.

- **Taking a Cruise:** Seattle is best seen from a boat, and there are plenty of vessels that will take you out on the water. Personally, I prefer sailboat outings from the waterfront, but for a more informative and diverse excursion, take the Argosy Cruises tour from Lake Union to the waterfront. If you don't mind flaunting the fact that you're a tourist, there's the daffy Seattle Duck Tour. See p. 147. X-ref is to "Boat Tours," in chapter 7.

- **Visiting Volunteer Park:** Whether the day is sunny or gray, this park on Capitol Hill is a great spot to spend an afternoon. You can relax in the grass, study Chinese snuff bottles in the Seattle Asian Art Museum, marvel at the orchids in the conservatory, or simply enjoy the great view of the city from the top of the park's water tower. See p. 135.

- **Riding the Water Taxi to Alki Beach:** The water taxi that operates between the Seattle waterfront and Alki Beach, on the far side of Elliott Bay, is practically the cheapest boat ride you can take in Seattle. Once you get to Alki Beach, you can dine with a killer view of the Seattle skyline, and then go for a walk or bike ride on the beachfront path. See p. 148.

- **Sea Kayaking on Lake Union:** Lake Union is a very urban body of water, but it has a great view of the Seattle skyline, and you can paddle right up to several waterfront restaurants. For more natural surroundings, kayak over to the marshes at the north end of the Washington Park Arboretum. See p. 153.

2 THE BEST SPLURGE HOTELS

- **Doubletree Arctic Club Hotel,** 700 Third Ave. (© **800/222-TREE**): If you love the romance of travel as much as I do, then you'll want to stay at this historic hotel. Built in 1917 as an exclusive men's club, the Arctic Club has a sort of art deco travel theme in its decor. It's delightfully retro and exotic. See p. 66.
- **The Edgewater,** Pier 67, 2411 Alaskan Way (© **800/624-0670**): For a sense of being immersed in all things Seattle, there is no better hotel choice than the Edgewater, which is located on a pier on the Seattle waterfront. The hotel is also only 5 blocks from Pike Place Market and the Seattle Aquarium and 3 blocks from the restaurants of Belltown. See p. 54.
- **The Fairmont Olympic Hotel,** 411 University St. (© **800/223-8772**): Built in 1924, this classic grande dame hotel is styled after an Italian Renaissance palace and is by far the most impressive of Seattle's handful of historic hotels. The grand lobby is unrivaled. See p. 58.
- **Four Seasons Seattle,** 99 Union St. (© **800/819-5053**): This modern luxury hotel has an enviable location adjacent to Pike Place Market and across the street from the Seattle Art Museum.

Add a year-round outdoor pool and spacious rooms with views of Elliott Bay and the Olympic Mountains, and you have the perfect hotel for a Seattle vacation. See p. 58.
- **Hotel Ändra,** 2000 Fourth Ave. (© **877/448-8600**): This is a city that likes to keep up with the trends, and the Hotel Ändra is a boldly contemporary lodging that competes directly with the W Seattle. Best of all, it's on the edge of the trendy Belltown neighborhood, which makes this an ideal base for foodies and club-crawling night owls. See p. 64.
- **Hotel 1000,** 1000 First Ave. (© **877/315-1088**): Big rooms have walls of glass that take in great views of the city and Elliott Bay, and the bathrooms are works of art. A special golf room even lets you play virtual golf at more than 50 famous golf courses. See p. 58.
- **Inn at the Market,** 86 Pine St. (© **800/446-4484**): Though Seattle has quite a few hotels that do well for a romantic weekend, the Inn at the Market, with its Elliott Bay views, European atmosphere, and proximity to many excellent (and romantic) restaurants, is sure to set the stage for lasting memories. See p. 65.

3 THE BEST MODERATELY PRICED HOTELS

- **Comfort Suites Downtown/Seattle Center,** 601 Roy St. (© **877/424-6423**): Only about 4 blocks from Seattle Center and the Space Needle, this modern budget hotel offers spacious rooms and a convenient location. Throw in some good restaurants within walking distance, and you have a little gem in a well-hidden corner of the city. See p. 67.

- **Gaslight Inn,** 1727 15th Ave. (© **206/325-3654**): Set in the Capitol Hill neighborhood, this B&B is in a lovingly restored and maintained Craftsman bungalow filled with original Stickley furniture. Lots of public spaces, very tasteful decor, and a swimming pool in the backyard all add up to unexpected luxury for a Seattle B&B. See p. 73.

- **Hotel Deca,** 4507 Brooklyn Ave. NE (℡ **800/899-0251**): This hotel is reasonably priced for what you get—it's one of the most stylish contemporary accommodations in Seattle. Ask for a room on an upper floor, and you'll also get good views. See p. 73.
- **Silver Cloud Inn–Lake Union,** 1150 Fairview Ave. N. (℡ **800/330-5812**): Situated across the street from Lake Union and close to Seattle Center, this hotel is just far enough from downtown to be affordable—and, best of all, it has a great location overlooking the lake. There's an indoor pool and several restaurants right across the street. See p. 71.
- **University Inn,** 4140 Roosevelt Way NE (℡ **800/733-3855**): Located close to the University of Washington and several museums, this hotel has attractive rooms and is an exceptional value. There's a small pool, and guests get to use the exercise room at a nearby sister property. See p. 74.

4 THE MOST UNFORGETTABLE DINING EXPERIENCES

- **Dahlia Lounge,** 2001 Fourth Ave. (℡ **206/682-4142**): You can't say that you've "done" Seattle if you haven't eaten at one of Tom Douglas's restaurants, and for my money, the Dahlia Lounge is the place to go if you're going to dine at only one of Tom's places. A dinner of crab cakes followed by coconut-cream pie captures the absolute essence of this place. See p. 92.
- **Elliott's,** Pier 56, 1201 Alaskan Way (℡ **206/623-4340**): The Northwest produces an astonishing variety of oysters, and locals are almost as obsessive about their bivalves as they are about coffee and beer. Elliott's almost always has the biggest and best selection of oysters in the city. Just remember that local oysters are less available in the summer than in other months. See p. 88.
- **The Herbfarm Restaurant,** 14590 NE 145th St., Woodinville (℡ **425/485-5300**): The Herbfarm is actually 30 minutes north of Seattle, but it is so famous and serves such unforgettable meals that people plan Seattle vacations around dinner here. This place is an absolute must for foodies, but be sure to make your reservation months in advance. See p. 249.
- **Rover's,** 2808 E. Madison St. (℡ **206/325-7442**): Want to feel like you've just discovered the best little hidden gem of a restaurant in Seattle? Book a table at chef Thierry Rautureau's Madison Valley neighborhood restaurant. Rautureau combines his love of local ingredients with his classic French training to produce his own distinctive take on Northwest cuisine. See p. 106.
- **Salumi,** 309 Third Ave. S. (℡ **206/621-8772**): Squeeze your way into this Pioneer Square hole-in-the-wall, stand in line, and then savor the finest, freshest artisan-made salami in the Northwest. The fact that this place is owned by celeb-chef Mario Batali's father guarantees that the lines are always long. See p. 100.

5 THE BEST THINGS TO DO FOR FREE (OR ALMOST)

- **Taking in the Sunset from the Waterfront:** On a clear summer day, the setting sun silhouettes the Olympic Mountains on the far side of Puget Sound and makes the view from the Seattle waterfront truly memorable. Try the rooftop park at the Bell Street Pier, Myrtle Edwards Park at the north end of the waterfront, the lounge at The Edgewater hotel, or, my personal favorite sunset spot, the Olympic Sculpture Park, which is adjacent to Myrtle Edwards Park. See "The Waterfront" in chapter 7.

- **Riding a Ferry Across Puget Sound:** Sure, you could spend $20 or $30 for a narrated tour of the Seattle waterfront, but for a fraction of that, you can take a ferry to Bremerton or Bainbridge Island and see not just Elliott Bay, but plenty more of Puget Sound. Keep an eye out for porpoises and bald eagles. See p. 30.

- **Relaxing over a Latte:** If the rain and gray skies start to get to you, there is no better pick-me-up (short of a ticket to the tropics) than a frothy latte in a cozy cafe. Grab a magazine and just hang out until the rain stops (maybe sometime in July). See "Coffee, Tea, Bakeries & Pastry Shops" in chapter 6.

- **Riding the Monorail:** Though the ride is short, covering a distance that could easily be walked in half an hour, the monorail provides a different perspective on the city. The retro-futurist transport, built for the Seattle World's Fair in 1962, ends at the foot of the Space Needle and even passes right through the Experience Music Project. See p. 29.

- **Exploring a Waterfront Park:** Seattle abounds with waterfront parks where you can gaze at distant shores, wiggle your toes in the sand, or walk through a remnant of old-growth forest. Some of my favorites include Discovery Park, Seward Park, Lincoln Park, and Golden Gardens Park. See "Parks & Public Gardens" and "Outdoor Pursuits" in chapter 7.

- **Museum-Hopping on First Thursday:** On the first Thursday of each month, almost all of Seattle's museums are open late, and most offer free admission for all or part of the day. Get an early start and be sure to check the opening and closing times of the museums. Talk about a great way to save bucks on your vacation! See chapter 7.

- **Taking a Free Boat Ride on Lake Union:** For 1 hour each Sunday afternoon, the Center for Wooden Boats on Lake Union offers free boat rides in classic wooden sailboats. You can watch noisy floatplanes landing and taking off as you sail serenely across the waves. See p. 128.

- **Strolling Through the Arboretum in Spring:** Winters in Seattle may not be long, but they do lack color. So when spring hits, the sudden bursts of brightness it brings are reverently appreciated. There's no better place in the city to enjoy the spring floral displays than the Washington Park Arboretum. See p. 145.

- **Stopping to Smell the Flowers:** Whether it's a cold rainy day or a sunny summer afternoon, a visit to the Volunteer Park Conservatory is a free ticket to the tropics. There are always plenty of beautiful orchids in bloom, as well as lots of other unusual tropical plants. See p. 136.

- **Cycling the Burke-Gilman Trail:** Seattle-area cyclists are blessed with a plethora of great cycling paths, and the granddaddy of them all is the Burke-Gilman Trail, which stretches for more than 14 miles from the Ballard neighborhood to the north end of Lake Washington. The Sammamish River Trail extends the trail for another dozen miles or so. There's even a gravel extension of the trail along the east shore of Lake Sammamish. See p. 152.

- **Going to an Outdoor Summer Movie or Concert:** When the summer sun shines, Seattleites spend as much time outdoors as they can, and among the city's favorite outdoor activities is attending outdoor concerts and movies. Whether in parks or parking lots, these outdoor performances bring out the lawn chairs and blankets. See "The Performing Arts" and "Movies," in chapter 10.

- **Hiking up Mount Si:** There's no getting around the fact that this hike is a real killer, but, ooh, the view from the top! Mount Si is less than 45 minutes east of Seattle and rises straight up from the valley of the Snoqualmie River. The trail also goes straight up, so if you aren't in good shape, don't even think of trying this hike. See p. 152.

- **Day-Tripping to Mount Rainier National Park:** With growling glaciers, meadows full of colorful wildflowers, and thousand-year-old trees, Mount Rainier National Park always gets my vote for best day trip from Seattle. In summer, the opportunities for hiking are absolutely breathtaking, and in winter, cross-country skiing and snowshoeing provide opportunities for exploring a snowy landscape. See "Mount Rainier," in chapter 11.

7 THE BEST OFFBEAT EXPERIENCES

- **Adding Your Contribution to the Gum Wall:** Hey, when your gum has lost its flavor, don't just spit it out on the sidewalk; instead, turn it into alfresco art by adding it to the "Gum Wall," Pike Place Market's self-adhesive display of ABC (already been chewed) art. See p. 127.

- **Making Music Even If You Can't Carry a Tune in a Bucket:** Even the musically challenged can make beautiful music (well, sort of) at a couple of unusual Seattle attractions. At the Experience Music Project, you can let your inner rock-'n'-roller go wild on simulated musical instruments, while at the Soundbridge Seattle Symphony Music Discovery Center, fans of classical music can

play a cello or conduct an orchestra. See p. 129 and 128.

- **Counting Salmon at Ballard's Chittenden Locks:** If you find yourself sleepless in Seattle, forget about counting sheep. Try counting salmon. In fact, even if you aren't suffering from insomnia, during the summer, the fish ladder and underwater viewing windows at the Hiram M. Chittenden (Ballard) Locks are great places to count salmon. See p. 137.

- **Believing It or Not at Ye Olde Curiosity Shop:** Two-headed calves, the Lord's Prayer on a grain of rice, a human mummy. These are just some of the unbelievable items on display at Ye Olde Curiosity Shop, Seattle's waterfront temple of the bizarre. See p. 138.

• **Buying a Flying Fish at Pike Place Market:** At Pike Place Market, the pigs may not fly, but the fish do. If you purchase a fresh salmon from the Pike Place Fish stall, you'll get to watch it go sailing over the counter as the overall-clad fishmongers put on one of the best floor shows in the market. See p. 182.

8 THE BEST THINGS TO DO ON A RAINY DAY

• **Hang Out at Elliott Bay Books:** Nothing beats hanging out in a big bookstore on a rainy day, especially when the bookstore feels as if it has been around for a century and has its own basement cafe. See p. 174.

• **Go Wine Tasting in Woodinville:** Who needs sunshine if you're going to be indoors sampling the fruits of the vine? This rainy-day outing is best on Saturdays, when dozens of wineries open their doors in the nearby Woodinville wine country. See "The Woodinville Wine Country" in chapter 11.

• **Get Jazzed Up at an Espresso Bar:** When it's cold and dark and wet out in Seattle, you need powerful medicine to keep the blues at bay. You need espresso. Bring a book or your laptop and sit and sip all day just like a Seattle native. See "Coffee, Tea, Bakeries & Pastry Shops" in chapter 6.

• **Spend the Day at Volunteer Park:** A park might not at first seem like the place to spend a rainy afternoon, but Volunteer Park, on Capitol Hill, is home to the Seattle Asian Art Museum, the Volunteer Park Conservatory, and a water tower with views over the city. See "The Neighborhoods" and "Parks & Public Gardens" in chapter 7.

9 THE BEST ACTIVITIES FOR FAMILIES

• **Wandering the Seattle Waterfront:** Yes, it's touristy, but with an aquarium, a carousel, boat-tour docks, and, best of all (at least as far as I'm concerned), Ye Olde Curiosity Shop, this is the sort of waterfront that keeps kids entertained for hours. See "The Waterfront" in chapter 7.

• **Seeing Seattle Center:** With a fun park, thrill rides, a science museum, an IMAX theater, a children's museum, a children's theater, and a choreographed multimedia fountain to play in, this is Seattle's ultimate kid zone. See "Seattle Center & Lake Union" and "Especially for Kids" in chapter 7.

• **An Outing to the Snoqualmie Valley:** Little ones enamored of Thomas the Tank Engine will adore the Northwest Railway Museum and affiliated Snoqualmie Valley Railroad. In summer, you can pick berries on local "U-pick" farms, and in the fall you can see salmon spawning at a fish hatchery. Then there's Camlann Medieval Village, where there are all sorts of fun activities all year. See "Snoqualmie Falls & the Snoqualmie Valley" in chapter 11.

• **Experience Music Project (EMP) and Science Fiction Museum (SFM):** If you've got teenagers in tow, drop them at this pair of affiliated museums and they'll stay happy for hours. EMP focuses on rock music with lots of cool interactive exhibits, while the SFM has loads of props from Hollywood's most famous sci-fi movies. See p. 129 and p. 132.

2

Seattle in Depth

Ever since 1851, when a boatload of settlers landed on a windswept beach on Puget Sound, Seattle has had grand aspirations. The pioneers who rowed ashore that day named their settlement New York Alki, appending the local Native American word for "by and by" to that of the East Coast's largest city, in hopes that this new community would one day be a bustling metropolis to rival New York. It took more than 150 years, but their dreams have come true, just not quite the way they had first imagined.

First, those early settlers discovered that the spot where they had set up camp was more than just windswept; it was downright blustery in winter. So they moved across Elliott Bay and changed the name of their community to Seattle in honor of a local Native American chief who had befriended the settlers. For nearly 50 years, Seattle remained a rough-and-tumble place surrounded by wilderness, but when gold was discovered in the Yukon and miners began emptying their pockets before and after they'd gone north to Alaska, Seattle turned from town to city.

However, even as Seattle has turned into a sprawling metropolis, it has remained tightly connected to its natural surroundings. With the waters of Puget Sound and lakes Union and Washington shaping the city's topography, Seattle is a city of splendid vistas, and many of those views are tinted a deep green, which has given the city its nickname—the Emerald City. Take a little time to read through this chapter, and you'll get a feel for this jewel of the Pacific Northwest.

1 SEATTLE TODAY

Despite the sluggish economy, Seattle is booming, as it has been for years. A walk around downtown can lead you to conclude that every vacant lot in the city is being turned into an office tower or some sort of combination hotel and condominiums. In the case of Paul Allen's new South Lake Union development, a neighborhood is being transformed from low-rise warehouses and apartments into high-rise condominiums and hotels. Even many of the city's once-sleepy neighborhoods have sprouted construction cranes. North Seattle's Ballard and Fremont neighborhoods have transformed from quiet urban backwaters into enclaves of hipness. Despite the economic hard times all across the U.S., Seattle still has a nearly palpable buzz. Electricity is in the air. Things may

have cooled in other parts of the country, but Seattle is still hot.

Much of the buzz in Seattle is due to Microsoft and the other high-tech companies, including Adobe and Amazon, which are either headquartered here or have large local facilities. These companies have helped shape the city's demographics to the point that Seattle is now a city of young, well-educated computer nerds. The city is also notoriously liberal and has a large gay and lesbian community. Consequently, Seattle today embraces diversity, as well as all the latest trends and technologies, and is constantly looking to the future.

Seattle began looking to the future way back in 1962 when it hosted Century 21, the Seattle World's Fair. Gazing into its future, the city envisioned bold new architectural landmarks, and so, for the World's Fair, the cloud-impaling Space Needle was erected. Today, this once-futuristic tower, with its flying saucer observation deck perched atop an enormous tripod, is the most recognizable structure on the Seattle skyline. Situated just north of downtown in the Seattle Center complex, which was the site of the World's Fair, the Space Needle provides stupendous views of the city and surrounding natural beauty. Today the design looks far less 21st century than it once did, and over the 45-plus years since the Space Needle was erected, the skyline it overlooks has changed radically—increasingly dominated by towering skyscrapers, symbols of Seattle's ever-growing wealth and its importance as a gateway to the Pacific Rim.

The 1962 World's Fair was far more than a fanciful vision of the future—it was truly prophetic for Seattle. The emergence of this city as a Pacific Rim trading center was a step toward a brighter future. The Seattle area has witnessed extraordinary growth in recent years—tens of thousands of people moving to the city in search of jobs, a better quality of life, and a mild climate. To keep pace with its sudden prominence on the Pacific Rim, Seattle has rushed to transform itself from a sleepy Northwest backwater into a cosmopolitan, world-class metropolis. New theaters, museums, sports stadiums, and even neighborhoods have cropped up around the city in recent years as new residents have demanded more from their city.

Positioning itself as a major metropolis has meant thinking big, and to this end Seattle has stayed busy in the past decade adding (and subtracting) large, sometimes controversial structures to its ever-changing cityscape. In 2000 Microsoft cofounder Paul Allen opened his Experience Music Project, a museum of rock 'n' roll that started out as a simple memorial to hometown rocker Jimi Hendrix. The

museum structure, designed by visionary architect Frank Gehry, is meant to conjure up images of a melted electric guitar and is one of the most bizarre-looking buildings on the planet. In 2004, Allen opened a Science Fiction Museum and Hall of Fame inside this same building.

Also in 2000, Seattle's venerable and much-disparaged Kingdome came crashing down in a cloud of dust as demolition experts imploded the massive cement structure to make way for a new football stadium for the Seattle Seahawks, the NFL team that happens to be owned by Paul Allen.

Allen has also been behind the redevelopment of land that once surrounded the Kingdome, and is currently working on a major development project north of downtown Seattle. This new neighborhood, still very much a work in progress, is known as South Lake Union, and connects the lake with downtown. The Seattle Streetcar's South Lake Union Line, inaugurated in December 2007, runs through the heart of the neighborhood and is a great way to get from downtown Seattle to Lake Union, where there is a new waterfront park.

In case you're beginning to think that sports stadiums and shrines to sci-fi and rock 'n' roll mean this city ain't got no culture, you should know that recent years have also seen the opening of both the new Seattle Central Library, designed by architect Rem Koolhaas, and the Marion Oliver McCaw Hall, which is home to the Seattle Opera and the Pacific Northwest Ballet. The former building is a strangely skewed multistory box of glass and steel that is filled with light (and books) and instantly became one of the city's most fascinating attractions. Best of all, there's no charge to visit. In 2007, a new and much-expanded Seattle Art Museum reopened to the public, as did the art museum's Olympic Sculpture Park. In 2007, the Seattle

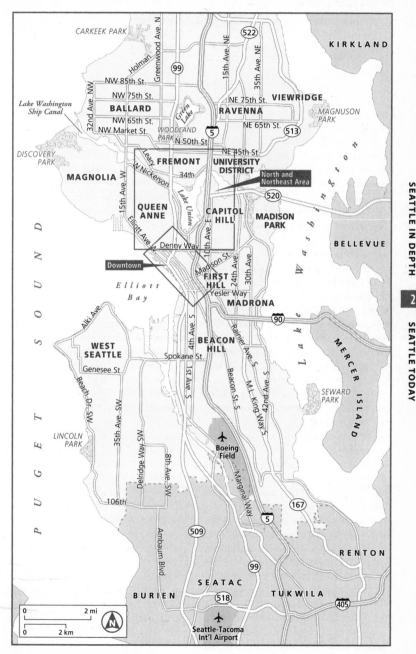

Local Wisdom

Every part of this country is sacred to my people. Every hillside, every valley, every plain and grove has been hallowed by some fond memory or some sad experience of my tribe.

—Chief Sealth, for whom Seattle is named

Aquarium also completed a major expansion and redesign project.

The urbanization and upscaling of this once sleepy city can be seen not only in its cultural edifices, but also on the shopping bags from downtown's Sixth Avenue and Pine Street shopping district. Where once the names were Nordstrom, Pendleton, Eddie Bauer, and REI (all Northwest companies), today they are just as likely to be Banana Republic, Pottery Barn, Williams-Sonoma, and even Cartier and Tiffany. Until 2 decades ago, Seattle was primarily a conglomeration of quaint neighborhoods from which people commuted into downtown. Today, however, people are both working and living in the city center. Throughout the Belltown neighborhood, along the waterfront, and in the South Lake Union neighborhood, high-rise water-view condominiums have sprouted, and today the downtown area is an active and vital urban center.

However, the change isn't limited to downtown, Belltown, and South Lake Union. North Seattle's Fremont neighborhood, long a bastion of artistic expression and hippie aesthetics, is now home to a campus of software giant Adobe. Amazon.com claims a hilltop location in south Seattle. Ballard, long a middle-class Scandinavian neighborhood, has also taken on a much more contemporary feel and is popular both as a place for young families to put down roots and as a busy nightlife district with a historical setting.

Seattle's youthful character is readily apparent on the streets of Belltown, Seattle's hippest neighborhood and main nightlife district. With upscale restaurants, stylish bars, and hip nightclubs, Belltown is where the beautiful people of Seattle spend their evenings. A walk through Belltown along First and Second avenues just north of Pike Place Market will turn up a tempting array of interesting (and often pricey) restaurants on almost every block. In summer the crowds spill out onto the sidewalks, waiting at sidewalk tables for the sun to go down and the action to begin.

In the past couple of years, Capitol Hill, long Seattle's main gay neighborhood has also become the epicenter of culinary expansionism. New restaurants have been opening at a surprising pace considering the state of the economy. Both at the north and south ends of the busy Broadway commercial corridor, there are groupings of great restaurants. The reason for so many new restaurants? A plethora of new condominiums in the neighborhood.

The city's high-tech industry has spawned an entire generation of cellphone-toting hipsters who don their very best basic black outfits whenever they head out for a night of bar-hopping in Belltown. By day, however, many of these same young Seattleites can be seen driving around with mountain bikes and sea kayaks on the roofs of their SUVs and Subaru Outbacks. So when you pack for your visit to Seattle, be sure to include lots of black clothes, a colorful rain jacket, hiking boots, and high heels. Just don't bother bringing the plaid flannel shirt—grunge is history, dude.

All the rapid growth in Seattle has, of course, had its drawbacks, and chief

That #@&*##? Hill

The section of First Hill that rises above the Pioneer Square area was once referred to as Profanity Hill because it was so #@&*##? hard to climb.

among these is traffic congestion. Spend even a short time in the city and you're likely to hear people griping about the traffic. Seattle's traffic congestion has become infamous on the West Coast, with frequent comparisons to the traffic of Los Angeles. However, a new light-rail system, inaugurated in 2009, now connects downtown, via the city's transit tunnel, with communities south of Seattle. By the beginning of 2010, light-rail should go all the way to Seattle-Tacoma International Airport. While the light rail will prove useful for visitors traveling to and from the airport, it is not likely to solve Seattle's traffic woes, so you can expect Seattle traffic to be bad when you visit (leave plenty of time in your schedule whenever you get behind the wheel). While visiting downtown Seattle, the best thing you can do is stay out of your car; it's best to use it only for excursions out of the city.

Traffic jams aside, Seattle is a lot of fun to visit, and if your life happens to revolve around boating, gardening, or food, you'll absolutely love it here. Boating is a Seattle obsession, and few cities anywhere can offer as wide a range of choices to get you on the water—from kayaks to cruise ships and everything in between. Want to paddle a kayak up to a restaurant and order a dozen raw oysters? You can do it here. Putter around in a steam-powered wooden boat? Easy. Sail off into the sunset? No problem. So boat-oriented is Seattle that the opening day of boating season is one of the city's biggest and most popular annual events. Tugboat and hydroplane races rank right up there in popularity as well.

The mild climate here, tempered by the waters of Puget Sound, has also made Seattle one of the most garden-obsessed cities in the nation. Spring vacations in Seattle should include visits to the city's public gardens, and a drive or walk around any residential neighborhood in the spring can serve as a de facto garden tour. I spend a lot of time in Seattle each spring and early summer, and just one visit to the Queen Anne neighborhood makes me wish I were back in my own garden dividing perennials and reconstructing my mixed borders.

Food, glorious food! These words seem to be a Seattle mantra, and as far as food goes, Pike Place Market is the gourmand's Valhalla. Sure, the market may be crowded with tourists most of the year, but it still serves as a source of produce and other hard-to-find cooking ingredients for both casual cooks and some of the city's best chefs. Pike Place Market is also fertile ground for new culinary concepts. The market has an artisan cheese maker, a wine bar specializing in Washington wines, a gourmet-to-go place, gelaterias, and even a shop specializing in truffle oils. What was once the only Starbucks in the world is also here in the market. You may be able to take a bite of the big apple in New York, but here in Seattle, you can take a bite of a Washington state apple (big or otherwise), a Rainier cherry, a marionberry, a Dungeness crab, a Willapa Bay oyster, and countless other great local food finds. And to wash it all down? Why, a double tall nonfat latte or a Washington state merlot, of course.

2 LOOKING BACK AT SEATTLE

By East Coast standards, Seattle got a late start in U.S. history. Although explorers visited the region as early as the late 1700s, the first settlers didn't arrive until 1851. Capt. George Vancouver of the British Royal Navy—who lent his name to both Vancouver, British Columbia, and Vancouver, Washington—had explored Puget Sound as early as 1792. However, there wasn't much to attract anyone permanently to this remote region. Unlike Oregon to the south, Washington had little rich farmland, only acres and acres of forest. It was this seemingly endless supply of wood that finally enticed the first settlers.

PIONEER YEARS

The region's first settlement was on Alki Point, in the area now known as West Seattle. Bad choice. Because this location was exposed to storms sweeping in off the Pacific Ocean, the settlers soon decided to move across Elliott Bay to a more protected spot that has since grown into the city of Seattle. The new location for the village was a tiny island surrounded by mud flats. Some early settlers wanted to name the town New York Alki—even then, Seattle had grand aspirations—but chose "Seattle" as a tribute to Chief Sealth, a local Native American who had befriended the newcomers.

In the middle of town, on the waterfront, Henry Yesler built the first steam-powered lumber mill on Puget Sound. It stood at the foot of what is now Yesler Way, which for many years was referred to as Skid Road, a reference to the way logs were skidded down to the sawmill from the slopes behind town. Over the years, Skid Road developed a reputation for its bars and brothels. Some say that after an East Coast journalist incorrectly referred to it as Skid Row in his newspaper, the name stuck and was subsequently applied to derelict neighborhoods all over the country. To this day, despite attempts to revamp the neighborhood, Yesler Way continues to attract the sort of visitors you would expect (due in part to the presence in the neighborhood of missions and homeless shelters), but it is also in the center of the Pioneer Square Historic District, one of Seattle's main tourist destinations.

UP FROM THE ASHES

By 1889, Seattle had more than 25,000 inhabitants and was well on its way to becoming the most important city in the Northwest. On June 6 of that year, however, 25 blocks in the center of town burned to the ground. By that time the city, which had spread out onto low-lying land reclaimed from the mud flats, had begun experiencing problems with mud and sewage disposal. The fire gave citizens the opportunity they needed to rebuild their town. The solution to the drainage and sewage problems was to regrade the steep slopes to the east of the town and raise the streets above their previous levels. Because the regrading lagged behind the rebuilding, the ground floors of many new buildings eventually wound up below street level. When the new roads and sidewalks

All Fired Up

The fire remembered as the Great Fire transformed Seattle from a town to a city.

—Greg W. Lange

Seattle's Really Not That Bad

I grew up in Seattle, but I always knew I wanted to leave.
—David Guterson, author of *Snow Falling on Cedars* and *The Other*

were constructed at the level that had previously been the second floor of most buildings, the former ground-floor stores and businesses moved up into the light of day and the spaces below the sidewalk were left to businesses of shady character. Today, you can tour sections of this Seattle underground (see "Good Times in Bad Taste" on p. 138).

Among the most amazing post-fire engineering feats was the leveling of two hills. Although Seattle once had eight hills, there are now only six—nothing is left of either Denny Hill or Jackson Street Hill. Hydraulic mining techniques, using high-powered water jets to dig into the hillsides, leveled both mounds. Today the Jackson Street Hill has become the flat area to the west of the International District, while Denny Hill is the flat neighborhood south of Seattle Center. This latter area was historically known as the Denny Regrade but today is known as Belltown.

Eight years after the fire, another event changed the city almost as much as the fire had. On July 17, 1897, the steamship *Portland* arrived in Seattle from Alaska, carrying a ton of gold from the recently discovered Klondike goldfields. Within the year, Seattle's population swelled with prospectors heading north. Few of them ever struck it rich, but they all stopped in

Seattle to purchase supplies and equipment, thus lining the pockets of local merchants and spreading far and wide the name of this obscure Northwest city. When the prospectors came south again with their hard-earned gold, much of it never left Seattle, sidetracked by beer halls and brothels.

THE BOEING YEARS

In 1916, not many years after the Wright brothers made their first flight, Seattle residents William Boeing and Clyde Esterveld launched their first airplane, a floatplane, from the waters of Lake Union. Their intention was to operate an airmail service to Canada. Their enterprise eventually became the Boeing Company, which grew to be the largest single employer in the area. Until recently, Seattle's fortunes were so inextricably bound to those of Boeing that hard times for the aircraft manufacturer meant hard times for the whole city. While Boeing still employs thousands of people in the Seattle metropolitan area, it no longer controls the city's economic fate. With the founding of a little computer software company called Microsoft, Seattle's economy began to diversify, and with that has come a new, broad-based prosperity that has profoundly changed Seattle's landscape and character.

3 SEATTLE IN POPULAR CULTURE: BOOKS, FILM, TV & MUSIC

BOOKS

If you're a hiker and want to get out on some of the nearby trails, be sure to pack a copy of John Zilly's hiking guide *Beyond*

Mount Si: The Best Hikes Within 85 Miles of Seattle. If, after a few hikes through the wild areas in and around Seattle, you decide you want to keep a bit of this wildness close at hand, pick up a copy of Terry Donnelly and Mary Liz Austin's *Wild Seattle: A Celebration of the Natural Areas In and Around the City,* a coffee-table book filled with beautiful photos.

David Guterson's immensely popular *Snow Falling on Cedars,* though not set in Seattle, does take place on a fictionalized Puget Sound island that sounds a lot like the Seattle bedroom community of Bainbridge Island.

Fans of murder mysteries should be sure to check out J. A. Jance's series of J. P. Beaumont mysteries, which feature a Seattle homicide detective. Although Seattle author Mary Daheim's Emma Lord mysteries aren't set right in Seattle, they take place in a fictitious town not far away.

If you've already been on the Seattle Underground tour, you know all about William Speidel's *Sons of the Profits.* This entertaining account of the first 50 years of Seattle history tells it like it was, much to the chagrin of straight-laced historians who didn't like the way Speidel dredged up the exploits of profiteers and prostitutes in writing this fun book. Despite the title, *Skid Road, an Informal Portrait of Seattle,* by Murray Cromwell Morgan, is a more straightforward history of Seattle, and equally readable. The book's title is a reference to the fact that the term "Skid Row" comes from early Seattle's Skid Road, down which logs were skidded to a lumber mill on the waterfront.

FILMS & TV

While the gray skies of Seattle aren't exactly the favorite backdrops of filmmakers, there have been some memorable films shot in Seattle over the years. Of course, *Sleepless in Seattle* (1993), starring Tom Hanks and Meg Ryan, is perhaps the best known of these, and boat tours of Seattle's Lake Union always point out the houseboat that was used in the movie. *Singles* (1992), directed by Cameron Crowe and starring Matt Dillon, Kyra

Sedgwick, and Bridget Fonda, features 20-somethings and the famous Seattle grunge music club scene. Long before the days of grunge, Elvis Presley made his way to Seattle in *It Happened at the World's Fair.* The 1963 film is set at the 1962 Seattle World's Fair, which gave Seattle the Space Needle. The Seattle jazz club scene is the backdrop for 1989's *The Fabulous Baker Boys,* which stars Jeff and Beau Bridges and Michelle Pfeiffer.

Early Seattle history was the focus of 1968's *Here Come the Brides,* about an 1870s logging company that brings 100 women to Seattle as wives for the lumberjacks. In 1960, John Wayne and Stewart Granger starred in *North To Alaska,* a story of romance and the lust for gold.

The Last Mimzy (2007), a family film about two kids who develop paranormal powers after they find a box of special toys, is set partly in Seattle and partly on nearby Whidbey Island. In *Life or Something Like It* (2002), Angelina Jolie stars as a Seattle TV reporter who is told by a psychic homeless man that she has only a few days to live. Nearby Tacoma serves as the backdrop for *10 Things I Hate About You* (1999), a retelling of Shakespeare's *The Taming of the Shrew.* In Bernardo Bertolucci's *Little Buddha* (1993), with Keanu Reeves, Bridget Fonda, and Chris Isaak, a reincarnated Tibetan lama turns up in Seattle. The red-hot dot.com days are the backdrop for *Disclosure* (1994), with Michael Douglas and Demi Moore.

ABC's *Grey's Anatomy* is set in Seattle, and, if you were a fan of the TV show *Frasier,* you've seen plenty of Seattle scenery and heard lots about this city.

MUSIC

Although many rock-music fans might think that Seattle music started and ended with grunge, that's just not true. Seattle has been producing noteworthy music and musicians for more than 60 years.

Long before grunge—in 1948, to be precise—a young, blind musician named Ray Charles moved to the Emerald City and made his first record. A decade later, legendary guitarist Jimi Hendrix, who was born in Seattle in 1942, began playing in his first local band. Although Hendrix's career would not take off until long after he had left Seattle, the musician is much celebrated here in his hometown. The Experience Music Project (EMP), Microsoft co-founder Paul Allen's music museum, started out as a place for Allen to show off his extensive collection of Hendrix memorabilia and eventually grew into a major shrine to popular music. Up on Capitol Hill, at the corner of Broadway Avenue and East Pine Street, there's a statue of Hendrix, and the guitarist's grave is at Greenwood Memorial Park in the nearby suburb of Renton.

In the mid-1980s, a new sound emerged in Seattle. It merged heavy metal with punk music and came to be known as grunge. The Sub Pop recording label was the premier grunge-music record company, and Seattle bands such as Nirvana, Pearl Jam, Alice in Chains, Mudhoney, and Soundgarden quickly came to dominate the airwaves with their new sound. The grunge scene effectively came to a screeching halt when Nirvana band-leader Kurt Cobain committed suicide in 1994.

4 EATING & DRINKING IN SEATTLE

Although it is mere coincidence that the words *Seattle* and *seafood* both start with the same three letters of the alphabet, it takes only a stroll through Pike Place Market to see for yourself that Seattle is a seafood-lover's nirvana. Silvery salmon, hefty Dungeness crabs, clams, mussels, and dozens of varieties of oysters are the seafood stars here in this city on the shores of Puget Sound. Salmon, although not always local, is a Northwest icon that shows up both fresh and smoked on Seattle menus. Wish you could take some salmon home with you? Not a problem. Pike Place Market fishmongers will pack fresh salmon for you to take home on the plane, and some vacuum-packed smoked salmon doesn't even need to be refrigerated. Oysters are such an obsession here that one of my favorite restaurants, Elliott's Oyster House, even has an oyster new year celebration each year in early November.

Washington's bounty doesn't end where the surf meets the turf. The state's temperate climate is ideal for growing everything from apples to zucchinis. Small farms grow such a wide variety of fresh produce throughout the year that the locavore movement (eating locally as much as possible) is rapidly gaining proponents among chefs at the city's top restaurants. *Fresh, organic, local,* and *sustainable* are the watchwords at an ever-increasing number of restaurants in town, such as Tilth, Agua Verde Cafe, and Portage Bay Café. Even espresso stands around town have jumped on the wagon, serving organic, fair-trade, and shade-grown coffees. Seattle's Theo Chocolate, a company that gives tours of its chocolate factory, roasts its own organic and fair-trade cocoa beans. Finally, guilt-free chocolate!

Of course, as nearly everyone on the planet knows, coffee leviathan Starbucks got its start here in Seattle, and espresso in Seattle has been raised to an art form. However, from dawn to dark, Seattle cups and glasses stay filled with more than just double-tall skinny lattes. Washington State is one of the nation's top wine producers, and many of the state's best and biggest wineries are within a 30-minute drive of Seattle in the town of Woodinville. Washington wineries are best known for their cabernet sauvignon and merlot, but you should also keep an eye out for excellent syrahs and Semillons. Many of the city's top restaurants emphasize Washington wines on their wine lists, and there are a handful of wine bars around the city where you can sip and sample regional fruits of the vine. Seattle is also home to quite a few craft breweries; some are tiny brewpubs, but others are major brewers that craft distinctive beers. While Pyramid Breweries and the Red Hook Ale Brewery are the two major players in the area, some of my favorite brewpubs include Big Time Brewery & Alehouse and the Elysian Brewing Company.

3

Planning Your Trip to Seattle

Seattle is one of the West Coast's most popular vacation destinations, which makes pre-visit planning essential. Try to make your hotel and car reservations as far in advance as possible—not only will you save money, but you'll also be more likely to find rooms available in the most recommendable hotels. Summer is the peak tourist season in Seattle, and from June through September downtown hotels are often fully booked for days or even weeks at a time. Consequently, reservations—for hotel rooms, rental cars, or tables at restaurants—are essential. If you plan to visit during the city's annual Seafair summer festival in late July and early August, when every hotel in town can be booked, reservations are especially important.

Oh, yeah, and about that rain. Seattle's rainy weather may be infamous, but Seattleites have ways of dealing with the dreary days. They either put on their rain gear and head outdoors just as if the sun were shining, or they retreat to the city's hundreds of excellent restaurants and cafes, its dozens of theaters and performance halls, its outstanding museums, its many movie theaters, and its excellent bookstores. They rarely let the weather stand in the way of having a good time, and neither should you.

Although summer is the best time to visit, Seattle offers year-round diversions and entertainment, and because it is still a seasonal destination, hotel rooms here are a real bargain during the rainy months between October and April.

For additional help in planning your trip and for more on-the-ground resources in Seattle, please turn to "Fast Facts" on p. 258.

1 WHEN TO GO

WEATHER

Let's face it: Seattle's weather has a bad reputation. As they say out here, "The rain in Spain stays mainly in Seattle." I wish I could tell you that it isn't so, but I can't. It rains in Seattle—and rains and rains and rains. However, when December 31 rolls around each year, a funny thing happens: They total up the year's precipitation, and Seattle almost always comes out behind such cities as Washington, Boston, New York, and Atlanta. So it isn't the *amount* of rain here that's the problem—it's the number of rainy or cloudy days, which far outnumber those of any of those rainy East Coast cities.

Most of Seattle's rain falls between October and April, so if you visit in the summer, you might not see a drop the entire time. But just in case, you should bring a rain jacket or at least an umbrella. Also, no matter what time of year you plan to visit Seattle, be sure to pack at least a sweater or light jacket. Summer nights can be quite cool, and daytime temperatures rarely climb above the low 80s Fahrenheit (upper 20s Celsius). Winters are not as cold as they are in the East, but snow does fall in Seattle.

Because of the pronounced seasonality of the weather here, people spend as much time outdoors during the summer as they can, and, accordingly, summer is when the city stages all its big festivals. Because it stays light until 10pm in the middle of summer, it's difficult to get Seattleites indoors to theater or music performances. But when the weather turns wet, Seattleites head for the theaters and performance halls in droves.

To make things perfectly clear, here's an annual weather chart:

Seattle's Average Temperature & Days of Rain

	Jan	Feb	Mar	Apr	May	June	July	Aug	Sept	Oct	Nov	Dec
Temp (°F)	41	44	46	51	57	61	65	65	61	54	47	43
Temp (°C)	5	6	7	10	13	16	18	18	16	12	8	6
Rain (days)	18	16	17	14	11	9	5	6	8	11	18	18

SEATTLE CALENDAR OF EVENTS

Seattleites will hold a festival at the drop of a rain hat, and summers here seem to revolve around the city's myriad celebrations. To find out what special events will be taking place while you're in town, check the "NW Ticket" arts-and-entertainment section of the Friday *Seattle Times* or pick up a copy of *Seattle Weekly*. Remember, festivals here take place rain or shine. For more specific dates than those listed here, take a look at the calendar of events on Seattle's Convention and Visitors Bureau website (**www.visitseattle.org**), which is updated as dates become available.

In addition to the festivals listed here, a series of more than a dozen cultural community festivals is held each year at Seattle Center. Called Festál, this series celebrates Seattle's cultural diversity. In the past they've held Vietnamese, African, Japanese, Filipino, Brazilian, and Tibetan festivals. For information, contact Seattle Center (© 206/684-7200; www.seattlecenter.com).

For an exhaustive list of events beyond those listed here, check http://events. frommers.com, where you'll find a searchable, up-to-the-minute roster of what's happening in cities all over the world.

JANUARY

Seattle Boat Show (© **206/634-0911;** www.seattleboatshow.com), Qwest Field Event Center and south Lake Union. At the West Coast's biggest boat show, more than 1,000 boats of every style and size are displayed. January 29 to February 6, 2010.

FEBRUARY

Northwest Flower & Garden Show (© **206/789-5333;** www.gardenshow. com), Washington State Convention and Trade Center. This massive show for avid gardeners has astonishing floral displays. February 3 to 7, 2010.

Chinatown/International District Lunar New Year Celebration (© **206/ 382-1197;** www.cidbia.org). Each year's date depends on the lunar calendar. In 2010, the Chinese New Year celebration will be in mid-February.

APRIL

Seattle Cherry Blossom and Japanese Cultural Festival (© **206/684-7200** or 206/723-2003; www.seattlecenter. com), Seattle Center. Traditional Japanese spring festival. Mid-April.

Skagit Valley Tulip Festival (© **360/ 428-5959;** www.tulipfestival.org), La Conner. An hour north of Seattle, acres and acres of tulips and daffodils cover the Skagit Valley with broad swaths of color each spring, creating an enchanting landscape. Lots of festivities. All month.

Opening Day of Boating Season (✆ 206/325-1000; www.seattleyacht club.org), Lake Union and Lake Washington. A parade of boats and much fanfare take place as Seattle boaters bring out everything from kayaks to yachts. First Saturday in May.

Seattle Maritime Festival (✆ 206/728-3163; www.portseattle.org). Tugboat races are the highlight of this annual Port of Seattle event. Festivities are centered on the Bell Street Pier (Pier 66) on the Seattle waterfront. Early May.

U District StreetFair (✆ 206/547-4417; www.udistrictstreetfair.org), University District. This is the first big street fair of the season in Seattle and includes lots of crafts booths, food vendors, and live music. Mid-May.

Giant Magnet (✆ 206/684-7338; www. seattleinternational.org), Seattle Center. Maori musicians, Persian puppets, Japanese storytellers, West African drummers and dancers—these are just some of the acts you might see at this children's festival that celebrates world cultures through the performing arts. Mid-May.

Seattle International Film Festival (✆ 206/324-9996; www.seattlefilm. com), at theaters around town. New foreign and independent films are screened over several weeks during this highly regarded film festival. Late May to mid-June.

Northwest Folklife Festival (✆ 206/684-7300; www.nwfolklife.org), Seattle Center. This is one of the largest folklife festivals in the country, with dozens of national and regional folk musicians performing on numerous stages. In addition, you'll find crafts vendors from all over the Northwest, lots of good food, and dancing. Memorial Day weekend.

Edmonds Arts Festival (✆ 425/771-6412; www.edmondsartsfestival.com). For a taste of what regional artists are up to, spend some time at this festival 30 minutes north of Seattle. Second weekend in June.

Fremont Fair (✆ 206/297-6801; www. fremontfair.com). A celebration of the summer solstice with a wacky parade, naked bicyclists, food, arts and crafts, and entertainment in one of Seattle's favorite neighborhoods. Third weekend in June.

Seattle Pride (✆ 206/322-9561; www. seattlepride.org), Capitol Hill. With several days of revelry leading up to and including the last weekend in June, this is the largest gay, lesbian, bisexual, and transgender march and festival in the Northwest. Last week in June.

JULY

Chase Family Fourth at Lake Union (✆ 206/281-7788; www.familyfourth. org). This is Seattle's main Fourth of July fireworks display. July 4.

Lake Union Wooden Boat Festival (✆ 206/382-2628; www.cwb.org), Center for Wooden Boats. Featured are classic speedboats and wooden boats, both old and new, from all over the Northwest. Races, demonstrations, food, and entertainment. July 3 to 5, 2010.

Out to Lunch (✆ 206/623-0340; www. downtownseattle.com). Free lunchtime music concerts in plazas and parks throughout downtown. July through August.

Seafair (✆ 206/728-0123; www.seafair. com). This is the biggest Seattle event of the year, with daily festivities—parades, hydroplane boat races, an air show with the Navy's Blue Angels, the Torchlight Parade, ethnic festivals, and sporting events. Events take place citywide. Mid-July to early August.

Chinatown/International District Summer Festival (✆ 206/382-1197; www.cidbia.org). Music, dancing, arts, and food of Seattle's Asian district. Second weekend in July.

Tivoli/Viking Days (✆ 206/789-5707; www.nordicmuseum.org), Ballard. Seattle's Ballard neighborhood was founded by Scandinavians, and that heritage is still celebrated each summer at the Nordic Heritage Museum. Lots of Scandinavian crafts and foods. Second weekend in July.

Pilchuck Glass School Open House (✆ 206/621-8422; www.pilchuck.com), Stanwood. If you're a fan of glass artist Dale Chihuly, you won't want to miss an opportunity to visit the school that helped him make a name for himself. The open house is immensely popular, so buy tickets early. Mid-July.

Bite of Seattle (✆ 425/283-5050; www.biteofseattle.com), Seattle Center. Sample bites from local restaurants or taste some wines. Third weekend in July.

Sequim Lavender Festival (✆ 877/681-3035 or 360/681-3035; www.lavenderfestival.com). Each summer the purple haze of lavender farms adds splashes of color to the landscape surrounding the town of Sequim on the Olympic Peninsula. This festival features farm visits and vendors selling lavender-themed art, crafts, cosmetics, and foods. Sequim is a 30-minute ferry ride and an hour's drive from Seattle. Third weekend in July.

Bellevue Arts Museum artsfair (✆ 415/519-0770; www.bellevuearts.org), Bellevue Square, Bellevue. This is the largest arts-and-fine-crafts fair in the Northwest. Last weekend in July.

Camlann Medieval Village Summer Village Festivals (✆ 425/788-8624; www.camlann.org), Carnation. Knights, ladies, jousting, and plenty of good cheer make this anachronistic festival great fun. You can even rent a costume for the day and attend a medieval banquet at Ye Bors Hede Inne. Mid-July through late August.

AUGUST

Chief Seattle Days (✆ 360/598-3311), Suquamish. A celebration of Northwest Native American culture across Puget Sound from Seattle. Third weekend in August.

SEPTEMBER

Bumbershoot, Seattle's Music & Arts Festival (✆ 206/281-7788; www.bumbershoot.org). Seattle's second-most-popular festival derives its peculiar name from a British term for an umbrella—an obvious reference to the rainy weather. Lots of rock music and other events pack Seattle's youthful set into Seattle Center and other venues. You'll find plenty of arts and crafts on display, too. Labor Day weekend.

OCTOBER

Issaquah Salmon Days Festival (✆ 425/392-0661; www.salmondays.org). This festival in Issaquah, 15 miles east of Seattle, celebrates the annual return of salmon that spawn within the city limits. First full weekend in October.

NOVEMBER

Seattle Marathon (✆ 206/729-3660; www.seattlemarathon.org), around the city. With all these hills, you have to be crazy to run a marathon in Seattle, but plenty of people do it every year. Sunday after Thanksgiving.

DECEMBER

Argosy Christmas Ship Festival (✆ 800/642-7816 or 206/623-1445; www.argosycruises.com), various locations. Boats decked out with imaginative Christmas lights parade past various waterfront locations. Argosy Cruises offers tours; see p. 149 for details. Throughout December.

New Year's at the Needle (☎ 206/905-2100; www.spaceneedle.com), Seattle Center. The Space Needle ushers in the new year with a big fireworks show at midnight sharp. December 31.

2 ENTRY REQUIREMENTS

PASSPORTS

Virtually every air traveler entering the U.S. is required to show a passport. All persons, including U.S. citizens, traveling by air between the United States and Canada, Mexico, Central and South America, the Caribbean, and Bermuda are required to present a valid passport. U.S. and Canadian citizens entering the U. S. at land and sea ports of entry from within the western hemisphere will need to present government-issued proof of citizenship, such as a birth certificate, along with a government-issued photo ID, such as a driver's license. A passport is not required for U.S. or Canadian citizens entering by land or sea, but it is highly encouraged to carry one.

VISAS

For information on obtaining a visa, please visit "Fast Facts," on p. 262.

The U.S. State Department has a **Visa Waiver Program (VWP)** allowing citizens of the following countries to enter the United States without a visa for stays of up to 90 days: Andorra, Australia, Austria, Belgium, Brunei, Denmark, Finland, France, Germany, Iceland, Ireland, Italy, Japan, Liechtenstein, Luxembourg, Monaco, the Netherlands, New Zealand, Norway, Portugal, San Marino, Singapore, Slovenia, Spain, Sweden, Switzerland, and the United Kingdom. Citizens of Czech Republic, Estonia, Hungary, Latvia, Lithuania, Malta, Republic of Korea, and Slovakia are soon to be admitted to the VWP. (*Note:* This list was accurate at press time; for the most up-to-date list of countries in

the VWP, consult http://travel.state.gov/visa.) Even though a visa isn't necessary, in an effort to help U.S. officials check travelers against terror watch lists before they arrive at U.S. borders, visitors from VWP countries must register online through the Electronic System for Travel Authorization (ESTA) before boarding a plane or a boat to the U.S. Travelers will complete an electronic application providing basic personal and travel eligibility information. The Department of Homeland Security recommends filling out the form at least 3 days before traveling. Authorizations will be valid for up to 2 years or until the traveler's passport expires, whichever comes first. Currently, there is no fee for the online application. *Note:* Any passport issued on or after October 26, 2006, by a VWP country must be an **e-Passport** for VWP travelers to be eligible to enter the U.S. without a visa. Citizens of these nations also need to present a round-trip air or cruise ticket upon arrival. E-Passports contain computer chips capable of storing biometric information, such as the required digital photograph of the holder. If your passport doesn't have this feature, you can still travel without a visa if it is a valid passport issued before October 26, 2005, and includes a machine-readable zone, or between October 26, 2005, and October 25, 2006, and includes a digital photograph. For more information, go to **http://travel.state.gov/visa**. Canadian citizens may enter the United States without visas; they will need to show passports (if traveling by air) and proof of residence, however.

Citizens of all other countries must have (1) a valid passport that expires at least 6 months later than the scheduled end of their visit to the U.S., and (2) a tourist visa.

CUSTOMS
What You Can Bring into the U.S.

Every visitor more than 21 years of age may bring in, free of duty, the following: (1) 1 liter of wine or hard liquor; (2) 200 cigarettes, 100 cigars (but not from Cuba), or 3 pounds of smoking tobacco; and (3) $100 worth of gifts. These exemptions are offered to travelers who spend at least 72 hours in the United States and who have not claimed them within the preceding 6 months. It is forbidden to bring into the country almost any meat products (including canned, fresh, and dried meat products such as buillion, soup mixes, and the like). Generally, condiments including vinegars, oils, spices, coffee, tea, and some cheeses and baked goods are permitted. Avoid rice products, as rice can often harbor insects. Bringing fruits and vegetables is not advised, though not prohibited. Customs will allow produce depending on where you got it and where you're going after you arrive in the U.S. International visitors may carry in or out up to $10,000 in U.S. or foreign currency with no formalities; larger sums must be declared to U.S. Customs on entering or leaving, which includes filing form CM 4790. For details regarding U.S. Customs and Border Protection, consult your nearest U.S. embassy or consulate, or **U.S. Customs** (www.customs.gov).

What You Can Take Home from Seattle

For information on what you're allowed to bring home, contact one of the following agencies:

U.S. Citizens: U.S. Customs & Border Protection (CBP), 1300 Pennsylvania Ave., NW, Washington, DC 20229 (© **877/287-8667;** www.cbp.gov).

Canadian Citizens: Canada Border Services Agency (© **800/461-9999** in Canada, or 204/983-3500; www.cbsa-asfc. gc.ca).

U.K. Citizens: HM Customs & Excise (© **0845/010-9000** from outside the U.K., or 020/8929-0152; www.hmce.gov. uk).

Australian Citizens: Australian Customs Service (© **1300/363-263;** www. customs.gov.au).

New Zealand Citizens: New Zealand Customs, The Customhouse, 17–21 Whitmore St., Box 2218, Wellington (© **04/473-6099** or 0800/428-786; www.customs.govt.nz).

MEDICAL REQUIREMENTS

Unless you're arriving from an area known to be suffering from an epidemic (particularly cholera or yellow fever), inoculations or vaccinations are not required for entry into the United States.

3 GETTING THERE & GETTING AROUND

GETTING TO SEATTLE
By Plane

The **Seattle–Tacoma International Airport** (© 206/433-5388; www.portseattle. org/seatac) is served by about 30 airlines. To find out which airlines travel to Seattle, please see "Airline, Hotel & Car Rental Websites," p. 263.

GETTING INTO TOWN FROM THE AIRPORT

BY CAR   To get to downtown from the airport, take the Wash. 518 exit from the airport. Driving east on Wash. 518 will connect you to I-5, where you'll then follow the signs north to Seattle. Generally, allow 30 minutes for the drive between the airport and downtown—45 minutes to an hour during rush hour.

During rush hour, it's sometimes quicker to take Wash. 518 west to Wash. 509 north to Wash. 99 (which becomes the Alaskan Way Viaduct along the Seattle waterfront).

BY TAXI, SHUTTLE, BUS, OR LIGHT RAIL A **taxi** into downtown Seattle will cost you $35 to $40 ($32 for the return ride to the airport). There are usually plenty of taxis around, but if not, call **Yellow Cab** (© **206/622-6500**) or **Orange Cab** (© **206/522-8800**). The flag-drop charge is $2.50; after that, it's $2.50 per mile.

Gray Line Downtown Airporter (© **800/426-7532** or 206/626-6088; www.graylineofseattle.com) is your best bet for getting to downtown. These shuttle vans provide service between the airport and downtown Seattle daily, every 30 minutes from 5:30am (5am from downtown) to 11pm. Passengers are picked up outside the baggage-claim area, at Door 00 just past baggage carousel 1. Shuttles stop at the following downtown hotels: Madison Renaissance, Crowne Plaza, The Fairmont Olympic, Seattle Hilton, Sheraton Seattle, Grand Hyatt, Westin Seattle, and Warwick Seattle. Fares are $11 one-way and $18 round-trip for adults, and $8.25 one-way and $13 round-trip for children 2 to 12. Connector service to and from the above hotels is also provided from numerous other downtown hotels, as well as from the Amtrak station, the Washington State Ferries terminal (Pier 52), and the Greyhound station. Connector service costs $3 one-way; call © **206/255-7159** an hour before you need service to arrange connector service. The biggest drawback of this shuttle service is that you may have to stop at several hotels before getting dropped off, so it could take you 45 minutes or more to get from the airport to your hotel. If you're traveling by yourself or with just one other person, though, this is the most economical choice besides a public bus.

Shuttle Express (© **800/487-7433** or 425/981-7000; www.shuttleexpress.com) provides 24-hour service between Sea-Tac and the Seattle, North Seattle, and Bellevue areas. Rates for scheduled shared-ride shuttles to downtown Seattle are $32 for one or two adults, $40 for three, and $52 for four. Rates to University District hotels are $37 for one adult ($19 on a scheduled shuttle), $45 for two adults ($38 on a scheduled shuttle), $53 for three ($57 on a scheduled shuttle), and $69 for four ($76 on a scheduled shuttle). There is a $10 discount for round-trip bookings on the shared-ride shuttle service. Children 12 and under ride free. There is also scheduled hotel service, which costs a bit more. On these shuttles, children 5 and under ride free with a paying adult. You need to make a reservation to get to the airport, but to leave the airport, simply head to the Ground Transportation Center on the third floor of the parking garage.

Metro Transit (© **800/542-7876** in Washington, or 206/553-3000; http://transit.metrokc.gov) operates two public buses between the airport and downtown. These buses leave from near door 2 of the baggage-claim area. It's a good idea to call for the current schedule when you arrive in town. Bus no. 194 runs every 15 to 30 minutes; it operates Monday through Friday from about 6am to 9:15pm, Saturday from about 6:30am to 9pm, and Sunday from about 6:30am to 7:30pm. Bus no. 174 runs every 25 to 30 minutes; it operates Monday through Friday from about 4:50am to 2:35am, Saturday from about 5:20am to 2:45am, and Sunday from about 6:25am to 2:40am. Bus trips to downtown take 30 to 45 minutes, depending on conditions. The fare is $1.75 during off-peak hours, $2.50 during peak hours.

If all goes according to plan, you should be able to take the **LINK** light-rail line from the airport to downtown Seattle in 2010. If the light-rail line is not yet completed to the airport when you visit, you will be able to take a bus to the nearby Tukwila Station. For information, contact **Sound Transit** (𝄢 **800/201-4900** or 206/398-5000; www.soundtransit.org)

By Car

Seattle is 110 miles from Vancouver, British Columbia, 175 miles from Portland, 810 miles from San Francisco, 1,190 miles from Los Angeles, 835 miles from Salt Lake City, and 285 miles from Spokane.

I-5 is the main north–south artery through Seattle, running south to Portland and north to the Canadian border. I-405 is Seattle's eastside bypass and accesses the cities of Bellevue, Redmond, and Kirkland on the east side of Lake Washington. I-90, which ends at I-5, connects Seattle to Spokane in the eastern part of Washington. Wash. 520 connects I-405 with Seattle just north of downtown and also ends at I-5. Wash. 99, the Alaskan Way Viaduct, is another major north–south highway through downtown Seattle; it passes through the waterfront section of the city.

CAR RENTALS Car-rental rates vary as widely and as wildly as airfares, so it pays to do some comparison shopping. In Seattle, a compact car will likely run you between $40 and $50 per day during the summer, with weekly rates ranging from $336 to $490. Rates are highest in the summer and lowest in the winter, but you'll almost always get lower rates the further ahead you reserve. Be sure to budget for the 19.2% car-rental tax (and, if you rent at the airport, additional airport concession fees and various other charges that will increase your total cost by around 40%!).

All the major car-rental agencies have offices in Seattle and at or near Seattle–Tacoma International Airport. Companies with a desk and cars inside the terminal include Alamo, Avis, Budget, Hertz, and National. Companies with desks inside the terminal but cars parked off the airport premises include Advantage, Dollar, Enterprise, and Thrifty. Off-site rental-car companies include Century/Rent Rite, Fox Rent A Car, and U Save.

International visitors should note that insurance and taxes are almost never included in quoted rental car rates in the U.S. Be sure to ask your rental agency about additional fees for these. They can add a significant cost to your car rental.

By Train

Amtrak (𝄢 **800/872-7245;** www.amtrak.com) service runs from Vancouver, British Columbia, to Seattle and from Portland and as far south as Eugene, Oregon, on the *Cascades* (a high-speed, European-style Talgo train). The train takes about 4 hours from Vancouver to Seattle and 3½ to 4 hours from Portland to Seattle. One-way fares from Vancouver to Seattle are usually around $35 and fares from Portland to Seattle are usually around $28. There is also Amtrak service to Seattle from San Diego, Los Angeles, San Francisco, and Portland on the *Coast Starlight,* and from Spokane and points east on the *Empire Builder.* Be aware that Amtrak also operates buses from Vancouver to Seattle.

Like the airlines, Amtrak offers several discounted fares; although they're not all based on advance purchase, you'll have more discount options by reserving early. Some discount fares can only be purchased on certain days; be sure to find out exactly what restrictions apply. Tickets for children 2 to 15 cost half the price of a regular coach fare when the children are accompanied by a fare-paying adult.

Also inquire about money-saving packages that include hotel accommodations, car rentals, tours, and so on with your train fare.

International visitors can buy a **USA Rail Pass,** good for 15, 30, or 45 days of unlimited travel on **Amtrak** (© **800/ USA-RAIL;** www.amtrak.com). The pass is available online or through many overseas travel agents. See Amtrak's website for the cost of travel within the western, eastern, or northwestern United States. Reservations are generally required and should be made as early as possible. Regional rail passes are also available.

By Boat

Seattle is served by **Washington State Ferries** (© **800/843-3779** or 888/808-7977 within Washington, or 206/464-6400; www.wsdot.wa.gov/ferries), the most extensive ferry system in the United States. Car ferries connect Seattle's Pier 52 and Colman Dock with both Bainbridge Island and Bremerton (on the Kitsap Peninsula). Car ferries also connect Fauntleroy (in West Seattle) with both Vashon Island and the Kitsap Peninsula at Southworth; Tahlequah (at the south end of Vashon Island) with Point Defiance in Tacoma; Edmonds with Kingston (on the Kitsap Peninsula); Mukilteo with Whidbey Island; Whidbey Island at Keystone with Port Townsend; and Anacortes with the San Juan Islands and Sidney, British Columbia (on Vancouver Island near Victoria). See "Getting Around," below, for fare information.

If you're traveling between Victoria, British Columbia, and Seattle, several options are available through **Victoria Clipper,** Pier 69, 2701 Alaskan Way (© **800/888-2535** or 206/448-5000; www.clippervacation.com). Ferries make the 2- or 3-hour trip throughout the year, at prices ranging from $83 to $155 round-trip for adults (the lower fare is for off-season advance-purchase tickets). You can also expect to pay some sort of fuel surcharge. Some scheduled trips also stop in the San Juan Islands.

By Bus

Greyhound (© **800/231-2222;** www. greyhound.com) bus service provides connections to almost any city in the continental United States. Seattle's Greyhound bus station is located at 811 Stewart St. (© **206/628-5561**), a few blocks northeast of downtown. Several budget chain motels are located nearby, and you can grab a free ride into downtown on a Metro bus. International visitors can obtain information about the **Greyhound North American Discovery Pass.** The pass, which offers unlimited travel and stopovers in the U.S. and Canada, can be obtained from foreign travel agents or through www.discoverypass.com

GETTING AROUND

Although downtown Seattle is fairly compact and can be easily navigated on foot, finding your way by car can be frustrating. Traffic, especially during rush hour, can be a nightmare. Drawbridges, one-way streets, I-5 cutting right through downtown, and steep hills all add up to challenging and confusing driving conditions. Here are some guidelines to help you find your way around.

MAIN ARTERIES & STREETS Three interstate highways serve Seattle. Seattle's main artery is I-5, which runs through the middle of the city. Take the James Street exit west if you're heading for the Pioneer Square area, take the Seneca Street exit for Pike Place Market, or take the Olive Way exit for Capitol Hill. I-405 is the city's north–south bypass and travels up the east shore of Lake Washington through Bellevue and Kirkland (Seattle's high-tech corridor). I-90 comes in from the east, crossing one of the city's two floating bridges, and ends at the south end of downtown.

Downtown is roughly defined as extending from the stadium district (just

Tips   Remembering Seattle's Streets

Locals use an irreverent little mnemonic device for remembering the names of Seattle's downtown streets, and since most visitors spend much of their time downtown, this phrase could be useful to you as well. It goes like this: "Jesus Christ made Seattle under protest." This stands for all the downtown east–west streets between Yesler Way and Olive Way/Stewart Street—Jefferson, James, Cherry, Columbia, Marion, Madison, Spring, Seneca, University, Union, Pike, Pine.

south of the Pioneer Square neighborhood) on the south to Denny Way on the north, and from Elliott Bay on the west to I-5 on the east. Within this area, most avenues are numbered, whereas streets have names. Exceptions to this rule are the first two roads parallel to the waterfront (Alaskan Way and Western Ave.) and avenues east of Ninth Avenue.

Many downtown streets and avenues are one-way. Spring, Pike, and Marion streets are all one-way eastbound, while Seneca, Pine, and Madison streets are all one-way westbound. Second and Fifth avenues are both one-way southbound, while Fourth and Sixth avenues are one-way northbound. First and Third avenues are both two-way streets.

To get from downtown to Capitol Hill, take Pike Street or Olive Way. Madison Street, Yesler Way, or South Jackson Street will get you over to Lake Washington on the east side of Seattle. If you're heading north across town, Westlake Avenue will take you to the Fremont neighborhood, while Eastlake Avenue will take you to the University District. These two roads diverge at the south end of Lake Union. To get to the arboretum from downtown, take Madison Street.

FINDING AN ADDRESS After you become familiar with the streets and neighborhoods of Seattle, there is really only one important thing to remember: Pay attention to the compass point of an address. Most downtown streets have no directional designation attached to them,

but once you cross I-5 going east, most streets and avenues are designated "East." South of Yesler Way, which runs through Pioneer Square, streets are designated "South." West of Queen Anne Avenue, streets are designated "West." The University District is designated "NE" (Northeast), and the Ballard neighborhood "NW" (Northwest). So if you're looking for an address on First Avenue South, head south of Yesler Way.

Another helpful hint is that odd-numbered addresses are likely to be on the west and south sides of streets, whereas even-numbered addresses will be on the east and north. Also, in the downtown area, address numbers jump by 100 with each block as you move away from Yesler Way going north or south and as you go east from the waterfront.

STREET MAPS If the streets of Seattle seem totally unfathomable to you, rest assured that even longtime residents sometimes have a hard time finding their way around. Don't be afraid to ask directions. You can obtain a free map of the city from the Seattle Visitor Center & Concierge Services (© **206-461-5888**).

You can buy a decent map of Seattle at most convenience stores and gas stations. For a greater selection, stop in at **Metsker Maps,** 1511 First Ave. (© **800/727-4430** or 206/623-8747; www.metskers.com).

If you're a member of AAA, you can get free maps of Seattle and Washington State either at your local AAA office or at the Seattle branch in the University District at

4554 Ninth Ave. NE (☎ **206/633-4222;** www.aaawa.com).

By Public Transportation

BY BUS   The best thing about Seattle's **Metro** (☎ **800/542-7876** in Washington or 206/553-3000; http://transit.metrokc.gov) bus system is that as long as you stay within the downtown area, you can ride for free between 6am and 7pm. The **Ride Free Area** is between Alaskan Way (the waterfront) to the west, Sixth Avenue and I-5 to the east, Battery Street to the north, and South Jackson Street to the south. Within this area are Pioneer Square, the waterfront attractions, Pike Place Market, the Seattle Art Museum, and almost all of the city's major hotels. Two blocks from South Jackson Street is Qwest Field (where the Seahawks play), 3 long blocks from South Jackson Street is Safeco Field (where the Mariners play), and 6 blocks from Battery Street is Seattle Center. Keeping this in mind, you can see a lot of Seattle without having to spend a dime on transportation.

The Ride Free Area also encompasses the **Downtown Seattle Transit Tunnel,** which allows buses and the new LINK light-rail cars to travel underneath downtown Seattle, thus avoiding traffic congestion. The tunnel extends from the International District in the south to the convention center in the north, with three stops in between. Commissioned artworks decorate each of the stations, making a trip through the tunnel more than just a way of getting from point A to point B. The tunnel is open Monday through Saturday from 5am to 1am and Sunday from 6am to midnight. When the tunnel is closed, buses operate on surface streets. Because the tunnel is within the Ride Free Area, there is no charge for riding through it, unless you are traveling to or from outside of the Ride Free Area.

If you travel outside the Ride Free Area, fares range from $1.75 to $2.50, depending on distance and time of day. (The higher fares are incurred during commuter hours.) On Saturday, Sunday, and holidays, you can purchase a **Regional Day Pass** for $4; it's available on any Metro bus, and it's good anywhere outside the Ride Free area. *Note:* When traveling out of the Ride Free Area between 6am and 7pm, you pay when you get off the bus; when traveling into the Ride Free Area, you pay when you get on the bus. Exact change is required; dollar bills are accepted.

BY MONORAIL   If you are planning a visit to Seattle Center, there is no better way to get there from downtown than on the **Seattle Monorail** (☎ **206/905-2620;** www.seattlemonorail.com), which leaves from Westlake Center shopping mall (Fifth Ave. and Pine St.). The elevated train covers the 1¼ miles in 2 minutes and passes right through the middle of the Experience Music Project, the Frank Gehry–designed rock-music museum. The monorail operates daily from 9am to 11pm. Departures are every 10 minutes. The one-way fare is $2 for adults and $1 for seniors, and 75¢ for children 5 to 12.

BY STREETCAR   Paul Allen's rapidly evolving South Lake Union development district, stretching from the north end of downtown Seattle to the south shore of Lake Union, is served by the **Seattle Streetcar** (☎ **206/553-3000;** www.seattlestreetcar.org). There are 11 stops along the 2½-mile route, including Lake Union Park, which is home to several historic ships, and the adjacent Center for Wooden Boats. Downtown, you can catch the streetcar at the corner of Westlake Avenue and Olive Way. Streetcars run every 15 minutes and operate Monday through Thursday from 6am to 9pm, Friday and Saturday from 6am to 11pm, and Sundays and holidays from 10am to 7pm. The fare is $2 for adults and 50¢ for seniors and students (children 5 and under are free). Metro passes and bus transfers are valid on the streetcar.

BY WATER TAXI April through October, the **King County Water Taxi** runs between the downtown Seattle waterfront (Pier 55) and Seacrest Park in West Seattle, providing access to West Seattle's popular Alki Beach and adjacent paved path. For a service schedule, check with Metro (© 206/684-1551; http://transit.metrokc.gov). The one-way fare is $3 (free for children under 6); $1 with a valid bus transfer; free with an all-day pass. A free shuttle, DART route 775, will take you to Alki Beach. In 2010, the water taxi is scheduled to begin operating year round.

BY FERRY **Washington State Ferries** (© 800/843-3779 or 888/808-7977 in Washington or 206/464-6400; www.wsdot.wa.gov/ferries) is the most extensive ferry system in the United States, and while these ferries won't help you get around Seattle itself, they do offer scenic options for getting out of town (and cheap "cruises," too). From downtown Seattle, car ferries sail to Bremerton (1-hr. crossing) and Bainbridge Island (35-min. crossing). From West Seattle, car ferries go to Vashon Island (15-min. crossing) and Southworth (35-min. crossing), which is on the Kitsap Peninsula. One-way fares between Seattle and Bainbridge Island or Bremerton, or between Edmonds and Kingston via car ferry, are $12 ($15 from May to the second Sat in Oct) for a car and driver, $6.70 for adult car passengers or walk-ons, $3.35 for seniors, and $5.40 for children 6 to 18. Car passengers and walk-ons pay fares only on westbound car ferries. One-way fares between Fauntleroy (West Seattle) and Vashon Island, or between Southworth and Vashon Island, are $15 ($19 from May to the second Sat in Oct) for a car and driver, $4.30 for car passengers or walk-ons, $2.15 for seniors, and $3.45 for children 6 to 18. There is also passenger-only ferry service to Vashon Island from Pier 50 on the Seattle waterfront.

By Car

Before you drive into downtown Seattle, keep in mind that traffic congestion is bad, parking is limited (and expensive), and streets are almost all one-way. You'll avoid a lot of frustration by leaving your car in your hotel parking garage.

Depending on what your plans are for your visit, you might not need a car at all. If you plan to spend your time in downtown Seattle, a car is a liability. The city center is well served by public transportation, with free buses in the downtown area. Then there are the monorail from downtown to Seattle Center, the Seattle Streetcar from downtown to Lake Union, and the King County Water Taxi from the waterfront to West Seattle. You can even take the ferries over to Bainbridge Island or Bremerton. Most Seattle neighborhoods that interest visitors are well served by public buses. But if your plans include any excursions out of the city—say, to Mount Rainier or the Olympic Peninsula—you'll definitely need a car.

If you're visiting from abroad and plan to rent a car in the United States, keep in mind that foreign driver's licenses are usually recognized in the U.S., but you may want to consider obtaining an international driver's license.

PARKING On-street parking in downtown Seattle is expensive, extremely limited, and, worst of all, rarely available near your destination. Most downtown parking lots (either above or below ground) charge from $18 to $25 per day, though many lots offer early-bird specials that allow you to park all day for around $12 or $14 if you arrive before a certain time in the morning (usually around 9am).

You can save money by leaving your car near the Space Needle, where parking lots charge $6 to $7 per day. Some Pike Place Market merchants validate parking permits.

DRIVING RULES & TIPS   A right turn at a red light is permitted after coming to a full stop. A left turn at a red light is permissible from a one-way street onto another one-way street after coming to a full stop.

If you park your car on a sloping street, be sure to turn your wheels to the curb. When parking on the street, check the time limit on your parking meter; some allow as little as 15 minutes of parking, while others are good for up to 4 hours. Also, be sure to check whether your parking space is restricted during rush hour.

Stoplights in the Pioneer Square area are particularly hard to see, so be alert at all intersections.

By Taxi

If you decide not to use the public transit system, call **Yellow Cab** (C 206/622-6500) or **Orange Cab** (C 206/522-8800). Taxis can be difficult to hail on the

street in Seattle, so it's best to call or wait at the taxi stands at major hotels. The flag-drop charge is $2.50; after that, it's $2.50 per mile. A maximum of four passengers can share a cab; the third and fourth passengers will each incur a surcharge of 50¢.

On Foot

Seattle is a surprisingly compact city. You can easily walk from Pioneer Square to Pike Place Market and take in most of downtown. However, the city is very hilly and when you head in from the waterfront, you will be climbing a very steep hill. If you get tired while strolling downtown, remember that between 6am and 7pm, you can always catch a bus for free as long as you stay within the Ride Free Area. Cross the street only at corners and only with the lights in your favor. Jaywalking, especially in the downtown area, is a ticketable offense.

[handwritten annotations:]
RED TOP (789-4949)   GRAY TOP (282-8222)
FAR WEST (622-1717)
STITA (246-9999) → airport

4 MONEY & COSTS

The Value of the U.S. Dollar vs. Other Popular Currencies

US$	Can$	UK£
1	1.15	0.61

Frommer's lists prices in the local cu... The currency conversions quoted ... were correct at press time. Howeve... fluctuate, so before departing con... currency exchange website such as ... **oanda.com/convert/classic** to chec... to-the-minute rates.

ATMs

Nationwide, the easiest and best way to get cash away from home is from an ATM (automated teller machine), sometimes referred to as a "cash machine" or "cashpoint." The **Cirrus** (C 800/424-7787; www.mastercard.com) and **PLUS** (www.visa.com) networks span the country; you

[inset box:]
How to Get There—Shuttle

For shared rides, Shuttle Express (800-487-7433) services areas within a 30 mile radius. Pick-up and drop-off is on the third floor of the Airport Garage. The check-in for scheduled Airporter services is on the Baggage Claim level. Airporter Shuttle (866-235-5247) serves Western Washington. Capital Aerporter serves Seattle (253-838-7431), Olympia (360-754-7113), Tacoma (253-927-6179), and outside of Western Washington (800-962-3579). Gray Line Downtown Airporter (800-426-7532) departs twice an hour until 11 pm to major downtown Seattle hotels. Check the website for Airport Express schedules and other service areas.

...impose a fee every time you use a card at another bank's ATM, and that fee is often higher for international transactions (up to $5 or more) than for domestic ones (where they're rarely more than $3). In addition, the bank from which you withdraw cash may charge its own fee. Visitors from outside the U.S. should also find out whether

What Things Cost in Seattle	U.S.$	British £
Weekly compact car rental (with taxes)	560.00	340.00
Bus fare (free in downtown)	1.75–2.50	1.07–1.53
Taxi from airport	35.00–40.00	21.35–24.40
Local telephone call	0.50	0.30
Double room at The Edgewater	200.00	122.00
Double room at the Mayflower Park Hotel	149.00	90.90
Double room at the Ramada Seattle Downtown	109.00	66.50
Dinner for one (without alcohol) at the Dahlia Lounge	50.00	30.50
Dinner for one (without alcohol) at Agua Verde Café	20.00	12.20
Pint of beer in a restaurant	4.50	2.75
Double latte	3.25	1.98
Admission to the Space Needle	16.00	9.76
Seattle Duck Tour	25.00	15.25

their bank assesses a fee on charges incurred abroad.

In Seattle, you'll find ATMs at most banks. You can also usually find them at gas station minimarts, although these machines usually charge a slightly higher fee than banks. You can sometimes avoid a fee by searching out a small community bank, a savings and loan, or a credit union ATM. To avoid fees, you can also go into a grocery store, make a purchase, and ask for cash back on your debit card.

CREDIT CARDS & DEBIT CARDS

Credit cards are the most widely used form of payment in the U.S. It's highly recommended that you travel with at least one major credit card; options include **Visa** (Barclaycard in Britain), **MasterCard** (Eurocard in Europe, Access in Britain, Chargex in Canada), **American Express, Diners Club,** and **Discover.** MasterCard and Visa are the two most commonly accepted credit cards. You must have a credit card to rent a car, and hotels and airlines usually require a credit card imprint as a deposit against expenses.

You can withdraw cash advances from your credit cards at banks or ATMs, but high fees make credit card cash advances a pricey way to get cash. Keep in mind that you'll pay interest from the moment of your withdrawal, even if you pay your monthly bills on time. Also, note that many banks now assess a 1% to 3% "transaction fee" on **all** charges you incur abroad (whether you're using the local currency or your native currency).

STAYING HEALTHY
What to Do if You Get Sick Away from Home

If you suffer from a chronic illness, consult your doctor before your departure. Pack **prescription medications** in your carry-on luggage, and carry them in their original containers, with pharmacy labels—otherwise they won't make it through airport security. Visitors from outside the U.S. should carry generic names of prescription drugs. For U.S. travelers, most reliable health-care plans provide coverage if you get sick away from home. Foreign visitors may have to pay all medical costs up front and be reimbursed later; see "Insurance" in the appendix (p. 260).

Additional **emergency numbers** are listed in the appendix (p. 258).

STAYING SAFE

Although Seattle is a relatively safe city, it has its share of crime. The most questionable neighborhood you're likely to visit is the Pioneer Square area, which is home to more than a dozen bars and nightclubs. By day, this area is quite safe (though it has a large contingent of street people), but late at night, when the bars are closing, stay aware of your surroundings and keep an eye out for suspicious characters and activities. Also take extra precautions with your wallet or purse when you're in the crush of people at Pike Place Market. Whenever possible, try to park your car in a garage at night. If you must park on the street, make sure there are no valuables in view—or anything that even looks as if it might contain something of worth. I once had my car broken into because I left a shopping bag full of trash on the back seat.

6 SPECIALIZED TRAVEL RESOURCES

In addition to the destination-specific resources listed below, please visit **Frommers.com** for additional specialized travel resources.

GAY & LESBIAN TRAVELERS

Seattle is one of the most gay-friendly cities in the country, with a large gay and lesbian community centered on Capitol Hill. Here in this neighborhood, you'll find numerous bars, nightclubs, stores, and bed-and-breakfasts catering to the gay community.

The first place to start looking for Seattle information is on the **Seattle Convention and Visitors Bureau**'s LGBT Web pages (**www.visitseattle.org/visitors/lgbt**). Once you're in Seattle, you can pick

up a copy of the *Seattle Gay News* (© 206/324-4297; www.sgn.org), which is the community's newspaper and is available at area bookstores and gay bars and nightclubs.

The **Greater Seattle Business Association (GSBA),** 400 E. Pine St., Ste. 322 (© 206/393-9188; www.thegsba.org), is Seattle's main GLBT business association and publishes a directory of gay-friendly Seattle businesses. This directory is a great resource and can be found wherever you find the *Seattle Gay News.*

The **Gaslight Inn** and **Bacon Mansion** are two gay-friendly bed-and-breakfasts in the Capitol Hill area; see p. 73 for full reviews on both B&Bs. For information on gay and lesbian bars and nightclubs, see p. 196.

For more gay and lesbian travel resources, visit **www.frommers.com**.

TRAVELERS WITH DISABILITIES

Most disabilities shouldn't stop anyone from traveling in the U.S. Thanks to provisions in the Americans with Disabilities Act, most public places are required to comply with disability-friendly regulations. Almost all public establishments (including hotels, restaurants, museums, and such, but not including certain National Historic Landmarks) and at least some modes of public transportation provide accessible entrances and other facilities for those with disabilities.

For anyone using a wheelchair, the greatest difficulty of a visit to Seattle is dealing with the city's many steep hills, which rival those of San Francisco. One solution for dealing with downtown hills is to use the elevator at Pike Place Market to get between the waterfront and First Avenue. There's also a public elevator at the west end of Lenora Street (just north of Pike Place Market). This elevator connects the waterfront with the Belltown neighborhood. If you stay at The Edgewater hotel, right on the waterfront, you'll have easy access to all of the city's waterfront attractions, and you'll be able to use the elevators to get to Pike Place Market.

Always mention your disability when making airline reservations. Airline policies differ regarding wheelchairs and Seeing Eye dogs.

Most hotels now offer wheelchair-accessible accommodations, and some of the larger and more expensive properties also offer TDD telephones and other amenities for the hearing and sight impaired.

For information on public bus accessibility, contact **Metro** (© **866/205-5001** in Washington State or 206/263-3113; http://transit.metrokc.gov/tops/accessible/accessible.html). For Metro TTY service,

call © **877/749-4286** in Washington State or 206/263-3116.

The **America the Beautiful—National Park and Federal Recreational Lands Pass—Access Pass** gives people who are visually impaired or have permanent disabilities (regardless of age) free lifetime entrance to federal recreation sites administered by the National Park Service (NPS), including the Fish and Wildlife Service, the Forest Service, the Bureau of Land Management, and the Bureau of Reclamation. This may include national parks, monuments, historic sites, recreation areas, and national wildlife refuges. If you plan to visit Mount Rainier National Park or Olympic National Park, this pass is a must.

The America the Beautiful Access Pass can be obtained in person at any NPS facility that charges an entrance fee. You need to show proof of a medically determined disability. Besides free entry, the pass also offers a 50% discount on some federal-use fees charged for such facilities as camping, swimming, parking, boat launching, and tours. For more information, go to www.nps.gov/fees_passes.htm or call the **United States Geological Survey (USGS),** which issues the passes, at © **888/275-8747.**

For more on organizations that offer resources to travelers with disabilities, go to **www.frommers.com**.

FAMILY TRAVEL

If you have enough trouble simply getting your kids out of the house in the morning, dragging them thousands of miles away may seem like an insurmountable challenge. But family travel can be immensely rewarding, giving you new ways of seeing the world through smaller pairs of eyes.

To locate accommodations, restaurants, and attractions that are particularly kid-friendly, refer to the "Kids" icon throughout this guide.

Many hotels in Seattle allow kids to stay free in a parent's room; some budget properties also allow children to eat for free in the hotel's restaurant. Keep in mind that most downtown hotels cater almost exclusively to business travelers and don't offer the sort of amenities that appeal to families—like swimming pools, game rooms, or inexpensive restaurants. For specific hotel recommendations, see "Family-Friendly Hotels" (p. 72).

Many of Seattle's larger restaurants, especially along the waterfront, offer children's menus. You'll also find plenty of variety and low prices at the many food vendors' stalls at Pike Place Market. And there's a food court in Westlake Center shopping mall. For information on restaurants that cater to families, see "Family-Friendly Restaurants" (p. 90).

For a list of more family-friendly travel resources, turn to the experts at **www. frommers.com**.

Note: If you plan to travel on to Canada during your Seattle vacation, be sure to bring your children's passports with you.

SENIOR TRAVEL

Don't be shy about asking for discounts, but always carry some kind of identification, such as a driver's license, that shows your date of birth. In Seattle, most attractions, some theaters and concert halls, tour companies, and the Washington State Ferries all offer senior discounts. These can add up to substantial savings, but you have to remember to ask.

The U.S. National Park Service offers an **America the Beautiful—National Park and Federal Recreational Lands Pass—Senior Pass** (formerly the Golden Age Passport), which gives seniors 62 years or older lifetime entrance to all properties administered by the National Park Service—national parks, monuments, historic sites, recreation areas, and national

wildlife refuges—for a one-time processing fee of $10. The pass must be purchased in person at any NPS facility that charges an entrance fee. Besides free entry, the America the Beautiful Senior Pass also offers a 50% discount on some federal-use fees charged for such facilities as camping, swimming, parking, boat launching, and tours. For more information, go to www. nps.gov/fees_passes.htm or call the **United States Geological Survey (USGS),** which issues the passes, at ✆ **888/275-8747.**

For more on organizations that offer resources to seniors, go to **www.frommers. com.**

STUDENT TRAVEL

Check out the **International Student Travel Confederation** (ISTC; www.istc. org) website for comprehensive travel services information and details on how to get an **International Student Identity Card (ISIC),** which qualifies students for substantial savings on rail passes, plane tickets, entrance fees, and more. It also provides a 24-hour help line. The card is valid for a maximum of 16 months. You can apply for the card online or in person at **STA Travel** (✆ **800/781-4040** in North America, 134-782 in Australia, 087/1230-0040 in the U.K.; www.sta travel.com), the biggest student travel agency in the world; check out the website to locate STA Travel offices worldwide.

If you're no longer a student but are still 25 or under, you can get an **International Youth Travel Card (IYTC)** from the same people, which entitles you to some discounts. **Travel CUTS** (✆ **800/592-2887;** www.travelcuts.com) offers similar services for both Canadians and U.S. residents. Irish students may prefer to turn to **USIT** (✆ **01/602-1906;** www.usit.ie), an Ireland-based specialist in student, youth, and independent travel.

Sustainable tourism is conscientious travel. It means being careful with the environments you explore and respecting the communities you visit. Two overlapping components of sustainable travel are **ecotourism** and **ethical tourism. The International Ecotourism Society (TIES)** defines ecotourism as responsible travel to natural areas that conserves the environment and improves the well-being of local people. TIES suggests that ecotourists follow these principles:

- Minimize environmental impact.
- Build environmental and cultural awareness and respect.
- Provide positive experiences for both visitors and hosts.
- Provide direct financial benefits for conservation and for local people.
- Raise sensitivity to host countries' political, environmental, and social climates.
- Support international human rights and labor agreements.

Before you even reach your hotel in Seattle, you can do your part for the environment by taking mass transit into town from the airport. By the time you read this, you should be able to ride the city's new LINK light rail (p. 26). If you must rent a car, you can get a hybrid car from Enterprise or Hertz.

If you want to sleep soundly at night knowing that you've done just a little bit more for the environment while on vacation, the **Hyatt at Olive 8** (p. 60) should be your first choice in Seattle. In 2009, this hotel became the first Seattle hotel certified by Leadership in Energy and Environmental Design (LEED), an organization that certifies environmentally sustainable construction practices. Although this is primarily a business and convention hotel, it is conveniently located and offers some great amenities, including a spa and a pool.

When it comes time to eat out, you've got loads of eco-friendly options in Seattle. See the "Meatless in Seattle" box in chapter 6 (p. 97) for some recommended vegetarian restaurants around town. At many of the restaurants listed in this book, you'll find that the chefs rely on local and organic produce as much as possible. The locavore movement (eating foods grown or raised nearby) has been wholeheartedly embraced here in Seattle. Restaurants emphasizing organic and sustainably produced ingredients include **Tilth** (p. 110), **Portage Bay Café** (p. 106), **Spinasse** (p. 107), and **Agua Verde Café** (p. 109).

There are even espresso bars that serve organic, fair-trade coffee (**Caffe Ladro;** p. 115) and a small chain of chocolate shops that serves both organic coffee and hot chocolate (**Chocolati;** p. 117). Keep an eye out for chocolate bars from **Theo Chocolate** (p. 178), a local chocolate maker that uses fair-trade cocoa beans in its chocolate bars and other confections. They even offer tours of their factory in the Fremont neighborhood.

If you plan on heading out of town on an adventurous outing, consider booking your tour with **EverGreen Escapes** (see below), which uses biodiesel tour vehicles.

General Resources for Green Travel

In addition to the resources for Seattle listed above, the following websites provide valuable wide-ranging information on sustainable travel. For a list of even more sustainable resources, as well as tips and explanations on how to travel greener, visit www.frommers.com/planning.

- **Responsible Travel** (www.responsibletravel.com) is a great source of sustainable travel ideas; the site is run by a spokesperson for ethical tourism in the travel industry. **Sustainable Travel International** (www.sustainable travelinternational.org) promotes ethical tourism practices, and manages an extensive directory of sustainable properties and tour operators around the world.
- In the U.K., **Tourism Concern** (www.tourismconcern.org.uk) works to reduce social and environmental problems connected to tourism. The **Association of Independent Tour Operators** (**AITO**; www.aito.co.uk) is a group of specialist operators leading the field in making holidays sustainable.
- In Canada, **www.greenlivingonline.com** offers extensive content on how to travel sustainably, including a travel and transport section and profiles of the best green shops and services in Toronto, Vancouver, and Calgary.
- In Australia, the national body which sets guidelines and standards for ecotourism is **Ecotourism Australia** (www.ecotourism.org.au). **The Green Directory** (www.thegreendirectory.com.au), **Green Pages** (www.thegreen pages.com.au), and **Eco Directory** (www.ecodirectory.com.au) offer sustainable travel tips and directories of green businesses.
- **Carbonfund** (www.carbonfund.org), **TerraPass** (www.terrapass.org), and **Carbon Neutral** (www.carbonneutral.org) provide info on "carbon offsetting," or offsetting the greenhouse gas emitted during flights.
- **Greenhotels** (www.greenhotels.com) recommends green-rated member hotels around the world that fulfill the company's stringent environmental requirements. **Environmentally Friendly Hotels** (www.environmentally friendlyhotels.com) offers more green accommodations ratings. The **Hotel Association of Canada** (www.hacgreenhotels.com) has a Green Key Eco-Rating Program, which audits the environmental performance of Canadian hotels, motels, and resorts.
- **Sustain Lane** (www.sustainlane.com) lists sustainable eating and drinking choices around the U.S.; also visit **www.eatwellguide.org** for tips on eating sustainably in the U.S. and Canada.
- For information on animal-friendly issues throughout the world, visit **Tread Lightly** (www.treadlightly.org). For information about the ethics of swimming with dolphins, visit the **Whale and Dolphin Conservation Society** (www.wdcs.org).
- **Volunteer International** (www.volunteerinternational.org) has a list of questions to help you determine the intentions and the nature of a volunteer program. For general info on volunteer travel, visit **www.volunteer abroad.org** and **www.idealist.org**.

8 SPECIAL-INTEREST TRIPS

ADVENTURE & WELLNESS TRIPS

If you want to turn a trip to Seattle into an adventure, book a multiday kayak tour with **Northwest Outdoor Center** (✆ **800/ 683-0637** or 206/281-9694; www.nwoc. com), which offers a variety of sea-kayak tours. Also see "The San Juan Islands" section of chapter 11 for kayak-tour companies offering trips through the San Juan Islands.

For a very different sort of hiking tour, contact **Deli Llama,** 17045 Llama Lane, Bow, WA 98232 (✆ **360/757-4212;** www. delillama.com), which offers llama trekking tours in Olympic National Park.

With its biodiesel vans and Jeeps, **Ever-Green Escapes** (✆ **866/203-7603** or 206/ 650-5795; www.evergreenescapes.com) is an environmentally conscious tour company specializing in adventurous getaways. Hiking, rafting, kayaking, and bicycling are all options on this company's tours.

FOOD & WINE TRIPS/ COOKING CLASSES

Seattle is the sort of city that foodies and wine lovers dream about—great restaurants with access to superb local ingredients and dozens of wineries within 30 minutes of the city. If you'd like to focus on food or wine on your vacation, check out some of the offerings from these cooking schools and wine-tour companies.

One of my favorite Seattle chefs, Tom Douglas, offers 5-day summer culinary camps ($2,500). To learn more, visit **www. tomdouglas.com**. Another local chef, Christine Keff, offers cooking classes through her restaurant, **Flying Fish,** 2234 First Ave. (✆ **206/728-8595;** www.flying fishseattle.com). The lunchtime classes cost $55.

Culinary Expeditions Tour Company, 1411 Fourth Ave., Ste. 1424, Seattle, WA 98101 (✆ **206/264-1270;** www.nw culinarytours.com), offers food-focused multiday tours in the Seattle area and also does a variety of special dinners.

If you'd like to hone your Asian-cooking skills, take a class with **NuCulinary,** 6253 California Ave. SW, PMB 250, Seattle, WA 98136 (✆ **206/932-3855;** www.nuculinary.com), which holds cooking classes at the Seattle area's two Uwajimaya Asian supermarkets.

At **L'Auberge Bed & Breakfast Inn/ Edge of Seattle Cooking School,** 16400 216th Ave. NE, Woodinville, WA 98072 (✆ **425/260-6213;** www.edgeof-seattle-cooking.com), you can stay in wine country and spend a couple of days learning new cooking techniques.

For a tour of the nearby Woodinville wine country, get in touch with **Bon Vivant Wine Tours** (✆ **206/524-8687;** www.bonvivanttours.com), which offers day tours of the area and also does 3-day tours to eastern Washington's wine country.

PACKAGES FOR THE INDEPENDENT TRAVELER

Package tours are simply a way to buy the airfare, accommodations, and other elements of your trip (such as car rentals, airport transfers, and sometimes even activities) at the same time and often at discounted prices.

One good source of package deals is the airlines themselves. Most major airlines offer air/land packages, including **American Airlines Vacations** (✆ 800/321-2121; www.aavacations.com), **Continental Airlines Vacations** (✆ 800/829-7777; www. covacations.com), **Delta Vacations** (✆ 800/ 654-6559; www.deltavacations.com), **United**

Vacations (© 888/854-3899; www.united vacations.com), and **US Airways Vacations** (© 800/455-0123; www.usairways vacations.com). Several big **online travel agencies**—Expedia, Travelocity, Orbitz, and Lastminute.com—also do a brisk business in packages.

For more information on Package Tours and for tips on booking your trip, see **www.frommers.com**.

9 STAYING CONNECTED

TELEPHONES

Generally, hotel surcharges on long-distance and local calls are astronomical, so you're better off using your **cellphone** or a **public pay telephone.** Many convenience groceries and packaging services sell **prepaid calling cards** in denominations up to $50; for international visitors, these can be the least expensive way to call home. Many public pay phones at airports now accept American Express, MasterCard, and Visa credit cards.

Most long-distance and international calls can be dialed directly from any phone. **For calls within the United States and to Canada,** dial 1 followed by the area code and the seven-digit number. **For other international calls,** dial 011 followed by the country code, city code, and the number you are calling.

Calls to area codes **800, 888, 877,** and **866** are toll-free. However, calls to area codes **700** and **900** (chat lines, bulletin boards, "dating" services, and so on) can be very expensive—usually a charge of 95¢ to $3 or more per minute, and they sometimes have minimum charges that can run as high as $15 or more.

For **reversed-charge or collect calls,** and for person-to-person calls, dial the number 0 and then the area code and number; an operator will come on the line, and you should specify whether you are calling collect, person-to-person, or both. If your operator-assisted call is international, ask for the overseas operator.

For **local directory assistance** ("information"), dial 411; for long-distance information, dial 1, then the appropriate area code and 555-1212.

CELLPHONES

Just because your cellphone works at home doesn't mean it will work everywhere in the U.S. (thanks to our nation's fragmented cellphone system). It's a good bet that your phone will work in major cities, but take a look at your wireless company's coverage map on its website before heading out; T-Mobile, Sprint, and Nextel are particularly weak in rural areas. If you need to stay in touch at a destination where you know your phone won't work, **rent** a phone that does from **Roberts rent-a-phone** (© **800/964-2468** or 781/596-2060; www.dollar-rent-a-phone.com).

INTERNET & E-MAIL
With Your Own Computer

More and more hotels, resorts, airports, cafes, and retailers are going Wi-Fi (wireless fidelity), becoming "hotspots" that offer free high-speed Wi-Fi access or charge a small fee for usage. Wi-Fi is even found in campgrounds, RV parks, and entire towns. Most laptops sold today have built-in wireless capability. To find public Wi-Fi hotspots at your destination, go to **www.jiwire.com**; its Hotspot Finder holds the world's largest directory of public wireless hotspots.

For dial-up access, most business-class hotels in the U.S. offer dataports for laptop modems, and many hotels in the U.S. now also offer free high-speed Internet access or wireless access either in the guest rooms or in the hotel lobby.

Wherever you go, bring a **connection kit** of the right power and phone adapters, a spare phone cord, and a spare Ethernet network cable—or find out whether your hotel supplies them.

For information on electrical currency conversions, see "Electricity," in the appendix (p. 258).

Without Your Own Computer

Most major airports have **Internet kiosks** that provide basic Web access for a per-minute fee that's usually higher than cybercafe prices. Also check out copy shops like **FedEx Office,** which offers computer stations with fully loaded software (as well as Wi-Fi).

For help locating cybercafes and other establishments where you can go for Internet access, visit **www.cybercaptive.com** and **www.cybercafe.com**.

Suggested Seattle Itineraries

When you're not familiar with a city, it can be daunting trying to figure out how to organize your time on a brief visit. In order to help you plan your trip to Seattle, I've put together three suggested itineraries. The first, a 1-day itinerary, hits all the must-see attractions and, I have to admit, packs a lot into a single day. Still, if you've got only a day to do Seattle, you probably want to get the most out of your time, and that's exactly what the first itinerary is for. The other two itineraries pick up some of Seattle's more interesting neighborhoods and outlying attractions.

THE NEIGHBORHOODS IN BRIEF

The Waterfront The Seattle waterfront, which stretches along Alaskan Way from roughly Washington Street in the south to Broad Street and Myrtle Edwards Park in the north, is the most touristy neighborhood in Seattle. In addition to the many tacky gift shops, greasy fish and chips windows, and tour-boat docks, you'll also find the city's only waterfront hotel (The Edgewater), the Seattle Aquarium, and a few excellent seafood restaurants. The waterfront is also a residential neighborhood. At the north end of Alaskan Way are waterview condominiums.

Downtown This is Seattle's main business district and can roughly be defined as the area from Pioneer Square in the south to around Pike Place Market in the north, and from First Avenue to Eighth Avenue. It's characterized by steep streets, high-rise office buildings, luxury hotels, and a high density of retail shops (primarily national chains). This is also where you'll find the Seattle Art Museum and Benaroya Hall, which is home to the Seattle Symphony. Because hotels in this area are convenient to both Pioneer Square and Pike Place Market, this is a good neighborhood in which to stay. Unfortunately, the hotels here are the most expensive in the city.

First Hill Because it is home to several large hospitals, this hilly neighborhood just east of downtown and across I-5 is called "Pill Hill" by Seattleites. First Hill is home to the Frye Art Museum and a couple of good hotels.

Pioneer Square The Pioneer Square Historic District, known for its restored 1890s buildings, is centered on the corner of First Avenue and Yesler Way. The tree-lined streets and cobblestone plazas make this one of the prettiest downtown neighborhoods. Pioneer Square (which refers to the neighborhood, not a specific square) is full of antiques shops, art galleries, restaurants, bars, and nightclubs. Because of the number of bars in this neighborhood, late nights are not a particularly pleasant time to wander here. Also, during the day, the number of street people in this area is off-putting to many visitors.

The Chinatown/International District Known to locals as the I.D., this is one of Seattle's most distinctive neighborhoods, and is home to a large Asian population. Here you'll find the Wing

Luke Asian Museum, Hing Hay Park (a small park with an ornate pagoda), Uwajimaya (an Asian supermarket), and many small shops and restaurants. The Chinatown/International District begins around Fifth Avenue South and South Jackson Street. This neighborhood is interesting for a stroll, but there aren't many attractions.

SoDo This neighborhood lies to the SOuth of DOwntown, and thus its name. It is home to Qwest Field and Safeco Field, and while primarily an industrial and warehouse district, it does have a smattering of interesting shops and restaurants.

Georgetown In this up-and-coming neighborhood south of SoDo and just north of Boeing Field, youthful urban pioneers are turning old industrial buildings into art galleries, nightclubs, cafes, and restaurants.

Belltown In the blocks north of Pike Place Market between Western and Fourth avenues, Belltown is ground zero for upscale Seattle restaurants and hip nightclubs. Keeping the restaurants in business are the residents of the neighborhood's many high-rise condominiums. Belltown's numerous nightclubs and bars attract crowds of the young, the hip, and the stylish—who, in turn, attract a lot of nighttime panhandlers.

Queen Anne Hill Queen Anne is just northwest of Seattle Center and offers great views of the city. This affluent neighborhood, one of the most prestigious in Seattle proper, is where you find some of Seattle's oldest homes. Today, the neighborhood is divided into the Upper Queen Anne and Lower Queen Anne neighborhoods. Upper Queen Anne is very peaceful and abounds in moderately priced restaurants. Lower Queen Anne, adjacent to

theaters and Marion Oliver McCaw Hall at Seattle Center, is something of a theater district and has a more urban character.

Capitol Hill To the northeast of downtown, centered along Broadway near Volunteer Park, Capitol Hill is Seattle's main gay neighborhood and has long been a popular youth-culture shopping district. Broadway sidewalks are always crowded, and it is nearly impossible to find a parking space here. However, in recent years, the area has been undergoing a renaissance. New condominiums are being built on Broadway, and along 12th Avenue, near the intersection with Pike Street, there are now more than half a dozen good restaurants. Capitol Hill is also where you'll find many bed-and-breakfasts, housed in some of the neighborhood's impressive old homes and mansions. Unfortunately, this neighborhood is Seattle's main hangout for runaways and street kids, many of whom are involved in the city's drug scene.

Madison Park One of Seattle's more affluent neighborhoods, Madison Park fronts the western shore of Lake Washington, northeast of downtown. The University of Washington Arboretum, which includes the Japanese Gardens, is the centerpiece of the neighborhood. Several excellent restaurants cluster here at the end of East Madison Street.

The University District As the name implies, this neighborhood in the northeast section of the city surrounds the University of Washington. The U District, as it's known to locals, provides all the amenities of a college neighborhood: cheap ethnic restaurants, pubs, clubs, espresso bars, and music stores. Several good hotels here offer substantial savings over comparable downtown accommodations.

Wallingford This is another of Seattle's quiet, primarily residential neighborhoods with an interesting commercial/ retail district. Located just west of the University District and adjacent to Lake Union, it's filled with small restaurants, some of which are quite good. You'll also find interesting little shops and an old school that has been renovated and is now home to boutiques and restaurants.

Fremont North of the Lake Washington Ship Canal between Wallingford and Ballard, Fremont is home to Seattle's best-loved piece of public art— *Waiting for the Interurban*—as well as the famous *Fremont Troll* sculpture. This is Seattle's wackiest neighborhood, filled with eclectic shops and ethnic restaurants. During the summer, there are outdoor movies on Saturday nights, a Sunday flea market, and a solstice festival.

Magnolia This affluent residential neighborhood lies to the west of Queen Anne Hill. Magnolia's few cafes, restaurants, and bars are frequented primarily by area residents, but it's also home to Palisade, one of Seattle's best waterfront restaurants. The west side of Magnolia borders sprawling Discovery Park, Seattle's largest green space.

Ballard If you have time to visit only one neighborhood outside of downtown, make it Ballard. In northwest Seattle, bordering the Lake Washington Ship Canal and Puget Sound, Ballard is a former Scandinavian community that retains visible remnants of its past. Known for its busy nightlife scene, Ballard, one of Seattle's most enjoyable neighborhoods, is also a great place to discover off-the-beaten-path gems. Art galleries and interesting boutiques and shops are set along the tree-shaded streets of the neighborhood's old commercial center. The neighborhood's Nordic Heritage Museum often has excellent art exhibits.

The Eastside Home to Bill Gates, Microsoft, countless high-tech spinoff companies, and seemingly endless suburbs, the Eastside lies across Lake Washington from Seattle proper and comprises the cities of Kirkland, Bellevue, Redmond, and a few other smaller communities. As the presence of Bill Gates's mansion attests, there are some pretty wealthy neighborhoods here; but wealth doesn't necessarily equal respect, and the Eastside is still much derided by Seattle citizens, who perceive it as an uncultured bedroom community.

West Seattle West Seattle, across the wasteland of the port facility from downtown, is not just the site of the terminal for ferries to Vashon Island and the Kitsap Peninsula. It's also the site of Seattle's favorite beach, Alki, which is as close to a Southern California beach experience as you'll find in the Northwest. Here, too, is the waterfront restaurant with the best view of Seattle: Salty's on Alki Beach.

Bainbridge Island Seattle's most exurban bedroom community is only a 35-minute ferry ride away, though Bainbridge feels quite far from the inner-city asphalt to the east. Green, green, green is the best way to characterize this rural residential island. Downtown Bainbridge Island (formerly known as Winslow), the island's main commercial area, has the feel of an upscale San Francisco Bay Area community. When you hear about Seattle's quality of life, this is what people are talking about.

1 THE BEST OF SEATTLE IN 1 DAY

Lace up your walking shoes, grab an umbrella if it looks like rain, and hit the streets early if you want to experience the best of Seattle in a single day. Luckily, two of the city's top attractions—Pike Place Market and the Olympic Sculpture Park—open early, so you should get started as early as possible. For visitors, the fact that the market is only 2 blocks from the waterfront makes connecting the dots in this town fairly easy. Late in the afternoon, after delving into the city's history, you'll visit Seattle Center, which is home to Seattle's most familiar icon, the Space Needle. Start: Walk or take a taxi to the Olympic Sculpture Park.

❶ Olympic Sculpture Park ★★★

Set at the north end of the waterfront and home to monumental sculptures by Alexander Calder, Claes Oldenburg, and Richard Serra, this multilevel park is the most beautiful open space in Seattle. There are stunning views across Puget Sound to the Olympic Mountains, native-plant gardens, and a tiny man-made beach that looks as wild as any beach on the Olympic Peninsula. See p. 124.

Walk south along the waterfront (or catch the free Waterfront Streetcar bus) to Pier 59 and the Pike Hill Climb.

❷ Pike Place Market ★★★

At the top of the hill-climb stairs, you'll find Pike Place Market, Seattle's sprawling historic market complex. Grab a grande latte at the Starbucks that kicked the whole espresso scene into high gear, and then pick out a pastry at one of the market bakeries. With fortification in hand, peruse the many stalls selling fresh salmon and Dungeness crabs, local and exotic produce, and cut flowers. By mid-morning, the market's arts-and-crafts vendors are usually set up and you can shop for distinctive gifts and souvenirs. Wander through the dark depths of the market to search out unusual specialty shops. See p. 126.

Take the Pike Hill Climb back down to the waterfront.

❸ The Waterfront ★★

Just as at San Francisco's Fisherman's Wharf, the Seattle waterfront is ground zero for tacky tourist shops, fish and chips counters, and mediocre, overpriced restaurants. However, the waterfront does have its redeeming features: On a clear day, the view across Elliott Bay to the Olympic Mountains is unforgettable. And a wide sidewalk along the waterfront is perfect for strolling. The real stars of the waterfront, though, are the Seattle Aquarium and, of course, the Olympic Sculpture Park. See p. 121.

Directly across the street from the stairs of the Pike Hill Climb is Pier 59.

❹ Seattle Aquarium ★★

Pier 59 is home to the Seattle Aquarium, where you can learn about the sea life of the region. Jellyfish, sea horses, salmon, and otters are just some of the popular attractions at this aquarium. See p. 125.

🍴 ALKI CRAB & FISH

In summer, head to Pier 55, where you can catch the water taxi across Elliott Bay to Alki in West Seattle. The view back across the water to the Seattle skyline is beautiful, and right at the water-taxi dock on Alki, there's this inexpensive little fish and chips place with a million-dollar view. If service is fast and you remembered to ask for a transfer when you got on the boat, you can ride back across the bay without having to buy another ticket. 1660 Harbor Ave. SW. ✆ 206/938-0975. See p. 114.

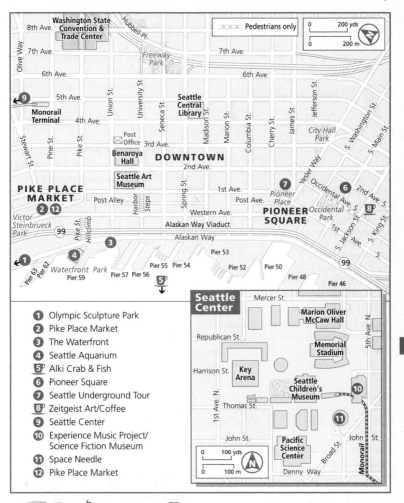

8th Ave. **Washington State Convention & Trade Center** Hubbell Pl.

☐☐☐☐ Pedestrians only

7th Ave.   *Freeway Park*   7th Ave.

Olive Way

6th Ave.   6th Ave.

5th Ave.   **Seattle Central Library**

Monorail Terminal   4th Ave.

Stewart St.   Pine St.   Pike St.   Union St.   University St.   Seneca St.   Spring St.   Madison St.   Marion St.   Columbia St.   Cherry St.   James St.   Jefferson St.   **City Hall Park**   S. Washington St.   S. Main St.

Post Office   3rd Ave.

Benaroya Hall   **DOWNTOWN**

2nd Ave.

Seattle Art Museum   1st Ave.

PIKE PLACE MARKET   Post Alley   Post Ave.   *Pioneer Place*   2nd Ave. S.

Pike St. Hillclimb   Harbor Steps

Victor Steinbrueck Park   **2** **12**   Western Ave.   **PIONEER SQUARE**   Occidental Park   Occidental Ave. S.   S. Washington St.   S. Main St.

99   **3**   Alaskan Way Viaduct   Yesler Way   Occidental Ave. S.   1st   S. Jackson St.   S. King St.

1   *Waterfront Park*   **4**   Alaskan Way

Pier 63   Pier 62   Pier 59   Pier 57   Pier 56   Pier 55   Pier 54   Pier 53   Pier 52   Pier 50   Pier 48   99   Pier 46

5

0   200 yds
0   200 m

Seattle Center   Mercer St.

Marion Oliver McCaw Hall

Republican St.   **Memorial Stadium**

5th Ave. N.

Harrison St.   **Key Arena**   **Seattle Children's Museum**   **10**

1st Ave. N.   Thomas St.   **11**

John St.   **Pacific Science Center**   John St.

Denny Way   Broad St.   Monorail

0   100 yds
0   100 m

- ① Olympic Sculpture Park
- ② Pike Place Market
- ③ The Waterfront
- ④ Seattle Aquarium
- ⑤ Alki Crab & Fish
- ⑥ Pioneer Square
- ⑦ Seattle Underground Tour
- ⑧ Zeitgeist Art/Coffee
- ⑨ Seattle Center
- ⑩ Experience Music Project/ Science Fiction Museum
- ⑪ Space Needle
- ⑫ Pike Place Market

SUGGESTED SEATTLE ITINERARIES

4

THE BEST OF SEATTLE IN 1 DAY

Take the water taxi back across Elliott Bay and then walk 5 blocks south. Head away from the water on Yesler Way.

⑥ Pioneer Square ★

The historic Pioneer Square area is where Seattle got its start back in the 1850s. Today, it is one of the city's only historic districts, and its tree-shaded streets are lined with brick buildings constructed after the Seattle fire of 1889. See "Walking Tour 2: The Pioneer Square Area," in chapter 8, for a recommended route to explore this area.

⑦ Seattle Underground Tour ★

To learn more about Seattle's early history, with an emphasis on the seamier side of life and the city's reconstruction after the fire of 1889, take the Underground Tour, which begins at the corner of First Avenue and Yesler Way. This tour provides a little fun and paints an interesting picture of the characters who founded Seattle. Be forewarned that participants need an appreciation for bad jokes and should not have a fear of dark, musty basements. See p. 138.

8 ZEITGEIST ART/COFFEE

With its big windows and local artwork, Zeitgeist Art/Coffee is popular with the Pioneer Square art crowd. A hip, low-key character makes this a pleasant place to kick back and get off your feet for a few minutes. 171 S. Jackson St. ℂ 206/583-0497. See p. 116.

If it's a weekday, head to the corner of James Street and Third Avenue, and catch a free bus through the Transit Tunnel to Westlake Station. On weekends, catch a free northbound Third Avenue bus to Westlake Center, an upscale shopping complex from which you can take a bus or the monorail to Seattle Center.

9 Seattle Center ★★

Built for the 1962 World's Fair, this 74-acre campus is the cultural heart of Seattle and the city's premier family attraction. Seattle Center is home to the Seattle Opera, the Pacific Northwest Ballet, numerous theater companies, a children's museum, and a science museum. For most people, however, Seattle Center is primarily known as the home of the Space Needle and the bizarre Frank Gehry–designed Experience Music Project/Science Fiction Museum building. See p. 128.

10 Experience Music Project/ Science Fiction Museum ★★

If you're a rock-music or science-fiction fan, explore this unusual pair of associated museums. They're both inside a huge blob of color that looks a bit like a melted-down electric guitar. If you're not interested in going inside, at least stroll around outside and marvel at the building's sweeping lines and colorful exterior. See p. 129 and 132.

11 Space Needle ★★

Of course, a visit to Seattle isn't complete without riding the elevator to the top of the Space Needle. From the observation deck, 520 feet above the ground, you have a superb panorama of Seattle and its surrounding mountains and many bodies of water. If it's summer and the sun is still shining, see if you can pick out the route you followed during your earlier tour of the city. Keep in mind that during the summer, sunset isn't until after 9pm. Other times of the year, you'll get to enjoy the city's twinkling lights. See p. 132.

12 Pike Place Market ★★★

Finish your day back at Pike Place Market. By nightfall, the fishmongers and flower vendors are long gone and the shops are all closed. However, some of the city's best restaurants and most enjoyable bars are here. Catch an eclectic musical act at The Pink Door, listen to Irish music at Kells, or enjoy a romantic late dinner at Il Bistro.

2 THE BEST OF SEATTLE IN 2 DAYS

On your second day, start and end your day with salmon. Up in north Seattle's Ballard neighborhood, you can take in salmon and locks (not lox) at the Hiram M. Chittenden Locks. Afterward, head back to Pike Place Market to shop for picnic supplies, and then hop aboard a ferry bound for Bainbridge Island. Once back in Seattle, take in world-class art at the Seattle Art Museum, and then head out for your second Puget Sound excursion of the day, this time to a state park island, where you'll be served a grilled salmon dinner (not lox this time, either). Start: Drive or take a bus to Ballard in north Seattle.

Map legend:

8th Ave.
Washington State Convention & Trade Center
Hubbell Pl.
7th Ave.
Freeway Park
7th Ave.
Stewart St.
Olive Way
6th Ave.
6th Ave.
Westlake Ave.
5th Ave.
5th Ave.
Union St.
University St.
Seattle Central Library
Seneca St.
Madison St.
Marion St.
Columbia St.
Cherry St.
James St.
Jefferson St.
Monorail Terminal
4th Ave.
4th Ave.
City Hall Park
Yesler Way
Virginia St.
Stewart St.
Pine St.
Pike St.
Post Office
3rd Ave.
Benaroya Hall
DOWNTOWN
2nd Ave.
PIKE PLACE MARKET
Seattle Art Museum **5**
6 ⓡ
Spring St.
1st Ave.
Pioneer Place
Occidental Ave. S.
1st Ave.
Post Alley
Harbor Steps
3
Post Ave.
PIONEER SQUARE
Occidental Park
1st Ave. S.
Occidental Ave. S.
2
Western Ave.
Victor Steinbrueck Park
Pike St. Hillclimb
99
Alaskan Way Viaduct
Alaskan Way
Jackson St.
Seattle Aquarium
7
Waterfront Park
Pier 55
Pier 54
Pier 53
4
Pier 50
99
Pier 63
Pier 62
Pier 59
Pier 57
Pier 56
Pier 55
To Blake Island
To Bainbridge Island
Pier 52
Pier 48
Pier 46

Pedestrians only
0   200 yds
0   200 m

1 Hiram M. Chittenden Locks
2 Pike Place Market
3 Harbor Steps
4 A Ferry Excursion to Bainbridge Island
5 Seattle Art Museum
6 Ancient Grounds
7 Tillicum Village Tour

SUGGESTED SEATTLE ITINERARIES

4

THE BEST OF SEATTLE IN 2 DAYS

Head to the corner of Third Avenue and Pike Street downtown and catch the no. 17 bus north to the Ballard neighborhood; get off at the Hiram M. Chittenden Locks stop.

❶ Hiram M. Chittenden Locks ★★

These locks separate the waters of Elliott Bay from those of Lake Union and allow everything from sea kayaks to commercial fishing boats to make their way between the two bodies of water. It's a slow, though fascinating, process that always draws crowds. However, for many summer visitors, the big attraction here is the fish ladder and its associated fish-viewing windows that allow visitors to watch salmon and steelhead migrating up-river. See p. 137.

Head back to downtown Seattle.

❷ Pike Place Market ★★

There's just so much to see at this market, you should visit again on your second day. Put together the ingredients for a picnic so you can have lunch on a ferry crossing Puget Sound. See p. 126.

❸ Harbor Steps ★

The Harbor Steps, 2 blocks south of Pike Place Market, may not be as beautiful as Rome's Spanish Steps, but they are by far the prettiest route from downtown to the waterfront and are a popular hangout both for footsore tourists and downtown office workers hoping to soak up a little sunshine on their lunch hour. Waterfalls, fountains, and sculptures grace the terraces of the Harbor Steps, and several restaurants and shops flank the stairs. Walk down the stairs to the waterfront.

❹ A Ferry Excursion to Bainbridge Island

No visit to Seattle is complete without a ride on a ferry, and because the Bainbridge Island ferry takes only 35 minutes for the crossing, it's a good choice for a ferry excursion if your time is limited. The big car ferries that shuttle back and forth across Puget Sound to both Bainbridge Island and Bremerton leave from Colman Dock at Pier 52. Once on Bainbridge Island, you can wander around the downtown area, where you'll find coffeehouses, restaurants, boutiques, galleries, and restaurants. You can even rent a sea kayak and paddle around Eagle Harbor while you're here. See "Ferry Excursions from Seattle," in chapter 11.

Once back in Seattle, head up the Harbor Steps for an afternoon of art.

❺ Seattle Art Museum ★★★

Looming over First Avenue at the corner of University Street is Jonathon Borofsky's *Hammering Man,* a three-story animated silhouette-like sculpture that stands outside the front door of the Seattle Art Museum. This huge museum has impressive permanent collections and hosts numerous traveling exhibits throughout the year. Any time of year, the Northwest Coast Indian and contemporary Northwest art exhibits are well worth a visit. See p. 127.

❻ ANCIENT GROUNDS ★
If you're interested in Native American artifacts, be sure to stop in at this eclectic establishment a half-block south of the Harbor Steps. Order a latte and then peruse the masks and wood carvings that fill the cases of this cabinet of curiosities. 1220 First Ave. ☏ **206/749-0747.** See p. 173.

❼ Tillicum Village Tour ★★

Although it is a bit touristy, the Tillicum Village Tour, which departs from Pier 55 on the waterfront, includes not only a boat excursion to Blake Island State Park, but also a salmon dinner and a performance of traditional Northwest Coast Native American masked dances. The "long house" where the dinner and dances are held was built as part of the same World's Fair that gave Seattle the Space Needle. The island setting is beautiful and the masked dances are fascinating. I especially recommend this tour for families. Be sure to check the schedule for these tours. See p. 148.

3 THE BEST OF SEATTLE IN 3 DAYS

On your third day, head out of the city to see some of the wild country for which the Northwest is famous. The only problem is that there are so many great choices that it can be difficult to decide where to go on a day trip from Seattle. Personally, I prefer the mountains, so I would steer you southeast to Mount Rainier, that great big bulk of a dormant volcano that looms over Seattle like a sleeping giant. The mountain and all its glaciers, wildflower meadows, and old-growth forests are preserved as Mount Rainier National Park. For this excursion, you'll need to rent a car. It's roughly 90 miles to the national park, and you should expect to take at least 2 hours to cover this distance. I recommend circling the mountain in a clockwise direction beginning at the park's northeast entrance, which is along Wash. 410 southeast of Enumclaw.

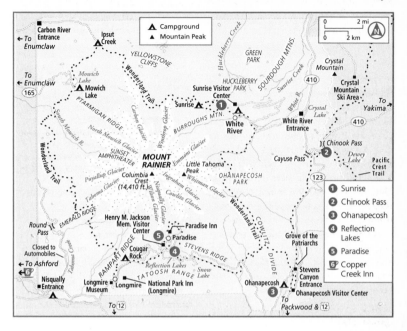

❶ Sunrise ★★★

This is the highest point in the park accessible by car, and the in-your-face view of Mount Rainier is unforgettable. Also in view is the Emmons Glacier, which is the largest glacier in the 48 contiguous states. Hiking trails of varying levels of difficulty radiate out from Sunrise, and every one of these trails has great views. Keep an eye out for mountain goats and elk. *Bonus:* Sunrise usually isn't as crowded as Paradise, on the other side of the mountain. See p. 240.

❷ Chinook Pass ★

At Cayuse Pass, on the east side of the park, take a short side trip off the main 'round-the-mountain road by staying on Wash. 410, which will bring you to the lovely Chinook Pass. Here the tiny Tipsoo Lakes flank the highway and Naches Peak rises above the road. A 4.5-mile loop trail leads alongside the lake and around Naches Peak through forests and meadows. This is a good place to lose the crowds. See p. 240.

Head back the way you just came and turn south on Wash. 123 to Ohanapecosh.

❸ Ohanapecosh ★★

You won't find any views of the mountain here, but you will find a .75-mile trail to some of the oldest trees in the state. The Grove of the Patriarchs trail, which begins just west of Wash. 123 near the park's Stevens Canyon entrance, leads to a streamside grove of Western red cedars that are estimated to be more than 1,000 years old. One of these trees is the largest red cedar in the park. See p. 240.

From Ohanapecosh, drive west through the park on Stevens Canyon Road.

❹ Reflection Lakes ★★

Make sure you have plenty of film in your camera or space on the compact flash card of your digital camera; the view of Mount

Rainier from these pretty little alpine lakes is hands-down the most photogenic view in the park. If there's no wind, the reflection of the mountain in the waters of these lakes provides the answer to how these bodies of water were named. See p. 240.

See p. 240.

Continue west on Stevens Canyon Road.

➎ Paradise ★★★

This place isn't called Paradise for nothing. Mountainside meadows burst into vibrant color each summer, usually starting in mid- to late July. Trails of different lengths meander through these wildflower meadows and lead to the edges of snowfields and viewpoints overlooking rumbling glaciers. Since you've probably already done quite a bit of hiking, you may want to head straight to the Nisqually Vista overlook, where you can gaze down on the Nisqually Glacier.

☕ COPPER CREEK INN

Just after you leave the park via the Nisqually entrance and Wash. 706, keep an eye out for this rustic roadside diner. Sure you can get a simple meal, but the real reason to stop here is for a slice of blackberry pie. It's the best in the area. 35707 Wash. 706 E., Ashford. ✆ **360/569-2326.**

Where to Stay

Seattle is close on the heels of San Francisco as a West Coast summer-in-the-city destination, so its hotels stay pretty much booked solid for July and August. Also keep in mind that if you aren't on an expense account, you may be faced with sticker shock when you see what these places charge. However, if you're willing to head out a bit from downtown, you'll find prices a little easier to swallow.

The hotel scene continues to grow ever more sophisticated. This year, there is a luxurious new Four Seasons hotel, as well as a new Hyatt that is a Leadership in Energy and Environmental Design (LEED)-certified environmentally aware hotel. Seattle also has several chic, postmodern hotels, as well as a number of historic properties, including the charming Doubletree Arctic Club Hotel, which celebrates adventure travel and the Alaska gold rush. This all adds up to plenty of options for the traveler planning a trip to Seattle.

Seattle's largest concentrations of hotels are downtown and near the airport, with a few good options in the University District and also over in the suburbs of Bellevue and Kirkland (on the east side of Lake Washington). If you don't mind high prices, downtown hotels are the most convenient, but if your budget won't allow for a first-class business hotel, try to stay near the Space Needle, in the Lower Queen Anne neighborhood, or in the University District, where prices are more reasonable.

Be sure to make reservations as far in advance as possible, especially if you plan to visit during Seafair or another major festival. See "Seattle Calendar of Events" (p. 20) for the dates of all the big festivals.

In the following listings, price categories are based on the high season, which generally runs from June through September (most hotels charge the same for single and double rooms). Keep in mind that the rates listed do not include taxes, which add up to 15.6% in Seattle. Also be sure to factor in hotel parking fees—about $30 or more per day in downtown Seattle.

For comparison purposes, I list what hotels call "rack rates," or walk-in rates—but you should never have to pay these highly inflated prices. Various discounts and specials are often available, so make it a point to ask if any are being offered during your stay (and be sure to check the hotel's website for online specials). At inexpensive chain motels, discounted rates are almost always available for AAA members and seniors.

Room rates can be considerably lower from October through April (the rainy season), and downtown hotels often have substantially reduced prices on weekends throughout the year (while budget hotels generally charge more on weekends).

A few hotels include breakfast in their rates; others provide complimentary breakfast only on certain deluxe floors. Most Seattle hotels offer nonsmoking rooms, while most bed-and-breakfast inns are exclusively nonsmoking. The majority of hotels, but few inns, offer wheelchair-accessible rooms.

SURFING FOR HOTELS

In addition to the online travel booking sites **Travelocity, Expedia, Orbitz, Priceline,** and **Hotwire,** you can book hotels through **Hotels.com, Quikbook** (www.quikbook. com), and **Travelaxe** (www.travelaxe.net). **HotelChatter.com** is a daily webzine offering

Tips   **Hotel Training**

You can often save quite a bit of money on your room by not staying right in downtown Seattle, and a couple of areas are particularly convenient due to good public transportation options. Stay at a hotel near Seattle Center, and you can take the monorail to downtown. Stay at a hotel on or near the south end of Lake Union and you can take the Seattle Streetcar to downtown.

smart coverage and critiques of hotels worldwide. For more tips on surfing for hotel deals online, visit **Frommers.com**.

SAVING ON YOUR HOTEL ROOM

The **rack rate** is the maximum rate that a hotel charges for a room. Hardly anybody pays this price, however, except in high season or on holidays. To lower the cost of your room:

- **Ask about special rates or other discounts.** You may qualify for corporate, student, military, senior, frequent flier, trade union, or other discounts.
- **Book online.** Many hotels offer Internet-only discounts or supply rooms to Priceline, Hotwire, or Expedia at rates much lower than the ones you can get through the hotel itself.
- **Remember the law of supply and demand.** Resort and many budget hotels are most crowded and therefore most expensive on weekends, so discounts are usually available for midweek stays. Business hotels in downtown locations are busiest during the week, so you can expect big discounts over the weekend.
- **Book an efficiency.** A room with a kitchenette allows you to shop for groceries and cook your own meals. This is a big money saver, especially for families on long stays.
- **Consider enrolling in hotel "frequent-stay" programs,** which are upping the ante lately to win the loyalty of repeat customers. Frequent guests can accumulate points or credits to earn free hotel nights, airline miles, in-room amenities, merchandise, tickets to concerts and events, and discounts on sporting facilities. Perks are awarded not only by many chain hotels and motels (Hilton HHonors, Marriott Rewards, and Wyndham ByRequest, to name a few), but also by individual inns and B&Bs. Many chain hotels partner with other hotel chains, car-rental firms, airlines, and credit card companies to give consumers additional incentive to do repeat business.

LANDING THE BEST ROOM

Somebody has to get the best room in the house. It might as well be you. You can start by joining the hotel's frequent-guest program, which may make you eligible for upgrades. A hotel-branded credit card usually gives its owner "silver" or "gold" status in frequent-guest programs for free. Always ask about a corner room. They're often larger and quieter, with more windows and light, and they often cost the same as standard rooms. When you make your reservation, ask if the hotel is renovating; if it is, request a room away from the construction. If you're a light sleeper, request a quiet room away from vending or ice machines, elevators, restaurants, and bars. Ask for a room that has most recently been renovated or redecorated. If you aren't happy with your room when you arrive, ask for another one. Most lodgings will be willing to accommodate you.

If you want to get a great deal on a great hotel (don't we all?), get in touch with Sheri Doyle at **Pacific Northwest Journeys** (© 800/935-9730 or 206/935-9730; www.pnw journeys.com). This company specializes in itinerary planning and also offers a reservation service. The charge is $45 per reservation; however, you can usually make that up in savings on just a 2-night stay. If you're going to be in town for longer than that, you'll definitely save money. Last-minute reservations are often possible, too. A consultation service is also available for people who would like a little assistance with an itinerary.

When planning your trip, you might also want to check with **Seattle Super Saver** (© 800/535-7071 or 206/461-5882; www.seattlesupersaver.com), a reservation service operated by Seattle's Convention and Visitors Bureau. Rates are comparable to what you might find at online booking sites.

I've listed some of my favorite B&Bs in the pages that follow, but to find other good options, contact the **Seattle Bed & Breakfast Association** (© 800/348-5630; www. lodginginseattle.com). **A Pacific Reservation Service** (© 800/684-2932 or 206/439-7677; www.seattlebedandbreakfast.com) books rooms at dozens of accommodations in the Seattle area. A wide range of rates is available.

1 BEST HOTEL BETS

- **Best Historic Hotel:** Built in 1924, the **Fairmont Olympic Hotel,** 411 University St. (© 800/223-8772 or 206/621-1700; www.fairmont.com/seattle), is styled after an Italian Renaissance palace and is by far the most impressive of Seattle's historic hotels. See p. 58.
- **Best for a Romantic Getaway:** Though Seattle has quite a few hotels that do well for a romantic weekend, the **Inn at the Market,** 86 Pine St. (© 800/446-4484 or 206/443-3600; www.innatthemarket.com), with its Elliott Bay views, European atmosphere, and proximity to many excellent (and romantic) restaurants, is sure to set the stage for lasting memories. See p. 65.
- **Best for Hipsters:** The **Hotel Ändra,** 2000 Fourth Ave. (© 877/448-8600 or 206/448-8600; www.hotelandra.com), has given Seattle a boldly contemporary lodging. Best of all, it's on the edge of the trendy Belltown neighborhood, which makes this an ideal base for club-crawling night owls. See p. 64.
- **Best for Families:** Just across the street from Lake Union, the **Silver Cloud Inn—Lake Union,** 1150 Fairview Ave. N. (© 800/330-5812 or 206/447-9500; www. silvercloud.com), is far enough from downtown to be affordable—but not far from Seattle Center. Plus it has a great location overlooking the lake. There are indoor and outdoor pools and several restaurants right across the street. See p. 71.
- **Best Budget Hotel:** With a hip vibe, rates that are easy on the wallet, and a great location in the heart of the Belltown restaurant-and-nightlife district, the **Ace Hotel,** 2423 First Ave. (© 206/448-4721; www.acehotel.com), is the best budget hotel in town. The only drawback is that you really need to be young and into staying up late to appreciate both the hotel and the location. See p. 64.
- **Best B&B:** Set in the Capitol Hill neighborhood, the **Gaslight Inn,** 1727 15th Ave. (© 206/325-3654; www.gaslight-inn.com), is a lovingly restored and maintained Craftsman bungalow filled with original Stickley furniture. Lots of public spaces, very

tasteful decor, and a swimming pool in the backyard all add up to unexpected luxury. See p. 73.

- **Best Location:** On a pier right on the Seattle waterfront, **The Edgewater,** Pier 67, 2411 Alaskan Way (© 800/624-0670 or 206/728-7000; www.edgewaterhotel.com), is only 5 blocks from Pike Place Market and the Seattle Aquarium, and 3 blocks from the restaurants of Belltown. Ferries to Victoria, British Columbia, leave from the adjacent pier. See below.

- **Best Views:** If you're not back in your room by sunset at the **Westin Seattle,** 1900 Fifth Ave. (© 800/937-8461 or 206/728-1000; www.westin.com/seattle), you may not turn into a pumpkin, but you will miss a spectacular light show. Because this is the tallest hotel in the city, the Westin boasts fabulous views from its upper floors, especially those facing northwest. See p. 62.

- **Best Health Club:** The **Bellevue Club Hotel,** 11200 SE Sixth St., Bellevue (© 800/ 579-1110 or 425/454-4424; www.bellevueclub.com), has a huge private health club complete with an indoor pool and tennis courts. See p. 75.

- **Best Pool:** Most hotels in the city center stick their swimming pool (if they have one at all) down in the basement or on some hidden terrace, but at the **Sheraton Seattle Hotel,** 1400 Sixth Ave. (© 800/325-3535 or 206/621-9000; www.sheraton.com/ seattle), you can do laps on the top floor with the lights of the city twinkling all around you. See p. 61.

- **Best Room Decor:** If you plan to spend a lot of time in your room, then the **Bellevue Club Hotel,** 11200 SE Sixth St., Bellevue (© 800/579-1110 or 425/454-4424; www. bellevueclub.com), is the place to be. The rooms are plush enough to please the most demanding of hedonists. See p. 75.

- **Best for Pets:** If you're traveling to Seattle with your pooch and don't mind shelling out big bucks for top-end accommodations, then the **Alexis Hotel,** 1007 First Ave. (© 888/850-1155 or 206/624-4844; www.alexishotel.com), should be your home away from home. Special pet amenities include designer doggie beds, dog treats, a dog bowl with distilled water, pet-sitting services, and even in-room dining for your pooch. See p. 55.

2 THE WATERFRONT

Seattle's most touristy neighborhood, the waterfront has the city's finest views and is home to several worthwhile attractions and activities. The Edgewater (see below) is the city's only true waterfront hotel, and it should be the top choice of anyone wanting to spend a Seattle vacation in the thick of things.

VERY EXPENSIVE

The Edgewater ★★   On a pier at the north end of the waterfront, the Edgewater is Seattle's only true waterfront hotel, and despite the urban setting, The Edgewater manages to capture the feel of a classic Northwest wilderness retreat. The views out the windows are among the best in Seattle, and sunsets can be mesmerizing. On a clear day, you can see the Olympic Mountains across Puget Sound. The mountain-lodge theme continues in the rooms, which feature fireplaces and lodgepole-pine furniture. The least expensive units overlook the city (and the parking lot), so it's worth it to spring for a waterview. The rooms with balconies are a bit smaller than other rooms, although the

When it first opened in the early 1960s, **The Edgewater** hotel (see above) advertised that you could fish from your room. Because the hotel is built on a pier jutting out into Elliott Bay, the claim was an easy one to make. In 1964, when The Beatles came to Seattle, they stayed at The Edgewater, and, of course, the Fab Four had to do a little fishing out the window of their room. The hotel has turned the room where John, Paul, George, and Ringo stayed into The Beatles Suite and filled it with Beatles memorabilia. Unfortunately, the hotel management now frowns on guests fishing from their room.

premium waterview rooms, with clawfoot tubs and walls that open out to those great views, are hard to beat.

Pier 67, 2411 Alaskan Way, Seattle, WA 98121. © **800/624-0670** or 206/728-7000. Fax 206/441-4119. www.edgewaterhotel.com. 223 units. $199–$729 double; $399–$2,500 suite. Children 17 and under stay free in parent's room. AE, DISC, MC, V. Valet parking $30. Pets accepted. **Amenities:** Restaurant, lounge; babysitting; bikes; concierge; exercise room and access to nearby health club; room service. *In room:* A/C, TV, hair dryer, minibar, Wi-Fi.

EXPENSIVE

Seattle Marriott Waterfront ★★ Across Alaskan Way from Elliott Bay, this sleek hotel doesn't have superb views like the nearby Edgewater, but it's the only other option if you want to stay on the waterfront. The hotel does a brisk business putting up people heading out on cruises (some cruise ships dock right across the street). If there isn't a cruise ship berthed across the street, the best views are from the large junior suites at the northwest corner of the property. Because of the way the hotel is designed, many standard rooms have only limited views, but they do have little balconies where you can stand and breathe in the salt air.

2100 Alaskan Way, Seattle, WA 98121. © **800/455-8254** or 206/443-5000. Fax 206/256-1100. www.seattle marriottwaterfront.com. 358 units. $229–$734 double. Children 17 and under stay free in parent's room. AE, DC, DISC, MC, V. Valet parking $40. **Amenities:** 2 restaurants, 2 lounges; concierge; executive-level rooms; exercise room and access to nearby health club; Jacuzzi; indoor/outdoor pool; room service; Wi-Fi. *In room:* A/C, TV, CD player, fridge, hair dryer, Internet.

3 DOWNTOWN & FIRST HILL

Downtown Seattle is the heart of the city's business community and home to numerous business hotels. Although these properties are among the most conveniently located Seattle accommodations, they are also the priciest, designed primarily for business travelers on expense accounts. Many offer discounted weekend and winter rates, however. The area has plenty of good restaurants, but mainly only cheap lunch spots or expense-account dinner places.

VERY EXPENSIVE

Alexis Hotel ★★ This century-old building is a sparkling gem in an enviable location: halfway between Pike Place Market and Pioneer Square and 3 blocks from the

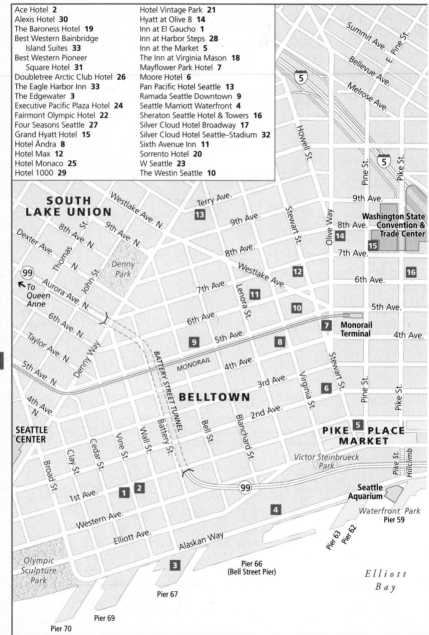

Ace Hotel **2**
Alexis Hotel **30**
The Baroness Hotel **19**
Best Western Bainbridge
    Island Suites **33**
Best Western Pioneer
    Square Hotel **31**
Doubletree Arctic Club Hotel **26**
The Eagle Harbor Inn **33**
The Edgewater **3**
Executive Pacific Plaza Hotel **24**
Fairmont Olympic Hotel **22**
Four Seasons Seattle **27**
Grand Hyatt Hotel **15**
Hotel Ändra **8**
Hotel Max **12**
Hotel Monaco **25**
Hotel 1000 **29**

Hotel Vintage Park **21**
Hyatt at Olive 8 **14**
Inn at El Gaucho **1**
Inn at Harbor Steps **28**
Inn at the Market **5**
The Inn at Virginia Mason **18**
Mayflower Park Hotel **7**
Moore Hotel **6**
Pan Pacific Hotel Seattle **13**
Ramada Seattle Downtown **9**
Seattle Marriott Waterfront **4**
Sheraton Seattle Hotel & Towers **16**
Silver Cloud Hotel Broadway **17**
Silver Cloud Hotel Seattle–Stadium **32**
Sixth Avenue Inn **11**
Sorrento Hotel **20**
W Seattle **23**
The Westin Seattle **10**

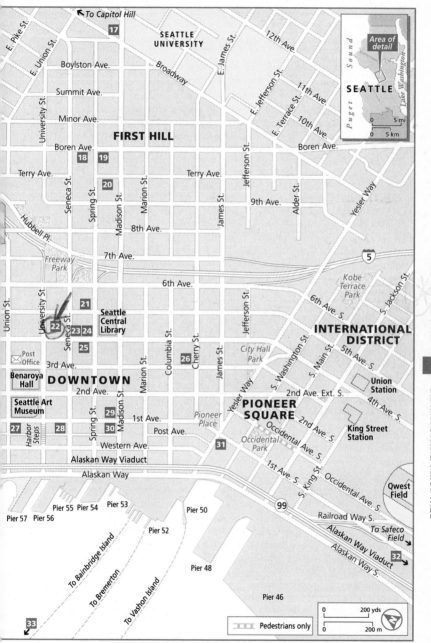

waterfront and the Seattle Art Museum. The Alexis is dedicated to the arts, and throughout the hotel, both in guest rooms and in public spaces, are numerous original works of art. The cheerful, personalized service and the pleasant mix of contemporary and antique furnishings give the Alexis a very special atmosphere. In the guest rooms, classic styling with a European flavor prevails. About a quarter of the rooms are suites, and the spa suites are real winners, offering whirlpool tubs in exceedingly luxurious bathrooms. Other suites have ties to the local arts community. The hotel also has complimentary evening wine tastings. As part of the Kimpton chain, the Alexis participates in the eco-friendly EarthCare program and does what it can to be green.

1007 First Ave. (at Madison St.), Seattle, WA 98104. ✆ **888/850-1155** or 206/624-4844. Fax 206/621-9009. www.alexishotel.com. 121 units. $299–$319 double; $355–$579 suite. Rates include evening wine reception. Children 17 and under stay free in parent's room. AE, DC, DISC, MC, V. Valet parking $30. Pets accepted. **Amenities:** Restaurant, 2 lounges; concierge; executive-level rooms; exercise room and access to nearby health club; room service; Aveda day spa. *In room:* A/C, TV, hair dryer, minibar, Wi-Fi.

The Fairmont Olympic Hotel ★★★ If you're looking for classically elegant surroundings, excellent service, and great amenities, then head straight for the Fairmont Olympic Hotel, a gorgeous facsimile of an Italian Renaissance palace. Without a doubt, this hotel has the grandest lobby in Seattle. Gilt-and-crystal chandeliers hang from the arched ceiling, while ornate moldings grace the glowing hand-burnished oak walls and pillars. Although many of the guest rooms tend to be rather small (with either two twin beds or one king bed), all are very elegant. If you crave extra space, opt for one of the suites, of which there are more than 200 (however, be aware that the executive suites aren't much bigger than the hotel's deluxe rooms). **The Georgian** (p. 88) is the most elegant restaurant in Seattle, with a menu that combines Northwest and Continental cuisines. Of all Seattle's luxury hotels, the Fairmont Olympic works the hardest at being eco-friendly.

411 University St., Seattle, WA 98101. ✆ **800/223-8772,** 800/821-8106 (in WA), 800/268-6282 (in Canada), or 206/621-1700. Fax 206/682-9633. www.fairmont.com/seattle. 450 units. $419–$429 double; $449–$3,500 suite. Children 18 and under stay free in parent's room. AE, DC, DISC, MC, V. Valet parking $36; self-parking $26. Pets accepted. **Amenities:** 2 restaurants (Continental/Northwest), lounge; concierge; executive-level rooms; health club w/indoor pool, exercise machines, Jacuzzi, and saunas; room service. *In room:* A/C, TV/VCR, CD player, hair dryer, minibar, Wi-Fi.

Four Seasons Seattle ★★★ This is one of the newest luxury hotels in Seattle, and it boasts a superb location adjacent to Pike Place Market and across the street from the Seattle Art Museum. The small lobby blends contemporary lines with natural stone and wood for a modern Northwest aesthetic. Guest rooms, which are wired to the max and have artworks by regional artists, feature walls of glass, and many of the rooms look out to Elliott Bay. An infinity-edge pool with a waterview may sound like it belongs in Hawaii or Mexico, but that's exactly what you'll find here on the hotel's rooftop terrace, which is just outside the hotel's huge exercise room and full-service spa. The hotel even has a long outdoor stairway that leads down to the waterfront.

99 Union St., Seattle, WA 98101. ✆ **800/819-5053** or 206/749-7000. Fax 206/749-7099. www.fourseasons.com/seattle. 147 units. $275–$395 double; $695–$5,000 suite. Children 18 and under stay free in parent's room. AE, DC, DISC, MC, V. Valet parking $36. Pets accepted. **Amenities:** Restaurant, lounge; babysitting; concierge; exercise room; year-round outdoor pool; room service; full-service spa. *In room:* A/C, TV/DVD, CD player, hair dryer, minibar, MP3 docking station, Wi-Fi.

Hotel 1000 ★★★ Geared toward techie business travelers and wired to the max, Hotel 1000 is the most luxurious and technologically advanced hotel in Seattle. However, what should really matter to you is that the rooms are bigger than those at most downtown hotels, and all have floor-to-ceiling walls of glass to let in lots of light and, if you're high enough up, take in views of Elliott Bay. Bathrooms in deluxe rooms are works of art, with freestanding Philippe Starck bathtubs that fill dramatically from the ceiling. Beautiful artwork lends a tranquil feel to both public spaces and guest rooms. Golfers take note: This is the only downtown Seattle hotel with its own golf course. In fact, the hotel's virtual-reality "golf club" has more than 50 golf courses from which to choose, including St. Andrews, Pinehurst No. 2, and Pebble Beach.

1000 First Ave., Seattle, WA 98104. © **877/315-1088** or 206/957-1000. www.hotel1000seattle.com. 120 units. $225–$500 double; $350–$5,500 suite. Children 17 and under stay free in parent's room. AE, DC, DISC, MC, V. Valet parking $32. Pets accepted ($40 fee). **Amenities:** Restaurant, lounge; babysitting; concierge; virtual golf course; exercise room and access to nearby health club; room service; sauna; small full-service spa. *In room:* A/C, TV, hair dryer, minibar, MP3 docking station, Wi-Fi.

W Seattle ★★ The W hotel chain has won plenty of national attention and devoted fans for its oh-so-hip accommodations, and here in the land of espresso and high-tech, the W is a natural. The lobby has the look and feel of a stage set, with dramatic lighting and sleek furniture, and in the evenings the space transforms into a lounge. Rooms are not only beautifully designed and filled with plush amenities, but they also tend to be larger than those at other W hotels. They're full of great perks, including goose-down comforters and plasma HDTVs. Although the "Cool Corner" rooms (ending in -09 and -02 on each floor) cost a bit more than regular units, they are much larger than standard rooms and have floor-to-ceiling windows. They're definitely worth requesting. The W also has an extensive array of amenities for your dog or cat, if yours happens to be traveling with you.

1112 Fourth Ave., Seattle, WA 98101. © **877/946-8357** or 206/264-6000. Fax 206/264-6100. www.whotels. com/seattle. 424 units. $299–$459 double; from $959 suite. Children 17 and under stay free in parent's room. AE, DISC, MC, V. Valet parking $35. Pets accepted ($100 fee). **Amenities:** Restaurant, lounge; babysitting; concierge; exercise room and access to nearby health club; room service. *In room:* A/C, TV/DVD, CD player, hair dryer, minibar, MP3 docking station, Wi-Fi.

EXPENSIVE

Grand Hyatt Seattle ★★★ If you're accustomed to staying in only the very finest hotels, book a room here. For classic luxury, contemporary styling, modern amenities, and attentive service, this hotel is first-rate. A spacious lobby full of regionally inspired glass art sets the tone the moment you arrive. There is, however, one catch: Unless you spring for something pricier than the basic "deluxe guest room," you're going to be a bit cramped; the least expensive units here are definitely designed for solo business travelers. The health club is well outfitted but doesn't have a swimming pool; families searching for deluxe accommodations should probably opt for the Fairmont instead. The hotel's restaurant is a Ruth's Chris Steak House.

721 Pine St., Seattle, WA 98101. © **800/492-8804** or 206/774-1234. Fax 206/774-6120. www.grandseattle. hyatt.com. 425 units. $199–$340 double; $1,250–$3,000 suite. Children 17 and under stay free in parent's room. AE, DC, DISC, MC, V. Valet parking $33; self-parking $28. **Amenities:** 2 restaurants, lounge; babysitting; concierge; executive-level rooms; health club w/Jacuzzi, sauna, and steam room; room service; day spa. *In room:* A/C, TV, CD player, hair dryer, minibar, MP3 docking station, Wi-Fi.

Hotel Monaco ★★ The Monaco is one of downtown Seattle's most stylish hotels, attracting a young and affluent clientele. If you appreciate cutting-edge style, you'll go for the eclectic, over-the-top, retro-contemporary design. The lobby has reproductions of ancient Greek murals, while in the guest rooms, you'll find wild color schemes, bold-striped wallpaper, flat-panel LCD TVs, DVD and CD players, and animal-print terry-cloth robes. Miss your pet back home? Call the front desk, and a staff member will send up a pet goldfish for the night. **Sazerac,** the hotel's Southern-inspired restaurant, is as boldly designed as the rest of the place. Be sure to order the restaurant's namesake cocktail, a New Orleans classic made with rye whiskey, at the adjacent bar. Among packages offered by this hotel are adventure tours with the eco-friendly EverGreen Escapes.

1101 Fourth Ave., Seattle, WA 98101. © **888/454-8397** or 206/621-1770. Fax 206/621-7779. www.monaco-seattle.com. 189 units. $179–$319 double; $229–$399 suite. Rates include evening wine tasting. Children 17 and under stay free in parent's room. AE, DC, DISC, MC, V. Valet parking $30. Pets accepted. **Amenities:** Restaurant, lounge; concierge; exercise room and access to nearby health club; room service. *In room:* A/C, TV, hair dryer, minibar, Wi-Fi.

Hotel Vintage Park ★★

Small, classically elegant, and exceedingly romantic, the Vintage Park is a must for both lovers and wine lovers. The guest rooms, which are named for Washington wineries, are perfect for romantic getaways, and each evening in the lobby, the hotel hosts a wine tasting featuring Washington wines. Throughout the hotel are numerous references to grapes and wine. Rooms vary quite a bit and boast bold colors and opulent furnishings that may convince you to forget your vacation plans and instead spend your days luxuriating amid the sumptuous surroundings. Deluxe rooms have the best views (including views of Mount Rainier), and although the bathrooms are small, they do have granite counters. Standard rooms, though smaller and less lavishly appointed, are still very comfortable, and, surprisingly, the bathrooms are larger than those in the deluxe rooms. Through its EarthCare program, this Kimpton hotel does its part to be eco-friendly.

1100 Fifth Ave., Seattle, WA 98101. © **888/853-3914** or 206/624-8000. Fax 206/623-0568. www.hotel vintagepark.com. 124 units. $139–$394 double; $475–$595 suite. Children 17 and under stay free in parent's room. AE, DC, DISC, MC, V. Valet parking $30. Pets accepted. **Amenities:** Restaurant (Italian), lounge; concierge; exercise room; room service. *In room:* A/C, TV, minibar, hair dryer, Wi-Fi.

Hyatt at Olive 8 ★★

This downtown hotel near the convention center is Seattle's first LEED-certified hotel. LEED (Leadership in Energy and Environmental Design) certifies environmentally sound buildings. To that end, this hotel has such green features as a living roof, lights that turn off when you leave your room, dual-flush toilets, water-reducing shower heads, and lots of natural light. The hotel's restaurant uses local and organic ingredients as much as possible, and even the spa features organic and environmentally aware products. On top of all that, the hotel is very stylish, boldly contemporary, and features relatively large guest rooms with all the electronic features you would expect in a modern business hotel.

1635 Eighth Ave., Seattle, WA 98101. © **888/591-1234** or 206/695-1234. Fax 206/676-4400. www.olive8. hyatt.com. 346 units. $179–$269 double; $379–$429 suite. Children 17 and under stay free in parent's room. AE, DC, DISC, MC, V. Valet parking $34. **Amenities:** 2 restaurants, lounge; babysitting; concierge; exercise room; room service; full-service spa w/lap pool and Jacuzzi. *In room:* A/C, TV, Wi-Fi, fridge, hair dryer, MP3 docking station.

Inn at Harbor Steps ★★

This inn's excellent location on the lower floors of a modern apartment building across the street from the Seattle Art Museum makes this inn convenient to all of downtown Seattle's major attractions. The guest rooms, which overlook a courtyard garden, feel spacious enough to be apartments. The surprisingly classical furnishings lend a comfortable, homey feel. Every unit has a gas fireplace, and the largest rooms have whirlpool tubs. The only real drawback is the lack of views.

1221 First Ave., Seattle, WA 98101. © 888/728-8910 or 206/748-0973. Fax 206/748-0533. www.innat harborsteps.com. 28 units. $195–$295 double. Rates include full breakfast and afternoon tea and appetizers. Children 4 and under stay free in parent's room. AE, DC, DISC, MC, V. Parking $18. **Amenities:** Concierge; health club; Internet; Jacuzzi; indoor pool; sauna. *In room:* A/C, TV/VCR/DVD, CD player, hair dryer, Internet.

Pan Pacific Hotel Seattle ★★ *III — clearly upgrade* This hotel, 3 long blocks north of the Westin, represents a new generation of Seattle hotels. Opening onto a central courtyard surrounded by condominium towers, the Pan Pacific feels entirely removed from the streets of Seattle. Although primarily a business hotel, the hotel's rooms are such plush retreats that they rightfully belong at some luxury resort, not at a business hotel. Rooms here are larger than at most Seattle downtown hotels, and even standard rooms have soaking tubs with pocket doors that open onto the bedroom area. Decor is minimalist and sleek, though with a soft edge, and walls of glass flood the rooms with light. Be sure to ask for a room with a view of the Space Needle.

2125 Terry Ave., Seattle, WA 98121. © 877/324-4856 or 206/264-8111. Fax 206/654-5049. www.pan pacific.com/seattle. 160 units. $200–$575 double; $1,000 suite. Children 17 and under stay free in parent's room. AE, DC, DISC, MC, V. Valet parking $33. Pets accepted ($50 fee). **Amenities:** Restaurant, lounge; concierge; exercise room and access to nearby health club; Jacuzzi; room service; full-service spa. *In room:* A/C, TV, hair dryer, minibar, Wi-Fi.

Sheraton Seattle Hotel ★★★ (Kids) This hotel, with 1,258 rooms, is the largest hotel in Seattle, and it is evident as soon as you arrive that big conventions are big business here. As an individual traveler, you're likely to feel a bit overlooked. However, despite the impersonal nature of this hotel, I still recommend it, especially for families. Kids (and many adults) will love the 35th-floor swimming pool with great city views. There's an exercise room on the same floor. You also get good views from guest rooms on the higher floors. All units are fairly large, but if you're not traveling with the kids and want the maximum space, book one of the king rooms, which are designed for business travelers. Throughout the hotel, you'll find artworks that are part of a $6-million collection.

1400 Sixth Ave., Seattle, WA 98101. © 800/325-3535 or 206/621-9000. Fax 206/621-8441. www.sheraton. com/seattle. 1,258 units. $169–$385 double; $300–$5,000 suite. Children 17 and under stay free in parent's room. AE, DC, DISC, MC, V. Valet parking $38. Pets accepted. **Amenities:** Restaurant, 2 lounges; concierge; executive-level rooms; health club; Jacuzzi; indoor pool; room service. *In room:* A/C, TV/DVD, hair dryer, Internet, minibar.

Sorrento Hotel ★★ With its wrought-iron gates, courtyard of palm trees, and plush seating in the octagonal Fireside Room, the Sorrento, which first opened in 1909, has a classic elegance. The guest rooms here are among the finest in the city: No two are alike, and while most are set up for business travelers, this hotel also makes a great choice for vacationers. Although more than half the units are suites, many provide little more space than you get in a standard room, so you may not want to splurge on an upgrade here. The hotel is set high on First Hill, yet downtown is only a few (steep) blocks away. If you'd rather not walk, there's a complimentary shuttle service. The hotel's dining room has the feel of a 1950s supper club, and in the Fireside Room, you can get afternoon tea and catch live jazz at night.

900 Madison St., Seattle, WA 98104. © 800/426-1265 or 206/622-6400. Fax 206/343-6155. www.hotel sorrento.com. 76 units. $189–$299 double; $199–$664 suite. Children 17 and under stay free in parent's room. AE, DC, DISC, MC, V. Valet parking $26. Pets accepted ($60 fee). **Amenities:** Restaurant, 2 lounges; concierge; executive-level rooms; exercise room and access to nearby health club; room service. *In room:* A/C, TV, fridge, hair dryer, minibar, Wi-Fi.

The Westin Seattle ★★★ (**Kids**)   With its distinctive cylindrical towers, the 47-story Westin is the tallest hotel in Seattle and consequently has the best views of any accommodations in the city. From rooms on the upper floors of the north tower's northwest side, you get breathtaking vistas of the Space Needle, Puget Sound, and the Olympic Mountains. Guest rooms here are also some of the nicest in town. Couple those great views (seen through unusual curved walls of glass) with the Westin's plush "Heavenly Beds," and you'll be sleeping—both literally and figuratively—on clouds. Although the pool here doesn't have the great views that the Sheraton's has, keep in mind that few downtown hotels have pools at all—which makes the Westin a good choice for families.

1900 Fifth Ave., Seattle, WA 98101. ℭ **800/937-8461** or 206/728-1000. Fax 206/728-2259. www.westin. com/seattle. 891 units. $169–$399 double; from $495 suite. Children 17 and under stay free in parent's room. AE, DC, DISC, MC, V. Valet parking $38; self-parking $35. Pets accepted. **Amenities:** 2 restaurants; 2 lounges; concierge; exercise room and access to nearby health club; Jacuzzi; large indoor pool; room service; sauna. *In room:* A/C, TV, hair dryer, minibar, Wi-Fi.

MODERATE

Executive Hotel Pacific ★   There aren't too many reasonably priced choices left in downtown Seattle, but this hotel, built in 1928 and completely renovated a few years ago, offers not only moderately priced rooms but also a prime location. It's situated halfway between Pike Place Market and Pioneer Square, and just about the same distance from the waterfront. Rooms have been updated and the lobby has a very stylish and contemporary look. However, the rooms are small (verging on tiny) and sometimes quite cramped. Consequently, I recommend this place primarily for solo travelers. Bathrooms, although very small, have all been completely upgraded.

400 Spring St., Seattle, WA 98104. ℭ **888/388-3932** or 206/623-3900. Fax 206/623-2059. www.executive hotels.net. 153 units. $129–$229 double; $299 suite. Children 15 and under stay free in parent's room. AE, DC, DISC, MC, V. Valet parking $28.; self-parking $19. Pets accepted. **Amenities:** 2 restaurants; concierge; exercise room and access to nearby health club. *In room:* A/C, TV, CD player, hair dryer, MP3 docking station, Wi-Fi.

Hotel Max ★   If you crave Philippe Starck–inspired furnishings but have an IKEA budget, this is the place for you. Before you even step through the door of your room, you'll know this place is different; every guest room door is covered with a black-and-white photo mural. In fact, art is the principal design theme here, and throughout the hotel there are works by dozens of regional artists. Flat-screen LCD TVs, stainless-steel sinks, and bold color schemes all make it clear that this place is designed to appeal to travelers with an artistic aesthetic. Rooms here can be tiny to the point of inducing claustrophobia, so the Max is best for solo travelers.

620 Stewart St., Seattle, WA 98101. ℭ **866/833-6299** or 206/728-6299. Fax 206/443-5754. www.hotel maxseattle.com. 163 units. $139–$299 double. Children 17 and under stay free in parent's room. AE, DC, DISC, MC, V. Valet parking $30. Pets accepted ($45 fee). **Amenities:** Restaurant; lounge; exercise room and access to nearby health club; room service. *In room:* A/C, TV, hair dryer, minibar, Wi-Fi.

Mayflower Park Hotel ★   If your favorite recreational activities include shopping or sipping martinis, the Mayflower Park is for you. Built in 1927, this historic hotel is connected to the upscale Westlake Center shopping plaza and is within a block of both Nordstrom and Macy's. Most rooms here are furnished with an eclectic blend of contemporary Italian and traditional European pieces. Some units still have small, old-fashioned bathrooms, but these have been renovated and are quite modern. The smallest guest rooms, though cramped, have also been renovated. If you crave space, ask for one of the larger corner rooms or a suite. Martini drinkers will want to spend time at **Oliver's**

lounge (p. 192), which serves the best martinis in Seattle and has free hors d'oeuvres in the evening. The hotel's **Andaluca** restaurant is a plush, contemporary spot serving highly creative cuisine Mediterranean-influenced Northwest.

405 Olive Way, Seattle, WA 98101. ℂ **800/426-5100,** 206/382-6990, or 206/623-8700. Fax 206/382-6997. www.mayflowerpark.com. 161 units. $149–$249 double; $169–$365 suite. Children 18 and under stay free in parent's room. AE, DC, DISC, MC, V. Valet parking $30. **Amenities:** Restaurant (Mediterranean/ Northwest), lounge; concierge; exercise room and access to nearby health club; Jacuzzi; room service. *In room:* A/C, TV, hair dryer, Wi-Fi.

INEXPENSIVE

The Baroness Hotel (Finds) Affiliated with the Inn at Virginia Mason and located right across the street, the Baroness is an apartment hotel that is primarily used by people here in Seattle for medical reasons. That said, it is a great value if you are not a demanding traveler. Rooms, though a bit dowdy, are comfortable, and some have kitchens. The surrounding neighborhood (aside from the hospital) is quite pretty. Downtown Seattle starts 4 blocks downhill from the Baroness. Although the rooms are not centrally air-conditioned, air conditioners can be requested.

1005 Spring St., Seattle, WA 98104. ℂ **800/283-6453** or 206/583-6453. Fax 206/223-7545. www.baroness hotel.com. 58 units. $85–$107 double; $114–$122 suite. Children 17 and under stay free in parent's room. AE, DISC, MC, V. Parking $13. *In room:* TV, Internet, kitchenette.

The Inn at Virginia Mason You may think I've sent you to a hospital rather than a hotel when you first arrive at this older establishment on Pill Hill—but don't worry. This is definitely a hotel, though it is adjacent to and managed by the Virginia Mason Hospital. Despite the fact that most guests are here because of the hospital, the hotel is a good choice for vacationers as well. Rates are economical, the location is quiet, and you're close to downtown. There's a rooftop deck and a shady little courtyard just off the lobby. Although the carpets and furniture here are in need of replacement, the rooms are still serviceable. Because this is an old building, room sizes vary. Deluxe rooms and suites can be quite large, and some have whirlpool baths and fireplaces.

1006 Spring St., Seattle, WA 98104. ℂ **800/283-6453** or 206/583-6453. www.innatvirginiamason.com. 79 units. $99–$109 double; $119–$189 suite. Children 17 and under stay free in parent's room. AE, DISC, MC, V. Parking $13. **Amenities:** Restaurant; concierge; room service. *In room:* TV, Wi-Fi.

Ramada Seattle Downtown ★ Located right on the monorail route and only a few blocks from downtown Seattle's main shopping district, this hotel may not look like much from the outside, but it has a very pretty lobby that belies the hotel's age. Guest rooms, though not as attractive as the lobby might suggest, were all completely renovated in 2007 and are comfortable and functional. You just won't find a more reliable budget hotel in downtown Seattle. Ask for a room with a view of the Space Needle; you just might get lucky.

2200 Fifth Ave., Seattle, WA 98121. ℂ **800/272-6232** or 206/441-9785. Fax 206/448-0924. www.ramada. com. 120 units. $109–$169 double. Children 17 and under stay free in parent's room. AE, DC, DISC, MC, V. Parking $12. **Amenities:** Restaurant; exercise room and access to nearby health club. *In room:* A/C, TV, hair dryer, Wi-Fi.

Sixth Avenue Inn ★ (Finds) It's never easy finding a decent budget hotel in a major city, but to find one within blocks of the main shopping district and almost as close to one of the city's top attractions is a real find. This older low-rise hotel has been around for years, but recent renovations have made it worth a stay once again. Pike Place Market is 6 blocks away, and Nordstrom and two other shopping centers are even closer. Rooms aren't fancy, but they're clean, comfortable, and functional.

2000 Sixth Ave., Seattle, WA 98121. © **206/441-8300.** Fax 206/441-9903. www.sixthavenueinn.com. 167 units. $100–$130 double. Children 16 and under stay free in parent's room. AE, DC, DISC, MC, V. Parking $15. **Amenities:** Restaurant, lounge; concierge; exercise room; room service. *In room:* A/C, TV, hair dryer, Wi-Fi.

4 BELLTOWN

Belltown, extending north from Pike Place Market, has for many years been one of Seattle's fastest-growing neighborhoods and has dozens of restaurants, an equal number of nightclubs, and several good hotels. If your Seattle travel plans include lots of eating out at hip restaurants or late-night partying, then Belltown is the place to stay.

EXPENSIVE

Hotel Ändra ★★   Located on the edge of the trendy Belltown neighborhood and only a few blocks from both downtown shopping and Pike Place Market, this hotel melds a vintage building with bold, contemporary styling and manages to succeed even better than the local W hotel. The location, close to lots of good restaurants and hot nightclubs, makes this a great place to stay if you're in Seattle to make the scene. Rooms are done in cool blues and kelp greens, with lots of wood and stainless-steel accents, Swedish modern furniture, ergonomic desk chairs, genuine alpaca headboards, retro clocks, and flat-screen TVs. Lights are on dimmers, so you can create just the right mood. Oh, and **Lola** (p. 93) is the hotel's Greek restaurant operated by Tom Douglas, one of my favorite Seattle chefs. Don't miss it.

2000 Fourth Ave., Seattle, WA 98121. © **877/448-8600** or 206/448-8600. Fax 206/441-7140. www.hotel andra.com. 119 units. $229–$299 double; $309–$2,500 suite. Children 17 and under stay free in parent's room. AE, DISC, MC, V. Valet parking $35. Pets accepted. **Amenities:** 2 restaurants (Greek, Italian), lounge; babysitting; concierge; exercise room and access to nearby health club; room service; in-room spa services. *In room:* A/C, TV, hair dryer, minibar, MP3 docking station, Wi-Fi.

MODERATE

Inn at El Gaucho ★★ (Finds)   While low-budget hipsters have the Ace hotel, those who are more flush can opt to stay at this plush little Belltown inn. It's located directly above, and affiliated with, the retro-swanky El Gaucho steakhouse. The nondescript street-level front door does nothing to prepare you for the luxurious little second-story lobby, which makes this place feel like a real find. After a night on the town, have breakfast in the luxurious feather bed. Leather chairs and sofas, plasma-screen TVs, and Bose radio/CD players all make rooms here well worth lingering in. Throw in fresh flowers and you have a great place for a romantic weekend on the town. One caveat: Be aware that the inn is up a flight of stairs.

2505 First Ave., Seattle, WA 98121. © **866/354-2824** or 206/728-1133. http://inn.elgaucho.com/inn. elgaucho. 18 units. $145–$275 suite. AE, MC, V. Valet parking $25. **Amenities:** Restaurant, 2 lounges; concierge; access to nearby health club; room service. *In room:* A/C, TV, CD player, hair dryer, Wi-Fi.

INEXPENSIVE

Ace Hotel   The Ace, in the heart of Belltown, is the city's hippest economy hotel. White-on-white and stainless steel are the hallmarks of the minimalist decor. Even the brick walls and wood floors have been painted white. Wall decorations are minimal, except in those rooms with 1970s photo murals of the great outdoors. Platform beds and wool blankets salvaged from foreign hotels add to the chic feel, as do the tiny stainless-steel sinks and shelves in the rooms with shared bathrooms. Basically, aside from the eight large rooms with private bathrooms (ask about the room with the shower behind the bed), this place is a step above a hostel; it's aimed at the 20- and 30-something crowd. Be aware that some walls are paper-thin and the clientele here tends to keep late hours. Don't plan on going to sleep early.

2423 First Ave., Seattle, WA 98121. ✆ **206/448-4721.** Fax 206/374-0745. www.acehotel.com. 28 units, 14 with shared bathroom. $99 double with shared bathroom; $165–$195 double with private bathroom. Rates include continental breakfast. Children 12 and under stay free in parent's room. AE, DC, DISC, MC, V. Parking $19. Pets accepted. *In room:* TV, Wi-Fi.

Moore Hotel   In a historic building 2 blocks from both Pike Place Market and the Belltown restaurant and nightlife district, the Moore is a decent downtown choice for young and adventurous travelers on a tight budget. If you've ever traveled through Europe on the cheap, you'll know what to expect from this place. It's not fancy, and if you aren't in a renovated room on a floor with renovated hallways, the place can seem a bit dreary. But if you request one of the updated suites, you'll be pleasantly surprised by the stylishly mod-ern large rooms with hardwood floors, full kitchens, and big windows. Ask for a room with a view of Puget Sound. The lobby, with its marble, tiles, and decorative moldings, hints at the Moore's historic character, but this is more budget accommodation than historic hotel. There's a hip restaurant/lounge, and an adjacent theater stages rock concerts.

1926 Second Ave., Seattle, WA 98101. ✆ **800/421-5508** or 206/448-4851. www.moorehotel.com. 120 units, 45 with shared bathroom. $71 double with shared bathroom; $86–$97 double with private bath-room; $117–$185 suite. Children 9 and under stay free in parent's room. MC, V. Parking $21. **Amenities:** Restaurant (American), lounge. *In room:* TV.

5 PIKE PLACE MARKET

Pike Place Market is one of Seattle's top attractions and a fascinating place to explore. In addition to all the small shops, produce stalls, and fishmongers, the market has lots of great restaurants and one of my favorite Seattle hotels. After the waterfront, this area is the next best place to soak up the essence of Seattle.

EXPENSIVE

Inn at the Market ★★★   For romance, convenience, and the chance to immerse yourself in the Seattle aesthetic, it's hard to beat this hotel in Pike Place Market. A roof-top deck overlooking Elliott Bay provides a great spot to soak up the sun on summer afternoons. Don't look for a grand entrance or large sign; there's only a small plaque on the wall to indicate that the building houses a tasteful and understated luxury hotel. Be sure to ask for one of the waterview rooms, which have large windows overlooking the bay (but cost roughly $150 more per night). Even if you don't get a waterview room, you'll still find spacious accommodations, with mold-to-your-body Tempur-Pedic beds, large bathrooms, and elegant decor that gives the feel of an upscale European beach resort. **Campagne,** the formal main dining room, serves French cuisine, while **Café Campagne** (p. 96) offers country-style French food amid casual surroundings.

86 Pine St., Seattle, WA 98101. ✆ **800/446-4484** or 206/443-3600. Fax 206/728-1955. www.innatthemarket.com. 70 units. $245–$490 double; $625 suite. Children 18 and under stay free in parent's room. AE, DC, DISC, MC, V. Parking $32. **Amenities:** 3 restaurants (French, country French, juice bar), 2 lounges; con-cierge; access to nearby health club; room service. *In room:* A/C, TV, hair dryer, minibar, Wi-Fi.

6 PIONEER SQUARE & THE INTERNATIONAL DISTRICT

The historic Pioneer Square area is Seattle's main nightlife district and can be a rowdy place on a Saturday night. By day, however, the area's many art galleries and antiques stores attract a very different clientele. Still, even in the daylight, be prepared to encounter a lot of street people. Warnings aside, this is one of the prettiest corners of Seattle and the only downtown neighborhood with historic flavor. The International District lies but a few blocks away from Pioneer Square.

EXPENSIVE

Doubletree Arctic Club Hotel ★★　　With distinctive ceramic walrus heads decorating the facade, this hotel was originally built in 1917 as an exclusive club for men who had struck it rich in the Alaska gold rush. Today, the Doubletree Arctic Club Hotel is one of the prettiest historic buildings in Seattle and should be your first choice in Seattle if you enjoy staying in historic hotels. The lobby, with its bar, billiards table, and travel-themed Art Deco furnishings, feels like it could be in Singapore or Nairobi; you half expect Humphrey Bogart to be sipping a gin and tonic in the corner. Guest rooms are decorated in keeping with the historic, adventure-travel theme. Be sure to sneak a peek inside the Northern Lights Dome Room, a grand hall with original frescoes, a stained-glass ceiling, and lots of ornate plasterwork and gilding.

700 Third Ave., Seattle, WA 98104. ⓒ **800/222-TREE** or 206/340-0340. Fax 206/340-0349. www.arctic clubhotel.com. 120 units. $129–$319 double. Children 17 and under stay free in parent's room. AE, DC, DISC, MC, V. Valet parking $29. Pets accepted. **Amenities:** Restaurant, lounge; concierge; exercise room; room service. *In room:* A/C, TV, hair dryer, minibar, MP3 docking station, Wi-Fi.

Silver Cloud Hotel Seattle—Stadium ★★ **(Kids)**　　If you're a Seattle Mariners baseball fan, there is no better place in town to stay than here; this hotel is directly across the street from Safeco Field. Even if you're not a baseball fan, this hotel is a great choice for its contemporary styling, and its beautiful, modern rooms, which have big windows and 42-inch high-definition TVs, are almost as impressive as those at the Pan Pacific Hotel on the other side of downtown. Families, take note: This is one of the few hotels in the area that has a swimming pool, and best of all, it's outside on a rooftop deck. The hotel is also adjacent to Qwest Field, where the Seattle Seahawks football team plays.

1046 First Ave. S., Seattle, WA 98134. ⓒ **800/497-1261** or 206/204-9800. Fax 206/381-0751. www.silver cloud.com/16home.htm. 211 units. $179–$259 double; $199–$319 suite. Children 17 and under stay free in parent's room. AE, DC, DISC, MC, V. Valet parking $20. **Amenities:** Restaurant, lounge; concierge; exercise room and access to nearby health club; Jacuzzi; outdoor pool; room service. *In room:* A/C, TV, fridge, hair dryer, MP3 docking station, Wi-Fi.

MODERATE

Best Western Pioneer Square Hotel ★　　This hotel, in a Romanesque-Victorian building listed on the National Register of Historic Places, is right in the heart of the Pioneer Square historic district, one of Seattle's main art gallery and nightlife neighborhoods. As such, things get especially raucous on weekend nights, and this hotel is recommended only for urban dwellers accustomed to dealing with street people and noise. However, if you're in town to party or to attend a Mariners or Seahawks game, there's no more convenient location. The Washington State Ferries terminal is also nearby. Guest rooms are fairly small (some are positively cramped) but are furnished in an attractive, classic style. Be aware of your surroundings if you're out on the streets late at night.

77 Yesler Way, Seattle, WA 98104. © **800/800-5514** or 206/340-1234. Fax 206/467-0707. www.pioneer square.com. 75 units. $120–$210 double. Rates include continental breakfast. Children 12 and under stay free in parent's room. AE, DC, DISC, MC, V. Parking $20. **Amenities:** Concierge; access to nearby health club; room service. *In room:* A/C, TV, hair dryer, Wi-Fi.

---

7 QUEEN ANNE & SEATTLE CENTER

The Queen Anne neighborhood is divided into Upper Queen Anne and Lower Queen Anne. The former is an upscale residential area with an attractive shopping district. The hotels listed here are in the lower neighborhood, which conveniently flanks Seattle Center and also offers lots of inexpensive restaurants.

EXPENSIVE

Hampton Inn Downtown/Seattle Center ★ Step out the front door of this hotel and you're staring straight at the Space Needle, which is only about 5 blocks away. That view and the convenient location within blocks of Seattle Center are the main reasons to stay here, and numerous good restaurants and cafes are also nearby. The standard rooms are comfortable enough, but if you plan to stay for more than a few days, consider one of the suites, which have fireplaces and balconies.

700 Fifth Ave. N., Seattle, WA 98109. © **800/426-7866** or 206/282-7700. Fax 206/282-0899. www.hampton innseattle.com. 198 units. Summer $189–$209 double, $249–$319 suite; other months $119–$149 double, $139–$209 suite. Rates include full breakfast. Children 18 and under stay free in parent's room. AE, DC, DISC, MC, V. Parking $13. **Amenities:** Exercise room. *In room:* A/C, TV, fridge, hair dryer, Internet.

MarQueen Hotel ★ (Kids) (Finds) This Lower Queen Anne hotel is in a renovated 1918 brick building that will appeal to travelers who enjoy lodgings with historic character. Seattle Center, with its many performance venues and family-oriented attractions, is only 3 blocks away, and from there you can take the monorail into downtown. Although the MarQueen's many high-tech amenities are geared toward business travelers, it's a good choice for vacationers as well. Guest rooms are spacious, although furnished very traditionally and a bit oddly laid out due to the hotel's previous incarnation as an apartment building. Lots of dark-wood trim and hardwood floors give an old-fashioned feel. Many units have separate little seating areas and full kitchens, which makes this a good choice for families. The hotel is adjacent to both an excellent espresso bar and several good restaurants.

600 Queen Anne Ave. N., Seattle, WA 98109. © **888/445-3076** or 206/282-7407. Fax 206/283-1499. www.marqueen.com. 59 units. $159–$220 double; $200–$360 suite. Rates include continental breakfast. Children 12 and under stay free in parent's room. AE, DC, DISC, MC, V. Valet parking $20. **Amenities:** Restaurant, 3 lounges; concierge; exercise room and access to nearby health club; room service; spa. *In room:* A/C, TV, hair dryer, kitchen, Wi-Fi.

MODERATE

Comfort Suites Downtown/Seattle Center ★ (Kids) Although it's none too easy to find this place (call and get specific directions), the bargain rates and spacious rooms make the Comfort Suites worth searching out. Since it's only 3 blocks from Seattle Center, you could feasibly leave your car parked at the hotel for most of your stay and walk or use public transit to get around. If you've brought the family, the suites are a good deal,

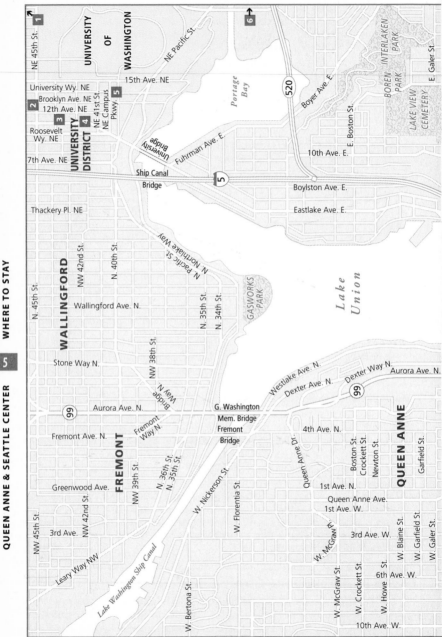

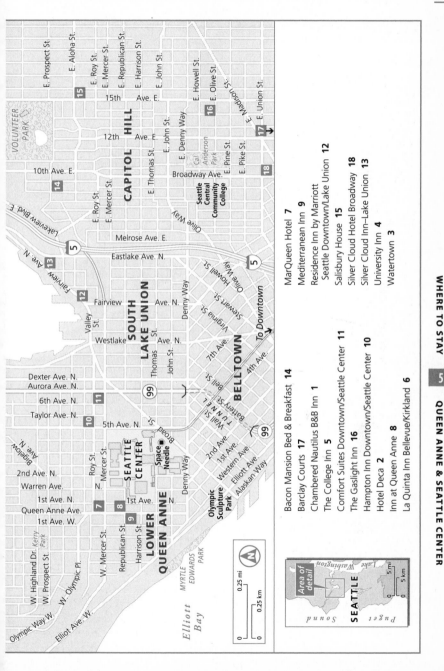

Bacon Mansion Bed & Breakfast **14**
Barclay Courts **17**
Chambered Nautilus B&B Inn **1**
The College Inn **5**
Comfort Suites Downtown/Seattle Center **11**
The Gaslight Inn **16**
Hampton Inn Downtown/Seattle Center **10**
Hotel Deca **2**
Inn at Queen Anne **8**
La Quinta Inn Bellevue/Kirkland **6**

MarQueen Hotel **7**
Mediterranean Inn **9**
Residence Inn by Marriott
Seattle Downtown/Lake Union **12**
Salisbury House **15**
Silver Cloud Hotel Broadway **18**
Silver Cloud Inn–Lake Union **13**
University Inn **4**
Watertown **3**

and the proximity to Seattle Center will help moms and dads keep the kids entertained. Ask for a room away from the busy highway that runs past the hotel.

601 Roy St., Seattle, WA 98109. ℂ **877/424-6423** or 206/282-2600. Fax 206/282-1112. www.comfort suites.com. 158 units. Early May to late Oct $130–$220 double, $225–$315 suite; late Oct to early May $100–$160 double, $175–$205 suite. Rates include continental breakfast. Children 18 and under stay free in parent's room. AE, DC, DISC, MC, V. Free parking. **Amenities:** Exercise room. *In room:* A/C, TV, fridge, hair dryer, Internet.

Mediterranean Inn ★   Don't be fooled by the name: This is not a bed-and-breakfast-type inn. But this modern apartment-hotel, in the Lower Queen Anne neighborhood, is just a couple of blocks from Seattle Center and is an ideal choice for extended stays. Because the Mediterranean Inn was designed with longer stays in mind, its rooms are much more comfortable than those at the nearby Inn at Queen Anne. With the exception of the least expensive rooms, you'll get plenty of space and a kitchenette. In summer, be sure to opt for a unit with air-conditioning. A Starbucks is just off the lobby.

425 Queen Anne Ave. N., Seattle, WA 98109. ℂ **866/525-4700** or 206/428-4700. Fax 206/428-4699. www.mediterranean-inn.com. 180 units. $95–$209 double. Children 12 and under stay free in parent's room. AE, DC, DISC, MC, V. Parking $15. **Amenities:** Exercise room. *In room:* TV/VCR, hair dryer, Internet, kitchenette.

INEXPENSIVE

Inn at Queen Anne   In the Lower Queen Anne neighborhood close to Seattle Center and numerous restaurants and espresso bars, this hotel is housed in a converted older apartment building. Though the rooms here aren't as nice as those at the nearby MarQueen, they're comfortable enough, albeit sometimes a bit cramped and not entirely modern. Deluxe units have window air conditioners. The convenient location and economical rates are the big pluses here, but there's also a pleasant garden surrounding the hotel. In summer, you should opt for a deluxe room with air-conditioning. On Wednesday and Saturday evenings, there are complimentary wine tastings.

505 First Ave. N., Seattle, WA 98109. ℂ **800/952-5043** or 206/282-7357. Fax 206/217-9719. www.innat queenanne.com. 68 units. $69–$149 double. Rates include continental breakfast. Children 12 and under stay free in parent's room. AE, DC, DISC, MC, V. Parking $18. **Amenities:** Concierge; exercise room and access to nearby health club. *In room:* TV, hair dryer, kitchenette, Wi-Fi.

8 LAKE UNION

Less than a mile from downtown, and lined with houseboats, marinas, and waterfront restaurants, Lake Union has a quintessentially Seattle character. Floatplanes use the lake as a runway, and you can rent boats from several places around the lake. If you are happiest when you're close to the water but want to avoid the crowds of the Seattle waterfront, this is an excellent alternative.

EXPENSIVE

Residence Inn by Marriott Seattle Downtown/Lake Union ★★   Right across the street from Lake Union, this Marriott Residence Inn is a good bet that's slightly removed from the city center. A seven-story atrium floods the hotel's plant-filled lobby with light, while the sound of a waterfall soothes traffic-weary nerves. All accommodations here, redone in 2008 in a bright, modern style, are suites, so you get more space for your money than you do at downtown hotels. Suites have full kitchens, so you can

prepare your own meals if you like (though breakfast is provided). There's no restaurant
on the premises, but several options are right across the street. Amenities include guest
receptions three nights each week and a grocery-shopping service.

800 Fairview Ave. N., Seattle, WA 98109. ℂ **800/331-3131** or 206/624-6000. Fax 206/223-8160. www.
marriott.com/sealu. 234 units. $199–$299 1-bedroom suite; $289–$429 2-bedroom suite. Rates include
full breakfast. Children 17 and under stay free in parent's room. AE, DC, DISC, MC, V. Parking $19. Pets
accepted ($10 per night). **Amenities:** Exercise room; Jacuzzi; indoor lap pool; sauna. *In room:* A/C, TV, hair
dryer, kitchen, Wi-Fi.

MODERATE

Silver Cloud Inn—Lake Union ★★ (Kids) (Value) Across the street from Lake

Union, this hotel offers good views (some of which take in the Space Needle). The rooms
are big and filled with lots of amenities, which make them convenient for long stays and
family vacations. Although the hotel doesn't have a restaurant of its own, plenty of waterfront options are within walking distance. The indoor swimming pool appeals to kids,
and floatplane tours leave from right across the street. This is a good value for such a great
location.

1150 Fairview Ave. N., Seattle, WA 98109. ℂ **800/330-5812** or 206/447-9500. Fax 206/812-4900. www.
silvercloud.com. 184 units. June–Sept $149–$269 double; Oct–May $119–$229 double. Rates include
continental breakfast. Children 17 and under stay free in parent's room. AE, DC, DISC, MC, V. Free parking.
Amenities: Exercise room; Jacuzzi; indoor pool. *In room:* A/C, TV, fridge, hair dryer, Wi-Fi.

---

9 CAPITOL HILL & EAST SEATTLE

A mile or so uphill and to the east of downtown Seattle, Capitol Hill has a split personality. It's a hangout for the 20-something crowd and contains the city's main gay neighborhood, yet it's also home to numerous large restored homes, a few of which have been
converted into bed-and-breakfast inns. If you prefer B&Bs to corporate hotels, this is the
best neighborhood in which to base yourself. The neighborhood has good public bus
connections to the city center.

MODERATE

Barclay Court ★★ (Finds) Across the street from Seattle University and less than a

mile from downtown Seattle, this pair of studios is a real find, but it's definitely not for
everyone. While the bold, contemporary styling and hand-blown-glass accents make
Barclay Court among the most attractive and stylish rentals in the city, you're on your
own when you stay here—check yourself in, check yourself out, and so forth. You can,
however, usually find the owner next door at his glass-blowing studio and gallery. Each
of the two rooms has its own beautiful garden patio. Inside are dyed concrete floors with
radiant heating, stylish modern furnishings, and lots of bright colors. The surrounding
neighborhood is one of Seattle's hip, up-and-coming areas. There's a great little espresso
place right around the corner. There are also two apartments available next door at the
affiliated Squire Park Guest House (www.squireparkguest.com).

1206 E. Barclay Court, Seattle, WA 98122. ℂ **206/329-3914.** Fax 206/329-3915. www.barclaycourteast.
com. 2 units. $128 double. 2-night minimum. AE, MC, V. No children allowed. *In room:* A/C, TV, hair dryer,
Internet, kitchen.

Salisbury House ★ On tree-lined 16th Avenue East, this grand old house has a wide

wraparound porch from which you can enjoy one of Seattle's prettiest residential streets.

(Kids) Family-Friendly Hotels

Best Western Bainbridge Island Suites (p. 77)   Rooms here are primarily large suites with kitchenettes and are ideal for trips with the family or for longer stays.

Comfort Suites Downtown/Seattle Center (p. 67)   The suites make this a good family choice, and the location near the Seattle Center will make the kids happy.

MarQueen Hotel (p. 67)   A few blocks from Seattle Center and its many attractions is this converted apartment building, which provides a convenient location for families, as well as spacious suites with kitchenettes.

Seattle Marriott Sea-Tac Airport (p. 75)   With a huge jungle-y atrium containing a swimming pool and whirlpool spas, kids can play Tarzan and never leave the hotel.

Silver Cloud Inn—Lake Union (p. 71)   Right across the street from Lake Union and several reasonably priced restaurants, this modern hotel has an indoor pool and spacious rooms.

Silver Cloud Hotel Seattle—Stadium (p. 66)   Adjacent to Qwest Field, where the Seattle Seahawks football team plays, this is one of few hotels in the area that has a swimming pool.

Westin Seattle (p. 62)   Parents will love the views from the tallest hotel in Seattle, while the kids will enjoy the pool—a rarity in downtown hotels.

Inside, there's plenty to admire as well. Two living rooms (one with a wood-burning fireplace) and a second-floor sun porch provide great spots for relaxing and meeting other guests. Four guest rooms have queen-size beds with down comforters, and a fifth one has a fireplace, whirlpool tub, and a king-size bed. Another room has an old clawfoot tub. Breakfasts here are deliciously filling and might include fresh fruit, juice, quiche, fresh-baked muffins or bread, and oatmeal pancakes.

750 16th Ave. E., Seattle, WA 98112. © **206/328-8682.** Fax 206/720-1019. www.salisburyhouse.com. 5 units. $139–$198 double. Rates include full breakfast. 2-night minimum in summer; 3-night minimum on holiday weekends. AE, MC, V. Children 13 and older are welcome. **Amenities:** Concierge. *In room:* Hair dryer, Wi-Fi.

Silver Cloud Hotel Broadway ★   At the Pill Hill end of Capitol Hill, this hotel is comfortable, reasonably priced, and close enough to downtown Seattle that anyone in good condition can walk there. (Although it's only a 10- to 15-min. walk, be forewarned that the way back is all uphill.) The Silver Cloud is a good bet if you want to check out the Capitol Hill nightlife scene, which is dominated by gay bars and clubs. There's even a hip bowling alley next door. Rooms are all attractively decorated; my favorites have in-room whirlpool tubs.

1100 Broadway, Seattle, WA 98122. © **800/590-1801** or 206/325-1400. Fax 206/324-1995. www.silvercloud.com. 179 units. $179–$259 double; $249–$269 suite. Rates include continental breakfast. Children 17 and under stay free in parent's room. AE, DC, DISC, MC, V. Parking $16. **Amenities:** Restaurant (Southwestern/American), lounge; concierge; exercise room and access to nearby health club; Jacuzzi; indoor pool; room service. *In room:* A/C, TV, fridge, hair dryer, Wi-Fi.

Bacon Mansion Bed & Breakfast ★   As the name implies, the Bacon Mansion is a big place—an 8,000-square-foot Tudor built in 1909, to be precise—and has all the accoutrements of a mansion: crystal chandelier, grand piano, huge dining-room table, library. Located on a shady stretch of Broadway, 2 blocks beyond Capitol Hill's busy commercial area, the inn combines a quiet residential feel with proximity to a youth-oriented shopping and dining scene. Decor includes a mix of antiques and period repro-ductions, with an abundance of floral prints. Although during the winter you may catch a glimpse of the Space Needle from the Capitol Suite, other rooms lack views. Two units are in the original carriage house.

959 Broadway E., Seattle, WA 98102. ✆ **800/240-1864** or 206/329-1864. Fax 206/860-9025. www.bacon mansion.com. 11 units, 2 with shared bathroom. $99–$129 double with shared bathroom; $119–$239 double with private bathroom. Rates include expanded continental breakfast. AE, DC, DISC, MC, V. Pets accepted in carriage house ($10 per night). **Amenities:** Concierge. *In room:* TV, hair dryer, Wi-Fi.

Gaslight Inn ★   Anyone enamored of Craftsman bungalows and the Arts and Crafts movement of the early 20th century should enjoy a stay in this 1906 home. Throughout the inn are numerous pieces of Stickley furniture, and everywhere you turn you'll see oak trim framing the doors and windows. The common rooms are decorated with a combina-tion of Western and Northwestern flair, and throughout the inn are lots of art-glass pieces. In summer, guests can swim in the backyard pool or lounge on the deck. Guest rooms continue the design themes of the common areas, with lots of oak furnishings and peeled-log beds in some units. The innkeepers can provide a wealth of information about the surrounding Capitol Hill neighborhood, the center of Seattle's gay community.

1727 15th Ave., Seattle, WA 98122. ✆ **206/325-3654.** Fax 206/328-4803. www.gaslight-inn.com. 8 units, 3 with shared bathroom. $98–$108 double with shared bathroom; $118–$159 double with private bath-room. Rates include continental breakfast. AE, MC, V. No children allowed. **Amenities:** Concierge; small seasonal heated outdoor pool. *In room:* TV, hair dryer, Wi-Fi.

10 NORTH SEATTLE (THE UNIVERSITY DISTRICT)

About 15 minutes north of downtown, the University District (more commonly known as the U District) appeals primarily to younger travelers, but it does offer less expensive accommodations than downtown and is still fairly convenient to Seattle's major attrac-tions. Also nearby are the Burke Museum, Henry Art Gallery, Museum of History and Industry, Woodland Park Zoo, and the University of Washington. As you would expect in a university neighborhood, there are lots of cheap restaurants, making this a good choice for anyone on a budget.

MODERATE

Hotel Deca ★★ Value   The 16-story Hotel Deca is one of Seattle's hippest hotels, and it offers excellent value. Consequently, it's one of my favorite hotels in the city. You'll be surrounded by modern Art Deco style as soon as you arrive, and the retro look is elegant, playful, and reminiscent of the 1930s. You'll also enjoy views of downtown Seattle, distant mountains, and various lakes and waterways. Every room is a corner unit, which means plenty of space to spread out. Small bathrooms are the biggest drawback.

Hotel Deca is considerably cheaper than comparable downtown options, and if you need to be near the university, it's definitely the top choice in the neighborhood.

4507 Brooklyn Ave. NE, Seattle, WA 98105. ⓒ 800/899-0251 or 206/634-2000. Fax 206/547-6029. www. hoteldeca.com. 158 units. June–Sept $149–$249 double; Oct–May $119–$189 double. Children 16 and under stay free in parent's room. AE, DC, DISC, MC, V. Parking $8. **Amenities:** Restaurant, lounge, coffee shop; concierge; exercise room; room service. *In room:* A/C, TV/DVD, CD player station, hair dryer, MP3 docking station, Wi-Fi.

University Inn ★   Within easy walking distance of the university, this hotel offers surprisingly attractive rooms. Although the least expensive units (called "traditional rooms") have bathrooms with showers but no tubs, small balconies and attractive furnishings make up for this shortcoming. The deluxe rooms, which have refrigerators and microwaves, are more spacious. For even more space and the best views, opt for one of the "premier rooms," which have large windows and extra-comfy beds (ask for room no. 331, which has a view of Mount Rainier). The upgraded rooms are definitely worth the extra money.

4140 Roosevelt Way NE, Seattle, WA 98105. ⓒ 800/733-3855 or 206/632-5055. Fax 206/547-4937. www. universityinnseattle.com. 102 units. $119–$169 double. Rates include continental breakfast. Children 17 and under stay free in parent's room. AE, DC, DISC, MC, V. Free parking. Pets accepted ($20 per night). **Amenities:** Restaurant; small outdoor pool; access to exercise room at nearby sister hotel. *In room:* A/C, TV, hair dryer, Wi-Fi.

Watertown ★★   Watertown is one of Seattle's U District entries in the hip boutique hotel market. Only blocks from the University of Washington, this beautifully designed hotel is definitely well placed for a trendy clientele. If you're into contemporary styling, you'll love it, even if you aren't in town on university business. Platform beds, streamlined built-ins, desks with frosted-glass tops and ergonomic chairs, and huge full-length mirrors are just a few of the interesting features in the guest rooms. Bathrooms are large and have granite countertops; when you see the frosted-glass portal on the door, you might imagine you're on a cruise ship.

4242 Roosevelt Way NE, Seattle, WA 98105. ⓒ 866/944-4242 or 206/826-4242. Fax 206/315-4242. www. watertownseattle.com. 100 units. $149–$209 double; $195–$265 suite. Rates include continental breakfast. Children 15 and under stay free in parent's room. AE, DC, DISC, MC, V. Free parking. **Amenities:** Bikes; exercise room and access to nearby health club. *In room:* A/C, TV, fridge, hair dryer, Wi-Fi.

INEXPENSIVE

Chambered Nautilus Bed & Breakfast Inn ★   This Georgian colonial inn sits high above an apartment-lined street atop an ivy-covered embankment, out of view of the sidewalk. Because the surrounding shady forest gives it a very secluded feel, you'll hardly realize you're in the middle of the city. The antiques-filled B&B, which dates from 1915, has a homey feel, and innkeeper Joyce Schulte makes sure guests are comfortable and well fed. Four of the rooms have porches; some have mountain views. Third-floor units have fireplaces and the best views. Be advised that this inn is not recommended for anyone who has trouble climbing stairs. Four suites, with DVD players, kitchens, and porches, are in an adjacent house, where children are welcome.

5005 22nd Ave. NE, Seattle, WA 98105. ⓒ 800/545-8459 or 206/522-2536. Fax 206/528-0898. www. chamberednautilus.com. 10 units. $104–$179 double; $124–$204 suite. Rates include full breakfast. AE, MC, V. Pets accepted in suites ($15 per day). Children 9 and older welcome in main house; children of all ages welcome in suites. **Amenities:** Concierge. *In room:* TV, hair dryer, Wi-Fi.

College Inn Built in 1909 for the Alaska-Yukon Exposition, this Tudor Revival building has loads of character and a great location right across the street from the University of Washington campus. That said, I really only recommend the College Inn for young travelers. All its rooms have shared bathrooms, and the inn itself, as with many budget accommodations in Europe, is up a couple of steep flights of stairs. The decor is a bit funky, but none of the guests seem to mind. Rooms range from tiny to spacious; all have washbasins. Parking can be a problem, so this is a good bet for anyone traveling without a car; there's good bus service into downtown.

4000 University Way NE, Seattle, WA 98105. ☏ **206/633-4441.** Fax 206/547-1335. www.collegeinnseattle. com. 27 units, all with shared bathroom. June–Oct $80–$100 double; Nov–May $75–$95 double. Rates include continental breakfast. MC, V. **Amenities:** Restaurant, lounge; Internet.

11 NEAR SEA-TAC AIRPORT

The airport is 30 to 45 minutes south of downtown (depending on the traffic). There's little to recommend this area besides its proximity to the airport.

MODERATE

Seattle Marriott Sea-Tac Airport ★★ Ⓚⁱᵈˢ With a steamy atrium garden in which you'll find plenty of tropical plants, a swimming pool, and two whirlpool tubs, this resortlike hotel is an excellent choice if you're visiting during the rainy season. There are even waterfalls and totem poles for that Northwest outdoorsy feeling; best of all, it's always sunny and warm in here (which is more than you can say for the real Northwest outdoors). Guest rooms are attractively furnished and comfortable, with good beds and great pillows. Ask for one of the rooms with a view of Mount Rainier.

3201 S. 176th St., Seattle, WA 98188. ☏ **800/314-0925** or 206/241-2000. Fax 206/248-0789. www.seattle airportmarriott.com. 459 units. $129–$219 double. Children 17 and under stay free in parent's room. AE, DC, DISC, MC, V. Valet parking $22; self-parking $18. **Amenities:** Restaurant, lounge; free airport transfers; concierge; executive-level rooms; exercise room; 2 Jacuzzis; indoor atrium pool; room service; sauna. *In room:* A/C, TV, hair dryer, MP3 docking station, Wi-Fi.

12 THE EASTSIDE

The Eastside (a reference to this area's location on the east side of Lake Washington) is Seattle's main high-tech suburb and comprises the cities of Bellevue, Kirkland, Issaquah, and Redmond. Should you be out this way on business, you may find that an Eastside hotel is more convenient than one in downtown. If it isn't rush hour, you can get to downtown in about 20 minutes via the I-90 or Wash. 520 floating bridge. During rush hour, however, it can take much longer. Two of the most luxurious hotels in the metropolitan area are here.

EXPENSIVE

Bellevue Club Hotel ★★★ In its gardens, architecture, and interior design, this hotel epitomizes contemporary Northwest style. Beautiful landscaping surrounds the entrance, and works of contemporary art are found throughout the public areas. The "club" in this hotel's name refers to a state-of-the-art health club that has everything from an indoor running track and three pools to indoor squash and outdoor tennis courts (there's also a full-service spa). But even if you aren't into aerobic workouts, this hotel has much to offer. You won't find more elegant rooms anywhere in the Seattle area. Accommodations are extremely plush, with the high-ceilinged club rooms among my favorites. These have floor-to-ceiling walls of glass, massive draperies, and private patios facing a beautiful garden. Luxurious European fabrics are everywhere, giving rooms a romantic feel. Bathrooms are resplendent in granite and glass, and most have whirlpool tubs.

11200 SE Sixth St., Bellevue, WA 98004. ☏ **800/579-1110** or 425/454-4424. Fax 425/688-3197. www.bellevueclubhotel.com. 67 units. $169–$335 double (from $129 on weekends); $450–$1,500 suite. Children 17 and under stay free in parent's room. AE, DC, DISC, MC, V. Valet parking $12. Pets accepted ($35 fee). **Amenities:** 3 restaurants (Pacific Rim), lounge; children's programs; concierge; expansive health club w/Jacuzzis, saunas, steam rooms; 2 indoor pools and 1 outdoor pool; room service; full-service spa; 10 tennis courts. *In room:* A/C, TV, hair dryer, minibar, Wi-Fi.

Woodmark Hotel, Yacht Club & Spa on Lake Washington ★★★ (Value)   This

resortlike hotel is so luxurious and in such a beautiful setting that it is the metro area's premier waterfront lodging—and well worth the 20-minute drive from downtown Seattle. Surrounded by a luxury residential community, the Woodmark has the feel of a beach resort and looks out over the very same waters that Bill Gates sees from his nearby Xanadu. There are plenty of lakeview rooms here, although you will pay a premium for them. For less expensive lodging, try the marinaview rooms. In addition to the hotel's dining room, several other restaurants are in the area. With advance reservations, guests can go out for a 2-hour cruise on the hotel's restored 1956 Chris-Craft boat. Beautiful surroundings, luxurious rooms, and boat tours all add up to one of Seattle's best hotel values.

1200 Carillon Point, Kirkland, WA 98033. ☏ **800/822-3700** or 425/822-3700. Fax 425/822-3699. www.thewoodmark.com. 100 units. $240–$320 double; $380–$2,000 suite. Children 17 and under stay free in parent's room. AE, DC, MC, V. Valet parking $15; self-parking $12. Pets accepted. **Amenities:** 2 restaurants, 2 lounges; babysitting; concierge; exercise room and access to nearby health club; room service; full-service spa; watersports equipment rentals. *In room:* A/C, TV, hair dryer, minibar, MP3 docking station, Wi-Fi.

MODERATE

Red Lion Hotel Bellevue ★   The Red Lion Hotel Bellevue is one of the few hotels

in the Seattle area that captures the feel of the Northwest in its design and landscaping. The sprawling two-story property is roofed with cedar-shake shingles, while the grounds are lushly planted with rhododendrons, ferns, azaleas, and fir trees. Guest rooms here are quite sophisticated and upscale, with elegant country French furnishings and decor, and bathrooms offer plenty of counter space.

11211 Main St., Bellevue, WA 98004. ☏ **800/733-5466** or 425/455-5240. Fax 425/455-0654. www.redlion.com. 181 units. $90–$180 double. Children 17 and under stay free in parent's room. AE, DC, DISC, MC, V. Free parking. Pets accepted ($20 per night). **Amenities:** Restaurant, lounge; exercise room and access to nearby health club; seasonal outdoor pool; room service. *In room:* A/C, TV, fridge, hair dryer, Wi-Fi.

INEXPENSIVE

Extended StayAmerica–Bellevue   Just off I-405 near downtown Bellevue, this

modern off-ramp motel caters primarily to long-term guests. To this end, the rooms are all large and have kitchenettes. However, you won't get daily maid service unless you are staying only a few days and pay extra for it. If you stay for a week, rates drop considerably.

11400 Main St., Bellevue, WA 98004. ☏ **800/804-3724** or 425/453-8186. Fax 425/453-8178. www.extendedstay.com. 148 units. Early May to early Oct $100–$115 double; early Oct to early May $65–$80 double. Children 17 and under stay free in parent's room. AE, DC, DISC, MC, V. Free parking. Pets accepted ($25 per day, $150 maximum). *In room:* A/C, TV, kitchen, Wi-Fi.

La Quinta Inn Bellevue/Kirkland   This budget chain hotel is located just across the Wash. 520 floating bridge (Evergreen Point Bridge), and while traffic across this bridge is heavy during rush hour, the location is surprisingly convenient. If traffic is light, you're only 15 minutes from downtown or the Seattle Center area. Guest rooms are basic but serviceable. Pluses include an outdoor pool, an exercise room, and a couple of casual restaurants right next door.

10530 NE Northrup Way, Kirkland, WA 98033. ⒸＣ **800/753-3757** or 425/828-6585. Fax 425/822-8722. www.lq.com. 119 units. $95–$139 double, $135–$149 suite. Rates include continental breakfast. Children 17 and under stay free in parent's room. AE, DISC, MC, V. Free parking. Pets accepted. **Amenities:** Exercise room; seasonal outdoor pool; Wi-Fi. *In room:* A/C, TV, hair dryer, Internet.

---

13 BAINBRIDGE ISLAND

Although Bainbridge Island is a 30-minute ferry ride away from Seattle, the ease of the commute to the city makes hotels in downtown Bainbridge Island eminently recommendable. Riding the ferry between the city and this idyllic island community captures the essence of the Seattle experience. The hotel and inn listed here are both within a short taxi or bus ride of the ferry terminal. If you're traveling light or don't have your bags with you, you can even walk.

MODERATE

Best Western Bainbridge Island Suites ★ ⓚ**Kids**   This is an all-suites hotel—a bit removed from quaint downtown Bainbridge Island, but still within walking distance of the ferry. Rooms are primarily large suites with kitchenettes and are ideal for trips with the family or for longer stays. By staying here, you get loads more space than you would get for this price in Seattle, and even when you add in the cost of taking the ferry to and from Seattle, rates are still very reasonable.

350 NE High School Rd., Bainbridge Island, WA 98110. ⒸＣ **866/396-9666** or 206/855-9666. Fax 206/855-9790. www.bestwestern.com/bainbridgeislandsuites. 51 units. $129–$169 double. Rates include continental breakfast. Children 12 and under stay free in parent's room. AE, DC, DISC, MC, V. Free parking. Pets accepted ($50 fee). **Amenities:** Concierge; exercise room. *In room:* A/C, TV, fridge, hair dryer, Internet.

The Eagle Harbor Inn ★★   Located a block from the water in downtown Bainbridge Island, this inn is the prettiest and most convenient inn on the island. You can easily walk between the inn and the ferry, and right across the street is a waterfront trail, a coffeehouse, a tavern, and a marina. This corner of town is quintessentially Bainbridge Island. With its colorful facade, varied rooflines, and residential feel, the Eagle Harbor Inn conjures up inns in small towns in Tuscany. Guest rooms, which vary in size and are done in a luxurious contemporary island-cottage style, are built around a small, attractively landscaped courtyard that is a pleasant place to sit in the sun over a cup of coffee. Keep in mind that this place is geared toward self-sufficient travelers.

291 Madison Ave. S. (P.O. Box 10386), Bainbridge Island, WA 98110. ⒸＣ **206/842-1446.** Fax 206/780-1715. www.theeagleharborinn.com. 8 units. $149–$199 double; $349–$499 town house. AE, MC, V. 2-night minimum summer and holiday weekends. Free parking. *In room:* A/C, TV/DVD, Internet.

6

Where to Dine

The fact that Pike Place Market, a public market filled with food stalls, is one of Seattle's top attractions should clue you in to the fact that this city takes food seriously. Throughout the summer, and other times of the year as well, the market overflows with a marvelous bounty of fresh salmon, Dungeness crabs, artisanal cheeses, Northwest berries, locally grown organic vegetables, wild mushrooms, and a wide variety of other produce.

Now, I realize that you'll probably be visiting Seattle on vacation and won't be doing your weekly grocery shopping here, but you'll be glad to know that the market's bounty also makes it onto the tables of lots of great Seattle restaurants, including quite a few right in the Pike Place Market neighborhood. So go ahead, ogle the market's offerings, and then make a reservation to eat at a nearby restaurant. When it comes time to order, just ask for something fresh and local. You'll have plenty of choices.

Of course, as everyone on earth seems to know by now, Seattle also takes coffee very seriously. This is where **Starbucks got its start**, and though the stylish espresso bars are now ubiquitous all across the country and around the world, there was a time when there was only one Starbucks—and, of course, it was (and still is) located in Pike Place Market (although this was not the first Starbucks; there was an earlier incarnation nearby).

While the market neighborhood gets my vote for best dining district in the city, nearby **Belltown,** which begins just a few blocks from Pike Place Market, also abounds with great restaurants. Be aware that most of these places are not cheap:

Entree prices at most places in these two neighborhoods average $20 or more, and there are a few places where you'll pay quite a bit more. However, if you happen to visit in spring or fall, keep an eye out for special prix-fixe menus. Recently, Capitol Hill has become the city's hottest restaurant neighborhood, and with lots of great restaurants within a few blocks of one another, this is a good place to go trolling for a place to eat.

If the area's high prices seem discouraging, rest assured that you can also find plenty of less expensive restaurants in the Pike Place Market neighborhood. In fact, because the market is such a tourist attraction, it has scads of cheap places to eat. Just don't expect haute cuisine at diner prices. You can, however, find a few gems, which I have listed in this chapter. Even trendy Belltown has a handful of good, inexpensive eateries.

For real dining deals, though, you'll need to head to the 'hoods. Seattle is a city of self-sufficient neighborhoods, and within these urban enclaves are dozens of good, inexpensive places to eat. These are neighborhood spots that aren't usually patronized by visitors to the city, but if you have a car and can navigate your way out into such neighborhoods as **Queen Anne, Madison Valley, Madison Park,** and **Ballard,** you'll have a seemingly endless number of choices. In the Upper Queen Anne neighborhood alone, I've counted more than a dozen restaurants within a 6-block area—and most of them have something or other to recommend them. I've listed my favorite, The 5 Spot, in this chapter.

So if you're up for a bit of culinary exploration, I recommend heading out of downtown to one of the city's residential neighborhoods. Stroll the compact commercial blocks of whichever district you find yourself in, and keep an eye out for newspaper reviews plastered in the front windows of restaurants. Pick one that the local paper liked, and you probably won't go wrong. And if you find someplace really great, be sure to drop me a line and let me know about it.

1   BEST DINING BETS

- **Best Waterfront Dining:** While the Seattle waterfront has plenty of touristy, in-your-face restaurants, you'll find the best waterfront dining experience in The Edgewater hotel. **Six-Seven Restaurant & Lounge,** Pier 67, 2411 Alaskan Way (© **206/269-4575;** www.edgewaterhotel.com), can claim not only superb food, but also very cool decor, a fabulous little deck, and one of the best views from any restaurant in the city. See p. 85.

- **Best View:** Without a doubt, **SkyCity at the Needle,** Space Needle, 400 Broad St. (© **800/937-9582** or 206/905-2100; www.spaceneedle.com), has the best views in Seattle—360 degrees worth of them. Sure it's expensive, but there's no place in town with views to rival these. See p. 100.

- **Best Outdoor Dining with a View:** Across Elliott Bay from downtown Seattle, **Salty's on Alki Beach,** 1936 Harbor Ave. SW (© **206/937-1600;** www.saltys.com), has a gorgeous view of the Seattle skyline. During the summer, you can get here by water taxi. See p. 113.

- **Best Budget Eatery with a View:** Of course, you could shell out big bucks to dine at Salty's, but you can get the same view at a fraction of the cost at the adjacent **Alki Crab & Fish,** 1660 Harbor Ave. SW (© **206/938-0975;** www.alkicrabandfish.com). Okay, so the menu is pretty limited but the fish and chips are excellent, and that view—wow! See p. 114.

- **Best Value:** While **Wild Ginger** usually gets all the accolades for its Pan-Asian cuisine, Belltown's little **Noodle Ranch,** 2228 Second Ave. (© **206/728-0463**), is every bit as good and much less expensive. The menu, however, is more limited. See p. 95.

- **Best Service: Canlis,** 2576 Aurora Ave. N. (© **206/283-3313;** www.canlis.com), is a Seattle tradition, the perfect place to close a big deal or celebrate a very special occasion. When you want to feel pampered, this is the place to dine. See p. 100.

- **Best French Cuisine:** Hidden away in the lower level of an artists' loft building at the north end of Belltown, the **Boat Street Cafe,** 3131 Western Ave. (© **206/632-4602;** www.boatstreetcafe.com), is a casual little restaurant that serves superb farmhouse French fare. Every last morsel on a plate here is given more attention than most restaurants give entire entrees. See p. 101.

- **Best Northwest Cuisine:** At **Rover's,** 2808 E. Madison St. (© **206/325-7442;** www.rovers-seattle.com), Chef Thierry Rautureau combines his love of local ingredients with classic French training to produce a distinctive take on Northwest cuisine. See p. 106.

- **Best Seafood:** Chef Tom Douglas can do no wrong, and at **Etta's Seafood,** 2020 Western Ave. (© **206/443-6000;** www.tomdouglas.com), he focuses his culinary talents on more than just his famed crab cakes. See p. 96.

ⓘ Tips   Al Fresco All Summer

Eight to nine months of rain and cloudy skies is a heavy price to pay for long summer days and sunsets that linger until almost 10pm. So can you blame Seattle's residents if they just won't go inside during the summer? The thought of eating indoors on a summer evening can be just too depressing to contemplate. If you happen to be here in the rain-free months (July, August, and September), and just don't want to eat indoors, here are some suggestions for al fresco meals.

If you got any closer to the water than the narrow little deck at the waterfront's **Six-Seven Restaurant** (see p. 85), you'd need a wetsuit. No deck in Seattle has a better view. Want a million dollar view for pennies on the dollar? Take the water taxi to Alki Beach and have fish and chips on the patio at **Alki Crab & Fish** (p. 114). You can get the same view and dine on more creative (and expensive) fare just down the street from Alki Crab & Fish at **Salty's on Alki** (p. 113). There's more high-end fish to be had with your views at **Ray's Boat House/Ray's Café** (see p. 112), a restaurant with a split personality and killer views. Keep an eye out for bald eagles.

If you don't have to have a view with your meal, try the shady little courtyard patio at **Volterra** (p. 112), an excellent Italian place in the Ballard neighborhood. **Serafina** (see p. 105), not far from the east shore of Lake Union, is another good Italian restaurant with a pretty garden patio. There's still more al fresco Italian at **The Pink Door** (see p. 98), Seattle's favorite "secret" Pike Place Market restaurant, which has a big deck with big view. If you're more in the mood for an urban sidewalk table experience, head to the **Virginia Inn** (see p. 94) near Pike Place Market. For a thoroughly Pike Place Market experience, grab a table at **El Puerco Lloron** (see p. 98), an inexpensive Mexican place on the Pike Hill Climb.

- **Best Place to Slurp Down Raw Oysters:** The Northwest produces an astonishing variety of oysters, and locals are almost as obsessive about their bivalves as they are about coffee and beer. For the best selection, head to **Elliott's,** Pier 56, 1201 Alaskan Way (ⓒ **206/623-4340;** www.elliottsoysterhouse.com). See p. 88.
- **Best Sushi:** If the sight of so much fresh fish in Pike Place Market has you craving sushi, then head up to the north end of Belltown to **Shiro's,** 2401 Second Ave. (ⓒ **206/443-9844**). All the Japanese businessmen here should give you a clue that this place is the real deal. See p. 94.
- **Best Steaks: Metropolitan Grill,** 820 Second Ave. (ⓒ **206/624-3287;** www.the metropolitangrill.com), in downtown Seattle, serves corn-fed, aged beef grilled over mesquite charcoal. Steaks just don't get any better than this. See p. 89.
- **Best Burgers:** We all have our own ideas of what constitutes the perfect burger, and Seattle has plenty of worthy contenders. I split my vote between the burgers at **Two Bells Bar & Grill,** 2313 Fourth Ave. (ⓒ **206/441-3050;** www.thetwobells.com), and those at the **74th Street Ale House,** 7401 Greenwood Ave. N. (ⓒ **206/784-2955;** www.seattlealehouses.com). See p. 95 and 112.
- **Best Desserts:** The **Dahlia Lounge,** 2001 Fourth Ave. (ⓒ **206/682-4142;** www. tomdouglas.com), has long been one of the best restaurants in Seattle, and while the

food is delicious, the triple coconut-cream pie is absolutely divine. The rest of the desserts are pretty good, too. See p. 92.

- **Best for Kids: Ivar's Salmon House,** 401 NE Northlake Way (© **206/632-0767;** www.ivars.net), resembles a Native American longhouse and is filled with cool stuff sure to fascinate kids. In sunny weather, the waterfront deck has a great view of Lake Union and the Seattle skyline. See p. 105.
- **Best Late-Night Dining: Palace Kitchen,** 2030 Fifth Ave. (© **206/448-2001;** www. tomdouglas.com), is an urbane palace of food, and it serves tasty specialties from the grill and rotisserie until 1am. The bar here is also a happening place. See p. 94.
- **Best Espresso:** Everyone in Seattle seems to have an opinion about where to get the best espresso drinks. My vote goes to **Caffé Vita,** 813 Fifth Ave. N. (© **206/285-9662;** www.caffevita.com) and 1005 E. Pike St. (© **206/709-4440**). The lattes served here have beautiful little works of art drawn onto the foam with espresso. See p. 117.

2 RESTAURANTS BY CUISINE

African
Pan Africa Market (Pike Place Market, $, p. 99)

American
Dick's (Queen Anne & Seattle Center, $, p. 101)

Icon Grill ★ (Belltown, $$, p. 94)

Lowell's ★ (Pike Place Market, $, p. 98)

Maggie Bluffs Marina Grill ★ (Queen Anne & Seattle Center, $, p. 104)

Portage Bay Café ★ (Lake Union & South Lake Union, $, p. 106)

Red Mill Burgers ★ (Wallingford, Fremont & Phinney Ridge, $, p. 111)

74th Street Ale House ★ (Wallingford, Fremont & Phinney Ridge, $, p. 112)

Sport Restaurant & Bar ★ (Queen Anne & Seattle Center, $, p. 104)

Two Bells Bar & Grill ★ (Belltown, $, p. 95)

Virginia Inn ★ (Belltown, $$, p. 94)

American Regional
Bluwater Bistro ★ (Lake Union & South Lake Union, $$, p. 104)

The 5 Spot ★ (Queen Anne & Seattle Center, $, p. 101)

Matt's in the Market ★★ (Pike Place Market, $$, p. 98)

Palace Kitchen ★ (Belltown, $$, p. 94)

Purple Café and Wine Bar ★ (Downtown & First Hill, $$, p. 90)

Bakeries & Pastry Shops
Bakery Nouveau ★ (West Seattle, $, p. 119)

Belle Epicurean (Downtown, $, p. 117)

The Confectional (Pike Place Market, $, p. 118)

Cow Chip Cookies (Pioneer Square & the International District, $, p. 118)

Crumpet Shop ★ (Pike Place Market, $, p. 118)

Cupcake Royale/Vérité Coffee (Ballard, $, p. 118)

Dahlia Bakery ★ (Belltown, $, p. 117)

Essential Bakery Cafe ★ (Wallingford, $, p. 118)

Grand Central Baking Company ★ (Pioneer Square & the International District, $, p. 118; Queen Anne & Seattle Center, $, p. 118)

Larsen's Danish Bakery (Ballard, $, p. 118)

Key to Abbreviations: $$$$ = Very Expensive; $$$ = Expensive; $$ = Moderate; $ = Inexpensive

Le Fournil (Queen Anne & Seattle Center, $, p. 118)

Le Panier (Pike Place Market, $, p. 118)

Macrina ★ (Belltown, $, p. 117; Queen Anne & Seattle Center, $, p. 118)

North Hill Bakery (Capitol Hill & Madison Valley, $, p. 118)

Three Girls Bakery (Pike Place Market, $, p. 118)

Top Pot Doughnuts (Belltown, $, p. 117)

Cafes, Coffee Bars & Tea Shops

Ancient Grounds ★ (Downtown & First Hill, $, p. 115)

Bauhaus Coffee & Books ★ (Capitol Hill & Madison Valley, $, p. 116)

Café Allegro (the University District, $, p. 117)

Caffe Ladro (Downtown & First Hill, $, p. 115; Caffe Ladro (Wallingford, Fremont & Phinney Ridge, $, p. 117)

Caffe Ladro Espresso Bar & Bakery ★ (Queen Anne & Seattle Center, $, p. 116)

Caffè Senso Unico (Downtown & First Hill, $, p. 115)

Caffè Umbria (Pioneer Square & the International District, $, p. 116)

Caffé Vita (Capitol Hill & Madison Valley, $, p. 117; Queen Anne & Seattle Center, $, p. 116)

Café Campagne ★★ (Pike Place Market, $$, p. 96)

Chocolati (Wallingford, Fremont & Phinney Ridge, $, p. 117)

Dilettante Mocha Martini Bar (Capitol Hill & Madison Valley, $, p. 117)

El Diablo Coffee Co. (Queen Anne & Seattle Center, $, p. 116)

Espresso Vivace Alley 24 ★ (Lake Union & South Lake Union, $, p. 116)

Fremont Coffee Company (Wallingford, Fremont & Phinney Ridge, $, p. 117)

Monorail Espresso (Downtown & First Hill, $, p. 115)

Panama Hotel Tea & Coffee House ★ (Pioneer Square & the International District, $, p. 116)

Starbucks (Pike Place Market, $, p. 115)

Uptown Espresso (Belltown & The Waterfront, $, p. 116; Queen Anne & Seattle Center, $, p. 116)

Vivace Espresso Bar at Brix ★ (Capitol Hill & Madison Valley, $, p. 117)

Zeitgeist Art/Coffee ★ (Pioneer Square & the International District, $, p. 116)

Caribbean

Pam's Kitchen (the University District, $, p. 109)

Chinese

Bamboo Garden (Queen Anne & Seattle Center, $, p. 97)

Jade Garden Restaurant (Pioneer Square & the International District, $, p. 99)

Continental

Canlis ★★★ (Queen Anne & Seattle Center, $$$$, p. 100)

The Georgian ★★★ (Downtown & First Hill, $$$$, p. 88)

Deli

Roxy's Deli ★ (Wallingford, Fremont & Phinney Ridge, $, p. 112)

French

Boat Street Café and Kitchen ★★ (Queen Anne & Seattle Center, $$, p. 101)

Café Campagne ★★ (Pike Place Market, $$, p. 96)

Café Presse ★ (Capitol Hill & Madison Valley, Pike Place Market, $, p. 108)

Joule ★★ (Wallingford, Fremont &
   Phinney Ridge, $$$, p. 110)
Le Pichet ★★ (Pike Place Market, $$,
   p. 96)
Matt's in the Market ★★ (Pike Place
   Market, $$, p. 98)
Virginia Inn ★ (Belltown, $$, p. 94)

Greek
Lola ★★ (Belltown, $$$, p. 93)

International
Baguette Box ★ (Downtown & First
   Hill, $, p. 91)
Beach Cafe at the Point ★★ (The
   Eastside, $$, p. 114)

Italian
Anchovies & Olives ★★ (Capitol Hill
   & Madison Valley, $$$, p. 106)
Bizzarro Italian Café ★ (Wallingford,
   Fremont & Phinney Ridge, $$,
   p. 110)
Il Bistro ★★ (Pike Place Market, $$$,
   p. 96)
The Old Spaghetti Factory (The
   Waterfront, $, p. 88)
Osteria La Spiga ★★ (Capitol Hill &
   Madison Valley, $$$, p. 107)
The Pink Door ★ (Pike Place Market,
   $$, p. 98)
Salumi ★★★ (Pioneer Square & the
   International District, $, p. 100)
Serafina ★ (Lake Union & South Lake
   Union, $$, p. 105)
Spinasse ★★ (Capitol Hill & Madi-
   son Valley, $$$, p. 107)
Volterra ★★ (Ballard, $$$, p. 112)

Japanese
I Love Sushi ★ (Lake Union & South
   Lake Union, $$, p. 105)
Shiro's Sushi Restaurant ★★ (Bell-
   town, $$, p. 94)
Wasabi Bistro ★ (Belltown, $$,
   p. 95)

Korean
Joule ★★ (Wallingford, Fremont &
   Phinney Ridge, $$$, p. 110)

Late-Night
Bluwater Bistro ★ (Lake Union &
   South Lake Union, $$, p. 104)
Brasa ★ (Belltown, $$$, p. 92)
El Gaucho ★★★ (Belltown, $$$$,
   p. 92)
The 5 Spot ★ (Queen Anne & Seattle
   Center, $, p. 101)
Flying Fish ★ (Belltown, $$$, p. 93)
Palace Kitchen ★ (Belltown, $$,
   p. 94)
The Pink Door ★ (Pike Place Market,
   $$, p. 98)
Wasabi Bistro ★ (Belltown, $$,
   p. 95)

Mediterranean
Brasa ★ (Belltown, $$$, p. 92)
Lark ★★ (Capitol Hill & Madison
   Valley, $$$, p. 107)
Palace Kitchen ★ (Belltown, $$,
   p. 94)
Palomino ★ (Downtown & First Hill,
   $$, p. 90)

Mexican
Agua Verde Cafe ★ (the University
   District, $, p. 109)
Cactus ★ (West Seattle, $$, p. 114)
El Camino ★ (Wallingford, Fremont
   & Phinney Ridge, $$, p. 111)
El Puerco Lloron (Pike Place Market,
   $, p. 98)

New American
Quinn's ★★ (Capitol Hill & Madison
   Valley, $$, p. 108)
Six-Seven Restaurant & Lounge ★★
   (The Waterfront, $$$, p. 85)
Spur Gastropub ★★ (Belltown, $$$,
   p. 93)
Tilth ★★ (Wallingford, Fremont &
   Phinney Ridge, $$$, p. 110)
Union ★★★ (Downtown & First
   Hill, $$$, p. 89)

Northwest
Canlis ★★★ (Queen Anne & Seattle
   Center, $$$$, p. 100)

Dahlia Lounge ★★★ (Belltown, $$$, p. 92)

Flying Fish ★ (Belltown, $$$, p. 93)

The Georgian ★★★ (Downtown & First Hill, $$$$, p. 88)

Lark ★★ (Capitol Hill & Madison Valley, $$$, p. 107)

Palomino ★ (Downtown & First Hill, $$, p. 90)

Palisade ★★ (Queen Anne & Seattle Center, $$$, p. 101)

Poppy ★★ (Capitol Hill & Madison Valley, $$$, p. 107)

Restaurant Zoë ★★ (Belltown, $$$, p. 93)

Rover's ★★★ (Capitol Hill & Madison Valley, $$$$, p. 106)

SkyCity at the Needle ★★ (Queen Anne & Seattle Center, $$$$, p. 100)

Pan-Asian

Dahlia Lounge ★★★ (Belltown, $$$, p. 92)

Noodle Ranch ★ (Belltown, $, p. 95)

Wild Ginger Asian Restaurant & Satay Bar ★★ (Downtown & First Hill, $$, p. 91)

Pan-Latin

Tango Tapas Restaurant & Lounge ★ (Downtown & First Hill, $$, p. 91)

Pizza

Pizzeria Pagliacci (Queen Anne & Seattle Center, $, p. 104)

Serious Pie ★ (Belltown, $, p. 95)

Quick Bites

Beecher's Handmade Cheese (Pike Place Market, $, p. 119)

Bottega Italiana (Pike Place Market, $, p. 120)

DeLaurenti ★ (Pike Place Market, $$, p. 119)

Dish D'Lish ★ (Ballard, $, p. 119)

Garlic Garden (Pike Place Market, $, p. 119)

Michou (Pike Place Market, $, p. 119)

Molly Moon's Homemade Ice Cream (Capitol Hill & Madison Valley, $, p. 120; Wallingford, Fremont & Phinney Ridge, $, p. 120)

Piroshky, Piroshky (Pike Place Market, $, p. 119)

Procopio (Pike Place Market, $, p. 120)

Spanish Table (Pike Place Market, $, p. 119)

Uli's Famous Sausage ★ (Pike Place Market, $$, p. 119)

Westlake Center food court (Downtown & First Hill, $, p. 119)

Seafood

Alki Crab & Fish (West Seattle, $, p. 114)

Anthony's Pier 66 & Bell Street Diner ★ (The Waterfront, $$, p. 85)

Brooklyn Seafood, Steak & Oyster House ★★ (Downtown & First Hill, $$$, p. 89)

Chinook's at Salmon Bay ★ (Ballard, $$, p. 113)

Elliott's ★★ (The Waterfront, $$, p. 88)

Etta's Seafood ★★ (Pike Place Market, $$, p. 96)

Flying Fish ★ (Belltown, $$$, p. 93)

Ivar's Salmon House ★★ (Lake Union & South Lake Union, $$, p. 105)

McCormick & Schmick's Seafood Restaurant ★ (Downtown & First Hill, $$, p. 89)

Pike Place Chowder (Pike Place Market, $, p. 99)

Ponti Seafood Grill ★★ (Wallingford, Fremont & Phinney Ridge, $$$, p. 110)

Ray's Boathouse/Ray's Cafe ★★ (Ballard, $$$, p. 112)

Salty's on Alki Beach ★★ (West Seattle, $$$, p. 113)

Spanish

The Harvest Vine ★★ (Capitol Hill & Madison Valley, $$, p. 108)

Txori Bar ★★ (Belltown, $$, p. 94)

Steak

El Gaucho ★★★ (Belltown, $$$$, p. 92)

Metropolitan Grill ★★ (Downtown & First Hill, $$$, p. 89)

Thai

Mae Phim (Downtown & First Hill, $, p. 91)

May ★ (Wallingford, Fremont & Phinney Ridge, $$, p. 111)

Thaiku ★ (Ballard, $, p. 113)

Vegetarian

Bamboo Garden (Queen Anne & Seattle Center, $, p. 97)

Cafe Flora ★ (Capitol Hill & Madison Valley, $, p. 108)

Carmelita ★★ (Wallingford, Fremont & Phinney Ridge, $$, p. 111)

Hillside Quickies Vegan Sandwich Shop (the University District, $, p. 97)

Rover's ★★★ (Capitol Hill & Madison Valley, $$$$, p. 106)

Silence-Heart-Nest (Wallingford, Fremont & Phinney Ridge, $, p. 97)

Vietnamese

Pho Than Brothers (Capitol Hill & Madison Valley, $, p. 109)

Tamarind Tree ★★ (Pioneer Square & the International District, $$, p. 99)

3 THE WATERFRONT

EXPENSIVE *BEST WATERFRONT DINING*

Six-Seven Restaurant & Lounge ★★ NEW AMERICAN   This stylish waterfront restaurant in The Edgewater hotel has more than just superb food to recommend it. The views of Elliott Bay and the Olympic Mountains are unforgettable, and the "robo-trees" that decorate the dining room are a curious blend of rustic and high-tech. If the weather is warm, try to get a seat on the narrow little deck; it's the best waterfront deck in Seattle. The menu changes regularly, so you never know what to expect. However, if the crab bisque is on the menu, don't miss it. The clam chowder here has won awards, too. The kitchen also does a great job with halibut, and its wood-roasted salmon is terrific.

Pier 67, 2411 Alaskan Way. ⓒ **206/269-4575.** www.edgewaterhotel.com. Reservations recommended. Main courses $12–$22 lunch, $22–$45 dinner. AE, DC, DISC, MC, V. Mon–Sat 7am–11pm; Sun 7am–2pm and 2:30–11pm.

MODERATE

Anthony's Pier 66 & Bell Street Diner ★ SEAFOOD   The Anthony's chain has several outposts around the Seattle area, but this complex is the most convenient and versatile. Not only does it have an upper-end, stylish seafood restaurant with good waterfront views, but also a moderately priced casual restaurant and a walk-up counter. The bold contemporary styling and abundance of art glass set Anthony's apart from most of the waterfront's restaurants. The upscale crowd heads upstairs for Asian- and Southwestern-inspired seafood dishes, while the more cost-conscious stay downstairs at the Bell Street Diner, where meals are much easier on the wallet (though far less creative). For the higher prices, you get better views. You can save money with the $19 four-course sunset dinners that are served Monday through Friday between 4 and 6pm.

WHERE TO DINE

6

THE WATERFRONT

Coffee, Tea, Bakeries, Pastry Shops & Quick Bites

Ancient Grounds **42**
Bauhaus Coffee & Books **1**
Beecher's Handmade Cheese **30**
Belle Epicurean **47**
Bottega Italiana **35**
Caffe Senso Unico **6**
Caffe Umbria **51**
The Confectional **34**
Cow Chip Cookies **49**
Crumpet Shop **34**
Dahlia Bakery **10**
DeLaurenti **35**
Garlic Garden **35**
Grand Central Baking Company **50**
Le Panier **29**
Macrina **21**
Michou **29**
Monorail Espresso **5**
Panama Hotel Tea & Coffee House **55**
Piroshky, Piroshky **29**
Procopio **39**
Spanish Table **37**
Starbucks **29**
Three Girls Bakery **34**
Top Pot Doughnuts **11**
Uli's Famous Sausage Co. **38**
Uwajimaya **54**
Zeitgeist Art/Coffee **52**

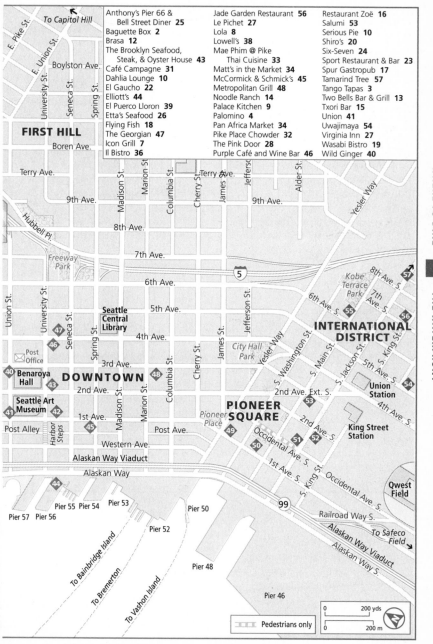

Anthony's Pier 66 & Bell Street Diner **25**
Baguette Box **2**
Brasa **12**
The Brooklyn Seafood, Steak, & Oyster House **43**
Café Campagne **31**
Dahlia Lounge **10**
El Gaucho **22**
El Puerco Lloron **39**
Etta's Seafood **26**
Flying Fish **18**
The Georgian **47**
Icon Grill **7**
Il Bistro **36**

Jade Garden Restaurant **56**
Le Pichet **27**
Lola **8**
Lowell's **38**
Mae Phim @ Pike Thai Cuisine **33**
Matt's in the Market **34**
McCormick & Schmick's **45**
Metropolitan Grill **48**
Noodle Ranch **14**
Palace Kitchen **9**
Palomino **4**
Pan Africa Market **34**
Pike Place Chowder **32**
The Pink Door **28**
Purple Café and Wine Bar **46**

Restaurant Zoë **16**
Salumi **53**
Serious Pie **10**
Shiro's **20**
Six-Seven **24**
Sport Restaurant & Bar **23**
Spur Gastropub **17**
Tamarind Tree **57**
Tango Tapas **3**
Two Bells Bar & Grill **13**
Txori Bar **15**
Union **41**
Uwajimaya **54**
Virginia Inn **27**
Wasabi Bistro **19**
Wild Ginger **40**

To Capitol Hill

E. Pike St.
E. Union St.
E. Pike St.
Boylston Ave.
University St.
Seneca St.
Spring St.

FIRST HILL
Boren Ave.

Terry Ave.
9th Ave.
8th Ave.
Hubbell Pl.
7th Ave.
Freeway Park
6th Ave.

Madison St.
Marion St.
Columbia St.
Cherry St.
James St.
Jefferson St.

Terry Ave.
9th Ave.

Alder St.

Yesler Way

5

Kobe Terrace Park
8th Ave. S.
7th Ave. S.
6th Ave. S.
5th Ave. S.

INTERNATIONAL DISTRICT

Union St.
University St.
Seneca St.
Spring St.

Seattle Central Library

5th Ave.
4th Ave.
3rd Ave.
2nd Ave.
1st Ave.

Jefferson St.

DOWNTOWN

Madison St.
Marion St.
Columbia St.
Cherry St.
James St.

City Hall Park

Yesler Way

S. Washington St.
S. Main St.
S. Jackson St.
5th Ave. S.
4th Ave. S.

Benaroya Hall
Seattle Art Museum
Post Office
Post Alley
Harbor Steps

Western Ave.

PIONEER SQUARE
Pioneer Place

Post Ave.

2nd Ave. Ext. S.

Union Station

King Street Station

Occidental Ave. S.
1st Ave. S.
King St.
Occidental Ave. S.

Qwest Field

Alaskan Way Viaduct
Alaskan Way

Pier 55 Pier 54 Pier 53
Pier 57 Pier 56
Pier 52
Pier 50
Pier 48

99

Railroad Way S.
To Safeco Field
Alaskan Way Viaduct
Alaskan Way S.

To Bainbridge Island
To Bremerton
To Vashon Island

Pier 46

0   200 yds
0   200 m

Pedestrians only

Many waterfront restaurants offer free or validated parking. When you make a reservation, be sure to ask where to park.

2201 Alaskan Way. *C* **206/448-6688.** www.anthonys.com. Reservations recommended at Pier 66, not taken at Bell Street Diner. Pier 66 main courses $18–$50; Bell Street Diner main courses $10–$40. AE, DISC, MC, V. Pier 66 Mon–Thurs 5–9:30pm, Fri–Sat 5–10pm, Sun 5–9pm; Bell Street Diner Mon–Thurs 11am–10pm, Fri–Sat 11am–10:30pm, Sun 11am–9pm.

Elliott's ★★ SEAFOOD   While most of its neighbors are content to coast along on tourist business, Elliott's actually aims to keep the locals happy by serving some of the best seafood in Seattle. Although the restaurant is right on the waterfront, the view isn't that great, which, I think, is partly why the food is good. Elliott's tries a little harder. Salmon and Dungeness crab are usually prepared several different ways, and are always a good bet here. However, the oyster bar, which can have more than 25 varieties, is the real reason to eat here. This is definitely the place to get to know your Northwest oysters. Monday through Friday, from 3 to 6pm, they have an "oyster hour" here; arrive early to get the best price.

Pier 56, 1201 Alaskan Way. *C* **206/623-4340.** www.elliottsoysterhouse.com. Reservations recommended. Main courses $9–$19 at lunch, $15–$40 at dinner. AE, DISC, MC, V. Sun–Thurs 11am–10pm; Fri–Sat 11am–11pm.

INEXPENSIVE

The Old Spaghetti Factory Kids ITALIAN   The Old Spaghetti Factory is a chain restaurant, which I don't normally recommend, but kids wandering the waterfront with their parents may be relieved to know that here at this palace of pasta they won't have to force down raw oysters, clam chowder, or any of that other icky stuff grown-ups eat at seafood restaurants. Anyone who's been to an Old Spaghetti Factory knows what to expect. If you haven't dined at one of the antiques-filled restaurants, I have two words for you—cheap pasta—and two other words for the kids—yummy noodles. Enough said? You'll find this place across from Pier 70 at the north end of the waterfront.

2801 Elliott Ave. *C* **206/441-7724.** www.osf.com. Reservations not accepted. Main courses $8–$13. AE, DISC, MC, V. Mon–Thurs 11:30am–2pm and 4:30–10pm; Fri 11:30am–2pm and 4:30–11pm; Sat noon–11pm; Sun noon–10pm (1st Mon in July to Labor Day also Mon–Fri 2–4:30pm).

4 DOWNTOWN & FIRST HILL

VERY EXPENSIVE

The Georgian ★★★ NORTHWEST/CONTINENTAL   The Georgian is as grand as they come, and if you're looking for haute cuisine, palatial surroundings, and superb service, no other restaurant in Seattle comes close. This is by far the most traditional and formal restaurant in the city. For the full Georgian experience, I recommend opting for the three-course or seven-course dinner. The seven-course dinner might include seared foie gras with pressed cherries, oysters with caviar and horseradish foam, seared scallops with truffle-bacon butter sauce, Dungeness crab bisque, bacon-wrapped pheasant with

black trumpet mushrooms, a local cheese served with huckleberries, and, a trio of small 89
cakes. The wine list is superb, and service is so attentive that you will likely feel as though
yours is the only table in the restaurant.

In the Fairmont Olympic Hotel, 411 University St. ℂ 206/621-7889. www.fairmont.com/seattle. Reservations highly recommended. Main courses $12–$19 lunch, $30–$49 dinner; 3-course prix-fixe menu $49 ($69 with wine); 7-course tasting menu $90 ($145 with wine). AE, DC, DISC, MC, V. Mon–Fri 6:30–11am and 11:30am–2:30pm; Sat–Sun 7am–2:30pm; Tues–Thurs 5:30–10pm; Fri–Sat 5:30–10:30pm.

EXPENSIVE

Brooklyn Seafood, Steak & Oyster House ★★ SEAFOOD   This classic seafood restaurant in the middle of the financial district looks as if it's been here since the Great Seattle Fire and is, in fact, housed in one of the city's oldest buildings. The specialty is oysters, with close to a dozen different types piled up at the oyster bar on any given night. Other tempting appetizers range from a cilantro-battered calamari steak to Dungeness crab cakes with wasabi aioli. The alder-planked wild salmon (roasted on a slab of alder wood) is an absolute Northwest classic and is your best bet if you aren't having oysters.

1212 Second Ave. ℂ 206/224-7000. www.thebrooklyn.com. Reservations recommended. Main courses $11–$15 lunch, $24–$44 dinner. AE, DC, DISC, MC, V. Mon–Thurs 11am–3pm and 5–10pm; Fri 11am–3pm and 5–10:30pm; Sat 4:30–10:30pm; Sun 4–10pm.

Metropolitan Grill ★★ STEAK   Fronted by massive granite columns that make it look more like a bank than a restaurant, the Metropolitan Grill is a traditional steakhouse that attracts a well-heeled clientele, primarily men in suits. When you walk in the front door, you'll immediately encounter a case full of meat that ranges from filet mignon to triple-cut lamb chops (with the occasional giant lobster tail tossed in). Perfectly cooked dry-aged steaks are the primary attraction; a baked potato and a pile of thick-cut onion rings complete the ultimate carnivore's dinner. Financial matters are a frequent topic of discussion here, and the bar even has a "Guess the Dow" contest. I hope you sold high, since it'll take some capital gains to finance a dinner for two here.

820 Second Ave. ℂ 206/624-3287. www.themetropolitangrill.com. Reservations recommended. Main courses $12–$56 lunch, $20–$82 dinner. AE, DC, DISC, MC, V. Mon–Fri 11am–3pm; Mon–Thurs 5–10pm; Fri 5–10:30pm; Sat 4–11pm; Sun 4–9pm.

Union ★★★ NEW AMERICAN   Across the street from the Seattle Art Museum, this beautiful, minimalist space is a don't-miss spot on any foodie's visit to Seattle. Chef Ethan Stowell is one of Seattle's finest chefs. Stowell's menu, designed to show off his culinary chops, is comprised of lots of small plates that should be assembled into a multicourse feast. The quality of the ingredients is incomparable and the presentation is gorgeous. Because the menu changes with the seasons and relies on whatever ingredients are freshest that day, you never know what might be available. Perhaps potato gnocchi with pork cheeks and marjoram; pasta with chanterelle mushrooms, prosciutto broth, and aged balsamic vinegar; or veal sweetbreads with bacon, prunes, celery root, and chestnuts. A light menu is also offered in the bar from 5 to 7pm and from 10pm to midnight.

1400 First Ave. ℂ 206/838-8000. www.unionseattle.com. Reservations recommended. Main courses $16–$18. DISC, MC, V. Daily 5–10pm.

MODERATE

McCormick & Schmick's Seafood Restaurant ★ SEAFOOD   Force your way past the crowds of business suits at the bar and you'll find yourself in a classic fish house—complete with cafe curtains, polished brass, leaded glass, and wood paneling.

(Kids) Family-Friendly Restaurants

Ivar's Salmon House (p. 105) is built to resemble a Northwest Coast Native American longhouse and is filled with artifacts that kids find fascinating. If they get restless, they can go out to the floating patio and watch the boats passing by.

At a marina overlooking Elliott Bay and downtown Seattle, economical **Maggie Bluffs Marina Grill** (p. 104) has food the kids will enjoy and provides crayons to keep them occupied while they wait. Before or after a meal, you can take a free boat ride across the marina to an observation deck atop the breakwater.

The Old Spaghetti Factory (p. 88) may be part of a chain, but with cheap food, a convenient location across the street from the waterfront, and loads of kid-friendly noodle dishes, this place is a good bet when you've worked up an appetite walking the length of the Seattle waterfront.

If you've got a young sports fan or two in your family, don't miss **Sport Restaurant & Bar** (p. 104), a sports-themed restaurant across the street from the Space Needle. If you aren't too hungry to wait, try to get one of the booths that has its own private wall-hung TV. You'll be so close to the on-screen action, you'll be able to make the calls before the refs do.

Daily menus commonly list more than 30 seafood entrees and feature well-prepared dishes such as grilled sturgeon, Dungeness crab and shrimp cakes with red-pepper aioli (a perennial favorite), and cedar-plank-roasted salmon with Northwest berry sauce. A half-dozen or more varieties of oysters are usually available. In late afternoon and late evening, bar appetizers start at only $1.95. If the restaurant is crowded and you can't get a table, consider sitting at the counter and watching the cooks perform amazing feats.

1103 First Ave. (C) **206/623-5500**. www.mccormickandschmicks.com. Reservations recommended. Main courses $9–$16 lunch, $9–$34 dinner. AE, DC, DISC, MC, V. Daily 11:30am–11pm.

Palomino ★ NORTHWEST/MEDITERRANEAN   On the upper level of the City Centre shopping center, only a block from Nordstrom and Pacific Place, this large, casual restaurant may be part of a chain, but its many art-glass chandeliers give it a decidedly Seattle feel. Anything from the wood-fired oven is a good bet, and the pizzas are particularly tasty, as are the juicy rotisserie chickens. For dessert, you'd be remiss if you didn't order the chocolate tiramisu.

In City Centre, 1420 Fifth Ave. (C) **206/623-1300**. www.palomino.com. Reservations recommended. Main courses $10–$19 lunch, $10–$38. AE, DC, DISC, MC, V. Mon–Sat 11am–3pm; Mon–Thurs 5–9:30pm; Fri–Sat 4:30–10pm; Sun 4–9pm.

Purple Café and Wine Bar ★ AMERICAN REGIONAL   Seattleites love this big, loud wine bar near Benaroya Hall and the Seattle Art Museum, and you probably will, too. The space, a beautiful bi-level dining room with tall walls of glass, has a very contemporary feel. The menu is almost intimidatingly long, and everything sounds so good that you won't know where to start or finish. If you have a hard time making decisions, just start ordering little bites off the tapas-style tasting menu. Portions are tiny, so you can sample lots of different flavors—maybe some beef carpaccio with a quail egg, arugula, and truffle oil, or gorgonzola-stuffed dates, or pork tenderloin crusted with fennel pollen. While there are occasional dishes that fall short, when you order enough little bites, you'll find plenty of winners.

1225 Fourth Ave. (C) **206/829-2280.** www.thepurplecafe.com. Reservations recommended. Main courses $10–$33. AE, DISC, MC, V. Mon–Thurs 11am–11pm; Fri 11am–midnight; Sat noon–midnight; Sun noon–11pm.

Tango Tapas Restaurant & Lounge ★ PAN-LATIN   In Spain, the appetizer-size plates of food known as *tapas* are traditionally served with drinks in bars. Here at Tango, however, tapas are front and center, taking cues from both classic and creative Spanish and Latin cuisine. Many of the items on the menu are substantial enough to serve as entrees, but you'll be much happier if you order lots of different plates and share everything with your dinner companions. Don't miss the *gambas picantes* (chipotle-pepper-flavored tiger prawns with a sauce made from pumpkin seeds and cilantro). On Monday nights all wines by the bottle are half-price, and every night, discounted tapas are served in the lounge between 4:30 and 6pm.

1100 Pike St. (C) **206/583-0382.** www.tangorestaurant.com. Reservations recommended. Tapas $2.50–$12; main courses $10–$19. AE, MC, V. Sun–Thurs 5–10:30pm; Fri–Sat 5pm–midnight.

Wild Ginger Asian Restaurant & Satay Bar ★★ PAN-ASIAN   This Pan-Asian restaurant has long been a Seattle favorite. It's across the street from Benaroya Hall, which makes it perfect for dinner before a symphony performance. I like to pull up a stool at the large satay bar and watch the cooks grill little skewers of everything from chicken to scallops to prawns to lamb. Each skewer is served with a small cube of sticky rice and pickled cucumber; order three or four satay sticks and you have yourself a meal. Of course, you can also sit at a table and have a more traditional dinner. Try the Panang beef curry (prime rib-eye steak in pungent curry sauce of cardamom, coconut milk, Thai basil, and peanuts). The restaurant is upstairs from the **Triple Door,** a classy live-music club, so be sure to check the performance schedule.

1401 Third Ave. (C) **206/623-4450.** www.wildginger.net. Reservations recommended. Satay sticks $2–$6.50; main courses $8.25–$19 at lunch, $10–$30 at dinner. AE, DC, DISC, MC, V. Mon–Sat 11:30am–3pm; Mon–Thurs 5–11pm; Fri 5pm–midnight; Sat 4:30pm–midnight; Sun 4–11pm.

INEXPENSIVE

Baguette Box ★ INTERNATIONAL   Sandwiches served on crunchy slices of baguette are the specialty of this casual little restaurant just a few blocks uphill from the convention center. The crispy drunken chicken sandwich, served with caramelized onions, cilantro, and a sweet-and-sour sauce, was inspired by a Vietnamese dish and is the house favorite, but I also like the grilled lemon grass skirt steak sandwich, which is also inspired by an Asian dish. There's a second Baguette Box in north Seattle's Fremont neighborhood at 626 N. 34th St. ((C) **206/632-1511**).

1203 Pine St. (C) **206/332-0220.** www.baguettebox.com. Main courses $6–$9. AE, MC, V. Daily 11am–8pm.

Mae Phim @ Pike Thai Cuisine (Value) THAI   Both my brother, who was born in Thailand, and my sister, who lived there for 12 years, love this restaurant. While the setting is as basic as it gets, the flavors are authentic, and the prices are great. It's hard to go wrong here with any of the Thai classic dishes. Mae Phim is less than 2 blocks from Pike

Place Market, but the tourist crowds rarely discover this great hole in the wall. That said, this place is immensely popular at lunch and usually has a line out the door. Try coming for an early dinner to avoid the crowds.

213 Pike St. ℂ **206/623-7453.** www.maephimpike.com. Main courses $7–$16. AE, DISC, MC, V. Daily 11am–9pm.

5 BELLTOWN

VERY EXPENSIVE

El Gaucho ★★★ LATE-NIGHT/STEAK   Conjuring up the ghosts of dinner clubs of the 1930s and 1940s, this high-end Belltown steakhouse looks as though it could be a Fred Astaire film set. Okay, you may find a better steak at one of the other high-end steakhouses in town, but you just can't duplicate the purely theatrical experience of dining at El Gaucho. Stage-set decor aside, the real stars of the show here are the 28-day dry-aged Angus beef steaks, definitely some of the best in town—but know that the perfect steak doesn't come cheap. All the classics are here, too, including Caesar salad tossed tableside and chateaubriand carved before your eyes. Not a steak eater? How about venison chops, an ostrich filet, or Australian lobster tail? There's also a classy bar off to one side.

2505 First Ave. ℂ **206/728-1337.** www.elgaucho.com. Reservations recommended. Main courses $17–$68 (steaks $37–$62). AE, DC, DISC, MC, V. Mon–Thurs 5pm–midnight; Fri–Sat 5pm–1am; Sun 5–11pm.

EXPENSIVE

Brasa ★ LATE-NIGHT/MEDITERRANEAN   Chef Tamara Murphy, much lauded over the years by national food magazines, is one of Seattle's finest chefs, and here, at her attractive Belltown restaurant, she has introduced many a Seattleite to the joys of Mediterranean cuisine. Because the space is equally divided between lounge and dining room, and because the lounge serves a long list of tapas until midnight on weekends, Brasa attracts a wide range of diners—from foodies out for an evening of haute cuisine and fine wine to revelers looking for a late-night bite. If you've got a few dinner companions, start with a variety of tapas.

2107 Third Ave. ℂ **206/728-4220.** www.brasa.com. Reservations highly recommended. Main courses $18–$31. AE, DC, MC, V. Sun–Thurs 5–10:30pm; Fri–Sat 5–midnight.

Dahlia Lounge ★★★ PAN-ASIAN/NORTHWEST   Out front, the neon chef holding a flapping fish may suggest that the Dahlia is little more than a roadside diner. However, a glimpse of the stylish interior will quickly convince you otherwise, and a single bite of any dish will assure you that this is one of Seattle's finest restaurants. Mouthwatering Dungeness crab cakes, a bow to chef Tom Douglas's Delaware roots, are the house specialty and should not be missed. The menu—influenced by the far side of the Pacific Rim—changes regularly, with the lunch menu featuring some of the same offerings at lower prices. It's way too easy to fill up on the restaurant's breads, which are baked in the adjacent Dahlia Bakery, and for dessert, it takes a Herculean effort to resist the crème caramel and the coconut-cream pie.

2001 Fourth Ave. ℂ **206/682-4142.** www.tomdouglas.com. Reservations highly recommended. Main courses $13–$29 lunch, $26–$38 dinner. AE, DC, DISC, MC, V. Mon–Fri 11:30am–2:30pm; Sat–Sun 9am–2pm; Mon–Thurs 5–10pm; Fri–Sat 5–11pm; Sun 5–9pm.

Flying Fish ★ LATE-NIGHT/NORTHWEST/SEAFOOD   Flying Fish is the main stage for local celebrity chef Christine Keff, and not only does this restaurant offer bold combinations of vibrant flavors, but it also serves dinner until midnight every night, keeping hip late-night partiers from going hungry. Every dish here is a work of art, and with small plates, large plates, and platters for sharing, diners can sample a wide variety of the kitchen's creations. The menu changes daily, so you can be sure that the latest seasonal ingredients will show up on the tables here. Desserts are festive little miniature parties on each plate, and the wine list is vast.

2234 First Ave. ✆ 206/728-8595. www.flyingfishseattle.com. Reservations recommended. Main courses $24–$34. AE, MC, V. Mon–Fri 11:30am–2pm; daily 5pm–1am.

Lola ★★ GREEK   Local celeb chef Tom Douglas celebrates his wife's Greek heritage with this restaurant in the über-hip Hotel Ändra. More akin to Douglas's Palace Kitchen than his plush Dahlia Lounge, Lola is a loud, lively, casual spot. Other than the words *kebab, tzatziki,* and *dolmades,* you won't find much common ground here with other Greek restaurants. Start things out with the supergarlicky *skordalia* spread and pita bread. I also recommend the salmon kabobs and the prawn kabobs with curried Muscat glaze. For the full family-dinner treatment, order the Lola Big Dinner, which gives you lots of tastes of the less adventurous dishes on the menu. By the way, the lamb burger is absolutely fabulous.

2000 Fourth Ave. ✆ **206/441-1430.** www.tomdouglas.com. Reservations highly recommended. Main courses $13–$17 lunch; $14–$32 dinner; big dinner $45. AE, DC, DISC, MC, V. Mon–Thurs 6–11am and 11:30am–4pm; Sat–Sun 7am–3pm; Sun–Thurs 4–10pm; Fri–Sat 4–11pm (late-night menu served until midnight).

Restaurant Zoë ★★ NORTHWEST   Belltown is packed with trendy, upscale restaurants where being seen is often more important than the food being served. This is definitely *not* one of those places, although the huge windows facing Second Avenue provide plenty of people-watching opportunities. Chef/owner Scott Staples mines the bounties of the Northwest to prepare his seasonal fare, preparing such dishes as roast steelhead with rhubarb compote, lamb loin with artichoke puree, and wild-boar Bolognese with arugula pappardelle pasta. Risotto here is reliably good and changes with the seasons. Desserts are as eclectic and creative as the entrees (apple cobbler with rosemary biscuit, Meyer lemon crepes with sweet basil syrup). The cocktails here are some of Seattle's most creative libations.

2137 Second Ave. ✆ **206/256-2060.** www.restaurantzoe.com. Reservations highly recommended. Main courses $19–$29. AE, MC, V. Sun–Thurs 5–10pm; Fri–Sat 5–11pm.

Spur Gastropub ★★ NEW AMERICAN   Set on one of the prettiest streets in Belltown, this restaurant serves high-style food in a casual setting. The menu includes some of the most daring dishes in Seattle, yet service is laid-back and there is a pronounced emphasis on the drinks served at the bar. Sustainability and the farm-to-table connection are emphasized here, with perfectly prepared dishes highlighting fresh, seasonal flavors. Dishes are simple and meant to be shared. However, portions are small, so to make a meal, you'll want to piece together several dishes. In the spring, you might find wonderfully crunchy sweetbreads served with fava-bean puree and spring-onion jam or pappardelle pasta with chanterelles, peas, and ricotta. Note that because this is officially a pub, you must be over 21 to dine here. And by the way, the cocktails here are excellent.

113 Blanchard St. ✆ **206/728-6706.** http://spurseattle.com. Reservations accepted only for parties of 8 or more. Main courses $9–$28. AE, DISC, MC, V. Daily 5pm–2am.

MODERATE

Icon Grill ★ AMERICAN   With colorful art glass hanging from chandeliers, overflowing giant vases, and every inch of wall space covered with framed artwork, the decor at the Icon Grill is way overboard, but that's what makes it so much fun. Basically, it's an over-the-top rendition of a Victorian setting gone 21st century. The menu leans heavily toward well-prepared comfort foods, such as a molasses-glazed meatloaf, which locals swear by, and a macaroni and cheese unlike anything your mother ever made. Liven things up with a grilled pear salad. The food here is usually pretty consistent, but the Icon is as much a Seattle experience as a culinary experience.

1933 Fifth Ave. ⓒ **206/441-6330.** www.icongrill.net. Reservations recommended. Main courses $11–$18 lunch, $18–$34 dinner. AE, MC, V. Mon–Fri 11:30am–2pm, Sat–Sun 11am–2pm; Sun–Thurs 5–10pm, Fri–Sat 5–11pm.

Palace Kitchen ★ AMERICAN REGIONAL/LATE-NIGHT/MEDITERRANEAN   Aside from Serious Pie, Tom Douglas's pizza place, this is the most casual of Douglas's five Seattle restaurants. The atmosphere is urban chic, with cement pillars, simple wood booths, and a few tables in the front window, which overlooks the monorail tracks. The menu is short and features a nightly selection of unusual cheeses and different preparations from the apple-wood grill. I like to begin a meal here with the creamy goat-cheese fondue (sometimes made with lavender). Entrees are usually simple and delicious, ranging from the Palace burger royale (a strong contender for best burger in Seattle) to applewood-grilled chicken with rhubarb and almonds. For dessert, the coconut-cream pie is an absolute must.

2030 Fifth Ave. ⓒ **206/448-2001.** www.tomdouglas.com. Reservations accepted only for parties of 6 or more. Main courses $15–$36. AE, DC, DISC, MC, V. Daily 5pm–1am.

Shiro's Sushi Restaurant ★★ JAPANESE   If ogling all the fish at Pike Place Market puts you in the mood for some sushi, then this is the place for you. Shiro's serves the best sushi in the city. It's fresh, flavorful, and perfectly prepared. Eat at the sushi bar and you'll be rubbing shoulders with locals and visiting Japanese businessmen, all of whom know that sushi maestro Shiro Kashiba has a way with raw fish. Be sure to order at least one of Shiro's special rolls. Also, the broiled black-cod *kasuzuke* should not be missed.

2401 Second Ave. ⓒ **206/443-9844.** www.shiros.com. Reservations recommended. Sushi $2–$16; main courses $20–$23. AE, MC, V. Daily 5–10pm.

Txori Bar ★★ SPANISH   If you keep up with dining trends, you're probably already familiar with Spanish *tapas* (small plates). However, here at Txori (pronounced *chorry*) the small plates are even smaller and are called *pinxtos* (pronounced *pinchos*). Meant to be simple accompaniments for wine or cocktails, these bite-sized morsels are intensely flavorful. The octopus leg on a slice of potato is one of my favorite dishes at Txori, and I once had a heavenly soft-shelled crab sandwich here. Although you'll have to eat a lot of pinxtos to make a meal, if you're just looking for a bite to eat, this place is perfect. If you're feeling adventurous, be sure to try the Basque-style sangria, which is made with red wine and Coca-Cola. Txori is a hole-in-the-wall with a very authentic feel and is affiliated with Harvest Vine, my favorite Seattle tapas restaurant.

2207 Second Ave. ⓒ **206/204-9771.** www.txoribar.com. Small plates $1.50–$5.25. AE, DISC, MC, V. Sun–Wed noon–11pm; Thurs–Sat noon–1am.

Virginia Inn ★ FRENCH   In business for more than a century, the Virginia Inn is a cozy spot for lunch or a cheap dinner in the Pike Place Market area. This place has long been a favorite local hangout, and since doubling in size a couple of years ago, has become less of a bar and more of a bistro. The menu includes lots of interesting small plates (grilled duck sausage, sunchoke brandade, cider-braised pork belly) for light eaters, as well as such French bistro classics as *moules frites* and cassoulet. Big windows let lots of light into the dining room, but if the sun is shining, most people try to get a seat on the sidewalk patio.

1937 First Ave. © 206/728-1937. www.virginiainnseattle.com. Reservations not accepted. Main courses $11–$22. MC, V. Mon–Fri 11:30am–3pm; Sat–Sun 11:30am–3:30pm; Sun–Thurs 5–10pm; Fri–Sat 5–11pm.

Wasabi Bistro ★ JAPANESE/LATE-NIGHT   This big, bright, and boldly styled Japanese restaurant is a hit with youthful habitués of Belltown. Not only is the sushi good, but the menu has plenty of other interesting options. To start, try the miso soup with clams and then maybe the kabocha squash dumplings with mushrooms. But be sure to save room for some of the creative sushi rolls *(makimono)*. I like the caterpillar roll (eel, cucumber, avocado, and flying-fish roe). There's live music (mostly jazz) here Sunday through Thursday nights.

2311 Second Ave. © 206/441-6044. www.wasabibistro.biz. Reservations recommended. Main courses $19–$36; sushi $1.50–$17. AE, DISC, MC, V. Mon–Fri 11:30am–2:30pm; daily 4pm–1am.

INEXPENSIVE

Noodle Ranch ★ Finds PAN-ASIAN   This Belltown hole-in-the-wall serves Pan-Asian cuisine for the hip but financially challenged crowd. It's a lively, boisterous scene, and the food is packed with intense, and often unfamiliar, flavors. The Mekong grill—rice noodles with a rice-wine/vinegar-and-herb dressing topped with grilled pork, chicken, beef, or tofu—should not be missed. You'll also find Laotian cucumber salad and many other vegetarian options. Although the place is frequently packed, the wait's not usually too long.

2228 Second Ave. © 206/728-0463. Reservations not accepted. Main courses $8–$13. AE, DISC, MC, V. Mon–Fri 11am–10pm; Sat noon–10pm; summer, Fri–Sat until 11pm).

Serious Pie ★ PIZZA   Another big hit from Seattle's own Tom Douglas, Serious Pie is a little pizza place around the corner from the Dahlia Lounge. With the feel of a *Ratskeller,* Serious Pie bakes beautiful crunchy-chewy crusts topped with the likes of chanterelle mushrooms and truffle cheese or morels and green-garlic pesto. The pizza list is short, and the pies are small enough that you can order several for your table. Top it all off with some Italian wine from the short wine list. Be sure to save room for dessert.

316 Virginia St. © 206/838-7388. www.tomdouglas.com. Reservations not accepted. Pizzas $14–$16. AE, DC, DISC, MC, V. Sun–Wed 11am–10pm; Thurs–Sat 11am–11pm.

Two Bells Bar & Grill ★ AMERICAN   Looking for the best burger in Seattle? Give the patties here a try. Although this is little more than an old tavern and a hangout for Belltown residents who can still remember the days before all the condos went up, the burgers are superb. They're thick, hand-formed patties served on chewy sourdough rolls. You can get yours with grilled onions and bacon, with blue cheese, or a few other ways. Accompany your burger with a pint of local beer and some mustardy coleslaw for the perfect burger-and-beer indulgence.

2313 Fourth Ave. © 206/441-3050. www.thetwobells.com. Reservations not accepted. Main courses $8–$10. AE, MC, V. Mon–Fri 11am–10pm; Sat 1–10pm; Sun 11:30am–10pm.

BEST BURGER

EXPENSIVE

Il Bistro ★★ ITALIAN   What with the fishmongers and crowds of tourists, Pike Place Market might not seem like the place for a romantic candlelit dinner, but romantic dinners are what Il Bistro is all about. This basement trattoria takes Italian cooking very seriously, and in so doing also puts the Northwest's bountiful ingredients to good use. The menu includes such mouthwatering starters as calamari sautéed with fresh basil, garlic, vinegar, and tomatoes. Hundreds of loyal fans insist that Il Bistro's rack of lamb with red-wine reduction sauce is the best in Seattle, and I'd have to agree. The pasta here can also be a true delight. You'll find Il Bistro tucked away down the cobblestone alley beside the market information kiosk.

93-A Pike St. (at First Ave.). ✆ **206/682-3049.** www.ilbistro.net. Reservations recommended. Main courses $17–$44. AE, DC, DISC, MC, V. Sun–Thurs 5:30–10pm; Fri–Sat 5:30–11pm; late-night menu until 1am.

MODERATE

Café Campagne ★★ (Value) FRENCH   Although this little cafe is in the heart of the Pike Place Market neighborhood, it's a world away from the market madness. I like to duck in here for lunch and escape the shuffling crowds. What a relief—so civilized, so very French. Most people leave this dark, cozy place feeling that they've discovered some secret hideaway. The menu changes with the seasons, but the rotisserie chicken is one of the house specialties. The daily three-course prix-fixe meal is a good deal. The cafe also doubles as a wine bar.

1600 Post Alley. ✆ **206/728-2233.** www.campagnerestaurant.com. Reservations recommended. Main courses $13–$23 lunch (2-course menu $19); $17–$23 dinner (3-course menu $35). AE, DC, DISC, MC, V. Mon–Thurs 11am–10pm; Fri 11am–11pm; Sat 8am–11pm; Sun 8am–10pm.

Etta's Seafood ★★ SEAFOOD   Seattle chef Tom Douglas's strictly seafood (well, almost) restaurant, Etta's, is located smack in the middle of the Pike Place Market neighborhood and, of course, serves Douglas's signature crab cakes (crunchy on the outside, creamy on the inside), which are not to be missed (and if they're not on the menu, just ask). Don't ignore your side dishes, either; they can be exquisite and are usually enough to share around the table. In addition to the great seafood, the menu always has a few other fine options. Stylish contemporary decor sets the mood, making this place as popular with locals as it is with tourists.   BEST SEAFOOD

2020 Western Ave. ✆ **206/443-6000.** www.tomdouglas.com. Reservations recommended. Main courses $12–$29. AE, DC, DISC, MC, V. Mon–Thurs 11:30am–9:30pm; Fri 11:30am–10pm; Sat 9am–3pm and 4–10pm; Sun 9am–3pm and 4–9pm.

Le Pichet ★★ FRENCH   Seattle seems to have a thing for French restaurants. They're all over the place, with a surprising number clustered around Pike Place Market. Le Pichet is one of my favorites. The name is French for "pitcher" and refers to the traditional ceramic pitchers used for serving inexpensive French wines. This should clue you in to the casual nature of the place, the sort of spot where you can drop by any time of day, grab a stool at the bar, and have a light meal. The menu is rustic French, and almost everything is made fresh on the premises. With lots of small plates and appetizers, it's fun and easy to piece together a light meal of shareable dishes. I like the country-style pâté, which is served with honey and walnuts. On Sunday afternoons, there's live music.

Meatless in Seattle

As far as food is concerned, Seattle may be best known for its multitude of seafood restaurants and its salmon-tossing fishmongers at Pike Place Market—but even strict vegetarians will find plenty of options in this incredibly veg-friendly city.

This is the kind of city where even **Safeco Field** (p. 155) sells veggie hot dogs. Baseball purists may sneer, but let's face it: It's tough being a vegetarian at hallowed ballparks that were legendary long before expansion teams like the Mariners came into existence. At the Safe, you can have your pick of wood-fired pizza, sushi, hummus, burritos, veggie stir-fry, and the stadium's legendary garlic fries (make sure everyone in your party eats some, or they may not be on speaking terms with you for a while).

Ready for a full meal? You don't have to be an Adam Yauch–lovin' Jew-Bu (Jewish Buddhist, in case you were wondering) or a Chinese kosher vegan or even a vegan, for that matter, to appreciate **Bamboo Garden,** 364 Roy St. (© **206/282-6616;** www.bamboogarden.net), conveniently located across from Seattle Center. It's one of the city's vegetarian standbys—and has the crowds to prove it (you'll see everything from business suits to yarmulkes to Tevas and tie-dye here). The restaurant's decor isn't much to speak of; it's the food––kosher Chinese––that's the draw. Go straight for no. 86, a sizzling curry hot pot filled with savory chunks of faux chicken, Napa cabbage, broccoli, and slightly mushy potato—pure comfort food, especially on a dreary day.

In the U District, there's **Hillside Quickies Vegan Sandwich Shop,** 4106 Brooklyn Ave. NE (© **206/632-3037;** www.hillsidequickie.com), a vegan soul-food cafe, and over in the Fremont neighborhood, the oddly named **Silence-Heart-Nest,** 3508 Fremont Place N. (© **206/633-5169;** www.silenceheartnest. com), is the local mecca of meatlessness.

In addition to these strict vegetarian restaurants, Seattle has plenty of nonveg establishments that are plenty veggie-friendly. For what just might be the best veggie burger in town, see **Red Mill Burgers** ★ (p. 111). Most garden-variety garden burgers leave me pining for a good ol' bacon double cheeseburger. But not Red Mill's Red Onion Veggie Burger: I can scarf one down for lunch, crave another come dinnertime, and wake up the next morning jonesing for yet another. Add a side of the best onion rings in Seattle, and you've got the perfect meal.

On the more refined side, there's **Rover's** ★★★ (p. 106), the most over-the-top veg-friendly experience in Seattle. Here, vegetarians get their own five-course tasting menu, and even vegans who give advance notice are eagerly accommodated.

If you just need some picnic fixings or a quick meal to go—and you've already done Pike Place Market—make like a local and head to one of the many branches of **Puget Consumers' Co-op (PCC),** a Seattle institution that's been around for over 50 years (see www.pccnaturalmarkets.com for locations). PCC features organic produce, fancy prepared foods, and specialty items such as "healing juices." Deli offerings vary, but don't be surprised if you find more than half a dozen different tofu dishes! For a superquick lunch, just head to the soup bar and grab some artisanal bread made by Essential Bakery.

—Leslie Shen

1933 First Ave. © **206/256-1499.** www.lepichetseattle.com. Reservations recommended. Small plates $8–$12; main courses $17–$19. MC, V. Sun–Thurs 8am–midnight; Fri–Sat 8am–2am.

Matt's in the Market ★★ (Finds) AMERICAN REGIONAL/FRENCH This casual gourmet restaurant boasts the best location in Pike Place Market. It's up on the third floor of the Corner Market Building facing the big neon clock that is the quintessential symbol of the market. The menu at Matt's changes regularly, with an emphasis on fresh ingredients from the market stalls that are only steps away. The latest culinary trends are always well represented. Recent starters included a classic seared foie gras as well as pork-belly carnitas (a contemporary spin on a Mexican classic). Keep an eye out for duck confit and leg of lamb. There's also a good selection of reasonably priced wines.

Corner Market Building, 94 Pike St. © **206/467-7909.** www.mattsinthemarket.com. Reservations highly recommended. Main courses $10–$19 lunch, $25–$38 dinner. AE, MC, V. Mon–Sat 11:30am–2:30pm and 5:30–10pm; Sun 11:30am–3pm.

The Pink Door ★ ITALIAN/LATE-NIGHT If I didn't tell you about this restaurant, you'd probably never find it. There's no sign out front—only the pink door for which the restaurant is named (look for it btw. Stewart and Virginia). On the other side of the door, stairs lead to a cellarlike space, which, on summer days, is almost always empty because no one wants to sit in a cellar when they can dine on the deck with a view of Elliott Bay. What makes this place so popular is as much the reliable Italian food as the fun atmosphere. You might encounter a tarot-card reader or a magician, and most nights there's some sort of Felliniesque cabaret performer (accordionists, trapeze artists, and the like). Be sure to start your meal with the antipasti plate. From there, you might move on to an Italian classic such as lasagna or something made with fresh seafood from the market.

1919 Post Alley. © **206/443-3241.** www.thepinkdoor.net. Reservations recommended. Main courses $7–$16 lunch; $14–$22 dinner. AE, DISC, MC, V. Mon–Thurs 11:30am–10pm; Fri–Sat 11:30am–11pm; Sun 4–10pm. *SEATTLE'S FAVE "SECRET" RESTAURANT*

INEXPENSIVE

El Puerco Lloron MEXICAN On one of the terraces of the Pike Hill Climb—a stairway that connects the waterfront with Pike Place Market—this Mexican fast-food place has a genuinely authentic feel, in large part because of the battered Mexican tables and chairs. And though the menu is limited, the food is as authentic as it gets. While you wait to place your order, you can watch tortillas being made by hand. A little patio seating area is very popular in summer.

1501 Western Ave. © **206/624-0541.** Main courses $6–$9. MC, V. Sun–Thurs 11am–7pm; Fri–Sat 11am–8pm.

Lowell's ★ AMERICAN Most of the time when I'm at Pike Place Market, I like to grab little bites here and there and savor lots of flavors, but when I've been on my feet for too many hours and just have to sit down, I head to Lowell's. This place is a market institution. I like the fish tacos, but there are also good steamer clams, decent fish and chips, salmon dishes, chowder, and burgers. However, what makes this place genuinely special is the view. Big walls of glass look out to Elliott Bay and the Olympic Mountains. It's so quintessentially Seattle and so unforgettable that you can't help wondering why you aren't being asked to pay a king's ransom to eat with this view. Altogether Lowell's has three floors (with a bar on the second floor), all of which have those same superb views.

Main Arcade, 1519 Pike Place. © **206/622-2036.** www.eatatlowells.com. Reservations not accepted. Main courses $9–$25. AE, DC, DISC, MC, V. Sun–Thurs 7am–6pm; Fri–Sat 7am–7pm (until later in summer).

Pan Africa Market (Value) AFRICAN   Pike Place Market is full of exotic foods, and you would be missing a big part of the market experience if you didn't try some sort of new cuisine you've never had before. My vote goes to African food, and this is the place to try it. Small and casual, with a few sidewalk tables, Pan Africa serves dishes from Ethiopia, Senegal, Morocco, and other African countries. I like the tangy chicken *yassa*, which gets its tanginess from lots of limes. There are also classic Ethiopian dishes served on *injera*, a crepe-like flatbread. This is a good bet for a filling lunch away from the tourist crowds.

1521 First Ave. © **206/652-2461.** www.panafricamarket.com. Reservations recommended. Main courses $8–$12 lunch, $11–$14 dinner. MC, V. Mon–Fri 11am–3pm and 5–10pm; Sat–Sun 9am–10pm.

Pike Place Chowder (Finds) SEAFOOD   This place does chowder, pure and simple. And while their great New England-style clam chowder has won a national award, they also do Manhattan clam chowder, smoked salmon chowder, mixed seafood chowder, and even a Southwestern-style chowder with chicken and corn. Can't decide which to get? Try the four-cup sampler and decide for yourself which is the best. You'll find this tiny place tucked away in Pike Place Market's Post Alley. There's a second restaurant in Pacific Place Shopping Center, 600 Pine St. (© **206/838-5680**).

1530 Post Alley. © **866/249-5890** or 206/267-2537. www.pikeplacechowder.com. Reservations not accepted. Main courses $6.25–$12. AE, MC, V. Daily 11am–5pm.

7 PIONEER SQUARE & THE INTERNATIONAL DISTRICT

In addition to the International District restaurants listed below, you'll find a large food court at **Uwajimaya,** 600 Fifth Ave. S. (© **206/624-6248;** www.uwajimaya.com), a huge Asian supermarket. Its stalls serve foods from various Asian countries. It all smells great, and everything is inexpensive, which makes it a great place for a quick meal.

MODERATE

Tamarind Tree ★★ (Finds) VIETNAMESE   In the back corner of the dingy Asian Plaza strip mall at the northwest corner of South Jackson Street and 12th Avenue South (on the eastern edge of the Chinatown/International District), this restaurant is a bit hard to find. Persevere: It's worth it. Step through the door and glance around at the packed tables, and you'll immediately get the idea that lots of Seattleites are in the know. Now take a deep breath and let the aromas of Vietnam fill your nose. Immediately order the fresh spring rolls, which are packed with great flavors and textures. The ultimate dinner here is the "seven courses of beef," which is just what it sounds like, and each course is packed with the zesty flavors that imbue all the dishes here with such exotic character. By the way, this place is way more stylish than the location would suggest and could hold its own in trendy Belltown.

1036 S. Jackson St. © **206/860-1404.** www.tamarindtreerestaurant.com. Reservations recommended. Main courses $6.50–$33. MC, V. Sun–Thurs 10am–10pm; Fri–Sat 10am–midnight.

INEXPENSIVE

Jade Garden Restaurant ★ CHINESE   It doesn't look like much from the outside (or from the inside for that matter), but the Jade Garden is considered by many to have the best dim sum in Seattle. Dim sum, if you aren't familiar, is a Chinese fast food that features little plates of steamed or fried dishes served from carts that are wheeled around the restaurant. Pick a few plates, perhaps some shrimp dumplings, or the popular honey-walnut shrimp, and eat your fill. See something you like? Order some more. Pace yourself; it all looks so tempting, it's easy to order too many plates. Just beware of the dish that looks just like chicken feet; it is!

424 Seventh Ave. S. © **206/622-8181.** Reservations not necessary. Main courses $6–$33; dim sum $2.10–$3.65. MC, V. Mon–Thurs 9am–2:30am; Fri–Sat 9am–3:30am; Sun 9am–1am.

Salumi ★★★ Finds ITALIAN Raise the bar on salami, and you have the artisan-cured meats of this closet-size eatery. The owner, Armandino Batali, who happens to be the father of New York's famous chef Mario Batali, makes all his own salami (as well as traditional Italian-cured beef tongue and other meaty delicacies). Order up a meat plate with a side of cheese, some roasted red bell peppers, and a glass of wine, and you have a perfect lunchtime repast in the classic Italian style. Did I mention the great breads and tapenades? Wow! If you're down in the Pioneer Square area at lunch, don't miss Salumi (even if there's a long line).

309 Third Ave. S. © **206/621-8772.** www.salumicuredmeats.com. Reservations not accepted. Main courses $7.50–$14. MC, V. Tues–Fri 11am–4pm.

WHERE TO DINE

6

8 QUEEN ANNE & SEATTLE CENTER

QUEEN ANNE & SEATTLE CENTER

VERY EXPENSIVE

Canlis ★★★ CONTINENTAL/NORTHWEST A local institution, Canlis has been in business since 1950 and yet still manages to keep up with the times. Its stylish interior mixes contemporary decor with Asian antiques, and its Northwest cuisine, with Asian and Continental influences, keeps both traditionalists and more adventurous diners content. Steaks from the copper grill are perennial favorites here, as are the Canlis salad and the spicy Peter Canlis prawns. To finish, why not go all the way and have the Grand Marnier soufflé? Canlis also has one of the best wine lists in Seattle. This is one of Seattle's most formal and traditional restaurants, the perfect place to celebrate a very special occasion.

2576 Aurora Ave. N. © **206/283-3313.** www.canlis.com. Reservations highly recommended. Main courses $28–$72; chef's tasting menu $70–$95 ($125–$190 with wines). AE, DC, DISC, MC, V. Mon–Thurs 5:30–9pm; Fri 5:30–10pm; Sat 5–10pm.

BEST VIEW

SkyCity at the Needle ★★ NORTHWEST Both the restaurant and the prices are sky high at this revolving restaurant, located just below the observation deck at the top of Seattle's famous Space Needle. However, because you don't have to pay extra for the elevator ride if you dine here, the charges start to seem a little bit more in line with those at other Seattle splurge restaurants. Okay, so maybe you can get better food elsewhere, but you won't get a more spectacular panorama anywhere else in Seattle. Simply prepared steaks and seafood make up the bulk of the offerings, with a couple of vegetarian options and some Northwest favorites thrown in. I recommend coming here for lunch; the menu includes some of the same dishes, prices are more reasonable, and the views, encompassing the city skyline, Mount Rainier, and the Olympic Mountains, are unsurpassed.

Space Needle, 400 Broad St. © **800/937-9582** or 206/905-2100. www.spaceneedle.com. Reservations highly recommended. Main courses $25–$34 lunch; $34–$54 dinner; weekend brunch $45 adults, $16

EXPENSIVE

Palisade ★★ NORTHWEST   With a panorama that sweeps from downtown to West Seattle and across the sound to the Olympic Mountains, Palisade has one of the best views of any Seattle waterfront restaurant and is always my choice for a splurge waterfront dinner. It also happens to have fine food and inventive interior design (incorporating a saltwater pond, complete with fish, sea anemones, and starfish, right in the middle of the dining room). The menu features a good mix of fish and meats prepared in both a wood-fired oven and a wood-fired rotisserie. The three-course sunset dinners, served before 6pm, cost $32 and are a great way to enjoy this place on a budget. Palisade also has an excellent and very popular Sunday brunch. *Note:* The restaurant is not easy to find; call for directions or to have the restaurant's complimentary limo pick you up at your hotel.

Elliott Bay Marina, 2601 W. Marina Place. © **206/285-1000.** www.palisaderestaurant.com. Reservations recommended. Main courses $11–$23 lunch, $23–$65 dinner; Sun brunch $35 ($12 for children 11 and under). AE, DC, DISC, MC, V. Mon–Fri 11:15am–2pm; Mon–Thurs 5–9pm; Fri 5–10pm; Sat 4–10pm; Sun 9:30am–2pm and 4–9pm.

MODERATE   *Best French*

Boat Street Café and Kitchen ★★ (Finds)   FRENCH   At the north end of Belltown 2 blocks north of the Olympic Sculpture Park, this hidden gem is one of my favorite Seattle restaurants. The setting, with its Japanese lanterns and rice-paper umbrellas hanging from the ceiling, is quintessential Seattle casual, while the menu is superbly prepared French cuisine at reasonable prices. Attention to the tiniest of details is what makes this place so special. I like to start with the pickle plate, which consists of an assortment of house-made pickled vegetables and fruits. Salads can be artfully composed and packed with distinctive flavors. Entrees lean toward hearty farmhouse French such as roast chicken with sautéed morels and pea vines. Crab cakes and the savory flan (maybe mushroom, maybe asparagus) are two other good bets.

3131 Western Ave. © **206/632-4602.** www.boatstreetcafe.com. Reservations recommended. Main courses $9.50–$13 lunch, $14–$30 dinner. AE, MC, V. Daily 10:30am–2:30pm; Tues–Sat 5:30–10pm.

INEXPENSIVE

Dick's (Value)   AMERICAN   If you're like me, sometimes you just have to have a burger. I don't mean one of those fancy shmancy Kobe beef burgers on an artisan foccacia roll. I mean a good, old-fashioned two-napkin fast-food burger. If that craving should strike while you're in Seattle Center, head to this class fast-food joint in the lower Queen Anne neighborhood. Dick's has been a local favorite for decades. In addition to burgers and shakes, they serve ice cream here.

500 Queen Anne Ave. N. © **206/285-5155.** www.ddir.com. Reservations not accepted. Main courses $1.50–$2.50. No credit cards. Daily 10:30am–2am.

The 5 Spot ★ AMERICAN REGIONAL/LATE-NIGHT   Every 3 months or so, this restaurant, one of Seattle's favorite diners, changes its menu to reflect a different regional U.S. cuisine. You might find Brooklyn comfort food featured, or perhaps Cuban-influenced Miami-style meals, but you can bet that whatever's on the menu will be filling and fun. The atmosphere here is pure kitsch—whenever the theme is Florida, the place is adorned with palm trees and flamingos and looks like the high-school gym done up for

WHERE TO DINE

6

QUEEN ANNE & SEATTLE CENTER

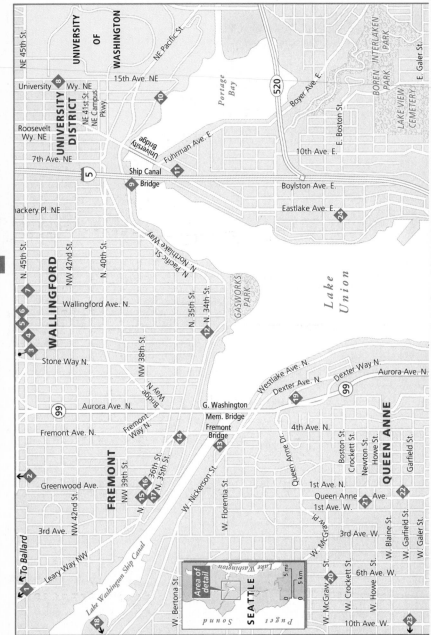

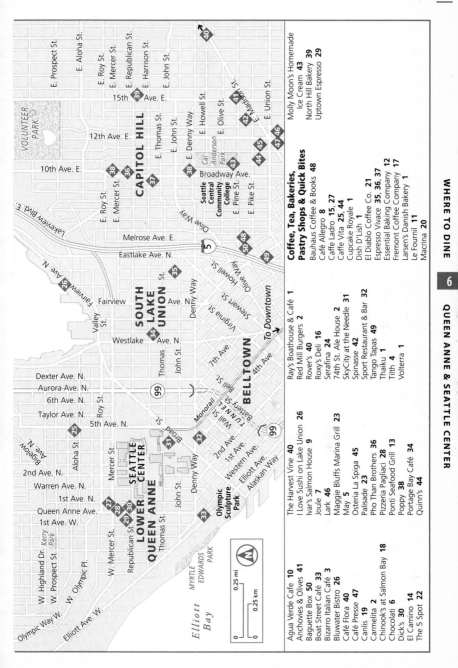

Agua Verde Cafe **10**
Anchovies & Olives **41**
Baguette Box **50**
Boat Street Café **33**
Bizarro Italian Café **3**
Bluwater Bistro **26**
Café Flora **40**
Café Presse **47**
Canlis **19**
Carmelita **2**
Chinook's at Salmon Bay **18**
Chocolati **6**
Dick's **30**
El Camino **14**
The 5 Spot **22**

The Harvest Vine **40**
I Love Sushi on Lake Union **26**
Ivar's Salmon House **9**
Joule **7**
Lark **46**
Maggie Bluffs Marina Grill **23**
May **5**
Osteria La Spiga **45**
Palisade **23**
Pho Than Brothers **36**
Pizzeria Pagliaci **28**
Ponti Seafood Grill **13**
Poppy **38**
Portage Bay Café **34**
Quinn's **44**

Ray's Boathouse & Café **1**
Red Mill Burgers **2**
Roxy's **40**
Roxy's Deli **16**
Serafina **24**
74th St. Ale House **2**
SkyCity at the Needle **31**
Spinasse **42**
Sport Restaurant & Bar **32**
Tango Tapas **49**
Thaiku **1**
Tilth **4**
Volterra **1**

**Coffee, Tea, Bakeries,
Pastry Shops & Quick Bites**
Bauhaus Coffee & Books **48**
Café Allegro **8**
Caffe Ladro **15, 27**
Caffe Vita **25, 44**
Cupcake Royale **1**
Dish D'Lish **1**
El Diablo Coffee Co. **21**
Espresso Vivace **35, 36, 37**
Essential Baking Company **12**
Fremont Coffee Company **17**
Larsen's Danish Bakery **1**
Le Fournil **11**
Macrina **20**

Molly Moon's Homemade
  Ice Cream **43**
North Hill Bakery **39**
Uptown Espresso **29**

prom night. This bustling diner is popular with all types who appreciate the fact that you won't go broke eating here. To find it, look for the neon sign of coffee pouring into a giant coffee cup, right at the top of Queen Anne Hill.

1502 Queen Anne Ave. N. *C* **206/285-SPOT.** www.chowfoods.com. Reservations recommended. Main courses $11–$18. MC, V. Mon–Fri 8:30am–midnight; Sat–Sun 8:30am–3pm and 5pm–midnight.

Maggie Bluffs Marina Grill ★ (Kids) AMERICAN   It's never easy to find affordable waterfront dining in any city, and Seattle is no exception. However, if you're willing to drive a few miles, you can save quite a few bucks at this casual marina restaurant at the foot of Magnolia Bluff (northwest of downtown Seattle). On sunny summer days, it's worth waiting for a patio table. The menu is fairly simple for the most part, offering the likes of burgers and fish and chips, but it also includes a few more creative dishes. The restaurant overlooks a marina full of pleasure boats, and though the view is partially obstructed by a breakwater, you can also see Elliott Bay, West Seattle, downtown, and even the Space Needle. Crayons are on hand to keep the kids entertained. After your meal, walk out on Pier G and take a free shuttle boat a few yards through the marina to an observation deck atop the breakwater.

Elliott Bay Marina, 2601 W. Marina Place. *C* **206/283-8322.** www.r-u-i.com/mag. Reservations not accepted. Main courses $9–$14. AE, DISC, MC, V. Mon–Thurs 11am–8pm; Fri 11am–9pm; Sat 9am–9pm; Sun 9am–8pm.

Pizzeria Pagliacci PIZZA   Pagliacci's pizza has repeatedly been voted the best in Seattle. There are lots of interesting pies on the menu, including a pesto pie and one made with pepperoni from local cured-meat purveyor Salumi. It's strictly counter service here, but there's plenty of seating. For those in a hurry or who just want a snack, Pagliacci has pizza by the slice. Luckily, because there are several Pagliaccis around town, you're never very far from a great slice.

550 Queen Anne Ave. N. *C* **206/726-1717** for delivery. www.pagliacci.com. Reservations not accepted. Pizza $8–$24. AE, MC, V. Sun–Thurs 11am–11pm; Fri–Sat 11am–midnight.

Sport Restaurant & Bar ★ (Kids) AMERICAN   If you've got sports fans for kids (or you're one yourself), this big restaurant right across the street from the Space Needle is a must. While the food is decent enough (especially the burgers), it's the in-booth plasma-screen TVs that make this place such a hit with sports fans. Be forewarned, however, that you can't reserve one of these way-cool booths, so arrive early or plan on a wait for one of these in-demand tables. For adults, there's a bar with a huge wall-hung TV, in addition to plenty of other standard-size screens.

140 Fourth Ave. N., Ste. 130. *C* **206/404-7767.** www.sportrestaurant.com. Reservations recommended. Main courses $9–$20. AE, DISC, MC, V. Sun–Thurs 11:30am–11pm; Fri–Sat 11:30am–1am.

9 LAKE UNION & SOUTH LAKE UNION

MODERATE

Bluwater Bistro ★ AMERICAN REGIONAL/LATE-NIGHT   Although it's on the shore of Lake Union, this place has limited views, which is probably why it's more popular with locals than with tourists. However, you *can* watch seaplanes take off and land right in front of the restaurant, which lends a strong sense of being in Seattle. Best of all, prices are considerably lower than at most tourist-targeted waterfront restaurants around town. Good choices include the New York steak topped with blue cheese and, at lunch, the grilled mahimahi sandwich with chipotle aioli. This is also a popular watering hole for marina types who arrive by boat.

Another Bluwater Bistro is near Woodland Park Zoo at 7900 E. Green Lake Dr. N. (*C* **206/524-3985**); a third is over on Lake Washington at 102 Lakeside Ave. (*C* **206/328-2233**); and a fourth is in Kirkland at Carillon Point, 2220 Carillon Point (*C* **425/822-4000**).

1001 Fairview Ave. N. (on Lake Union). *C* **206/447-0769.** www.bluwaterbistro.com. Reservations recommended. Main courses $11–$19 lunch, $11–$28 dinner. AE, MC, V. Daily 11:30am–1am.

I Love Sushi on Lake Union ★ JAPANESE   This locals-favorite sushi bar is right on Lake Union at the south end of the lake, and although it's a bit difficult to find, it's well worth searching out. Not only is the sushi excellent, but there are also some tasty, exotic cocktails. The views of the lake are limited, which is probably why the food is so good. Be sure to try the Seattle roll, which is made with flying-fish roe and salmon (a nod to the flying fish at Pike Place Market perhaps). If you're not a fan of sushi, try the black cod *kasuzuke*, which is marinated in sake curd.

1001 Fairview Ave. N. *C* **206/625-9604.** www.ilovesushi.com. Reservations recommended. Main courses $16–$30; sushi $2.50–$13. AE, MC, V. Mon–Thurs 11:30am–2pm and 4–10pm; Fri 11:30am–2pm and 4–10:30pm; Sat noon–2:30pm and 5–10:30pm; Sun 4:30–9:30pm.

Ivar's Salmon House ★★ (Kids) SEAFOOD   With a view of the Space Needle on the far side of Lake Union, flotillas of sea kayaks silently slipping by, sailboats racing across the lake, and powerboaters tying up at the dock out back, this restaurant on the north side of Lake Union is quintessential Seattle. Add a building designed to resemble a Northwest Coast Indian longhouse, and you have what just might be the very best place in town for a waterfront meal. This place is a magnet for weekend boaters who abandon their own galley fare in favor of Ivar's clam chowder and famous alder-smoked salmon. Lots of artifacts, including long dugout canoes and historic photos of Native American chiefs, make Ivar's a hit with both kids and adults. Bear in mind that this restaurant's popularity means that service can be slow; just relax and keep enjoying the views.

401 NE Northlake Way. *C* **206/632-0767.** www.ivars.net. Reservations recommended. Main courses $9–$20 lunch, $14–$30 dinner. AE, MC, V. Mon–Thurs 11am–9pm; Fri–Sat 11am–10pm; Sun 9:30am–2pm and 3:30–9pm.

Serafina Osteria & Enoteca ★ ITALIAN   A bit off the beaten tourist track but close to downtown, Serafina is one of my favorite Seattle dining spots. It has a nice touch of sophistication, but overall it's a relaxed neighborhood place where the rustic, romantic atmosphere underscores the earthy, country-style dishes. It's hard to resist ordering at least one of the bruschetta appetizers, which come with any of three different toppings. Among the pasta offerings, don't pass up the delicious veal meatballs in a green olive–tomato sauce served over penne. Also be sure not to miss the *melanzane alla Serafina* (thinly sliced eggplant rolled with ricotta cheese, basil, and Parmesan and baked in tomato sauce). Live music (mostly jazz and Latin) plays Friday through Sunday nights and for Sunday brunch.

2043 Eastlake Ave. E. *C* **206/323-0807.** www.serafinaseattle.com. Reservations recommended. Main courses $10–$18 lunch, $18–$26 dinner. AE, MC, V. Mon–Fri 11:30am–2:30pm; Sun 10am–2:30pm; Sun–Thurs 5–10pm; Fri–Sat 5–11pm (bar menu nightly until midnight).

Portage Bay Café ★ AMERICAN   After years of slow development, the South Lake Union neighborhood is finally become someplace worth exploring, and this restaurant, right on the streetcar line, is currently my favorite neighborhood spot. Local, organic, and sustainable ingredients are used as much as possible, and the portions, especially at breakfast, are huge. Order pancakes, waffles, or French toast, and you'll get to make a trip to the toppings bar, which is loaded with fresh fruit, organic maple syrup, nuts, and other goodies. There are even breakfast choices for the gluten-intolerant (buckwheat pancakes and rice-flour pancakes). At lunch, you can get sandwiches and burgers, but this place is really all about breakfast, which is served all day.

391 Terry Ave. N. ✆ **206/462-6400.** www.portagebaycafe.com. Reservations not accepted. Main courses $7–$15. AE, DISC, MC, V. Mon–Fri 7:30am–3pm; Sat–Sun 8am–3pm.

10 CAPITOL HILL & MADISON VALLEY

The section of Capitol Hill near the intersection of 12th Avenue and Pike Street has in the past few years become one of Seattle's hottest restaurant neighborhoods. I've listed some of my favorite neighborhood restaurants here (Lark, Quinn's, Café Presse), but there are plenty of others that are worth trying. If you feel like finding your own favorite restaurant, stroll around this neighborhood and check out the menus.

VERY EXPENSIVE   *BEST NW CUISINE*

Rover's ★★★ NORTHWEST/VEGETARIAN   Tucked away in a quaint clapboard house behind a chic little shopping center in the Madison Valley neighborhood east of downtown, Rover's is one of Seattle's most acclaimed restaurants. Thierry Rautureau, the restaurant's award-winning chef, received classical French training before falling in love with the Northwest and all the wonderful ingredients it has to offer. *Voilà!* Northwest cuisine with a French accent. The delicacies on the frequently changing menu are enough to send the most jaded of gastronomes into fits of indecision. Luckily, you can simply opt for one of the fixed-price dinners and leave the decision making to a professional. Notable creations include lobster with a tapioca cake and Osetra caviar; lime-ginger granite with carrot foam; and Guinea fowl confit with grilled leeks, red quinoa, and smoked goose jus. Vegetarians, take note: You won't find many vegetarian feasts to compare with what's served here.

2808 E. Madison St. ✆ **206/325-7442.** www.rovers-seattle.com. Reservations required. Main courses $15–$20; prix-fixe 3-course lunch $35; 4-course bistro menu $45; 5-course dégustation menu $80 (vegetarian) and $95; chef's 8-course grand menu $130. AE, MC, V. Tues–Thurs 6–9:30pm; Fri noon–1:30pm and 5:30–9:30pm; Sat 5:30–9:30pm; Sun 10am–2pm and 5–8pm.

EXPENSIVE

Anchovies & Olives ★★ ITALIAN   Ethan Stowell is one of Seattle's top chefs, and his Union restaurant downtown is one of my favorite Seattle restaurants. Here on Capitol Hill, in a bright, minimally decorated urban-hip dining room, he focuses on simple, seasonal Italian food with the emphasis on seafood, and as the name implies, anchovies show up in quite a few dishes. I know, I know, either you love 'em or you hate 'em. Personally, I fall into the former camp, which is why I like this restaurant so much. The menu also includes several *crudos,* which are the Italian version of sashimi or ceviche.

Because the portions here are all quite small, you can get a lot of great tastes over the course of a meal; however, if you have a big appetite, your bill can really add up.

1550 15th Ave. ℂ **206/838-8080.** www.anchoviesandolives.com. Reservations not accepted. Main courses $9–$18. DC, MC, V. Daily 5pm–midnight.

Lark ★★ NORTHWEST/MEDITERRANEAN   You wouldn't think to look at it, but this unpretentious Capitol Hill restaurant has an impressive pedigree. Chef John Sundstrom formerly headed the kitchen at the W Seattle's Earth & Ocean restaurant, but Sundstrom fled the downtown financial district in favor of the 'hoods and opened this far more casual bistro. The menu consists of dozens of small plates that you should assemble into a meal to fit your appetite. The menu changes with the seasons, and it pays to be adventurous. You might try carpaccio of yellowtail with preserved lemons and green olives; foie gras terrine with cashews and vanilla-poached apricots; or beef tartare with a raw quail egg and onion crackers. The cheese list here is one of the best in the city, so be sure to order some either as an appetizer or as an end to your meal.

926 12th Ave. ℂ **206/323-5275.** www.larkseattle.com. Reservations accepted only for parties of 6 or more. Small plates $8–$20. MC, V. Tues–Sun 5–10:30pm.

Osteria La Spiga ★★ ITALIAN   In recent years, Italian restaurants serving regional cuisines have been giving Seattleites a sample of Italian cooking that does *not* include tomato sauce. At La Spiga, you can sample the cuisine of Italy's Emilia-Romagna region. The restaurant is a big, contemporary space in the heart of Capitol Hill's restaurant district, and on warm summer days, the tables on the sidewalk patio are the place to be. Be sure to start a meal with the *piadina,* a flatbread made from faro (an ancient wheat-like grain); the bread is served with a variety of meats and cheeses. The menu changes seasonally, so you might also start with zucchini blossoms stuffed with mozzarella and an anchovy fillet. There are always lots of interesting pasta dishes and a short list of more substantial entrees. Don't miss the condiments list, which includes a variety of olive oils and aged balsamic vinegar.

1429 12th Ave. ℂ **206/323-8881.** www.laspiga.com. Reservations highly recommended. Main courses $12–$28. AE, MC, V. Sun–Thurs 5–11pm; Fri–Sat 5pm–midnight.

Poppy ★★★ NORTHWEST   When chef Jerry Traunfeld, long head of the kitchen at the fabled Herbfarm restaurant, struck out on his own, he did not go the expected route of opening a French restaurant or a trendy tapas place. Instead, he took as inspiration the compartmentalized platters that are common in India and are known as *thalis.* That is where the similarity to Indian food begins and ends. Your thali might include carrot-orange thyme soup; salmon with sea beans, bacon, and pinot noir sauce; snap peas with peppermint and sesame seeds; zucchini-basil gratin; fritters made with green rice and ricotta; and pickles made from spring onions and strawberries. The flavors are very reminiscent of dishes at the Herbfarm, but the presentation is very casual. If your appetite isn't ready for 10 courses, you can get a *smalli,* an option which comes with fewer courses. Happy hour here is a great deal; there are $5 drinks and $5 sampler thalis.

622 Broadway E. ℂ **206/324-1108.** www.poppyseattle.com. Reservations highly recommended. Prix-fixe dinner $20–$32. AE, DISC, MC, V. Sun and Tues–Thurs 5:30–10pm; Fri–Sat 5:30–11pm.

Spinasse ★★ ITALIAN   This little hole in the wall on Capitol Hill is the most authentic-feeling Italian restaurant in Seattle. The menu is written in Italian on a blackboard (though with English translations on the paper menu), candles light the dining room, and a long wooden table down one side of the restaurant provides communal seating. Highlighting the cuisine of Italy's Piedmont region, the menu lets the simple flavors of each ingredient shine through. You might start your meal with anchovies in a green sauce or a spinach frittata with shaved black truffles. Pastas are made in-house (all the pasta-making equipment is on view at dinner), so be sure to have a pasta course, perhaps Jerusalem artichoke ravioli with sage butter and toasted pine nuts. As much as possible, the restaurant relies on organic ingredients.

1531 14th Ave. ✆ **206/251-7673.** www.spinasse.com. Reservations recommended. Main courses $19–$28; family-style dinners $32–$75. AE, DISC, MC, V. Sun–Mon and Wed–Thurs 5–10pm; Fri–Sat 5–11pm.

MODERATE

The Harvest Vine ★★ SPANISH   Madison Valley is one of Seattle's prettiest neighborhoods and is easily reached from downtown Seattle (just follow Madison St. from the edge of downtown). Here, in a stretch of a few blocks, you'll find half a dozen good restaurants, including the most authentic tapas restaurant in the city. From the sidewalk, the Harvest Vine appears to be little more than a tiny bar, but downstairs is a cozy wine cellar-like dining room. The menu consists exclusively of traditional Spanish small plates, and though prices can sometimes be quite high for what you get, it's still possible to piece together a very satisfying and economical meal. The menu changes daily, but you can always count on the cured meat plates and assorted cheeses. Also keep an eye out for such delicacies as Navarran pork sausage, air-cured duck breast, and grilled venison.

2701 E. Madison St. ✆ **206/320-9771.** www.harvestvine.com. Reservations recommended. Tapas $5.50–$21. AE, MC, V. Daily 5–10pm.

Quinn's ★★ NEW AMERICAN   Patterned after the much-lauded gastropubs of London, Quinn's is the latest restaurant concept from local kitchen legend Scott Staples, whose Restaurant Zoë is one of my favorite Belltown eateries. This place is casual and boisterous, but the food is great and the beer list, heavy on Belgian beers, is one of the best in the city. If you're looking for comfort food, consider the wild-boar sloppy joe or the fish and chips. Foodies looking for something more creative might want to opt for the foie gras, the frog legs, or the marrow bones. Be forewarned: this is a mix-and-match small-plates sort of place, and your tab will add up quickly.

1001 E. Pike St. ✆ **206/325-7711.** www.quinnspubseattle.com. Reservations not accepted. Main courses $10–$19. AE, DISC, MC, V. Mon–Thurs 11am–3pm and 5pm–midnight; Fri–Sat 11am–3pm and 5pm–1am; Sun 5–10pm.

INEXPENSIVE

Cafe Flora ★ VEGETARIAN   Big, bright, and airy, this Madison Valley cafe will dispel any ideas you might have about vegetarian food being boring. This meatless gourmet cooking draws on influences from around the world, which makes this a vegetarian's dream come true. One of the house specialties is a portobello Wellington made with mushroom-pecan pâté and sautéed leeks in a puff pastry. Keep an eye out for unusual pizzas such as apple-and-Stilton-cheese. On weekends a casual brunch features interesting breakfast fare.

2901 E. Madison St. ✆ **206/325-9100.** www.cafeflora.com. Reservations accepted only for parties of 8 or more. Main courses $9.50–$18. MC, V. Mon–Thurs 11:30am–9pm (until 10pm in spring and summer); Fri 11:30am–10pm; Sat 9am–2pm and 5–10pm; Sun 9am–2pm and 5–9pm.

Café Presse ★ FRENCH   Under the same ownership as Belltown's Le Pichet (my favorite Seattle French cafe), Café Presse is modeled after a traditional Parisian bar-cafe,

This is an all-day sort of place. You can start with eggs or a pastry for breakfast, get a ham sandwich on a baguette for lunch, and at dinner order steak *frites* or a salad with boneless quail. At the end of the day, you can wind down with a drink at the bar. This is a casual neighborhood place that's popular with students from Seattle University, which is only half a block away. There's even a little newsstand with imported magazines and soccer games on the TV.

1117 12th Ave. ℂ 206/709-7674. www.cafepresseseattle.com. Reservations not accepted. Main courses $5–$16. MC, V. Daily 7am–2am.

Pho Than Brothers VIETNAMESE Seattleites are crazy about Vietnamese food, and restaurants serving traditional *pho* (noodle soup) can be found all over the city. The Pho Than Brothers chain, which has 10 restaurants around the region, is one of the most reliable of these noodle shops. Try the *chin nam,* which is made with beef brisket and flank steak. Be sure to finish your meal with a cream puff. Other convenient Pho Than Brothers restaurants can be found in Ballard at 2021 NW Market St. (ℂ 206/782-5715), and in the University District at 4207 University Way NE (ℂ 206/633-1735).

516 Broadway E. ℂ 206/568-7218. www.thanbrothers.com. Main courses $4.25–$7. No credit cards. Daily 11am–9pm.

11 THE UNIVERSITY DISTRICT

INEXPENSIVE

Agua Verde Cafe ★ (Finds) MEXICAN Set on the shore of Portage Bay, between Lake Union and Lake Washington, this casual Mexican restaurant is a big hit with University of Washington students. Consequently, there's often a line out the door. The menu is limited to tacos, Mexican-style sandwiches, empanadas, quesadillas, and, at dinner, a handful of more substantial entrees. It's hard to go wrong, but I especially recommend the tacos, which come three to an order. Try the grilled mahimahi or yam versions, both of which are topped with a delicious avocado sauce. Add a couple of sides—cranberry slaw, pineapple-jicama salsa, or chile-mashed potatoes—for a filling and inexpensive meal. Agua Verde also serves pretty good margaritas and rents kayaks for $15 to $18 per hour. This is Mexican food with a conscience—Agua Verde uses wild-caught fish, free-range chickens, shade-grown coffee, and organically farmed shrimp.

1303 NE Boat St. ℂ 206/545-8570. www.aguaverde.com. Reservations taken only for large parties and not at all in summer. Main courses $3.50–$10 lunch, $5.75–$16 dinner. AE, DISC, MC, V. Mon–Sat 11am–3:30 and 4–9pm; Sun noon–6pm (takeout window Mon–Fri 7:30am–2:30pm).

Pam's Kitchen (Finds) CARIBBEAN Imagine a burrito stuffed full of curried beef or chicken and you have an idea of what *rotis* are like. Now throw in a bit of Trinidadian flavor and you'll get some idea of what to expect from Pam's Kitchen, a casual little place on the north side of the University District's main retail area. Although Pam's serves chicken rotis, most regulars agree that the beef rotis are the best item on the menu. Wash down your roti with some house-made punch or hibiscus tea.

5000 University Way NE. ℂ 206/696-7010. www.pams-kitchen.com. Reservations not accepted. Main courses $12–$15. MC, V. Tues–Thurs 4–9pm; Fri–Sat noon–9:30pm; Sun 5–8:30pm.

12 WALLINGFORD, FREMONT & PHINNEY RIDGE

EXPENSIVE

Joule ★★ KOREAN-FRENCH FUSION   With a casual, laid-back urban feel, this little restaurant brings a bit of Belltown vibe to the family-oriented Wallingford neighborhood and is well worth an excursion out from downtown Seattle. The menu, an eclectic blend of Korean and French, is divided into such categories as tossed (salads), simmered (soups), crisped (hot side dishes), sparked (grilled meats and seafood), and pickled. This latter category is where you'll find various *kimchis*. Flavor combinations may at first seem bizarre, but, are often truly inspired. There's even bacon butter to go with the bread. Obviously, this restaurant is for adventurous eaters, but if you're the been-there, done-that sort of culinary explorer, Joule should not be missed.

1913 N. 45th St. ⓒ **206/632-1913.** www.joulerestaurant.com. Reservations recommended. Main courses $15–$24. AE, DISC, MC, V. Tues–Thurs 5–10pm; Fri–Sat 5–11pm; Sun noon–8pm.

Ponti Seafood Grill ★★ SEAFOOD   At the south end of the Fremont Bridge overlooking the Lake Washington Ship Canal (not officially in North Seattle), Ponti is one of Seattle's most elegant and sophisticated restaurants. The menu, which changes regularly, roams the globe from Thailand to Italy, while also offering some solidly Northwestern creations. Perennial favorites among the appetizers include the Cajun barbecued prawns and the Dungeness-crab spring rolls with the dipping sauce of the moment. Don't-miss dishes among the entrees include the grilled wild salmon and the outstanding Thai penne pasta with grilled scallops, Dungeness crab, and tomato-ginger chutney. There's also a more casual cafe side to this restaurant. Before or after you dine here, take a walk around Fremont to check out the funky shops and eclectic public art.

3014 Third Ave. N. ⓒ **206/284-3000.** www.pontiseafoodgrill.com. Reservations recommended. Main courses $20–$42. AE, DC, MC, V. Daily 5–9:30pm.

Tilth ★★ NEW AMERICAN   Tilth is one of the nation's only restaurants to receive organic certification from Oregon Tilth (an organization that sets organic standards), but don't confuse organic with granola-crunchy hippie food. Chef Maria Hines, one of Seattle's most creative chefs, oversaw the kitchen at the W Seattle's acclaimed Earth & Ocean before opening this restaurant in a cute little cottage in the Wallingford neighborhood. The menu emphasizes fresh, seasonal ingredients in dishes that seem simple yet are packed with flavor. While the menu changes with the seasons, you can almost always count on finding the mini duck burgers on the menu. One of my favorite aspects of the menu here is that most dishes are available as appetizers or entrees, so if you want to try several dishes, you can.

1411 N. 45th St. ⓒ **206/633-0801.** www.tilthrestaurant.com. Reservations recommended. Main courses $25–$29. MC, V. Mon–Thurs 5–10pm; Fri 5–10:30pm; Sat 10am–2pm and 5–10:30pm; Sun 10am–2pm and 5–10pm.

MODERATE

Bizzarro Italian Café ★ (Finds) ITALIAN   The name neatly sums up this casual Italian restaurant, where a party atmosphere reigns most nights. The tiny room is filled with mismatched thrift-store furnishings, and strange things hang from the walls and ceiling. Also around the restaurant are numerous paintings of the namesake "Bizzarro," a character who looks like a deranged Italian cook. The food changes with the seasons and emphasizes pasta dishes. Bizzarro is at the west end of the Wallingford neighborhood, just off Stone Way North.

1307 N. 46th St. ℂ **206/632-7277.** www.bizzarroitaliancafe.com. Sun–Thurs, reservations accepted only for parties of 6 or more; Fri–Sat reservations not accepted. Main courses $15–$20. MC, V. Daily 5–10pm.

Carmelita ★★ VEGETARIAN   Who says vegetarianism and decadence have to be mutually exclusive? Here at Carmelita's, the two coexist quite nicely. Located in the Phinney Ridge neighborhood north of Woodland Park Zoo, this very Northwestern restaurant features lots of natural woods, a relaxed ambience, and a seasonal menu that incorporates the best local ingredients. In warm weather, there's seating out on the lovely garden patio. Main courses might include pizza with garlic, artichoke pesto, and fresh buffalo mozzarella; asparagus risotto, toasted cumin-pumpkin seed pesto, lemon oil, and wood sorrel; and wild nettle spaetzle with sautéed sun-dried tomatoes and morels, crispy sunchokes, and truffle oil. And for dessert, definitely go for the warm chocolate "muck muck" (a fallen chocolate cake with seasonal compote).

7314 Greenwood Ave. N. ℂ **206/706-7703.** www.carmelita.net. Reservations recommended. Main courses $16–$18. DISC, MC, V. Sun and Tues–Thurs 5–9pm; Fri–Sat 5–10pm.

El Camino ★ MEXICAN   Maybe it's the implied promise of sunshine and warm weather in every bite, but Seattle seems to have an obsession with Southwestern and Mexican food. If you, too, need a dose of spicy flavors, hit the road *(el camino)* in the Fremont neighborhood. As soon as you sit down, order a margarita; the house margarita here is the best I've had north of Tucson. As you sip your cocktail, you'll notice that the menu here is unlike just about any Mexican restaurant menu you've ever seen. Forget the cheesy chalupas. Here you might find salmon in tart tamarind sauce or enchiladas in *pipian* (pumpkin-seed sauce). Daily fresh-fish specials are available, and the fish of the day also goes into the delicious fish tacos.

607 N. 35th St. ℂ **206/632-7303.** www.elcaminorestaurant.com. Reservations recommended. Main courses $9–$22. AE, MC, V. Tues–Thurs 5–10pm; Fri–Sat 5–11pm; Sun 5–9pm. Late-night menu until midnight Fri–Sat.

May ★ THAI   I've spent a lot of time in Thailand, and even if the food at this second-floor Wallingford restaurant weren't some of the best Thai food in Seattle, I would love May for its architecture. From the outside it looks just like a Thai Buddhist temple, complete with shiny blue glass along the steeply pitched eaves, and from the inside, it duplicates the old teak houses that are so rare in Thailand in the 21st century. Throw in a street-level bar lifted straight off a beach on the Gulf of Siam, and you have a fun restaurant in a pleasant Seattle neighborhood. The *phad Thai,* made the traditional way (with tamarind sauce, not ketchup) is a must, as is the grilled squid appetizer. Seafood dishes, such as the *phad grapao Samui* (made with scallops, prawns, and squid) are a highlight here.

1612 N. 45th St. ℂ **206/675-0037.** Main courses $8–$12 lunch, $10–$24 dinner. AE, MC, V. Daily 11:30am–1am.

INEXPENSIVE

Red Mill Burgers ★ AMERICAN   Just a little north of Woodland Park Zoo, this retro burger joint is tiny and always hoppin' because everyone knows it does one of the best burgers in Seattle. Try the verde burger, made with Anaheim peppers for just the right amount of fire. Don't miss the onion rings. And don't come dressed in your finest attire—burgers here are definitely multinapkin affairs.

A second Red Mill Burgers is at 1613 W. Dravus St. (© **206/284-6363**), which is midway between downtown Seattle and Ballard. Lines often seem to be shorter here.

312 N. 67th St. © **206/783-6362**. www.redmillburgers.com. Burgers $3.50–$6.50. No credit cards. Tues–Sat 11am–9pm; Sun noon–8pm.

Roxy's Deli ★ DELI   With pastrami and corned beef sandwiches that come in regular and New York sizes, Roxy's takes the concept of traditional New York Jewish deli very seriously. Lucky Seattle! Only the best pastrami and corned beef are used here, and if you're a fan of hot pastrami sandwiches, you'll want to be sure to search out this little gem. Also, if you've dedicated your life to the quest for the perfect Reuben sandwich, be sure to try Roxy's. Definitely a contender for best in Seattle. Breakfast is served all day.

462 N. 36th St. © **206/632-3963**. www.pastramisandwich.com. Main courses $5.25–$16. AE, MC, V. Daily 7am–7pm.

74th Street Ale House ★ AMERICAN   This neighborhood pub, designed to resemble pubs in England, not only serves a good variety of locally brewed ales, but also has some of the best pub fare in the city. The burger—made with lean ground beef, served on a hunk of French baguette, and covered with grilled onions and red bell peppers—is terrific. The gumbo is another winner; this rich, dark stew is perfect on a cold, rainy night. Both the Caesar salad and the chicken sandwich are also excellent. Located about a mile north of Woodland Park Zoo, this is a great spot for lunch before or after visiting the zoo. *Note:* Because it is a tavern, children are not allowed.

7401 Greenwood Ave. N. © **206/784-2955**. www.seattlealehouses.com. Main courses $10–$16. MC, V. Sun–Thurs 11:30am–11pm; Fri–Sat 11:30am–midnight. BEST BURGER

13 BALLARD

EXPENSIVE

Ray's Boathouse/Ray's Cafe ★★ SEAFOOD   When Seattleites want to impress visiting friends and relatives, this restaurant often ranks right up there with the Space Needle, the ferries, and Pike Place Market. The view across Puget Sound to the Olympic Mountains is guaranteed to impress out-of-towners. You can watch the boat traffic coming and going from the Lake Washington Ship Canal, and bald eagles are often seen fishing just offshore. Then there's Ray's dual personality—Ray's Cafe upstairs is a lively (and loud) cafe and lounge, while Ray's Boathouse downstairs is a much more formal, sedate scene. The downstairs menu is more creative, the upstairs menu less expensive (but even upstairs you can order from the downstairs menu). The crab cakes are delicious and packed full of crab. If you see any sort of fish in *sake kasu* (a typically Northwest/Pacific Rim preparation), order it.

6049 Seaview Ave. NW. © **206/789-3770** for Boathouse or 206/782-0094 for Cafe. www.rays.com. Reservations recommended. Main courses $22–$39 at Boathouse, $11–$25 at Cafe. AE, DC, DISC, MC, V. Boathouse Mon–Fri 5–9pm, Sat–Sun 4:30–9pm; Cafe Sun–Thurs 11:30am–9:30pm, Fri–Sat 11:30am–10pm.

Volterra ★★ ITALIAN   It would be hard to imagine a more picture-perfect little restaurant than Volterra. Set on a shady tree-lined street of historic brick buildings, this place is made for romantic dinners. It's also a wonderful place for a weekend brunch. Rest **113** assured that this is not your typical southern Italian joint. Start your meal with polenta stuffed with fontina cheese and served with truffle-scented wild mushroom ragu, then move on to the wild boar tenderloin with gorgonzola sauce. At brunch, be sure you order something with hash browns—they're to die for. Whenever you come here to dine, be sure to do a little shopping along Ballard Avenue before or after your meal.

5411 Ballard Ave. NW. © 206/789-5100. www.volterrarestaurant.com. Reservations recommended. Main courses $15–$29. AE, DISC, MC, V. Mon–Thurs 5–10pm; Fri 5–11pm; Sat 9am–2pm and 5–11pm; Sun 9am–2pm and 5–9pm.

MODERATE

Chinook's at Salmon Bay ★ SEAFOOD Fishermen's Terminal, the winter home of the large Alaska fishing fleet, is just across the Lake Washington Ship Canal from the Ballard neighborhood, and overlooking all of the moored commercial fishing boats is one of Seattle's favorite seafood restaurants. This big, boisterous place has walls of windows looking out onto the marina and a long menu featuring seafood fresh off the boats. My favorite meal here is a cup of the oyster stew followed by the alder-plank-roasted salmon.

The only problem with Chinook's is that it isn't very easy to reach. Take Elliott Avenue north from the downtown waterfront, continue north on 15th Avenue West, take the last exit before crossing the Ballard Bridge, and follow the signs to Fishermen's Terminal. Before or after a meal, you can stroll around the marina and have a look at all the fishing boats.

1900 W. Nickerson St. © 206/283-4665. www.anthonys.com. Reservations not accepted. Main courses $8–$30. AE, DISC, MC, V. Mon–Thurs 11am–10pm; Fri 11am–11pm; Sat 7:30am–11pm; Sun 7:30am–10pm.

INEXPENSIVE

Thaiku ★ (Finds) THAI Ballard Avenue is one of the prettiest streets in Seattle: Its sidewalks are shaded by trees, and the old brick commercial buildings have been converted into boutiques, galleries, restaurants, and nightclubs. Amid these pleasant historic surroundings, you'll find my favorite Thai restaurant in town. Known to locals as the Noodle House, Thaiku is a dark place with lots of wooden Asian antiques hanging from the walls and ceilings. The fun atmosphere is just a bonus, though, since it's the great noodle dishes that are the main attraction. I don't think you'll find a better *phad Thai* anywhere in Seattle. The bar here, which is known for its unusual herb-infused cocktails, gets lively on weekends, and there's even live jazz on Wednesday and Thursday nights.

5410 Ballard Ave. NW. © 206/706-7807. www.thaiku.com. Reservations not necessary. Main courses $7–$13. AE, DISC, MC, V. Mon–Thurs 11:30am–9:30pm; Fri 11:30am–10:30pm; Sat–Sun noon–9:30pm.

14 WEST SEATTLE

EXPENSIVE

Salty's on Alki Beach ★★ SEAFOOD Although the prices here are almost as out of line as those at the Space Needle, and the service is unpredictable, this restaurant has *the* waterfront view in Seattle, and the food is usually pretty good. Because Salty's is on the northeast side of the Alki Peninsula, it faces downtown Seattle on the far side of Elliott Bay. Come at sunset for dinner and watch the setting sun sparkle off skyscraper windows as the lights of the city begin to twinkle. On sunny summer days, lunch on one of the two decks is a sublimely Seattle experience. Don't be discouraged by the ugly industrial/port area you drive through to get here; Salty's marks the start of Alki Beach, the closest Seattle comes to a Southern California beach scene.

1936 Harbor Ave. SW. (C) **206/937-1600.** www.saltys.com. Reservations recommended. Main courses $10–$29 lunch, $15–$50 dinner. AE, DC, DISC, MC, V. Mon–Thurs 11am–3pm and 5–9pm; Fri 11am–3pm and 5–9pm; Sat 9:30am–1pm and 4–9:30pm; Sun 8:45am–1:30pm and 4:15–9pm (slightly longer hours in summer).

MODERATE

Cactus ★ MEXICAN   Maybe you're not a fish-and-chips kind of person or maybe long sandy beaches remind you of Mexico. If either of these describe you and you happen to be hungry out Alki Beach way, check out this modern Mexican place. It's a big, colorful place with glass garage doors that open to the fresh air on warm summer days (perfect for sipping a margarita or a cold beer). The blue-corn calamari and wild-mushroom quesadillas are good bets for starters. Personally, I like the soft-shell carnitas (pork) tacos, but you should also consider the Chimayo enchilada and the chile relleno. If you've never had it, try the Navajo fry bread. There are other Cactus restaurants in the Madison Park neighborhood at 4220 E. Madison St. ((C) **206/324-4140**); and in Kirkland at 121 Park Lane ((C) **425-893-9799**).

2820 Alki Ave. SW (C) **206/933-6000.** www.cactusrestaurants.com. Call-ahead wait list; reservations accepted for parties of 6 or more. Main courses $13–$18. AE, DISC, MC, V. Mon–Thurs 11:30am–3pm and 5–10pm; Fri–Sat 11:30am–11pm; Sun 11:30am–10pm.

INEXPENSIVE

Alki Crab & Fish (Value) SEAFOOD   Sure, there are plenty of places on the Seattle waterfront to get fish and chips, but for an unforgettable cheap meal, catch the water taxi over to Alki Beach. Right at the dock, you'll find this little fish-and-chips joint that boasts one of the best views in Seattle. In fact, next-door-neighbor Salty's on Alki Beach has made its reputation almost solely based on this very vista. So if you want the city's best view of the Seattle skyline but don't want to blow your budget, this is the place. The cost of the water taxi from the Seattle waterfront plus the halibut and chips doesn't even come close to what you would spend on a meal at Salty's. If you're just coming over to eat, you can even ask for a transfer and get back to Seattle without having to pay for the return ride!

1660 Harbor Ave. SW. (C) **206/938-0975.** Main dishes $5–$15. MC, V. Daily 9am–9pm.

---

15 THE EASTSIDE

The Eastside, the high-tech suburb on the east side of Lake Washington, includes the cities of Bellevue, Kirkland, Issaquah, and Redmond.

MODERATE

Beach Cafe at the Point ★★ INTERNATIONAL   This casual waterfront cafe is the Eastside's best bet for an economical and creative meal with a view. In summer, the patio dining area just can't be beat. The menu circles the globe, bringing a very satisfying mélange of flavors to Eastside diners. Because the offerings change daily, you never know what you might find when you drop by.

16 COFFEE, TEA, BAKERIES & PASTRY SHOPS

CAFES, COFFEE BARS & TEA SHOPS

Unless you've been on Mars for the past 20 years, you're likely aware that Seattle has become the espresso capital of America. Seattleites are positively rabid about coffee, which isn't just a hot drink or a caffeine fix anymore, but rather a way of life. Wherever you go in Seattle, you're rarely more than a block from your next cup. There are espresso carts on the sidewalks, drive-through espresso windows, espresso bars, espresso counters at gas stations, espresso milkshakes, espresso chocolates, even eggnog lattes at Christmas.

Starbucks (www.starbucks.com), the ruling king of coffee, is seemingly everywhere you turn. It sells some 30 types and blends of coffee beans. **Seattle's Best Coffee/SBC** (www.seattlesbest.com), another of Seattle's favorite espresso-bar chains, is also owned by Starbucks. Close on the heels of Starbucks and SBC in popularity and citywide coverage is the **Tully's** (www.tullys.com) chain, which seems to have an espresso bar on every corner that doesn't already have a Starbucks or an SBC. Serious espresso junkies, however, swear by **Caffe Ladro** (www.caffeladro.com) and **Caffé Vita** (www.caffevita.com). If you see one of either of these chains, check it out and see what you think.

As places to hang out and visit with friends, coffeehouses and cafes are as popular as bars and pubs. Among my favorite Seattle cafes and espresso bars are the following (organized by neighborhood):

DOWNTOWN & FIRST HILL   If you're a total espresso fanatic and want to sip a triple latte where it all started, head to **Monorail Espresso,** a walk-up window at the northeast corner of Fifth and Pike streets. Although this is not the espresso stand's original location, in its previous incarnation (way back in 1980), Monorail was the very first espresso cart in Seattle.

Ancient Grounds ★, 1220 First Ave. (☎ **206/749-0747**), is hands down the coolest and most unusual espresso bar in Seattle. This coffeehouse doubles as an art gallery specializing in antique Mexican, Japanese, and Northwest Coast Indian masks and ethnic artifacts from around the world. Cases are full of colorful minerals and insects in glass boxes. It's all very dark and Victorian.

Caffe Ladro, a small local chain of espresso bars, is one of my favorite places to get coffee in Seattle. Downtown, you'll find cafes at 801 Pine St. (☎ **206/405-1950**) and 108 Union St. (☎ **206/267-0600**). The coffee served here is 100% fair-trade, organic, and shade grown.

Not far away from Caffe Ladro, you'll find **Caffé Senso Unico,** 622 Olive Way (☎ **206/264-7611;** www.caffesensounico.com), which is right across the street from the Pacific Place shopping mall and yet has a very Italian feel.

PIKE PLACE MARKET, BELLTOWN & THE WATERFRONT   Seattle is legendary as a city of coffeeholics, and Starbucks is the main reason. This company has coffeehouses all over town (and all over the world), but the **Starbucks** in Pike Place Market, at 1912 Pike Place (☎ **206/448-8762**), was once the only Starbucks anywhere (although it was not the first Starbucks). Today it is the only chain store allowed in the market. Although you won't find any tables or chairs here, Starbucks fans shouldn't miss an opportunity to get their coffee at the source. Be sure to notice the bare-breasted-mermaid sign out front, which is how the Starbucks logo started out before becoming modest enough for mass-market advertising.

If you need to sit down while you drink your latte, or simply don't want to drink Starbucks coffee, then try **Local Color,** 1606 Pike Place (© **206/728-1717;** www.local colorseattle.com), a combination cafe and art gallery that has live jazz on Friday and Saturday nights.

If you're wandering around checking out the hip shops in Belltown and need a pick-me-up, head over to **Uptown Espresso,** 2504 Fourth Ave. (© **206/441-1084;** www. uptownespresso.net). Down on the waterfront, try the branch at Pier 70, 2801 Alaskan Way (© **206/770-7777**).

For hot chocolate, sipping chocolate (basically warm liquid chocolate), and a wide variety of chocolates and chocolate confections, don't miss **Chocolate Box,** 108 Pine St. (© **800/861-6188** or 206/443-3900; www.sschocolatebox.com), which is just a half block from Pike Place Market.

PIONEER SQUARE & THE INTERNATIONAL DISTRICT   **Zeitgeist Art/Coffee** ★, 171 S. Jackson St. (© **206/583-0497;** www.zeitgeistcoffee.com), with its big windows and local artwork, is popular with the Pioneer Square art crowd. For a classically Italian cafe experience, sit and sip at **Caffè Umbria,** 320 Occidental Ave. S. (© **206/624-5847;** www.caffeumbria.com), which is on a pretty, shady plaza.

In the International District, don't miss the atmospheric **Panama Hotel Tea & Coffee House** ★, 607 S. Main St. (© **206/515-4000;** www.panamahotelseattle.com), which is filled with historic photos and offers a fascinating glimpse into the neighborhood's past. This is a great place to relax over a pot of rare Chinese tea and a slice of the cafe's unusual green-tea cake.

QUEEN ANNE/SEATTLE CENTER   In the heart of the pleasant Upper Queen Anne area, **Caffe Ladro Espresso Bar & Bakery** ★, 2205 Queen Anne Ave. N. (© **206/282-5313**), has the feel of a cozy neighborhood coffeehouse. Another Caffe Ladro is in the MarQueen Hotel building in Lower Queen Anne, at 600 Queen Anne Ave. N. (© **206/282-1549**).

Uptown Espresso, 525 Queen Anne Ave. N. (© **206/285-3757**), with its crystal chandelier and gilt-framed classical paintings, has a very theatrical European feel. Good baked goodies, too.

Caffé Vita is one of Seattle's finest coffee roasters. In the Lower Queen Anne neighborhood, you can sample these superb coffees at Caffé Vita's own coffeehouse, at 813 Fifth Ave. N. (© **206/285-9662**).

If you've tired of double tall raspberry mochas and are desperately seeking a new coffee experience, make a trip to Upper Queen Anne's **El Diablo Coffee Co.,** 1811 Queen Anne Ave. N. (© **206/285-0693;** www.eldiablocoffee.com), a Latin-style coffeehouse. The Cubano, made with two shots of espresso and caramelized sugar, and the café con leche (a Cubano with steamed milk) are both devilishly good drinks. Viva la revolución!

LAKE UNION & SOUTH LAKE UNION   A Seattle friend insists that the espresso at **Espresso Vivace Alley 24** ★, 227 Yale Ave. N. (© **206/388-5164;** www.espressovivace. com), across the street from the REI flagship store, is the best in Seattle. Give it a try and see if you agree.

CAPITOL HILL & MADISON VALLEY   On the downtown edge of Capitol Hill, **Bauhaus Coffee & Books** ★, 301 E. Pine St. (© **206/625-1600**), is a great place to hang out and soak up the atmosphere of Seattle's main gay neighborhood. You can always find lots of interesting 30-something types hanging out reading or carrying on heated discussions.

Caffé Vita, 1005 E. Pike St. (© **206/709-4440**), has a devoted following of espresso fanatics who swear by the perfectly roasted coffee beans and lovingly crafted lattes served here.

Capitol Hill has two outposts of Espresso Vivace, a locals' favorite. There's **Vivace Espresso Bar at Brix** ★, 532 Broadway Ave. E. (© **206/860-2722;** www.espressovivace.com), a curved marble bar, and a sidewalk cart at 321 Broadway Ave. E. (no phone). By the way, this coffee roastery participates in a carbon-sequestration program.

If hot chocolate and chocolate cake are more your style, stop in at **Dilettante Mocha Martini Bar,** 538 Broadway Ave. E. (© **206/329-6463;** www.dilettante.com), which is located in a modern space at the north end of the Capitol Hill commercial district not far from Volunteer Park.

NORTH SEATTLE In the U District, you'll find Seattle's oldest coffeehouse: **Café Allegro,** 4214 University Way NE (© **206/633-3030;** www.cafeallegromusic.com), down an alley around the corner from "the Ave" (as University Way is called by locals). This is a favored hangout of University of Washington students. Keep looking; you'll find it.

In Wallingford, I give up espresso so I can sip one of the wonderful gourmet hot chocolates served at **Chocolati,** 1716 N. 45th St. (© **206/633-7765;** www.chocolati.com). There are two other Chocolati cafes in the Greenlake neighborhood near the zoo—7810 E. Greenlake Dr. N. (© **206/527-5467**) and 8319 Greenwood Ave. N. (© **206/783-7078**). These cafes also serve organic, fair-trade espresso.

In Fremont, try **Caffe Ladro,** 452 N. 36th St. (© **206/675-0854**), or the pretty little **Fremont Coffee Company,** 459 N. 36th St. (© **206/623-3633;** www.fremontcoffee.net), in the quaint little Frank Rosche house, which was built in 1904.

BAKERIES & PASTRY SHOPS

DOWNTOWN If you happen to be staying downtown in one of the city's business hotels and want a delicious treat, drop by **Belle Epicurean,** Fairmont Olympic Hotel, 1206 Fourth Ave. (© **206/262-9404;** www.belleepicurean.com), which specializes in sweet brioche buns.

BELLTOWN For some of the best baked goodies in the city, head to **Macrina** ★, 2408 First Ave. (© **206/448-4032;** www.macrinabakery.com), a neighborhood bakery/cafe that's a cozy place for a quick, cheap breakfast or lunch. In the morning, the smell of baking bread wafts down First Avenue and draws in many passersby.

Tom Douglas's restaurants—Dahlia Lounge, Palace Kitchen, Etta's, Lola, and Serious Pie—are all immensely popular, and there was such a demand for the breads and pastries served at these places that Douglas opened his own **Dahlia Bakery** ★, 2001 Fourth Ave. (© **206/441-4540;** www.tomdouglas.com). The croissants here are the best in Seattle—and you can even get Douglas's fabled coconut-cream pie to go.

Leave it to Seattle to take the doughnut craze and turn it into something sophisticated. **Top Pot Doughnuts,** 2124 Fifth Ave. (© **206/728-1966;** www.toppotdoughnuts.com), is housed in a former showroom building with big walls of glass. Books now line the walls; doughnuts fill the display cases.

WHERE TO DINE

6

COFFEE, TEA, BAKERIES & PASTRY SHOPS

The **Crumpet Shop** ★, 1503 First Ave. (© **206/682-1598**), specializes in its British namesake pastries but does scones as well. It's almost a requirement that you accompany your crumpet or scone with a pot of tea. **Le Panier,** 1902 Pike Place (© **206/441-3669;** www.lepanier.com), is a great place to get a croissant and a latte and watch the market action. With a wall of glass cases filled with baked goods and a window facing one of the busiest spots in the market, **Three Girls Bakery,** 1514 Pike Place, stall no. 1 (© **206/622-1045**), is a favorite place to grab a few pastries or other goodies to go. If cheesecake is your vice, head to **The Confectional,** 1530 Pike Place (© **206/282-4422;** www.theconfectional.com), which specializes in individual cheese-cakes. Just don't expect me to absolve you of your weight gain.

PIONEER SQUARE & THE INTERNATIONAL DISTRICT **Grand Central Baking Company** ★, 214 First Ave. S. (© **206/622-3644;** www.grandcentralbakery.com), in Pioneer Square's Grand Central Arcade, is responsible for awakening Seattle to the plea-sures of rustic European-style breads. This bakery not only turns out great bread, but also does good pastries and sandwiches.

Although the name is none too appealing, **Cow Chip Cookies,** 102A First Ave. S. (© **206/292-9808;** www.cowchipcookies.com), bakes Seattle's best chocolate-chip cook-ies, which come in different sizes depending on the size of your craving.

QUEEN ANNE/SEATTLE CENTER & LAKE UNION My favorite Belltown bakery, **Macrina,** also has an outpost at 615 W. McGraw St. (© **206/283-5900;** www.macrina bakery.com), which is near the top of Queen Anne Hill at the north end of the neighbor-hood's business district.

Over on the east side of Lake Union, you can drool over beautiful French pastries at **Le Fournil,** 3230 Eastlake Ave. E. (© **206/328-6523;** www.le-fournil.com). Alterna-tively, check out the rustic breads at **Grand Central Baking Company** ★, 1616 Eastlake Ave. E. (© **206/957-9505**).

CAPITOL HILL & MADISON VALLEY If you've been on your feet at Volunteer Park for a while and need a snack, try the **North Hill Bakery,** 518 15th Ave. E. (© **206/325-9007;** www.northhillbakery.com), just a few blocks east of the park. There's always a good selection of baked goods in the cases.

NORTH SEATTLE Let's say you've spent the morning or afternoon at the zoo and you're suddenly struck with a craving for a fresh apple tart or an almond croissant. What's a person to do? Make tracks to the **Essential Bakery Cafe** ★, 1604 N. 34th St. (© **206/545-0444;** www.essentialbaking.com), a Wallingford rustic-bread bakery and pastry shop. You can also get sandwiches here. A second Essential Bakery Cafe is east of down-town in the Madison Valley neighborhood, at 2719 E. Madison St. (© **206/328-0078**). When nothing else will satisfy but a rich cupcake slathered with butter-cream frosting, stop in at Ballard's **Cupcake Royale/Vérité Coffee,** 2052 NW Market St. (© **206/782-9557;** www.cupcakeroyale.com), which also has locations in West Seattle at 4556 Cali-fornia Ave. SW (© **206/932-2971**), and east of downtown in the Madrona neighborhood at 1101 34th Ave. (© **206/709-4497**). This was Seattle's very first specialty cupcake bakery. For *stollen, kringles,* and other classic Danish pastries, head to **Larsen's Danish Bakery,** 8000 24th Ave. NW (© **800/626-8631;** www.larsensbakery.com) in Ballard, Seattle's Scandinavian neighborhood.

If you've been out on Alki Beach and are suddenly struck with a craving for a *pain au chocolate* or a slice of opera cake, don't despair. Just head to **Bakery Nouveau** ★, 4737 California Ave. SW (© **206/923-0534;** www.bakerynouveau.com), which many Seattleites swear is the best bakery in the city.

17   QUICK BITES

For variety, it's hard to beat the food court on the top floor of **Westlake Center,** 400 Pine Street in downtown Seattle. However, if you're a fan of Asian food, then be sure to have a quick meal from one of the vendors in the food court at **Uwajimaya,** 600 Fifth Ave. S. (© **206/624-6248;** www.uwajimaya.com), a huge Asian supermarket in the International District. If you're up in Ballard and decide you'd like to have a picnic on the beach at Golden Gardens Park (a great idea, by the way), I suggest stopping in at **Dish D'Lish** ★, 5136 Ballard Ave. NW (© **206/789-8121;** www.kathycasey.com), a gourmet-to-go shop in the heart of historic Ballard. Owner Kathy Casey has been a mover and shaker on the Seattle restaurant scene for years.

MARKET MUNCHING

Few Seattle activities are more enjoyable than munching your way through Pike Place Market. The market has dozens of fast-food vendors, and it's nearly impossible to resist the interesting array of finger foods and quick bites. Here are some of my favorite places:

If you're planning a picnic, **DeLaurenti** ★, 1435 First Ave. (© **800/873-6685** or 206/622-0141; www.delaurenti.com), near the market's brass pig, is the perfect spot to get your pâté, sandwiches, and wine.

Sausage lovers should be sure to have at least one sausage sandwich at **Uli's Famous Sausage,** 1511 Pike Place (© **206/839-1000;** www.ulisfamoussausage.com). Pick from the long list of sausages and have it grilled up with your choice of toppings. Whether you crave a German bratwurst or a French merguez, you'll find it here.

If you're a fan of the stinking rose, don't miss the **Garlic Garden,** 93 Pike St., #3 (© **877/207-5166** or 206/405-4022; www.garlicgarden.com), just around the corner from the pig statue. The Lebanese Breeze garlic dip/spread is so good, you're allowed to have only one free sample. Buy a container to spread on some bread from Le Panier.

Michou, 1904 Pike Place (© **206/448-4758),** has cases full of delicious French- and Italian-inspired gourmet foods to go and is located right next door to Le Panier, a good French bakery.

Piroshky, Piroshky, 1908 Pike Place (© **206/441-6068;** www.piroshkybakery.com), lays it all out in its name. The sweet or savory Russian filled rolls are the perfect finger food.

At **Beecher's Handmade Cheese,** 1600 Pike Place (© **206/956-1964;** www.beechers cheese.com), you can watch cheese being made and sample some of the products. But what brings me back here again and again is the awesome macaroni and cheese. Get some to go, and have a picnic down on the waterfront.

The **Spanish Table,** 1426 Western Ave. (© **206/682-2827;** www.spanishtable.com), is a specialty food shop on one of the lower levels of the market. You can get simple Spanish-style sandwiches, great soups, cheeses, and other light meal items, and then shop for a paella pan. This quiet corner of the market is a great place to get away from the crowds and try some food you might never have encountered before.

Moments Picnic Spots

To give focus to a tour of Pike Place Market, why not spend the morning or afternoon shopping for interesting picnic items, then head up to the north end of the waterfront to the **Olympic Sculpture Park** or **Myrtle Edwards Park?** Or, since a picnic of foods from Pike Place Market should be as special as the food-shopping experience, consider heading a bit farther afield, perhaps to **Discovery Park,** Seattle's waterfront urban wilderness (take Western Ave. north along Elliott Bay to Magnolia and follow the signs). Another good place for a picnic is **Volunteer Park,** high atop Capitol Hill. Alternatively, you could have your picnic aboard a **ferry** headed to Bainbridge Island (a 30-min. trip) or to Bremerton (a 1-hr. trip).

And when you just have to have something sweet, cold, and creamy, try the much-lauded gelato at **Bottega Italiana,** 1425 First Ave. (© **206/343-0200;** www.bottegaitaliana. com), or **Procopio,** 1501 Western Ave. (© **206/622-4280;** www.procopiogelati.com), which is on the Pike Hillclimb that links the waterfront with Pike Place Market. For some of the best and most unusual ice cream in Seattle, head on up to Capitol Hill, and get in line at **Molly Moon's Homemade Ice Cream,** 917 E. Pine St. (© **206/708-7947;** www.mollymoonicecream.com), on Capitol Hill. Alternatively, you can stand in line in Wallingford at 1622 N. 45th St. (© **206/547-5105**), their second location. Flavors here include such untraditional ice creams as salted caramel, cardamom, rosemary-meyer lemon, honey lavender, and pomegranate-curry sorbet.

Exploring Seattle

I hope you've got a good pair of walking shoes and a lot of stamina (a double latte helps), because Seattle is a walking town. The city's two biggest attractions—the waterfront and Pike Place Market—are the sorts of places where you'll spend hours on your feet. When your feet are beat, you can relax on a tour boat and enjoy the views of the city from the waters of Puget Sound, or you can take a 2-minute rest on the monorail, which links downtown with Seattle Center, home of the Space Needle. If your energy level sags, don't worry; there's always an espresso bar nearby.

By the way, that monorail ride takes you right through the middle of Paul Allen's Experience Music Project, the Frank Gehry–designed rock-music museum also located in Seattle Center. Paul Allen, who made his millions as one of the co-founders of Microsoft, has spent many years changing the face of Seattle. He has renovated Union Station and developed the area adjacent to Qwest Field, which was built for the Seattle Seahawks football team, which is owned by . . . you guessed it: Paul Allen. The stadium is adjacent to the Seattle Mariners' Safeco Field, which is one of the few ballparks in the country with a retractable roof. Paul Allen is now working on a large-scale development project at the south end of Lake Union.

Despite Seattle's many downtown diversions, the city's natural surroundings are still its primary attraction. You can easily cover all of Seattle's museums and major sights in 2 or 3 days. Once you've seen what's to see indoors, you can begin exploring the city's outdoor life.

If you plan to spend all your time in downtown Seattle, a car is a liability. However, when it comes time to explore beyond downtown, say, to the University District, Fremont, or Ballard, a car can be handy (although there are also good bus connections to these neighborhoods). If you want to head farther afield—to Mount Rainier or the Olympic Peninsula, for example—then a car is a must.

1 THE WATERFRONT

What Fisherman's Wharf is to San Francisco, the waterfront is to Seattle. Stretching along Alaskan Way from Yesler Way, in the south, to Bay Street, Myrtle Edwards Park, and the Olympic Sculpture Park, in the north, the waterfront is Seattle's most popular and touristy destination. Tacky gift shops, candy stores selling fudge and saltwater taffy, sidewalk T-shirt vendors, overpriced restaurants, and walk-up counters serving greasy fish and chips—they're all here. Why bother fighting the jostling crowds? Well, for one thing, this is where you'll find the Seattle Aquarium and Ye Olde Curiosity Shop, which is king of the tacky gift shops and as fun as a Ripley's Believe It or Not museum. Ferries to Bainbridge Island and Bremerton, as well as several different boat tours, also operate from the waterfront. Oh, and then there's the view, that incomparable view across Elliott Bay to the Olympic Mountains. So stay focused and stay out of the shopping arcades inside the piers (unless, of course, you really need salt-and-pepper shakers shaped like the Space Needle).

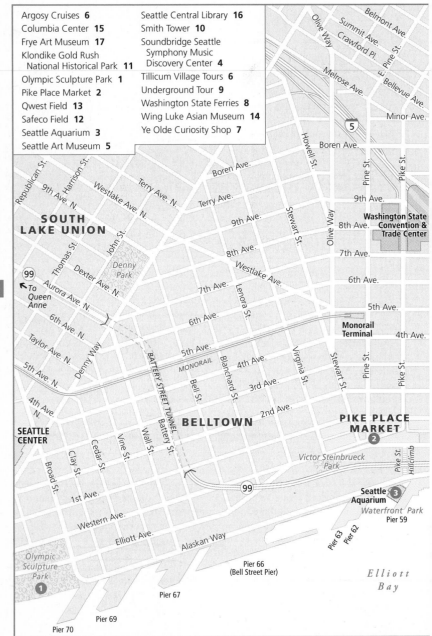

Argosy Cruises **6**
Columbia Center **15**
Frye Art Museum **17**
Klondike Gold Rush
  National Historical Park **11**
Olympic Sculpture Park **1**
Pike Place Market **2**
Qwest Field **13**
Safeco Field **12**
Seattle Aquarium **3**
Seattle Art Museum **5**

Seattle Central Library **16**
Smith Tower **10**
Soundbridge Seattle
  Symphony Music
  Discovery Center **4**
Tillicum Village Tours **6**
Underground Tour **9**
Washington State Ferries **8**
Wing Luke Asian Museum **14**
Ye Olde Curiosity Shop **7**

EXPLORING SEATTLE

7

THE WATERFRONT

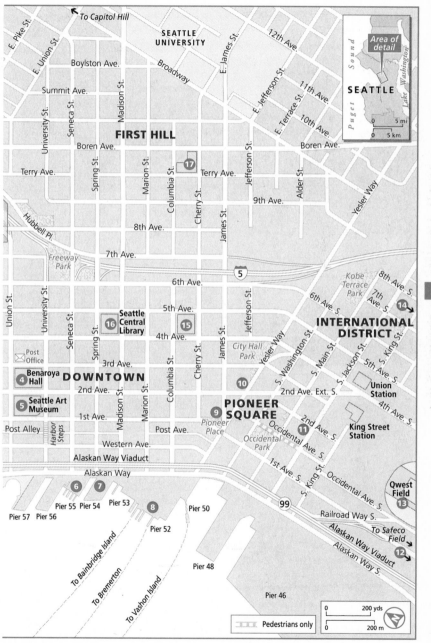

> **Value** **Saving Money on Sightseeing**
>
> If you're a see-it-all, do-it-all kind of person, you'll definitely want to buy a **City-Pass** (© **888/330-5008** or 208/787-4300; www.citypass.com), which gets you into the Space Needle, Seattle Aquarium, Pacific Science Center, Woodland Park Zoo, and the Museum of Flight or the Experience Music Project/Science Fiction Museum, and also lets you take a boat tour of the harbor with Argosy Cruises, all at a savings of almost 50% if you visit all five attractions and do the harbor tour. The passes, good for 9 days from the date of first use, cost $54 for adults and $39 for children 3 to 12. Purchase your CityPass at any of the participating attractions.
>
> The **Go Seattle Card** (© **866/628-9029**; www.goseattlecard.com) is another interesting option for the see-it-all, do-it-all travelers who are able to plan out a daily tour route in advance. It takes careful planning to get your money's worth out of this card, but it can be done. The way this card works is that you pay $55 ($38 for children ages 3–12) for a card that will get you into as many participating attractions as you can visit in 1 day. There's a discount for 2-, 3-, 5-, and 7-day cards, and your best bet would probably be the 3-day card.

You'll find the Washington State Ferries terminal at **Pier 52,** which is at the south end of the waterfront near Pioneer Square. (A ferry ride makes for a cheap cruise.) **Pier 55** has excursion boats offering harbor cruises and trips to Tillicum Village on Blake Island. At **Pier 56,** cruise boats leave for trips through the Chittenden (Ballard) Locks to Lake Union. See "Organized Tours," p. 146, for details on these excursions. At **Pier 57** you'll find the **Bay Pavilion,** which has a vintage carousel and a video arcade to keep the kids busy.

Pier 59 is home to the Seattle Aquarium (see below for details) and a small waterfront park. If you continue up the waterfront, you'll find **Pier 66,** also called the Bell Street Pier, which has a rooftop park. Anthony's (p. 85), one of the best seafood restaurants on the waterfront, is also on this pier. At **Pier 67** is The Edgewater hotel (p. 54), a great place to take in the sunset over a drink or dinner.

Next door, at **Pier 69,** you can see the dock for the ferries that ply the waters between Seattle and Victoria, British Columbia. Just north of this pier is the **Olympic Sculpture Park** and the grassy **Myrtle Edwards Park,** which together make all the waterfront schlock worth enduring, a nice finale to the waterfront. Myrtle Edwards Park has a popular bicycling-and-skating trail and is a great spot for a sunset stroll or a picnic. The Olympic Sculpture Park (p. 124), which covers a hillside overlooking the north end of the waterfront, is my favorite Seattle attraction, offering not only monumental sculptures, but gardens of native plants and superb views of the Seattle skyline, Elliott Bay, and the Olympic Mountains.

Olympic Sculpture Park ★★★ Covering 9 acres of hillside, the Olympic Sculpture Park stretches from Belltown down to the waterfront at Myrtle Edwards Park. Modern and contemporary monumental sculptures are the focus of the collection, which includes works from regional, national, and international artists, including Alexander Calder, whose sculpture *Eagle* is one of the highlights of the collection. From just the right perspective, this sculpture perfectly frames the distant Space Needle. What a view! Other noteworthy works include Claes Oldenburg and Coosje van Bruggen's *Typing* shadowy *Hammering Man,* an animated three-story steel sculpture that pounds out a silent beat in front of the museum. Inside the museum, white cars go tumbling through the air with colored lights shooting out of them in Cai Guo-Qiang's sculpture *Inopportune: Stage One.* Once you finally get inside the museum proper, you'll find one of the nation's premier collections of Northwest Coast Indian art and artifacts, and an equally large collection of African art. The museum is particularly strong in modern and contemporary art, but there are also good collections of European and American art ranging from ancient Mediterranean works to pieces from the medieval, Renaissance, and baroque periods. Of course, the Northwest contemporary art collection is also quite extensive. (The museum also has a smattering of Asian art, but the city's major collection of Asian art is at the affiliated Seattle Asian Art Museum in Volunteer Park; p. 136.)

1300 First Ave. ✆ **206/654-3100.** www.seattleartmuseum.org. Admission $15 adults, $12 seniors, $9 children 13–17, free for children 12 and under. Free for all on 1st Thurs of each month; free for seniors on 1st Fri of each month; free for teens on 2nd Fri of each month 5–9pm. Tues–Wed and Sat–Sun 10am–5pm; Thurs–Fri 10am–9pm. Closed Columbus Day, Thanksgiving, Christmas Eve, Christmas, New Year's Eve, and New Year's Day (open some holiday Mon). Bus: Any downtown bus.

Soundbridge Seattle Symphony Music Discovery Center Perhaps you're an accomplished musician but have always longed to conduct an orchestra, or perhaps you've never had much musical talent at all but dream of playing the cello like Yo-Yo Ma. At this fascinating little music exploration center, you can find out what it feels like to wield the baton or be first chair in the string section of the symphony. Not only do interactive exhibits allow you to play a cello, tickle the ivories, or conduct a virtual orchestra, but you can also check out more than 500 classical recordings at the listening bar. There's an exhibit on the science of music as well.

Benaroya Hall, Second Ave. and Union St. ✆ **206/336-6600.** www.soundbridge.org. Admission $7 adults, $5 children 5–18, free for children 4 and under. Mon 9am–4pm; Wed 9–11am; Thurs–Sat 9am–4pm; Sun 10am–4pm. Bus: Any downtown bus.

3 SEATTLE CENTER & LAKE UNION

Built in 1962 for the World's Fair, Seattle Center is today not only the site of Seattle's famous Space Needle, but also a cultural and entertainment park that doubles as the city's favorite festival grounds. Within Seattle Center's boundaries you'll find the Experience Music Project (EMP), the affiliated Science Fiction Museum, the Pacific Science Center, the Seattle Children's Museum, the Seattle Children's Theatre, Key Arena (former home of the NBA's Seattle SuperSonics), the Marion Oliver McCaw Hall, the Intiman Theatre, the Bagley Wright Theatre, a children's amusement park, and a fountain that's a favorite summertime hangout. The "Especially for Kids" section (p. 145) lists further details on Seattle Center attractions that young travelers will enjoy. Not far away, you'll find Lake Union, with a couple of nautical attractions.

Center for Wooden Boats ★ This unusual little museum is basically a collection of wooden boats. Most are tied up to the docks surrounding the museum's floating boathouse, but some are stored on the dock itself. Dedicated to the preservation of historic wooden boats, the center is unique in that many exhibits can be rented and taken out on the waters of Lake Union. There are both rowboats and sailboats; rates range from $20 to $50 per hour (call for hours of availability). Free classic boat rides are held on Sunday from 2 to 3pm (sign up as early as 10am). Adjacent to the center, you'll find the 12-acre

Eraser, Scale X, Richard Serra's massive plate-steel *Wake,* and *Split,* a life-size stainless-steel tree by Roxy Paine. If the sculptures aren't enough to hold your attention, turn your eyes toward the views of Elliott Bay and the distant Olympic Mountains. Down along the water, you'll also find a perfect little beach that was constructed as part of the sculpture park. This diminutive stretch of shoreline feels as wild as any beach on the Olympic Peninsula.

2901 Western Ave. ✆ **206/654-3100.** www.seattleartmuseum.org. Free admission. Park: Daily 30 min. before sunrise to 30 min. after sunset; PACCAR Pavilion: May to Labor Day Tues–Sun 10am–5pm, day after Labor Day to Apr Tues–Sun 10am–4pm. Pavilion closed Columbus Day, Thanksgiving, Christmas Eve, Christmas, New Year's Eve, and New Year's Day. Bus: 1, 2, 3, 13, 15, 16, 18, 19, 24, 33, 81, 82. Waterfront Streetcar Bus (Rte. 99): Pier 69 stop.

Seattle Aquarium ★★ (Kids) Although it's not nearly as large and impressive as the Monterey Bay Aquarium or the Oregon Coast Aquarium, the Seattle Aquarium is a fabulous introduction to the sea life of the Northwest. The "Window on Washington Waters" exhibit, a huge tank just inside the entrance, is a highlight of a visit, especially when divers feed the fish. There's also a tank that generates crashing waves, and, in the *Life on the Edge* tide pool exhibit that focuses on life along Washington's shores, you can reach into the water to touch starfish, sea cucumbers, and anemones (kids love these tanks). The aquarium's main focus is on the water worlds of the Puget Sound region, but there are also fascinating exhibits of sea life from around the world, including a beautiful coral-reef tank. The star attractions, however, are the playful river otters and sea otters, as well as the giant octopus. From the underwater viewing dome you get a fish's-eye view of life beneath the waves, and each September you can watch salmon return up a fish ladder to spawn.

Pier 59, 1483 Alaskan Way. ✆ **206/386-4300.** www.seattleaquarium.org. Admission $16 adults, $11 children 4–12, free for children 3 and under. Daily 9:30am–5pm. Bus: 10, 12, 15, 18, or 81, and then walk through Pike Place Market to the waterfront. Waterfront Streetcar Bus (Rte. 99): Pike St. stop.

2 PIKE PLACE MARKET TO PIONEER SQUARE

Pike Place Market and the Pioneer Square historic district lie at opposite ends of First Avenue; midway between the two is the Seattle Art Museum.

The **Pioneer Square** area, with its historic buildings, interesting shops, museum, and Underground Tour (see "Good Times in Bad Taste," later in this chapter), is well worth a morning or afternoon of exploration. See chapter 8 for a walking tour of the area.

Klondike Gold Rush National Historical Park "At 3 o'clock this morning the steamship *Portland,* from St. Michaels for Seattle, passed up (Puget) Sound with more than a ton of gold on board and 68 passengers." When the *Seattle Post-Intelligencer* published that sentence on July 17, 1897, it started a stampede. Would-be miners heading for the Klondike goldfields in the 1890s made Seattle their outfitting center and helped turn it into a prosperous city. When they struck it rich up north, they headed back to Seattle, the first U.S. outpost of civilization, and unloaded their gold, making Seattle doubly rich. Although this place isn't in the Klondike (that's in Canada) and isn't really a park (it's more of a museum in a historic building), it's still a fascinating place, and it seems only fitting that it should be here in Seattle. (Another unit of the park is in Skagway, AK.) During the summer, free walking tours of the Pioneer Square neighborhood are scheduled daily.

On the Trail of Dale Chihuly

For many years now, Northwest glass artist Dale Chihuly, one of the founders of the Pilchuck School for art glass north of Seattle, has been garnering international attention for his fanciful, color-saturated contemporary art glass. From tabletop vessels to huge chandeliers and massive window installations, his creations in glass have a depth and richness of color treasured by collectors around the world. His sensuous forms include vases within bowls reminiscent of Technicolor birds' eggs in giant nests. Works in his ikebana series, based on the traditional Japanese flower-arranging technique, are riotous conglomerations of color that twist and turn like so many cut flowers waving in the wind.

No one place in Seattle features a large collection of his work, but numerous public displays exist around the city. Up on the third floor of the **Washington State Convention and Trade Center,** Pike Street and Eighth Avenue, is a case with some beautifully lighted pieces. The **City Centre shopping arcade,** 1420 Fifth Ave., has displays by numerous glass artists, including Chihuly. Don't miss the large wall installation that is beside this upscale shopping arcade's lounge. You'll also find two Chihuly chandeliers inside **Benaroya Hall,** Third Avenue between Union and University streets, which is the home of the Seattle Symphony.

Want to take home an original Chihuly as a souvenir of your visit to Seattle? Drop by the **Foster/White Gallery,** 220 Third Ave. S. (© **206/622-2833**), in Pioneer Square.

If you're a serious fan of Chihuly's work and art glass in general, then you have to take the time for an excursion to **Tacoma,** 32 miles south of Seattle. Here you'll find the **Museum of Glass,** 1801 Dock St. (© **866/468-7386**), which is devoted to art glass in all its forms and is connected to downtown Tacoma via a pedestrian bridge designed by Chihuly. You can see more of Chihuly's work at the **Tacoma Art Museum,** 1701 Pacific Ave. (© **253/272-4258**). Just up the street from here, at Tacoma's restored **Union Station,** 1717 Pacific Ave. (© **253/863-5173**), which is now the federal courthouse, there is a fascinating large Chihuly installation in a massive arched window. For more information on visiting Tacoma, see "Tacoma's Museums & Gardens," in chapter 11.

319 Second Ave. S. © **206/220-4240.** www.nps.gov/klse. Free admission. Daily 9am–5pm. Closed New Year's Day, Thanksgiving, and Christmas. Bus: Any downtown bus. Waterfront Streetcar Bus (Rte. 99): Occidental Park stop.

Pike Place Market ★★★   Pike Place Market, originally a farmers market, was founded in 1907 when housewives complained that middlemen were raising the price of produce. The market allowed shoppers to buy directly from producers and thus save on grocery bills. For several decades, the market thrived. However, World War II deprived the market of nearly half its farmers when Japanese Americans were moved to internment camps. With the postwar flight to the suburbs, the market was never able to recover from the war years, and by the 1960s, the market was no longer the popular spot it had been.

If you find giant spiders more fascinating than frightening, then you should drop by Pike Place Market's unusual **Seattle Bug Safari,** 1501 Western Ave. (© **206/285-BUGS;** www.seattlebugsafari.com), which is located on the Pike Hill Climb and is home to more than 40 species of large and unusual insects, spiders, scorpions, centipedes, and millipedes. The zoo is open Tuesday through Saturday from 10am to 6pm and Sunday from 11am to 5pm (Mon hours vary seasonally). Admission is $8 for adults and $6 for children 4 to 12.

MARKET INFO CTR
1st Ave + Pike SW corner 10-6 daily

When it was announced that the site was being eyed for a major redevelopment project, a grass-roots movement arose to save the 9-acre market and, eventually, the market was declared a National Historic District.

These days the market bustles from dawn to dusk, but the 100 or so farmers and fishmongers who set up shop on the premises are only a small part of the attraction. You'll also find more than 150 local craftspeople and artists selling their creations as street performers serenade milling crowds. Hundreds of small specialty shops are scattered throughout the market, plus dozens of restaurants, including some of the city's best. At the **information booth** almost directly below the large PIKE PLACE MARKET sign, you can pick up a free map and guide to the market. Keep an eye out for low-flying fish at the **Pike Place Fish** stall, and be sure to save some change for *Rachel,* the market's giant charity piggy bank.

Victor Steinbrueck Park, at the north end of the market at the intersection of Pike Place, Virginia Street, and Western Avenue, is a popular lounging area for both the homeless and those just looking for a grassy spot in the sun. In the park, you'll see two 50-foot-tall totem poles.

The market's **"Gum Wall"** is a bit of a sticky subject. No one can agree whether it is art or just a disgusting form of litter. Maybe you'll have to decide for yourself. You'll find the chewing-gum-covered wall just down Pike Street (actually a cobbled alley) from the market information booth. The wall is across the street from the Alibi Room bar.

See "Market Munching" in chapter 6 for a rundown of some of my favorite market food vendors. Also, if you're going to be in town in October, consider attending the annual **Feast at the Market** (© **206/548-3266;** www.pikemed.org/feast), a showcase for food from market restaurants.

In summer, there are free guided tours of the market on Saturday mornings at 10am. These tours leave from *Rachel,* the market piggy bank. No reservations are necessary.

Btw. Pike and Pine sts. at First Ave. © **206/682-7453.** www.pikeplacemarket.org. Pike Place/First A businesses Mon–Sat 10am–6pm, Sun 11am–5pm; Down Under stores daily 11am–5pm; many produ vendors open at 8am in summer; restaurant hours vary. Closed New Year's Day, Thanksgiving, and Chr mas. Bus: 5, 10, 11, 12, 15, 18, 19, 21, 22, 24, 33, 41, 56, 71, 72, 73, 81, 84, 113, 121, or 122. Waterf Streetcar Bus (Rte. 99): Pike St. Hillclimb stop.

Seattle Art Museum (SAM) ★★★   This large museum verges on world-class should not be missed on a visit to Seattle. With acres of gallery space and cutting exhibit designs, this is definitely not your typical, stodgy art museum. Before you step inside the museum, you'll come face to faceless silhouette with Jonathon Bor

PICASSO tickets ★

Pole to Pole

Totem poles are the quintessential symbol of the Northwest, and although this Native American art form actually comes from farther north, there are quite a few totem poles around Seattle. The four in **Occidental Park** at Occidental Avenue South and South Washington Street were carved by local artist Duane Pasco. The tallest is 35-foot-tall *The Sun and Raven,* which tells the story of how Raven brought light into the world. Next to this pole is *Man Riding a Whale.* This type of totem pole was traditionally carved to help villagers during their whale hunts. The other two figures that face each other are symbols of the Bear Clan and the Welcoming Figure.

A block away, in the triangular plaza of **Pioneer Place,** you can see Seattle's most famous totem pole. This totem pole is a replacement for the plaza's original pole, which was damaged by an arsonist's fire in 1938. Seattle businessmen on a cruise to Alaska stole the original pole from a Tlingit village near Fort Tongass, Alaska, in 1899. According to local legend, after the pole caught fire in 1938, the city fathers sent a check to the tribe with a request for a new totem pole. The Tlingit response was, "Thanks for paying for the first one. Send another check for the replacement." The truth is far more prosaic: As part of a Civilian Conservation Corps program, the U.S. Forest Service paid Tlingit carver Charles Brown to create a new totem pole.

Up near Pike Place Market, at **Victor Steinbrueck Park,** which is at the intersection of Pike Place, Virginia Street, and Western Avenue, are two 50-foot-tall totem poles. To see the largest concentration of totem poles in the city, visit the **University of Washington's Burke Museum** (see p. 136 for details). If you take the Tillicum Village tour, you'll also see totem poles outside the longhouse on **Blake Island** where the dinner and masked-dance performances are held.

Lake Union Park and the South Lake Union Historic Ships Wharf, which is home to a handful of historic vessels.

1010 Valley St. (Waterway 4, south end of Lake Union). ℂ **206/382-2628.** www.cwb.org. Free admission. Early May to late Sept daily 10am–8pm; late Sept to early May Tues–Sun 10am–5pm. Bus: 5, 17, 26, 28, 70, 71, 72, or 73. South Lake Union Streetcar: Lake Union Park stop.

Experience Music Project (EMP) ★★   The brainchild of Microsoft co-founder Paul Allen and designed by avant-garde architect Frank Gehry, who is known for pushing the envelope of architectural design, this rock-'n'-roll museum is a massive, multicolored blob at the foot of the Space Needle. Originally planned as a memorial to Seattle native Jimi Hendrix, the museum grew to encompass not only Hendrix, but all of the Northwest rock scene (from "Louie Louie" to grunge) and the general history of American popular music.

The most popular exhibits here (after the Jimi Hendrix room) are the interactive rooms. In one room, you can play guitars, drums, keyboards, or even DJ turntables. In another, you can experience what it's like to be onstage performing in front of adoring fans. Another exhibit focuses on the history of guitars and includes some of the first

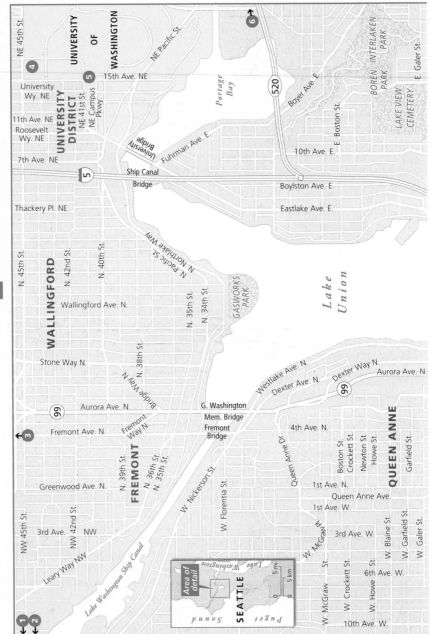

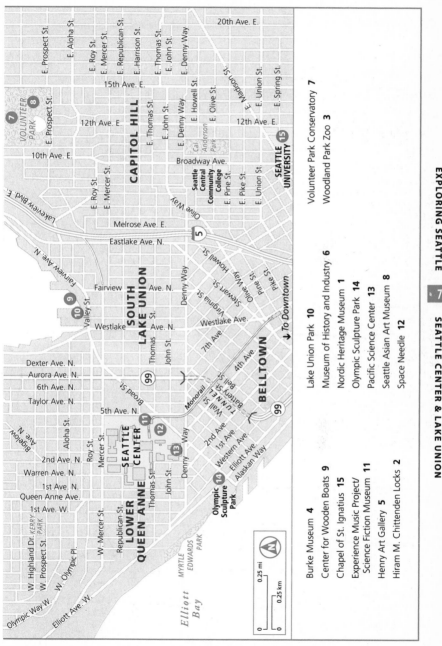

20th Ave. E.

E. Prospect St.
E. Aloha St.
E. Roy St.
E. Mercer St.
E. Republican St.
E. Harrison St.
E. Thomas St.
E. John St.
E. Denny Way

15th Ave. E.

E. Prospect St.
VOLUNTEER PARK **8**
7
12th Ave. E.
E. Thomas St.
E. John St.
E. Denny Way
E. Howell St.
E. Olive St.
12th Ave. E.

10th Ave. E.

CAPITOL HILL

Cal Anderson Park

Broadway Ave.

Seattle Central Community College

E. Madison St.
E. Union St.
E. Spring St.

SEATTLE UNIVERSITY **15**

E. Roy St.
E. Mercer St.
E. Pine St.
E. Pike St.
E. Union St.

Olive Way

Melrose Ave. E.

Lakeview Blvd. E.

Eastlake Ave. N.
5

Fairview Ave. N.

Fairview Ave. N.

SOUTH LAKE UNION

Denny Way
Virginia St.
Stewart St.
Howell St.
Olive Way
Pine St.
Pike St.

9
10
Valley St.
Westlake Ave. N.
Thomas St.
John St.
Westlake Ave.
7th Ave.

→ To Downtown

Dexter Ave. N.
Aurora Ave. N.
6th Ave. N.
Taylor Ave. N.

Broad St.
99
4th Ave
Monorail
Bell St.
BELLTOWN
Wall St.
TUNNEL
99

5th Ave. N.

Bigelow Ave. N.

11
12
SEATTLE CENTER
Mercer St.
Roy St.
Aloha St.
2nd Ave. N.
13
Denny Way
2nd Ave.
1st Ave.
Western Ave.

Warren Ave. N.
1st Ave. N.
Queen Anne Ave.
LOWER QUEEN ANNE
John St.
Thomas St.
Elliott Ave.
Alaskan Way

1st Ave. W.
Republican St.
KERRY PARK
Olympic Sculpture Park **14**

W. Highland Dr.
W. Prospect St.
W. Olympic Pl.
W. Mercer St.
MYRTLE EDWARDS PARK

Olympic Way W.
Elliott Ave. W.

Elliott Bay

0 0.25 mi
0 0.25 km

Ⓐ

Burke Museum **4**

Center for Wooden Boats **9**

Chapel of St. Ignatius **15**

Experience Music Project/
Science Fiction Museum **11**

Henry Art Gallery **5**

Hiram M. Chittenden Locks **2**

Lake Union Park **10**

Museum of History and Industry **6**

Nordic Heritage Museum **1**

Olympic Sculpture Park **14**

Pacific Science Center **13**

Seattle Asian Art Museum **8**

Space Needle **12**

Volunteer Park Conservatory **7**

Woodland Park Zoo **3**

[handwritten at top: Battlestar Galactica the Exhibit / closed Tues. Jimi Hendrix]

[handwritten in left margin, vertical: Lives science show = 11, 12:30 3:30 daily (1st day) / circus/thunder Mountain; toots; (art; etc) every ½ hr]

electric guitars, which date from the early 1930s. Give yourself plenty of time to explore this unusual museum.

Seattle Center, 325 Fifth Ave. N. ✆ **877/367-7361** or 206/770-2702. www.emplive.org. Admission (valid for Science Fiction Museum) $15 adults, $12 seniors and children 5–17, free for children 4 and under. Free admission 1st Thurs of each month 5–8pm. Memorial Day to Labor Day daily 10am–7pm; Labor Day to Memorial Day Wed–Mon 10am–5pm (until 8pm 1st Thurs of each month). Closed Thanksgiving and Christmas. Bus: 1, 2, 3, 4, 5, 13, 15, 16, 18, 19, 24, 26, 28, 30, 33, 81, or 82. Monorail: From Westlake Center at Pine St. and Fourth Ave.

[handwritten: LASER SHOW Th, F, Sat Sun]

Pacific Science Center ★★ (Kids) Although its exhibits are aimed primarily at children, the Pacific Science Center is fun for all ages. The main goal of this sprawling complex at Seattle Center is to teach kids about science and to instill a desire to study it. To that end, kids can investigate life-size robotic dinosaurs, a butterfly house and insect village (with giant robotic insects), technology exhibits where they can play virtual-reality soccer or challenge a robot to tic-tac-toe, and dozens of other fun hands-on exhibits addressing the biological sciences, physics, and chemistry. Throughout the year there are special events that are guaranteed to keep your kids entertained for hours. There's a planetarium for learning about the skies (and laser shows for the fun of it), plus an IMAX theater. Be sure to check the schedule for special exhibits when you're in town.

Seattle Center, 200 Second Ave. N. ✆ **206/443-2001**, 206/443-4629 for IMAX information, or 206/443-2850 for laser-show information. www.pacsci.org. Admission $11 adults, $9.50 seniors, $8 ages 6–12, $6 ages 3–5, free for children 2 and under. IMAX $8–$12 adults, $7.50–$11 seniors, $7–$10 ages 6–12, $6–$10 ages 3–5, free for children 2 and under. Laser show $5–$8. Various discounted combination tickets available. Mon–Fri 10am–5pm; Sat–Sun 10am–6pm. Closed Christmas. Bus: 1, 2, 3, 4, 5, 13, 15, 16, 18, 19, 24, 26, 28, 30, 33, 81, or 82. Monorail: From Westlake Center at Pine St. and Fourth Ave.

Science Fiction Museum and Hall of Fame (SFM) ★ Located inside the Experience Music Project, this is another pet project of Seattle's own billionaire nerd Paul Allen. This museum is packed with more pop-culture icons, in this case from the world of science fiction. With displays of actual props and costumes from such historic sci-fi films and TV shows as *Star Trek, Star Wars, Alien, Dr. Who,* and *Terminator,* this place is an absolute must for devoted fans of one of literature's least-respected yet best-loved genres. The museum spends a lot of time chronicling the history of science fiction, including displays of 1930s and 1940s pulp fiction magazines. Other displays focus on the fans themselves (and the conventions they stage), as well as the connections to science. But for most visitors, it's the movie props that are the real draw. From robots to jet packs to space suits and ray guns, it's all here.

Seattle Center, inside Experience Music Project building, 325 Fifth Ave. N. ✆ **877/367-7361** or 206/770-2702. www.empsfm.org. Admission (also valid for EMP) $15 adults, $12 seniors and children 5–17, free for children 4 and under. Free admission 1st Thurs of each month 5–8pm. Memorial Day to Labor Day 10am–7pm; other months daily 10am–5pm (until 8pm 1st Thurs of each month). Closed Thanksgiving and Christmas. Bus: 1, 2, 3, 4, 5, 13, 15, 16, 18, 19, 24, 26, 28, 30, 33, 81, or 82. Monorail: From Westlake Center at Pine St. and Fourth Ave.

Space Needle ★★ From a distance it looks like a flying saucer on a tripod, and when it was built for the 1962 World's Fair, the 605-foot-tall Space Needle was meant to suggest future architectural trends. Today the Space Needle is the quintessential symbol of Seattle, and at 520 feet above ground level, its observation deck provides superb views of the city and its surroundings. Displays identify more than 60 sites and activities in the Seattle area, and high-powered telescopes let you zoom in on them. You'll also find a pricey restaurant, SkyCity (p. 100), atop the tower. If you don't mind standing in line

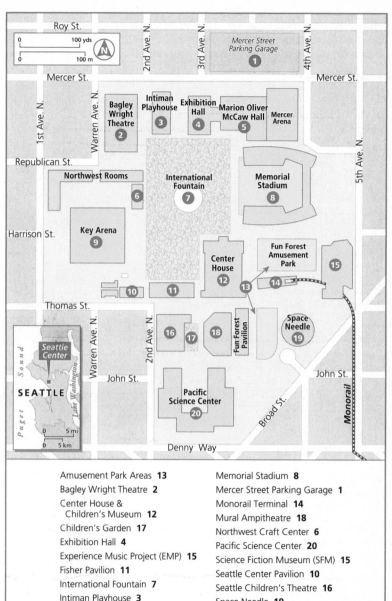

Amusement Park Areas **13**

Bagley Wright Theatre **2**

Center House &
Children's Museum **12**

Children's Garden **17**

Exhibition Hall **4**

Experience Music Project (EMP) **15**

Fisher Pavilion **11**

International Fountain **7**

Intiman Playhouse **3**

Key Arena **9**

Marion Oliver McCaw Hall **5**

Memorial Stadium **8**

Mercer Street Parking Garage **1**

Monorail Terminal **14**

Mural Ampitheatre **18**

Northwest Craft Center **6**

Pacific Science Center **20**

Science Fiction Museum (SFM) **15**

Seattle Center Pavilion **10**

Seattle Children's Theatre **16**

Space Needle **19**

Space Needle Alternatives

If you don't want to deal with the crowds at the Space Needle but still want an elevated downtown view, you have some alternatives. One is the big, black **Columbia Center** (✆ **206/386-5151**), at the corner of Fifth Avenue and Columbia Street. At 943 feet, this is the tallest building in Seattle, with more stories (76, to be exact) than any other building west of the Mississippi. Up on the 73rd floor, you find an observation deck with views that dwarf those from the Space Needle. Admission is only $5 for adults and $3 for seniors and children 6 to 12. It's open Monday through Friday from 8:30am to 4:30pm.

Not far from the Bank of America Tower is the **Smith Tower,** 506 Second Ave. (✆ **206/622-4004**; www.smithtower.com). Opened in 1914, this was Seattle's first skyscraper and, for 50 years, the tallest building west of Chicago. Although the Smith Tower has only 42 stories, it still offers excellent views from its 35th-floor observation deck, which surrounds the ornate Chinese Room, a banquet hall with a carved ceiling. A lavish lobby and original manual elevators make this a fun and historic place to take in the Seattle skyline. May through September, the deck is open daily from 10am to sunset; April and October, it's open daily from 10am to 5pm; November through March, it's open Saturday and Sunday from 10am to 4pm. However, the deck is sometimes closed for special events. Admission is $7.50 for adults, $6 for seniors and students, and $5 for children 6 to 12.

If you've ever seen a photo of the Space Needle framed by Mount Rainier and the high-rises of downtown Seattle, it was probably taken from **Kerry Viewpoint,** on Queen Anne Hill. If you want to take your own drop-dead gorgeous photo of the Seattle skyline from this elevated perspective, head north from Seattle Center on Queen Anne Avenue North, and turn left on West Highland Drive. When you reach the park, you'll immediately recognize the view.

Another great panorama is from the water tower in **Volunteer Park,** on Capitol Hill at East Prospect Street and 14th Avenue East (p. 135).

and paying quite a bit for an elevator ride, make this your first stop in Seattle so that you can orient yourself. (However, cheaper alternatives exist if you just want a view of the city—see "Space Needle Alternatives," below.)

Seattle Center, 400 Broad St. ✆ **206/905-2100.** www.spaceneedle.com. Admission $16 adults ($20 for day-and-night ticket), $16 seniors ($21 for day-and-night ticket), $9 ages 4–13 ($13 for day-and-night ticket), free for children 3 and under. No charge if dining in the SkyCity restaurant. Mon–Thurs 9:30am–11pm; Fri–Sat 9am–11:30pm; Sun 9am–11pm. Valet parking $12 for 4-hr. parking. Bus: 1, 2, 3, 4, 5, 13, 15, 16, 18, 19, 24, 26, 28, 30, 33, 81, or 82. Monorail: From Westlake Center at Pine St. and Fourth Ave.

4 THE NEIGHBORHOODS

See chapter 8 for walking tours of Pike Place Market, Pioneer Square, and Fremont.

Seattle today boasts of its strategic location on the Pacific Rim, but its ties to Asia are nothing new. This is evident in the International District, Seattle's main Asian neighborhood, which is centered between Fifth Avenue South and 12th Avenue South (btw. S. Washington St. and S. Lane St.). Called both Chinatown and the International District (because so many Asian nationalities have made this area home), the neighborhood has been the center of the city's Asian communities for more than a century. You can learn about the district's history at the **Wing Luke Asian Museum** (see below).

At the corner of Maynard Avenue South and South King Street is **Hing Hay Park,** the site of an ornate and colorful pavilion given to Seattle by the city of Taipei, Taiwan.

The International District has many restaurants, import stores, and food markets. The huge **Uwajimaya** (p. 180) is all of these rolled into one.

Wing Luke Asian Museum Despite much persecution in the 19th and 20th centuries, Asians, primarily Chinese and Japanese, have played an integral role in developing the Northwest, and today the connection between this region and the far side of the Pacific has opened both economic and cultural doors. Named for the first Asian American to hold public office in the Northwest and located in the heart of Seattle's International District, this small museum has exhibits that explore the roles various Asian cultures have played in the settlement and development of the region. Other exhibits help explain Asian customs to non-Asians. If you're walking around the International District, this place will give you a better appreciation of the neighborhood, but the exhibits tend to have a narrow range of appeal.

719 S. King St. © **206/623-5124.** www.wingluke.org. Admission $8 adults, $6 students and seniors, $5 children 5–12, free for children 4 and under. Free admission 1st Thurs and 3rd Sat of each month. Tues–Sun 10am–5pm (until 8pm 1st Thurs and 3rd Sat of each month). Closed major holidays. Bus: 7, 14, 36, 42, 99 (Waterfront Streetcar Bus), or any bus using the transit tunnel.

FIRST HILL (PILL HILL) & CAPITOL HILL

Seattle is justly proud of its parks, and **Volunteer Park** ★★ on Capitol Hill at 14th Avenue East and East Prospect Street (drive north on Broadway and watch for signs) is one of the most popular. Here you'll find not only acres of lawns, groves of trees, and huge old rhododendrons, but also an old water tower that provides one of the best panoramas in the city. A winding staircase leads to the top of the water tower, from which you get 360-degree views. The observatory level also has an interesting exhibit about the Olmsted Brothers and the system of parks they designed for Seattle. To find the water tower, park near the Seattle Asian Art Museum if you can; then walk back out of the parking lot to where the road splits. The view from directly in front of the museum, by Isamu Noguchi's *Black Sun* sculpture, isn't bad either.

Frye Art Museum ★ On First Hill not far from downtown Seattle, this museum is primarily an exhibit space for the extensive personal art collection of Charles and Emma Frye, Seattle pioneers who began collecting art in the 1890s. The collection focuses on late-19th-century and early-20th-century representational art by European and American painters, with works by Andrew Wyeth, Thomas Hart Benton, Edward Hopper, Albert Bierstadt, and Pablo Picasso, as well as a large collection of engravings by Winslow Homer. In addition to galleries filled with works from the permanent collection, temporary exhibitions, often of more contemporary works, are held throughout the year.

704 Terry Ave. (at Cherry St.). © **206/622-9250.** www.fryeart.org. Free admission. Tues–Wed and Fri–Sat 10am–5pm; Thurs 10am–8pm; Sun noon–5pm. Closed New Year's Day, July 4th, Thanksgiving, and Christmas. Bus: 3, 4, or 12.

Finds **It's a Mystery to Me**

> The **Seattle Museum of the Mysteries,** 623 Broadway Ave. E. (© **206/328-6499;**
> www.seattlechatclub.org), is the city's very own center for the paranormal.
> Located in the basement of a building at the north end of the main Capitol Hill
> shopping district, this little privately owned museum of the bizarre has exhibits
> on Bigfoot, UFOs, and ghosts. Museum admission is $2 for adults and $1 for
> youths 9 to 17. Call for hours. Ghost tours of Capitol Hill are also offered.

Seattle Asian Art Museum ★ Housed in an Art Deco building in Volunteer Park,
the collection at this museum places an emphasis on Chinese and Japanese art, but also
includes works from Korea, Southeast Asia, South Asia, and the Himalayas. Among the
museum's most notable pieces are Chinese terra-cotta funerary art, Chinese snuff bottles,
and Japanese *netsuke* (belt decorations). Entire rooms are devoted to Japanese and Chinese ceramics. The central hall contains stone religious sculptures from South Asia (primarily India).

Volunteer Park, 1400 E. Prospect St. © **206/654-3100.** www.seattleartmuseum.org. Admission $7
adults, $5 seniors and youths 13–17, free for children 12 and under. Free admission for all on 1st Thurs of
each month; free for seniors on 1st Fri of each month; free for families on 1st Sat of each month. Tues-
Wed and Fri-Sun 10am–5pm; Thurs 10am–9pm (closed Tues in winter). Closed New Year's Eve, New Year's
Day, Columbus Day, Thanksgiving, Christmas Eve, and Christmas. Bus: 10.

Volunteer Park Conservatory ★ This stately old Victorian conservatory, built in
1912, houses a large collection of tropical and desert plants, including palm trees,
orchids, and cacti, and features seasonal floral displays. Both the plants and the building
are beautiful and should not be missed. It's especially rewarding to visit on a rainy day.

Volunteer Park, 1400 E. Galer St. © **206/684-4743.** www.seattle.gov/parks/parkspaces/VolunteerPark/
conservatory.htm. Free admission. Memorial Day to Labor Day daily 10am–6pm; other months daily
10am–4pm. Bus: 10.

NORTH SEATTLE (INCLUDING BALLARD, FREMONT, MONTLAKE & THE U DISTRICT)

The **Fremont District,** which begins at the north end of the Fremont Bridge—near the
intersection of Fremont Avenue North and North 36th Street—is one of Seattle's funki-
est and most unusual neighborhoods. Even livelier, though not nearly as eclectic or
artistic, the **University District** (known locally as the U District) has loads of cheap
restaurants and the types of shops you would associate with a college-age clientele. But
the main attractions for visitors are the two excellent museums on the university campus
and the nearby Museum of History and Industry, which is just across the Montlake
Bridge from the U District.

Burke Museum ★★ At the northwest corner of the University of Washington campus, the Burke Museum features exhibits on the natural and cultural heritage of the
Pacific Rim and is the Northwest's foremost museum of paleontology, archaeology, and
ethnology. Permanent exhibits include *Life & Times of Washington State,* which covers
500 million years of Washington history (and prehistory) with lots of fossils, including a
complete mastodon. The second permanent exhibit, *Pacific Voices,* focuses on the many
cultures of the Pacific Rim and their connections to Washington State. In front of the

EXPLORING SEATTLE

7

THE NEIGHBORHOODS

Parking on the University of Washington campus is expensive on weekdays and Saturday mornings, so try to visit the Burke Museum or Henry Art Gallery on a Saturday afternoon or a Sunday, when parking is free.

museum stand several modern totem poles that are replicas of poles carved in the late 19th century. Because this museum is fairly large, it mounts touring shows that often make only a few other stops in the U.S., so be sure to check the exhibition schedule when you are in town.

[handwritten: EPIC TOTEM POLE COLLECTION]

University of Washington, 17th Ave. NE and NE 45th St. ℂ **206/543-5590** or 206/543-7907. www.burke museum.org. Admission $9.50 adults, $7.50 seniors, $6 children 5–18, free for children 4 and under. For $1 more, you can get admission to the nearby Henry Art Gallery. Free admission 1st Thurs of each month. Daily 10am–5pm (1st Thurs of each month until 8pm). Closed New Year's Day, July 4th, Thanksgiving, and Christmas. Bus: 30, 43, 49, 70, 71, 72, 73, or 74.

Henry Art Gallery   Expect the unexpected here—and prepare to be challenged in your concept of what constitutes art. The focus of the Henry Art Gallery, on the west side of the UW campus, is on contemporary art with retrospectives of individual artists, as well as exhibits focusing on specific themes or media. The museum benefits from large, well-lit gallery spaces illuminated by pyramidal and cubic skylights that can be seen near the main entrance. Photography and video are both well represented, and for the most part, the exhibits are the most avant-garde in the Seattle area. The museum's permanent Skyspace installation by James Turrell, who uses light to create his artwork, is worth the price of admission if you're the contemplative type. The Skyspace is a small room with an oval ceiling opening that frames the sky. At night, the outside of the glass Skyspace is illuminated by an ever-changing light show. The museum also has a cafe and a small sculpture courtyard. Parking is often available at the Central Parking Garage, at NE 41st Street and 15th Avenue NE. *[handwritten: 4100 15th Ave N h. Tues by UW. never working]*

University of Washington, 15th Ave. NE and NE 41st St. ℂ **206/543-2280.** www.henryart.org. Admission $10 adults, $6 seniors, free for students and children 13 and under. For $1 more, you can get admission to the nearby Burke Museum. Free admission 1st Thurs of each month. Tues–Wed and Fri–Sun 11am– 5pm; Thurs 11am–8pm. Closed New Year's Day, July 4th, Thanksgiving, Christmas Eve, and Christmas. Bus: 30, 43, 49, 70, 71, 72, 73, or 74.

Hiram M. Chittenden (Ballard) Locks ★★   For some strange reason, many people are intrigued by the concept of two side-by-side bodies of water on two different levels. Consequently, the Hiram M. Chittenden Locks are among the most popular attractions in the city. These locks, operated by the Army Corps of Engineers, consist of a small lock and a large lock. The latter accommodates barges and commercial fishing vessels, while the small lock stays busy shuttling small private boats between Puget Sound and the Lake Washington Ship Canal, which connects to both Lake Union and Lake Washington.

On the south side of the locks, there are fish ladders and fish-viewing windows that provide opportunities for salmon viewing during the summer months. The chance to see salmon in a fish ladder is as much of a draw as the locks themselves, and in the past the fish runs have also attracted hungry sea lions that at times become salmon-swallowing pests.

Good Times in Bad Taste

If your kids (or you) love bad jokes and are fascinated by the bizarre, you won't want to miss the Underground Tour and a visit to Ye Olde Curiosity Shop. Together, these two attractions should reassure you that espresso, traffic jams, and Microsoft aside, Seattle really does have a sense of humor.

If you have an appreciation for off-color humor and are curious about the seamier side of Seattle history, the **Underground Tour,** 608 First Ave. (© **206/ 682-4646;** www.undergroundtour.com), will likely entertain and enlighten you. The tours wander around below street level in the Pioneer Square area, where you can still find the vestiges of Seattle businesses built just after the great fire of 1889. Learn the lowdown dirt on early Seattle, a town where plumbing was problematic and a person could drown in a pothole. Tours are held daily. The cost is $15 for adults, $12 for seniors and students 13 to 17 or with college ID, and $7 for children 7 to 12; children 6 and under are discouraged from participating.

Ye Olde Curiosity Shop, Pier 54, 1001 Alaskan Way (© **206/682-5844;** www. yeoldecuriosityshop.com), is a cross between a souvenir store and Ripley's Believe It or Not! It's weird! It's wacky! It's tacky! The collection of oddities was started in 1899 by Joe Standley, who developed a more-than-passing interest in strange curios. See Siamese-twin calves, a natural mummy, the Lord's Prayer on a grain of rice, a narwhal tusk, shrunken heads, a 67-pound snail, fleas in dresses—all the stuff that may have fascinated you as a kid.

10-6 daily 9-9 F & Sat

Also here at the locks, you can stroll the grounds of the **Carl S. English, Jr. Botanical Gardens,** a park filled with rare and unusual shrubs and trees. March through November, there are free tours of the grounds Monday through Friday at 1 and 3pm, Saturday and Sunday at 11am and 1 and 3pm.

The locks are located a 10- to 15-minute drive north of downtown. Follow Elliott Avenue north along the waterfront from downtown Seattle; after crossing the Ballard Bridge, drive west on Northwest Market Street.

3015 NW 54th St. © **206/783-7059.** Free admission. Daily 7am–9pm (visitor center: May–Sept daily 10am–6pm; Oct–Apr Thurs–Mon 10am–4pm). Bus: 17.

Museum of History and Industry (MOHAI) ★ *COLLECTIBES* If the Underground Tour's (see "Good Times in Bad Taste," below) vivid description of life before the 1889 fire has you curious about what the city's more respectable citizens were doing back in those days, you can find out here, where re-created storefronts provide glimpses into their lives. Located at the north end of the Washington Park Arboretum, this museum explores Seattle's history with frequently changing exhibits on more obscure aspects of the city's past. While many of the displays will be of interest only to local residents, anyone wishing to gain a better understanding of the city's history may also enjoy the exhibits here. There's a Boeing mail plane from the 1920s, plus an exhibit on the 1889 fire that leveled the city. MOHAI also hosts touring exhibitions that address Northwest history. Although not

Montlake

Photos & Voices, Richard Bennel prints 1922 Ford Model T, 1930's Seattle in Legos, 1971 Motorcross Bike

WTO protests in Seatt, Boeing Plant I (WW II + Cold War)

actually in north Seattle, this museum is just across the Montlake Bridge from the University District.

McCurdy Park, 2700 24th Ave. E. ✆ **206/324-1126.** www.seattlehistory.org. Admission $8 adults, $7 seniors, $6 youths 5–17, free for children 4 and under; free admission 1st Thurs of each month. Daily 10am–5pm (until 8pm 1st Thurs of each month). Closed Thanksgiving and Christmas. Bus: 25 or 43. From I-5, take Wash. 520 east (exit 168B) to the Montlake exit, go straight through the stoplight to 24th Ave. E, and turn left.

Nordic Heritage Museum ★ **Finds**　Housed in a former school building, this is primarily a neighborhood museum focusing on the experiences of Scandinavian immigrants in Seattle's Ballard neighborhood. However, it also mounts exhibits of Scandinavian and Scandinavian-inspired art, and these temporary exhibits are what make the Nordic Heritage Museum worth seeking out for those who aren't of Scandinavian heritage. The Dream of America exhibit on the first floor does an excellent job of explaining why Scandinavians began immigrating to the United States and how they ended up settling in Ballard. Up on the third floor, each of the Nordic countries gets a display room of its own. In mid-July each year, the museum sponsors the Viking Days festival, which includes booths serving Nordic foods.

3014 NW 67th St. ✆ **206/789-5707.** www.nordicmuseum.org. Admission $6 adults, $5 seniors and college students, $4 5 years to 12th grade, free for children 4 and under. Tues–Sat 10am–4pm; Sun noon–4pm. Closed New Year's Day, Easter, Thanksgiving, Christmas Eve, and Christmas. Bus: 17 or 18.

Woodland Park Zoo ★★ **Kids**　This sprawling zoo has outstanding exhibits focusing on Alaska, tropical Asia, the African savanna, and the tropical rainforest. The brown-bear enclosure, one of the zoo's best exhibits, is a very realistic reproduction of an Alaskan stream and hillside. In the savanna, zebras gambol and giraffes graze contentedly near a reproduction of an African village. An elephant forest provides plenty of space for the zoo's pachyderms, and the gorilla and orangutan habitats are also nicely done. A farm-animal area is a big hit with the little ones, and young kids like the Zoomazium, an interactive educational play area where they can see what it's like to be wild animals.

750 N. 50th St. ✆ **206/548-2500.** www.zoo.org. Admission May–Sept $17 adults, $15 seniors, $11 children 3–12, free for children 2 and under; Oct–Apr $11 adults, $9 seniors, $8 children 3–12, free for children 2 and under. May–Sept daily 9:30am–6pm; Oct–Apr daily 9:30am–4pm. Parking $5. Bus: 5 or 82.

SOUTH SEATTLE

Museum of Flight **Kids**　Right next door to Boeing Field, at an active airport 15 minutes south of downtown Seattle, this museum will have aviation buffs walking on air. Housed inside the six-story glass-and-steel repository are some of history's most famous planes.

The collection of planes starts with a replica of the Wright brothers' 1903 plane and continues through to the present state of flight. Suspended in the Great Hall are more than 20 planes, including a 1935 DC-3, the first Air Force F-5 supersonic fighter, and the *Gossamer Albatross*, a human-powered airplane. The Personal Courage Wing houses 28 World War I and World War II fighter planes. You'll also see one of the famous Blackbird spy planes, which at one time were the world's fastest jets (you can even sit in the cockpit of one of these babies). There's also a rare World War II Corsair fighter that was rescued from Lake Washington and restored to its original glory. Visitors also get to board a retired British Airways Concorde supersonic airliner. An exhibit on the U.S. space program features an Apollo command module. Of course, you'll also see plenty of Boeing planes, including a reproduction of Boeing's first plane, which was built in 1916. The museum also incorporates part of Boeing's old wooden factory building, a remnant from the company's earliest years.

While any air-and-space museum lets you look at mothballed planes, not many have their own air-traffic control tower and let you watch aircraft taking off and landing at an active airfield. You can even take to the air here during the summer, when biplane rides are usually offered from in front of the museum.

The **Museum of Flight Restoration Center,** 2909 100th St. SW, Everett (© **425/745-5150**) is 30 minutes north of Seattle at Paine Field. Here you'll see planes in various stages of restoration. The center is open Tuesday through Thursday from 8am to 4pm and Saturday from 9am to 5pm. Call for directions. Paine Field is also where you'll find the **Future of Flight Aviation Center and Boeing Tour** (see below). Together, these two make a fascinating half-day outing.

9404 E. Marginal Way S. © **206/764-5720.** www.museumofflight.org. Admission $14 adults, $13 seniors, $7.50 children 5–17, free for children 4 and under. Free admission 1st Thurs of each month 5–9pm. Daily 10am–5pm (until 9pm 1st Thurs of each month). Closed Thanksgiving and Christmas. Bus: 174. Take exit 158 off I-5.

NORTH OF SEATTLE

Flying Heritage Collection Because of the Boeing connection, the Seattle area has an abundance of airplane-related attractions. Here at the Flying Heritage Collection, you can marvel at the 15 immaculately restored fighter planes that belong to Microsoft co-founder Paul Allen. Old fighter planes are another of Allen's interests, along with professional football (he owns the Seattle Seahawks) and rock music and science fiction (he owns the Experience Music Project and the Science Fiction Museum). Many of the rare planes in this collection are in flyable condition, and two to three times a month during the summer, planes take to the air over Paine Field. If you're visiting the Future of Flight Aviation Center (see below), you'll also want to stop by this little air museum.

Paine Field, 3407 109th St. SW, Everett. © **877/342-3404.** www.flyingheritage.com. Admission $12 adults, $10 seniors, $8 children 6–15, free for children 5 and under. Memorial Day to Labor Day daily 10am–5pm; other months closed Mon. Closed Thanksgiving, Christmas.

Future of Flight Aviation Center & Boeing Tour ★★ Before Bill Gates and Microsoft, **Boeing** was by far the largest employer in the Seattle area. Although the airplane manufacturer no longer has its corporate headquarters in Seattle, Boeing is still a major presence in the city, and it still has something that Microsoft can never claim: the single largest building, by volume, in the world. The company's Everett assembly plant could easily hold 911 basketball courts; 74 football fields; 2,142 average-size homes; or all of Disneyland (with room left over for covered parking). This impressive building is open to the public by guided tour, and a visit to the plant is one of the most interesting tourist activities in Seattle. On the tour, you'll get to see how huge passenger jets are assembled. In the Future of Flight Aviation Center, from which the tours leave, you can stick your head inside a giant jet engine, climb into the cockpit of a Boeing 727, design your own jet on a computer, or go for a ride in a flight simulator.

The guided 90-minute tours are offered on the hour from 9am to 3pm, and tickets for same-day use are sold on a first-come, first-served basis; in summer, tickets for any given day's tours often sell out by noon. To check availability of same-day tickets, call the number below. It's also possible to make reservations 24 hours or more in advance by calling © **800/464-1476** or 360/756-0086 daily between 9am and 5pm, or by booking online at the website below. If making reservations, you'll pay an extra $2.50 per ticket.

If you're in town without a car, you can book a tour to the plant through **Customized Tours** (© **800/770-8769** or 206/878-3965; www.customizedtours.net), which charges $56 and will pick you up at your Seattle hotel.

8415 Paine Field Blvd., Mukilteo. © **888/467-4777** or 425/438-8100. www.futureofflight.org. Admission $15 adults, $14 seniors, $8 children 4 ft. tall to age 15 (no children under 4 ft. tall on Boeing tour); exhibit hall only admission $9 adults, $4 children 6–15, free for children 5 and under. Daily 8:30am–5:30pm. Closed Thanksgiving, Christmas, and New Year's Day. Drive 30 miles north from Seattle on I-5, take exit 189 to Wash. 526 W., and continue 4 miles to the intersection of Paine Field Blvd. and 84th St. SW.

THE EASTSIDE

Bellevue Arts Museum ★ Located on the east side of Lake Washington a 20- to 30-minute drive from downtown Seattle, Bellevue was once just an upscale suburb but has become a city in its own right. With several large galleries that host shows and installations by regional and national artists, the Bellevue Arts Museum is one of the cultural underpinnings of this city's newfound urbanism. This museum also gives the public opportunities to interact with artists. To this end, the museum stages each July the Northwest's largest and most highly regarded art fair. During the rest of the year, it features frequent artist demonstrations. Stop by if you happen to be on the Eastside and are an art aficionado.

510 Bellevue Way NE, Bellevue. © **425/519-0770.** www.bellevuearts.org. Admission $9 adults, $7 seniors and students, free for children 5 and under. Free admission for everyone first Fri of each month. Mon–Thurs 11am–5pm; Fri 11am–8pm; Sat–Sun noon–5pm. Closed major holidays. From Seattle, take I-90 east over Lake Washington to the Bellevue Way exit, and drive north on Bellevue Way for approx. 2 miles.

Rosalie Whyel Museum of Doll Art ★ (Kids) If you're a doll collector or happen to be traveling with a child who likes playing with dolls, this Bellevue museum should definitely be part of your Seattle itinerary. Displays include more than 1,200 dolls from around the world, including 17th-century wooden dolls, 19th-century china dolls, and the original Barbie. Throughout the year, the museum has special exhibits that focus on different types of dolls.

1116 108th Ave. NE, Bellevue. © **425/455-1116.** www.dollart.com. Admission $8 adults, $7 seniors, $5 children 5–17, free for children 4 and under. Mon–Sat 10am–5pm; Sun 1–5pm. Closed New Year's Day, Easter, July 4th, Thanksgiving, and Christmas. From Seattle, take Wash. 520 east over the Evergreen Point Bridge to I-405 S.; then take the NE Eighth St. westbound exit and turn right on 108th Ave. NE.

5 ARCHITECTURAL GEMS

Of course, Seattle's most famous architectural landmark is the **Space Needle** (p. 132), which, when it was built for the 1962 World's Fair, was envisioned as the look of things to come. Now that the 21st century is upon us, the reality of 21st-century architecture is far stranger than was imagined. Frank Gehry's design for the building that now houses both the **Experience Music Project** (p. 129) and the **Science Fiction Museum and Hall of Fame** (p. 132) is one of the city's most bizarre buildings, but it faces stiff competition from the skewed glass-cube architecture of the **Seattle Central Library.**

Chapel of St. Ignatius ★ Lest you think subtlety is a concept unknown to architects commissioned to design contemporary buildings in Seattle, pay a visit to this tasteful little chapel on the campus of Seattle University, a Catholic institution. Designed by architect Steven Holl, the chapel was conceived as "seven bottles of light in a stone box," with each of those bottles reflecting an aspect of Catholic worship. The "bottles" are basically a means of channeling light into the chapel, and though the exterior seems rather stark and angular, on the inside, soft, multihued light suffuses the rooms. The chapel is something of an exploration of the ways natural light can illuminate a building, and the overall effect is positively enchanting.

Seattle University, E. Marion St. and 12th Ave. E. ℭ 206/296-5588. www.seattleu.edu/chapel. Free admission. Mon–Thurs 7am–10pm; Fri 7am–7pm; Sat 8am–5pm; Sun 8am–10pm. Bus: 12.

Seattle Central Library ★★ It isn't often that the library is considered one of the coolest places in town, but Seattle's downtown library is such an architectural wonder that it is one of the city's highlights. When the building opened in 2004, its design created a rift among many locals, who either loved it or hated it. Indeed, there wasn't much of a middle ground with this giant glass cube and its diamond-patterned steel girders and strange angles. Regardless of your reaction to architect Rem Koolhaas's design, you can't help but notice that in a town known for its gray skies, this library abounds with natural light. There are also colorful spongy chairs, floors of bamboo and brushed metal, carpets printed to look like plants, and an outdoor garden designed to meld with the indoor carpets. On the first and third Monday of each month, from noon to 1pm, you can catch "Thrilling Tales! A Storytime for Adults," a program of lunchtime readings aimed not at kids, as is usually the case, but at adults. Oh, and if you need to use the Internet, this place has hundreds of computer terminals, too.

1000 Fourth Ave. ℭ 206/386-4636. www.spl.org. Free admission. Mon–Thurs 10am–8pm; Fri–Sat 10am–6pm; Sun noon–6pm. Closed New Year's Day, Martin Luther King, Jr. Day, Presidents Day, Easter, Memorial Day, July 4th, Labor Day, Veterans Day, Thanksgiving, Christmas Eve, and Christmas. Bus: Any Fourth Ave. bus.

6 PARKS & PUBLIC GARDENS

PARKS

Seattle's many parks are part of what make it such a livable city and an enjoyable place to visit. In the downtown area, **Myrtle Edwards Park** ★, 3130 Alaskan Way W. (ℭ 206/684-4075), at the north end of the waterfront, is an ideal spot for a sunset stroll with views of Puget Sound and the Olympic Mountains. The park includes a 1.25-mile paved pathway. At its north end, this park connects with the Port of Seattle's **Elliott Bay Park.**

Freeway Park, at Sixth Avenue and Seneca Street, is one of Seattle's most unusual parks. Built right on top of busy I-5, this green space is more like a series of urban plazas, with terraces, waterfalls, and cement planters creating walls of greenery. You'd never know that a roaring freeway lies beneath your feet. Unfortunately, although the park is convenient, the isolated nature of its many nooks and crannies often gives it a deserted and slightly threatening feel.

For serious communing with nature, nothing will do but 534-acre **Discovery Park** ★★, 3801 W. Government Way (ℭ 206/386-4236). Occupying a high bluff and sandy point jutting into Puget Sound, this is Seattle's largest and wildest park. You can easily spend a day wandering its trails and beaches. The visitor center is open Tuesday through Sunday from 8:30am to 5pm. Discovery Park is a 15-minute drive from downtown; to get here, follow the waterfront north from downtown Seattle toward the Magnolia neighborhood and watch for signs to the park. Alternatively, you can take bus 24 or 33 from downtown.

Fish Gotta Swim

It's no secret that salmon in the Puget Sound region have dwindled to dangerously low numbers. But it's still possible to witness the annual return of salmon in various spots around the sound.

In the autumn, on the waterfront, you can see returning salmon at the **Seattle Aquarium** (p. 125), which has its own fish ladder. But the very best place to see salmon is at the **Hiram M. Chittenden (Ballard) Locks,** 3015 NW 54th St. (© **206/783-7059;** see p. 137 for directions and hours). Between June and September (July–Aug are the peak months), you can view salmon through underwater observation windows as they leap up the locks' fish ladder.

East of Seattle, in downtown Issaquah, salmon can be seen year-round at the **Issaquah Salmon Hatchery,** 125 W. Sunset Way (© **425/391-9094** or 425/427-0259). However, it is in the fall that adult salmon can be seen returning to the hatchery. Each year on the first weekend in October, the city of Issaquah holds the Issaquah Salmon Days Festival to celebrate the return of the natives.

When you reach the park, follow signed trails down to the beach and out to the lighthouse at the point. Although the lighthouse is only occasionally open to the public, the views from the beach make this a good destination for an hour's walk. The beach and park's bluff-top meadows both make good picnic spots.

Up on Capitol Hill, at East Prospect Street and 14th Avenue East, you'll find **Volunteer Park ★★,** 1247 15th Ave. E. (© 206/684-4075), which is surrounded by the elegant mansions of this old neighborhood. It's a popular spot for sunning and playing Frisbee™, and is home to the Seattle Asian Art Museum (p. 136), an amphitheater, a water tower with a superb view of the city, and a conservatory filled with tropical and desert plants. With so much variety, you can easily spend a morning or afternoon exploring this park.

On the east side of Seattle, along the shore of Lake Washington, you'll find not only swimming beaches but also 300-acre **Seward Park ★,** 5902 Lake Washington Blvd. S. (© 206/684-4396). This large park's waterfront may be its biggest attraction, but it also has a dense forest with trails winding through it. Keep an eye out for the bald eagles that nest here. The park is south of the I-90 floating bridge off Lake Washington Boulevard South. From downtown Seattle, follow Madison Street northeast and turn right onto Lake Washington Boulevard.

Near Alki Beach in West Seattle, **Jack Block Park,** 2130 Harbor Ave. SW (© 206/728-3654), is well worth a visit. The park, wedged between the port and Elliott Bay, has a .25-mile paved walkway that meanders along beside the water. The path eventually leads to a viewing tower overlooking both the water and the port. Kids will love watching all the port's cool equipment and the boats coming and going. Now, I know I've made this park sound like it's in the middle of an industrial area, but it actually has plenty of natural shoreline. For the little ones, there's even a play area that incorporates old buoys. You'll find the park adjacent to Terminal 5 on Harbor Avenue.

North Seattle has several parks worth visiting, including the unique **Gas Works Park** ★, 2101 N. Northlake Way, at Meridian Avenue North (✆ **206/684-4075**), at the north end of Lake Union. In the middle of its green lawns looms the rusting hulk of an old industrial plant; the park's small Kite Hill is the city's favorite kite-flying spot.

Moving farther north, on Green Lake Drive North near Woodland Park Zoo, you'll find **Green Lake Park** ★★, 7201 E. Green Lake Dr. N. (✆ **206/684-4075**), a center for exercise buffs who jog, bike, and skate on its 2.8-mile paved path. It's also possible to picnic on the many grassy areas and swim in the lake (there are changing rooms and a beach with summer lifeguards).

North of the Ballard neighborhood is **Golden Gardens Park** ★★, 8498 Seaview Place NW (✆ **206/684-4075**), which, with its excellent views of the Olympic Mountains and its somewhat wild feeling, is my favorite Seattle waterfront park. It has great views, some small wetlands, and a short trail. Golden Gardens is best known as one of Seattle's best beaches, too, and even though the water here is too cold for swimming, the sandy beach is a pleasant spot for a sunset stroll. People often gather on summer evenings to build fires on the beach. To reach this park, drive north from the waterfront on Elliott Avenue, which becomes 15th Avenue West; after crossing the Ballard Bridge, turn left on Market Street and follow this road for about 2 miles (it will change names to become NW 54th St. and then Seaview Ave. NW).

PUBLIC GARDENS

See also the listings for the **Volunteer Park Conservatory** (p. 136) and the **Hiram M. Chittenden Locks** (p. 137).

Bellevue Botanical Garden ★   Any avid gardener should be sure to make a trip across one of Seattle's two floating bridges to the city of Bellevue and its Bellevue Botanical Garden. This 53-acre garden is one of the Northwest's most-talked-about perennial gardens. The summertime displays of flowers, in expansive mixed borders, are absolutely gorgeous. You can also see a Japanese garden, a shade border, and a water-wise garden (designed to conserve water). April through October, free guided tours of the garden are offered Saturday and Sunday at 2pm.

Wilburton Hill Park, 12001 Main St., Bellevue. ✆ **425/452-2750**. www.bellevuebotanical.org. Free admission. Daily dawn to dusk; visitor center daily 9am–4pm. From Seattle, take Wash. 520 east over the Evergreen Point Bridge to I-405 S.; then take the NE Eighth St. exit east, turn right on 120th Ave. NE, continue ³/₄ mile and turn left on Main St.

Japanese Garden   Covering 3½ acres, the Japanese Garden is a perfect little world unto itself, with a cherry orchard (for spring color), babbling brooks, and a lake rimmed with Japanese irises and filled with colorful koi (Japanese carp). A special tea garden encloses a teahouse, where several times each month between April and October, you can attend a traditional tea ceremony ($10). Unfortunately, noise from a nearby road can be distracting. Between April and October, there are free guided tours of the gardens Wednesday at 12:30pm and Saturday and Sunday at 12:30 and 2:30pm (May–Aug, there are also tours Mon at 12:30pm).

Washington Park Arboretum, 1075 Lake Washington Blvd. E. (north of E. Madison St.). ✆ **206/684-4725**. Admission $5 adults; $3 seniors, college students, and youths 6–17; free for children 5 and under. Late Mar to early May Tues–Sun 10am–7pm; early May to mid-Aug daily 10am–8pm; mid-Aug to mid-Sept daily 10am–7pm; mid-Sept to mid-Oct Tues–Sun 10am–6pm; mid-Oct to late Oct Tues–Sun 10am–5pm; early Nov to mid-Nov Tues–Sun 10am–4pm. Closed mid-Nov to late Mar. Bus: 11.

Kubota Garden ★ This 20-acre Japanese-style garden, in a working-class neighbor- hood not far from the shores of Lake Washington in South Seattle, was the life's work of garden designer Fujitaro Kubota. Today the gardens are a city park, and the mature landscaping and hilly setting make this the most impressive and enjoyable Japanese garden in the Seattle area. Kubota began work on this garden in 1927, and over the years built a necklace of ponds, a traditional stroll garden, and a mountainside garden complete with waterfalls. A tall, arched moon bridge is a highlight. The self-taught Kubota went on to design gardens at Seattle University and at the Bloedel Reserve on Bainbridge Island. Between April and October, free tours of the gardens are offered at 10am on the fourth Saturday of the month.

9817 55th Ave. S. (at Renton Ave. S). ℭ **206/684-4584.** www.kubota.org. Free admission. Daily dawn to dusk. From downtown, take I-5 south to exit 158 (Pacific Hwy. S/E. Marginal Way), turn left toward Martin Luther King Jr. Way, and continue uphill on Ryan Way; turn left on 51st Ave. S., right on Renton Ave. S., and right on 55th Ave. S. Bus: 106.

Washington Park Arboretum ★ The acres of trees and shrubs in Washington Park Arboretum stretch from the far side of Capitol Hill all the way to the Montlake Cut (a canal connecting Lake Washington to Lake Union). Within the 230-acre arboretum are 4,600 varieties of plants and quiet trails that are pleasant throughout the year but are at their most beautiful in spring, when the azaleas, cherry trees, rhododendrons, and dogwoods are all in bloom. The north end of the arboretum, a marshland that is home to ducks and herons, is popular with bird-watchers as well as kayakers and canoeists (see "Outdoor Pursuits," later in this chapter, for places to rent a canoe or kayak). A boardwalk with views across Lake Washington meanders along the waterside in this area (though noise from the adjacent freeway detracts considerably from the experience).

2300 Arboretum Dr. E. ℭ **206/543-8800.** www.depts.washington.edu/wpa/general.htm. Free admission. Daily dawn to dusk; visitor center daily 10am–4pm. Enter on Lake Washington Blvd. E. off E. Madison St.; or take Wash. 520 off I-5 north of downtown, take the Montlake Blvd. exit, and go straight through the 1st intersection. Bus: 43.

---

7 ESPECIALLY FOR KIDS

In addition to the listings below, kids will also enjoy many of the attractions described earlier in this chapter, including the **Seattle Aquarium** (p. 125), the **Pacific Science Center** (p. 132), and **Woodland Park Zoo** (p. 139).

Adolescent and preadolescent boys seem to unfailingly love **Ye Olde Curiosity Shop** and the **Underground Tour** (see p. 138 for both). Younger kids also love the **Museum of Flight** (p. 139).

And even the surliest teenagers will think you're pretty cool for taking them to the **Experience Music Project** (p. 129).

Do the kids need to burn off some energy? See "Parks & Public Gardens" (p. 142) for descriptions of Seattle's best recreational areas; "Outdoor Pursuits" (p. 150) for the lowdown on beaches, biking, and in-line skating; and "Spectator Sports" (p. 155) for details on Seattle's professional football, baseball, and soccer teams.

You might also be able to catch a performance at the **Seattle Children's Theatre** (ℭ **206/441-3322;** www.sct.org), in Seattle Center (see below); or at the **Northwest Puppet Center,** 9123 15th Ave. NE (ℭ **206/523-2579;** www.nwpuppet.org).

Children's Museum (Kids) The Children's Museum is in the basement of the Center House at Seattle Center, which is partly why Seattle Center is such a great place to spend a day with the kids. The museum includes plenty of hands-on cultural exhibits, a child-size neighborhood, a Discovery Bay for toddlers, a mountain wilderness area, a global village, and other special exhibits to keep the little ones busy learning and playing for hours.

Seattle Center, Center House, 305 Harrison St. © **206/441-1768.** www.thechildrensmuseum.org. Admission $7.50 adults and children, $6.50 seniors, free for children under 1. Mon–Fri 10am–5pm; Sat–Sun 10am–6pm. Closed New Year's Day, Thanksgiving, and Christmas. Bus: 1, 2, 3, 4, 5, 13, 15, 16, 18, 19, 24, 26, 28, 30, 33, 81, or 82. Monorail: From Westlake Center at the corner of Pine St. and Fourth Ave.

Seattle Center ★ (Kids) If you want to keep the kids entertained all day long, head to Seattle Center. This 74-acre cultural center and amusement park stands on the northern edge of downtown at the end of the monorail line. The most visible building at the center is the **Space Needle** (p. 132), which provides an outstanding panorama of the city from its observation deck. However, of much more interest to children are the **Fun Forest** (© **206/728-1585;** www.funforest.com), with its roller coaster, log flume, merry-go-round, Ferris wheel, arcade games, and minigolf; the **Children's Museum** (see above); and **Seattle Children's Theatre** (see above). This is also Seattle's main festival site, and in the summer months hardly a weekend goes by without some special event filling its grounds. On hot summer days, the **International Fountain** is a great place for kids to keep cool (bring a change of clothes).

305 Harrison St. © **206/684-7200.** www.seattlecenter.com. Free admission; pay per ride or game (various multiride tickets available). Fun Forest outdoor rides: Days and hours vary with season (call for hours). Indoor attractions open year-round at 11am (closing time varies). Bus: 1, 2, 3, 4, 5, 13, 15, 16, 18, 19, 24, 26, 28, 30, 33, 81, or 82. Monorail: From Westlake Center at the corner of Pine St. and Fourth Ave.

8 ORGANIZED TOURS

For information on the **Underground Tour,** see p. 138.

WALKING TOURS

In addition to the walking tours mentioned here, there are Pike Place Market tours offered by the market itself. See the Pike Place Market listing on p. 126 for details.

If you'd like to explore downtown Seattle with a knowledgeable guide, join one of the informative walking tours offered by **See Seattle Walking Tours** (© **425/226-7641;** www.see-seattle.com). These tours visit Pike Place Market, the waterfront, the Pioneer Square area, and the International District. Tours cost $20 and can last as much as 6 hours, depending on how much stamina you have. There must be a minimum of six people signed up before a tour begins.

You can also learn a lot about local history and wander through hidden corners of the city on the 2-hour tours run by **Duse McLean/Seattle Walking Tours** (© **425/885-3173;** www.seattlewalkingtours.com). These tours wind their way from the International District to Pike Place Market, taking in historic buildings, public art, and scenic vistas. Tours are $15 per person, are offered year-round by reservation, and require a minimum of three people to go out.

For an insider's glimpse of life in Seattle's Chinatown/International District, hook up with **Chinatown Discovery Tours** (© **206/623-5124;** www.seattlechinatowntour.com). On these walking tours, which last 1½ hours, you learn the history of this colorful and

Bus Tours

If you'd like an overview of Seattle's main tourist attractions, or if you're pressed for time during your visit, you can pack in a lot of sights on a city tour with **Gray Line of Seattle** (© 800/824-8897 or 206/626-5200; www.graylineseattle.com). Half-day tours cost $35 for adults, $18 for children. Many other options, including tours to Mount Rainier National Park and to the Boeing plant in Everett, are also available. Gray Line also operates a **Double-Decker Tour** in open-top buses. These city tours run from June through September and cost $21 for adults and $11 for children. Buses depart from seven stops around the city; call for details or keep an eye out for a parked double-decker bus. To glimpse a bit more of Seattle on a guided van tour, try the "Explore Seattle Tour" offered by **Customized Tours** (© **800/770-8769** or 206/878-3965; www.customizedtours.net), which charges $46 per person. This tour stops at Pike Place Market, the Hiram M. Chittenden Locks and Fish Ladder, and the Klondike Gold Rush Historical Park. The company also offers a Boeing plant tour ($56 per person) and a Snoqualmie Falls and wineries tour ($70 per person).

historic neighborhood. Rates (for four or more on a tour) start from $17 for adults, $12 for students, and $10 for children.

Foodies, take note. You're probably already aware that you should spend lots of time in Pike Place Market, sampling all the great foods and eating in the many excellent restaurants. If you want a real behind-the-scenes look at how local chefs utilize the market, take one of the **Chef's Tours of the Market.** On these tours, local chefs (often from some of my favorite area restaurants) lead you through the market stalls to select ingredients. Once you've learned the ins and outs of shopping the market, you get to watch as the day's chef prepares a meal with the ingredients purchased that morning. Best of all, you get to eat what's been created. The tours, which are held once or twice a month, last 3½ hours and cost $95. For information and reservations, contact the **Market Foundation** (© **206/774-5249;** www.pikeplacemarketfoundation.org).

Food-focused tours of the market are also offered by **Savor Seattle** (© **888/987-2867;** www.savorseattletours.com), which charges $41 for a 2-hour tour and also offers a coffee-and-chocolate tour, and **Seattle Food Tours** (© **206/725-4483;** http://seattlefoodtours.com), which charges $42 for a 2½-hour tour and also offers a tour of Belltown restaurants. If you want to learn more about the famous Seattle coffee culture, go on a coffee crawl with **Seattle by Foot** (© **800/838-3006;** www.seattlebyfoot.com). These 2-hour tours, which leave from under the neon coffee mug (Pike St. and Post Alley) in Pike Place Market, cost $24 if you make a reservation and $27 if you just show up. This company also does an evening Seattle pub crawl.

BOAT TOURS

In addition to the boat tours and cruises mentioned below, you can do your own low-budget "cruise" simply by hopping on one of the ferries operated by **Washington State Ferries** (© **800/843-3779** or 888/808-7977 in Washington, or 206/464-6400; www.wsdot.wa.gov/ferries). Try the Bainbridge Island or Bremerton ferries out of Seattle for a 1½- to 2½-hour round-trip. For more information on these ferries, see p. 30.

On the Water on the Cheap

If you don't go boating a few times while you're in Seattle, then you've missed the point. This city is defined by its waterways, and on sunny summer afternoons it sometimes seems as if half the population is out on the water. However, you don't have to take an expensive dinner cruise to see Seattle from sea level. The city has lots of inexpensive options for getting out on the water. If these suggestions don't float your boat, I don't know what will.

How about an hour on Lake Union in a classic wooden boat for absolutely nothing? On Sunday afternoons, the **Center for Wooden Boats** (see p. 128) offers free boat rides. Just be sure to sign up early. Just north of downtown Seattle, you can also take a very short, though free, boat ride at the **Elliott Bay Marina** at the foot of Magnolia Bluff. The boat ride crosses barely a few yards of water at the marina and drops you at a jetty with a stupendous view of Elliott Bay and the city skyline. The listing for Maggie Bluffs Marina Grill (see p. 104) has details.

For $3, you can ride the **King County Water Taxi** (see p. 30) from the Seattle waterfront to Alki Beach in West Seattle. For $6.70, you can ride a **Washington State Ferry** (see p. 30) to Bainbridge Island (a 35-minute trip) or Bremerton (a one-hour trip). Even better, as a walk-on passenger, your return trip is free. For only $7.50 per hour, you can rent a canoe or rowboat at the University of Washington's **Waterfront Activities Center** (p. 153) and paddle around the marshes at the north end of the Washington Park Arboretum.

However, for the best free boat ride in Seattle, you will, unfortunately (or fortunately), have to stay at the metro area's most luxurious waterfront hotel. Guests at the **Woodmark Hotel, Yacht Club & Spa on Lake Washington** (see p. 76) can arrange to go for a two-hour cruise on the hotel's restored 1956 Chris-Craft speedboat.

If you don't have enough time for an overnight trip to the **San Juan Islands,** it's still possible to get a feel for these picturesque islands by riding the San Juan Islands ferry from Anacortes to Friday Harbor. These ferries depart from Anacortes, 75 miles north of Seattle. If you get off in Friday Harbor, you can spend a few hours exploring this town before returning to Anacortes. Alternatively, if you have more money to spend (and even less time), boat tours of the San Juan Islands depart from the Seattle waterfront. For information on ferries and boat excursions to the San Juan Islands, see chapter 11, "Side Trips from Seattle."

If you opt for only one tour while in Seattle, the **Tillicum Village Tour** ★★, Pier 55 (© **800/642-7816** or 206/623-1445; www.tillicumvillage.com) should be it—it's unique and truly Northwestern. The tour includes a boat excursion, a salmon dinner, and Northwest Coast Indian masked dances. The salmon dinner is pretty good, and the traditional dances are fascinating (although more for the craftsmanship of the masks than for the dancing itself). Located in Blake Island State Park, across Puget Sound from Seattle, and accessible only by boat, Tillicum Village was built in conjunction with the 1962 Seattle World's Fair. The "village" is actually just a large restaurant and performance

Seattle by Duck

Paul Revere would have had a hard time figuring out what to tell his fellow colonists if the British had arrived by Duck. A Duck, if you don't know, is a World War II amphibious vehicle that can arrive by land or by sea, and these odd-looking vehicles now provide tours of Seattle on both land and water. Duck tours take in the standard city sights, but then plunge right into Lake Union for a tour of the Portage Bay waterfront, with its many houseboats and great views. The 90-minute tours leave from a parking lot across from the Space Needle; they cost $25 for adults and $15 for kids. Contact **Seattle Duck Tours** ★, 516 Broad St. (✆ **800/817-1116** or 206/441-DUCK; www.seattleducktours.net). Because these tours encourage visitors to get a little daffy, they're very popular; reservations are recommended.

hall fashioned after a traditional Northwest Coast longhouse, but with the totem poles standing vigil out front, the forest encircling the longhouse, and the waters of Puget Sound stretching out into the distance, Tillicum Village is a beautiful spot. After the dinner and dances, you can strike out on forest trails to explore a bit of the island. There are even beaches on which to relax. Tours are $80 for adults, $73 for seniors, $30 for children 5 to 12, and free for children 4 and under. They're offered daily from May through September and on weekends in October and April.

Seattle is a city surrounded by water; so while you're here, you should be sure to set sail one way or another. **Argosy Cruises** ★ (✆ 800/642-7816 or 206/623-1445; www.argosycruises.com) offers the greatest variety of boat-tour options. If you're short on time, just do the 1-hour harbor cruise that departs from Pier 55 ($18–$22 adults, $8.50–$10 children 5–12) or the 2½-hour cruise from Lake Union through the Hiram M. Chittenden Locks to Elliott Bay ($34–$41 adults, $12–$13 children). This latter tour departs from Pier 56 and includes a bus connection between the waterfront and Lake Union. Argosy also operates two Lake Washington cruises that will take you past Bill Gates's fabled waterfront Xanadu. The 2-hour cruise departs from the AGC Marina at the south end of Lake Union ($27–$33 adults, $11–$12 children), while the 1½-hour cruise departs from the city dock in downtown Kirkland on the east side of the lake ($31 adults, $11 children). Of these options, I recommend the cruise through the locks; it may be the most expensive outing, but you get good views and the chance to navigate the locks. Reservations are recommended for all cruises; in rate ranges above, the higher rates are for cruises between mid-March and early September. Want a meal with your cruise? Try one of Argosy's lunch, brunch, or dinner cruises aboard this company's *Royal Argosy.* Lunch and brunch cruises are $51 to $62 for adults and $24 for children 5 to 12; dinner cruises are $87 to $98 for adults and $33 to $43 for children. These cruises get my vote for best dinners afloat.

I also like the "Sunday Ice Cream Cruises" offered on Sunday afternoon by the *m/v Fremont Avenue.* These 45-minute cruises, operated by **Seattle Ferry Service** (✆ 206/284-2828 or 206/713-8446; www.seattleferryservice.com), putter around Lake Union in a cute little tour boat. These tours cost $11 for adults, $10 for seniors, $7 for children 5 to 13, and $2 for children 4 and under. They even allow pets on board the boat! Ice cream is sold on board, as are chocolate root beer floats. During the summer, there are

Seattle Noir

If your tastes run to the macabre, you might be interested in the tours offered by **Private Eye on Seattle** ★ (✆ **206/365-3739;** www.privateeyetours.com). These somewhat bizarre van tours are led by a private eye named Jake, who shares stories of interesting and unusual cases from the Emerald City. Tours are $25 per person. Another option is a tour of some of the city's haunted locales. The ghoulishly inclined might also want to take a **Market Ghost Tour** (✆ **206/322-1218;** www.seattleghost.com) and get in touch with the souls that haunt Pike Place Market. Tours cost $15 per person.

also 1-hour cruises on Fridays and Saturdays. These tours cost $15 for adults, $7 for children 5 to 13, and $2 for children 4 and under. The *m/v Fremont Avenue* departs from Lake Union Park at the south end of Lake Union (take the Seattle Streetcar to the Lake Union Park station).

If you prefer a quieter glimpse of Seattle from the water, from May to mid-October **Emerald City Charters/Let's Go Sailing,** Pier 54 (✆ **206/624-3931;** www.sailingseattle. com), offers 1½- and 2½-hour sailboat cruises. The longer excursions are at sunset. The cruises cost $25 and $40 for adults, $20 and $35 for seniors, and $18 and $30 for children 11 and under.

SCENIC FLIGHTS & HOT-AIR BALLOON RIDES

Seattle is one of the few cities in the United States where floatplanes are a regular sight in the skies and on the lakes. If you want to see what it's like to take off and land from the water, you've got a couple of options.

Seattle Seaplanes ★, 1325 Fairview Ave. E. (✆ **800/637-5553** or 206/329-9638; www. seattleseaplanes.com), which takes off from the southeast corner of Lake Union, offers 20-minute scenic flights over the city for $88. This company also offers flights to nearby waterfront restaurants for dinner.

If you'd rather pretend you're back in the days of the Red Baron, you can go up in a vintage biplane with **Olde Thyme Aviation** ★ (✆ **206/730-1412;** www.oldethyme aviation.com), which operates from Boeing Field. A 20-minute flight along the Seattle waterfront to the Space Needle costs $135 for two people; other flights range in price from $165 to $549 for two people. Keep in mind that these flights operate only when weather conditions are appropriate.

Seattle isn't known as a hot-air-ballooning center, but if you'd like to try floating over the Northwest landscape not far outside the city, contact **Over the Rainbow** (✆ **206/ 364-0995** or 425/861-8611; www.letsgoballooning.com), which flies over the wineries of the Woodinville area. Flights are offered in both the morning and the afternoon and cost $169 to $225 per person.

9 OUTDOOR PURSUITS

See "Parks & Public Gardens" (p. 142) for a rundown of great places to play.

BEACHES

Alki Beach ★, across Elliott Bay from downtown Seattle, is the city's most popular beach and is the nearest approximation you'll find in the Northwest to a Southern California beach scene. The paved path that runs along this 2½-mile beach is popular with skaters, walkers, and cyclists, and the road that parallels the beach is lined with shops, restaurants, and beachy houses and apartment buildings. But the views across Puget Sound to the Olympic Mountains confirm that this is indeed the Northwest. (Despite those views, this beach lacks the greenery that makes some of the city's other beaches so much more appealing.) From April through October, a water taxi operates between the downtown Seattle waterfront and Alki Beach; see p. 30 for details. By the way, Alki rhymes with *sky,* not *key.*

For a more Northwestern beach experience (which usually includes a bit of hiking or walking), head to one of the area's many waterfront parks. **Lincoln Park,** 8011 Fauntleroy Way SW (© **206/684-4075**), south of Alki Beach in West Seattle, has bluffs and forests backing the beach. Northwest of downtown Seattle in the Magnolia area, you'll find **Discovery Park** ★★, 3801 W. Government Way (© **206/386-4236**), where miles of beaches are the primary destination of most park visitors. To reach Discovery Park, follow Elliott Avenue north along the waterfront from downtown Seattle, take the W. Dravus Street exit and go west across the overpass, and turn right on 20th Avenue W./ Gilman Avenue W., which becomes W. Government Way and leads to the park's main entrance.

Golden Gardens Park ★★, 8498 Seaview Place NW (© **206/684-4075**), north of Ballard and Shilshole Bay, is my favorite Seattle beach park. Although the park isn't very large and is backed by railroad tracks, the views of the Olympic Mountains are magnificent, and on summer evenings people build fires on the beach. Lawns and shade trees make Golden Gardens ideal for a picnic.

Several parks along the shores of Lake Washington have small stretches of beach, many of which are popular with hardy swimmers. **Seward Park** ★, 5902 Lake Washington Blvd. S. (© **206/684-4396**), southeast of downtown Seattle, is a good place to hang out by the water and do a little swimming. From downtown, take Madison Street east to Lake Washington Boulevard and turn right. Although this isn't the most direct route to Seward Park, it's the most scenic. Along the way, you'll pass plenty of other small parks, including Mount Baker Beach.

BIKING

Montlake Bicycle Shop, 2223 24th Ave. E. (© **206/329-7333;** www.montlakebike. com), rents bikes by the day for $25 to $100. This shop is just south of the Montlake

Seeing the Light

When the first settlers arrived in the Seattle area, their ship dropped them at Alki Point. Today this point of land jutting out into Puget Sound is still important to mariners as the site of the **Alki Lighthouse,** 3201 Alki Ave. SW (© **206/217-6203**). The lighthouse is open for tours from June through August on Saturday and Sunday afternoons from 1:30 to 4pm.

Bridge and is convenient to the **Burke-Gilman/Sammamish River Trail** ★★, a 27-mile paved pathway created mostly from an old railway bed. This immensely popular path is a great place to take the family for a bike ride or to get in a long, vigorous ride without having to deal with traffic. The Burke-Gilman portion of the trail starts in the Ballard neighborhood of North Seattle, but the most convenient place to start a ride is at **Gas Works Park,** on the north shore of Lake Union. From here you can ride north and east, by way of the University of Washington, to **Kenmore Logboom Park,** at the north end of Lake Washington. Serious riders can continue on from Kenmore Logboom Park on the Sammamish River portion of the trail, which leads to **Marymoor Park,** at the north end of Lake Sammamish. Marymoor Park is the site of a velodrome (bicycle racetrack). This latter half of the trail is my favorite part; it follows the Sammamish River and passes through several pretty parks. Riding the entire trail out and back is a ride of more than 50 miles and is popular with riders in training for races. Plenty of great picnicking spots can be found along both sections of the trail.

The West Seattle bike path along **Alki Beach** is another good place to ride; it offers great views of the sound and the Olympics. If you'd like to pedal this pathway, you can rent single-speed bikes at **Alki Kayak Tours,** 1660 Harbor Ave. SW (✆ **206/953-0237;** www.kayakalki.com), which charges $7 per hour. Because this outfitter has a limited number of bikes, it's a good idea to call ahead and make a reservation. You can then take the water taxi from the downtown waterfront to West Seattle; the dock is right at the Alki Kayak Tours building.

GOLF

While Seattle isn't a name that springs immediately to the minds of avid golfers, the sport inspires just as much passion here as it does across the country. Should you wish to get in a round while you're in town, Seattle has three conveniently located municipal golf courses: **Jackson Park Golf Course,** 1000 NE 135th St. (✆ **206/363-4747**); **Jefferson Park Golf Course,** 4101 Beacon Ave. S. (✆ **206/762-4513**); and **West Seattle Golf Course,** 4470 35th Ave. SW (✆ **206/935-5187**). This latter course has great views of the Seattle skyline and gets my vote as the best of the city's municipal courses. All three charge very reasonable green fees of between $30 and $35. For more information on these courses, see **www.seattlegolf.com.**

HIKING

Within Seattle itself there are several large nature parks laced with enough trails to allow for a few good, long walks. Among these are **Seward Park,** 5902 Lake Washington Blvd. S., southeast of downtown, and **Lincoln Park,** 8011 Fauntleroy Way SW, south of Alki Beach in West Seattle.

The city's largest natural park, and Seattleites' favorite spot for a quick dose of nature, is **Discovery Park,** 3801 W. Government Way (✆ **206/386-4236**), northwest of downtown, at the western tip of the Magnolia neighborhood. Covering more than 500 acres, this park has many miles of trails and beaches to hike—not to mention gorgeous views, forest paths, and meadows in which to laze away after a long walk. To reach Discovery Park, follow Elliott Avenue north along the waterfront from downtown Seattle, take the W. Dravus Street exit and go west across the overpass, and turn right on 20th Avenue W./ Gilman Avenue W., which becomes W. Government Way and leads to the park's main entrance.

My favorite area hike, the trail up **Mount Si** ★★, is also the most challenging hike near Seattle. The rugged, glacier-carved peak, which is just a 30- to 45-minute drive east

of downtown on I-90, rises abruptly from the floor of the Snoqualmie Valley outside the **153**
town of North Bend and has an exhausting trail to its summit. However, the payoff is
awesome views. (Take lots of water—it's an 8-mile round-trip hike.) From I-90, take the
North Bend exit (exit 31), drive into town, turn right at the stoplight onto North Bend
Way, continue through town, turn left onto Mount Si Road, and continue 2 miles to the
trail head.

Farther east on I-90, at **Snoqualmie Pass** and just west of the pass, are several trail
heads. Some trails lead to mountain summits, others to glacier-carved lakes, and still
others past waterfalls deep in the forest. Because of their proximity to Seattle, these trails
can be very crowded, and you will need a Northwest Forest Pass ($5 for a 1-day pass) to
leave your car at national-forest trail heads (though not at the Mount Si trail head, which
is on state land). My favorite trail in this area is the 8-mile round-trip hike to beautiful
Snow Lake, a cool pool of subalpine waters surrounded by granite mountains. The trail
head is just north of I-90 on Alpental Road (take exit 52). For more information and to
purchase a Northwest Forest Pass, contact the **Snoqualmie Ranger District,** 902 SE
North Bend Way (© **425/888-1421;** www.fs.fed.us/r6/mbs), in North Bend.

JOGGING

The **waterfront,** from Pioneer Square north to Myrtle Edwards Park, where a paved path
parallels the water, is a favorite downtown jogging route. The residential streets of **Capitol Hill,** when combined with roads and sidewalks through **Volunteer Park,** are another
good choice. If you happen to be staying in the University District, you can access the
27-mile **Burke-Gilman/Sammamish River Trail** or run the ever-popular trail around
Green Lake. Out in West Seattle, the **Alki Beach** pathway is also very popular and
provides great views of the Olympics. Spring through fall, you can access this trail via
water taxi; see p. 30 for details.

SEA KAYAKING, CANOEING, ROWING & SAILING

If you'd like to try your hand at **sea kayaking** ★★, head to the **Northwest Outdoor
Center** ★★, 2100 Westlake Ave. N. (© **800/683-0637** or 206/281-9694; www.nwoc.
com), on the west side of Lake Union. Here you can rent a sea kayak for between $13
and $20 per hour. You can also opt for guided tours lasting from a few hours to several
days, and there are plenty of classes available for those who are interested.

Moss Bay Rowing, Kayaking and Sailing Center, 1001 Fairview Ave. N. (© **877/
244-8896** or 206/682-2031; www.mossbay.net), rents sea kayaks, rowing shells, and
sailboats at the south end of Lake Union near Chandler's Cove. Rates range from $13 per
hour for a single kayak to $18 per hour for a double. Because this rental center is a little
closer to downtown Seattle, it's a better choice if you are here without a car.

If you're interested in renting a wooden rowboat or sailboat on Lake Union, see the
listing for the **Center for Wooden Boats,** on p. 128.

On the University of Washington campus behind Husky Stadium is the **Waterfront
Activities Center** (© **206/543-9433;** www.depts.washington.edu/ima/IMA_wac.php),
which is open to the public and rents canoes and rowboats for $8 per hour. With the
marshes of the Washington Park Arboretum directly across a narrow channel from the
boat launch, this is an ideal place for beginner canoeists to rent a boat.

In this same general area, you can rent kayaks at the **Agua Verde Paddle Club,** 1303
NE Boat St. (© **206/545-8570;** www.aguaverde.com), at the foot of Brooklyn Avenue
on Portage Bay (the body of water between Lake Union and Lake Washington). Kayaks
can be rented from March through October and go for $15 to $18 per hour. Best of all,

this place is part of the Agua Verde Cafe, a great Mexican restaurant! Before or after a paddle, be sure to get an order of tacos. See chapter 6 for details.

At **Green Lake Boat Rental,** 7351 E. Green Lake Dr. N. (② **206/527-0171;** www.greenlakeboatrentals.net), in North Seattle not far from Woodland Park Zoo, you can rent canoes, paddleboats, sailboats, and rowboats for a bit of leisurely time on the water. A paved path circles the park, which is one of the most popular in Seattle (it's a great place to join crowds of locals enjoying one of the city's nicest green spaces). Kayaks, canoes, rowboats, and paddleboats all rent for $14 per hour, and sailboats go for $20 per hour.

And now for something completely different. If you're not up for paddling, how about an electric boat? The **Electric Boat Company,** Westlake Landing Building, 2046 Westlake Ave. N. (② **206/223-7476;** www.theelectricboatco.com), rents boats that will hold your whole family (up to 10 people). The boats rent for $89 per hour (2-hr. minimum) and are a fun and safe way to cruise around Lake Union and check out the houseboats. You can even stop at one of the lakefront restaurants for a meal or drinks. I'm sure you'll get asked lots of questions about the boat.

SKIING

One of the reasons Seattleites put up with long, wet winters is because they can go skiing within an hour of the city. And with many slopes set up for night skiing, it's possible to leave work and hit the slopes before dinner, ski for several hours, and be back home in time to get a good night's rest. The ski season in the Seattle area generally runs from late November to late April. Equipment can be rented at the ski area listed below or at **REI,** 222 Yale Ave. N. (② **888/873-1938** or 206/223-1944; www.rei.com).

CROSS-COUNTRY SKIING In the Snoqualmie Pass area of the Cascade Range, less than 50 miles east of Seattle on I-90, the **Summit Nordic Center** (② **425/434-6708;** www.summitatsnoqualmie.com) offers rentals, instruction, and many miles of groomed trails.

Several Sno-Parks (designated cross-country ski areas) are along I-90 at Snoqualmie Pass. Some have groomed trails; others have trails that are marked but not groomed. Be sure to get a **Sno-Park permit** ($10–$11 for a 1-day pass; $30–$31 for a season pass), which is required if you want to park at a cross-country ski area. Sno-Park permits are available at ski shops; pick one up when renting your skis.

DOWNHILL SKIING Jointly known as the **Summit at Snoqualmie** (② **425/434-7669** for information, or 206/236-1600 for the snow report; www.summit-at-snoqualmie.com), the Alpental, Summit West, Summit Central, and Summit East ski areas are all located at Snoqualmie Pass, less than 50 miles east of Seattle off I-90. Together, these four ski areas offer more than 65 runs, rentals, and lessons. Adult all-day lift tickets cost $55. Call for hours of operation.

TENNIS

Seattle Parks and Recreation operates dozens of outdoor tennis courts all over the city. The most convenient are at **Volunteer Park,** 1247 15th Ave. E. (at E. Prospect St.).

If it happens to be raining and you have your heart set on playing tennis, indoor public courts are available at the **Amy Yee Tennis Center,** 2000 Martin Luther King, Jr. Way S. (② **206/684-4764**). Rates here are $25 for singles and $30 for doubles for 1¼ hours. This center also has outdoor courts that cost $10 for 1½ hours.

Although in 2008, Seattle lost the Supersonics, its NBA basketball team, it is still home to professional football, baseball, ice hockey, soccer, and women's basketball, as well as the various University of Washington Huskies teams.

Ticketmaster (© **206/346-1660;** www.ticketmaster.com) sells tickets to almost all sporting events in the Seattle area. You'll find Ticketmaster outlets at area Fred Meyer stores.

BASEBALL

Seattle's most popular professional sports team is the **Mariners** (© **206/346-4000** or 206/346-4001; www.seattlemariners.com), part of Major League Baseball's American League. The team has a devoted following, so buy your tickets well in advance if you want to see a game.

The Mariners' retro-style **Safeco Field** ★★★ is one of the most beautiful ballparks in the country. It's also one of only a handful of stadiums with a retractable roof (which can open or close in 10–20 min.), allowing the Mariners a real grass playing field without the worry of getting rained out.

Ticket prices range from $8 to $75. Though you may be able to buy a single ticket on game day at the Safeco Field box office, it's tough to get two seats together. If you want to ensure that you get good seats, order in advance at **Mariners Team Stores** (there are locations at Fourth and Stewart sts. downtown and in the Bellevue Square shopping mall) or through **Ticketmaster** (© **206/622-HITS;** www.ticketmaster.com), which has outlets at Fred Meyer stores. Parking is next to impossible in the immediate vicinity of Safeco Field, so plan to leave your car behind.

If you'd like a behind-the-scenes look at the ballpark, you can take a **1-hour tour,** which costs $9 for adults, $7 for seniors, and $7 for kids 3 to 12. Tickets can be purchased at the Mariners Team Store at Safeco Field, at other Mariners Team Stores around the city, or through Ticketmaster. Tour times vary, and tours are not offered on days when day games are scheduled.

BASKETBALL

With the Seattle SuperSonics leaving on a jet plane for Oklahoma City in 2008, Seattle is without an NBA team. However, for the time being, the WNBA's **Seattle Storm** (© **206/217-WNBA;** www.stormbasketball.com) is still playing pro ball in Seattle Center's Key Arena. Ticket prices range from $15 to $160; they're available at the arena box office or through Ticketmaster (© **877/962-2849**).

The **University of Washington Huskies** women's basketball team has also been very popular for years. For information on both the women's and the men's Huskies basketball games, call © **206/543-2200** or go to www.gohuskies.com.

FOOTBALL

Ever since they made it to the Super Bowl in 2006, the **Seattle Seahawks** (© **888/635-4295** or 425/203-8000; www.seahawks.com) have been getting way more respect in their home town than they used to get. So, you may find it difficult to get your hands on tickets if you decide on the spur of the moment to attend a Seahawks game. The Seahawks play at **Qwest Field,** 800 Occidental Ave. S. (© **206/381-7500;** www.qwest field.com), which is adjacent to Safeco Field. Tickets to games run from around $49 to more than $394 and are sold through **Ticketmaster** (© 206/622-HAWK; www.ticket master.com). Regardless of how the Seahawks are doing in a particular year, games against Oakland, Denver, and a couple of other teams usually sell out as soon as tickets go on sale in July or August. Traffic and parking in the vicinity of Qwest Field is a night-mare on game days, so take the bus if you can. If you want a behind-the-scenes look at Qwest Field, you can take a tour of the stadium. Tours operate daily at 12:30 and 2:30pm between June and August and only on Friday and Saturday in other months. *Note:* No tours are given on game days or when other events are scheduled. Tours cost $7 for adults and $5 for seniors and children 4 to 12.

Not surprisingly, the **University of Washington Huskies** (© 206/543-2200; www. gohuskies.com), who play in Husky Stadium on the university campus, have a loyal fol-lowing. Big games (Nebraska or Washington State) sell out as soon as tickets go on sale in the summer. Other games can sell out in advance, but obstructed-view tickets are usu-ally available on game day. Ticket prices range from $65 to $70 for reserved seats, and from $30 to $35 for general admission.

HORSE RACING

The state-of-the-art **Emerald Downs,** 2300 Emerald Downs Dr., Auburn (© 888/931-8400 or 253/288-7000; www.emeralddowns.com), is south of Seattle, in Auburn, off Wash. 167 (reached from I-405 at the south end of Lake Washington). To get to the racetrack, take the 15th Street Northwest exit. Admission is $7. The season runs from mid-April to September.

THE MARATHON

The **Seattle Marathon** (© 206/729-3660; www.seattlemarathon.org), which attracts more than 12,000 participants, takes place the Sunday after Thanksgiving. The race starts and ends at Seattle Center and crosses the I-90 floating bridge to Mercer Island.

SOCCER

If you're a soccer fan, you can catch the United Soccer League's **Seattle Sounders** (© 877/ MLS-GOAL; www.soundersfc.com) at Qwest Field. Tickets, which sell for $20 to $85, are available through Ticketmaster (© 206/628-0888).

---

11 DAY SPAS

Seattle has plenty of day spas scattered around the metro area. These facilities offer such treatments as massages, facials, seaweed wraps, mud baths, and the like. Expect to pay $170 to $295 or more for a half-day of pampering and $330 to more than $650 for a full day.

Convenient Seattle day spas include **Gene Juarez Salons,** 607 Pine St. (© 206/326-6000; www.genejuarez.com), and **Etherea Salon and Spa,** 2001 First Ave. (© 206/441-5511; www.ethereasalon.com) and 1015 First Ave. (© 206/628-9605).

North of downtown, good choices include **Habitude at the Locks,** 2801 NW Market St. (© 206/782-2898; www.habitude.com), and its sister location, **Habitude Fremont,** 513 N. 36th St. (© 206/633-1339).

City Strolls

Downtown Seattle is compact and easily explored on foot (if you don't mind hills), and, among visitors to the city, the most popular stroll is along the waterfront, from Pioneer Square to Pike Place Market. Everything along the waterfront is right there to be seen, so you don't really need me to outline the specifics. Instead, I've focused on spots that can be a little confusing, the sorts of places where you might overlook some of the gems.

Although you can easily enjoy Pike Place Market simply by getting lost in the market maze for several hours, you might want to consult the first walking tour I've outlined below just so you don't miss any of the highlights.

Some people make the mistake of dismissing the Pioneer Square area as a neighborhood of street people, but it is much more than that. To help you get the most out of downtown Seattle's only historic neighborhood, my second walking tour takes in interesting shops, art galleries, and historic buildings.

The third walking tour will take you through the Fremont District. Home to counterculture types, Fremont is a quirky area filled with tongue-in-cheek art and unusual shops.

WALKING TOUR 1   PIKE PLACE MARKET

Start:	At the corner of Pike Street and First Avenue.
Finish:	At the corner of Pike Street and First Avenue.
Time:	Approximately 4 hours, including shopping and dining.
Best Times:	Weekends, when crafts vendors set up along Pike Place.
Worst Times:	Weekends, when the market is extremely crowded.

Despite the crowds of tourists and locals, Pike Place Market, a sprawling complex of historic buildings and open-air vendors' stalls, remains Seattle's most fascinating attraction. You'll find aisles lined with fresh produce, cut flowers, and seafood, as well as unusual little shops tucked away in the many hidden corners of this multilevel maze. Street performers also take to the streets here, adding another level of fun to a meander through the market.

Because Pike Place Market is so large, it is easy to overlook some of its more interesting businesses and its many quirky works of public art. The following walking tour is meant to lead you through the market, past the many places you wouldn't want to miss. For more information on the market, see p. 126.

Start your tour at the corner of Pike Street and First Avenue at the:

❶ Pike Place Market Information Kiosk

This tiny cubicle is one of the most important buildings in the market. Here you can pick up a copy of the market newspaper, which has a map of the market.

Directly behind the information kiosk rises the famous Pike Place Market neon sign and clock. Just below this sign you'll find:

② Rachel the Pig

This life-size bronze statue of a pig is the unofficial Pike Place Market mascot and also doubles as the market piggy bank. Each year, people deposit thousands of dollars into *Rachel*. Hardly any visitor to the market goes home without a shot of some friend or family member sitting on the pig.

It's sometimes difficult to spot *Rachel* because of the crowds that gather here to watch the flying fish at:

③ Pike Place Fish

The antics of the fishmongers at Pike Place Fish are legendary. No, they don't actually sell flying fish, but if you decide to buy, say, a whole salmon, your fish will go flying through the air (amid much shouting and gesticulating) from the front of the stall to the back, where someone will steak it or fillet it for you and even pack it on dry ice so that you can take it home with you on the plane.

To the right of Pike Place Fish begin the market's main:

④ Produce Stalls

In summer, look for fresh cherries, berries, peaches, and melons; in the fall it's Washington State apples. Stalls full of colorful cut flowers also line this section of the market.

As you wander through this crowded section of the market, keep an eye out for: M-Sat 8-5

⑤ Chukar Cherries Sun 10-5

This Washington State candy company, at 1529-B Pike Place (℗ **206/623-8043**), specializes in chocolate-covered dried cherries. Samples are always available.

A little farther along, you'll come to the North Arcade, where you'll find lots of:

⑥ Crafts Vendors

This is a good place to shop for handmade souvenirs. These craftspeople know their clientele, so most of the work here is small enough to fit in a suitcase.

On weekends, you can find more crafts vendors along this side of the street just past the end of the covered

market stalls. Across Western Avenue from the last of these outdoor crafts stalls is:

⑦ Steinbrueck Park

Although this small, grassy park is favored by the homeless, it is also home to a pair of impressive totem poles and offers a superb view of Elliott Bay. Watch for the comings and goings of the giant car ferries that link Seattle to Bainbridge Island and Bremerton on the far side of Puget Sound.

From the park, walk back across Western Avenue and Pike Place and head toward your starting point. You'll now be on the opposite side of Pike Place from the produce stalls. This stretch of the market has lots of great prepared-food stalls, so be sure to do a little grazing. If you've become convinced that Pike Place Market is strictly for tourists, climb the stairs to the:

⑧ Lisa Harris Gallery

This art gallery, at 1922 Pike Place (℗ **206/443-3315**), always seems to have interesting contemporary artwork, largely by Northwestern artists.

A little way up the street, you'll find what was once the only: 6-7:45; 6:30

⑨ Starbucks

That's right, years ago this narrow space, at 1912 Pike Place (℗ **206/448-8762**), was the only Starbucks in the world. Unlike today's Starbucks, this espresso bar has no tables or chairs; it's strictly a grab-it-and-go spot. Since you've already been on your feet for a while and still have a lot of the market to see, you may want to stop in and order a grande mocha to see you through the rest of your walking tour. Also be sure to notice how different the mermaid here looks compared to today's official logo. By the way, this was not the first Starbucks; it had been in a previous location before moving to the market.

How about a little something tasty to go with that mocha?

⑩ Le Panier

Located at 1902 Pike Place (℗ **206/441-3669**), this French-style bakery has good croissants and other pastries to accompany your espresso. They also have breads to go with that pepper jelly you bought earlier.

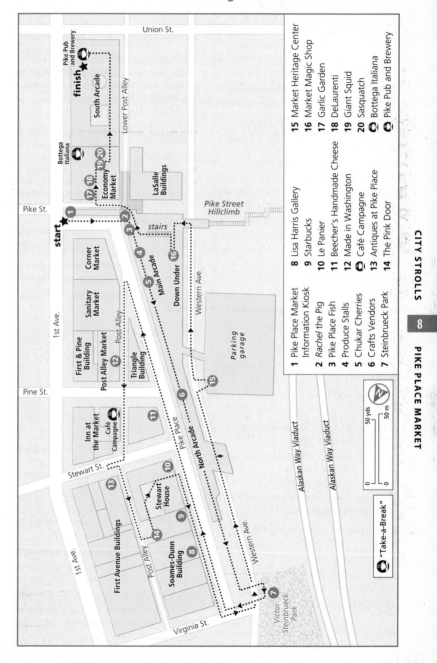

Union St.

Pike Pub and Brewery

finish ★

South Arcade

Lower Post Alley

Bottega Italiana

17 18

Economy Market

19 20

LaSalle Buildings

Pike St.

1 start ★

2

3

stairs

4

Corner Market

Sanitary Market

5

Main Arcade

Down Under 16

First & Pine Building

Post Alley Market 12

Post Alley

Triangle Building

1st Ave.

Pine St.

Inn at the Market

Café Campagne

11

Western Ave.

Pike Street Hillclimb

6

15

Parking garage

Stewart St.

13

Stewart House

10

9

Pike Place

North Arcade

First Avenue Buildings

Post Alley

14

Soames-Dunn Building

8

1st Ave.

Western Ave.

Virginia St.

Victor Steinbrueck Park

Alaskan Way Viaduct

Alaskan Way Viaduct

N

0 ────── 50 yds
0 ────── 50 m

"Take-a-Break"

1 Pike Place Market Information Kiosk
2 *Rachel*/the Pig
3 Pike Place Fish
4 Produce Stalls
5 Chukar Cherries
6 Crafts Vendors
7 Steinbrueck Park

8 Lisa Harris Gallery
9 Starbucks
10 Le Panier
11 Beecher's Handmade Cheese
12 Made in Washington
13 Antiques at Pike Place
14 The Pink Door

15 Market Heritage Center
16 Market Magic Shop
17 Garlic Garden
18 DeLaurenti
19 Giant Squid
20 Sasquatch
Bottega Italiana
Pike Pub and Brewery

Café Campagne

CITY STROLLS

8

PIKE PLACE MARKET

Continue along Pike Place in the same direction, and in the next block you'll see: 9-6

⑪ Beecher's Handmade Cheese
Here, at 1600 Pike Place (☎ **206/956-1964**), you can watch cheese being made and taste samples of the goods. This place also does a yummy macaroni and cheese.

Continue along Pike Place for another block, passing several more prepared-food stalls, and then turn left into Post Alley. This narrow lane cuts through several blocks of the market, and many shops and restaurants open onto it. For Seattle souvenirs, it's hard to beat:

⑫ Made in Washington
Shortly after you start up the narrow lane, you'll come to this store, at 1530 Post Alley (☎ **206/467-0788**). It carries smoked salmon, prepared foods, crafts, books, and plenty of other inexpensive stuff from here in Washington.

TAKE A BREAK
Pike Place Market is full of surprises, not the least of which are the many excellent restaurants hidden away in quiet corners of the complex. One of my very favorites is Café Campagne, 1600 Post Alley (☎ **206/728-2233**), a classy little French cafe serving delicious lunches. The atmosphere is très French. Don't confuse this restaurant with the much more expensive and formal Campagne, which is above the cafe.

Continue up the alley, and at Stewart Street, on the north side of the street, you'll see:

⑬ Antiques at Pike Place
This large antiques mall, at 92 Stewart St. (☎ **206/441-9643**), has more than 80 dealers. The stalls are packed full of interesting collectibles.

Back on Post Alley, watch for:

⑭ The Pink Door
This restaurant, at 1919 Post Alley (☎ **206/443-3241**), is one of the market's most famous dinner spots. No sign marks it out front, just the pink door. A flight of stairs leads down to an Italian restaurant and cabaret/bar. The deck is *the* place to eat on summer evenings.

From Post Alley, descend to Pike Place via the staircase to the left of The Pink Door. These stairs lead down to a building with a shady courtyard. After walking through the building, turn right and go to the corner of Virginia Street. Cross Pike Place, turn left, and walk down Western Avenue to the:

⑮ Market Heritage Center
At 1533 Western Avenue, in this open-air exhibit on the history of Pike Place Market, you can learn all about the various incarnations of the market since its inception. If you'd like to do a guided walking tour similar to this one, you can contact the Market Foundation at the number above.

Continue down Western Avenue, and in a couple of blocks you'll come to the Pike Street Hill Climb, a network of stairways that connect the waterfront with Pike Place Market. If you head up the stairs, you'll find the market's Down Under area, which consists of long hallways lined with small shops. My favorite shop in the Down Under is the:

⑯ Market Magic Shop
Located on the Down Under's fourth level, the Market Magic Shop (☎ **206/624-4271**) sells all kinds of tricks and paraphernalia for magicians. Kids love this shop, as do aspiring magicians. Directly across the hall from this shop are some unusual coin-operated window displays of giant shoes. Don't miss them!

If you leave the Down Under by way of the market stairs that are an extension of the Pike Hill Climb, you will find yourself back in the vicinity of *Rachel* the pig and Pike Place Fish. From here, make your way through the crowd of people waiting to see the fish fly and head into the Economy Building. In the walkway leading toward First Avenue, you'll find the:

⑰ Garlic Garden
This stall, at 93 Pike St. #3 (☎ **206/405-4022**), is famous for its pungent Lebanese Breeze garlic spread, which is great on bread. Just be sure that everyone in your group has some; this stuff may not be pure garlic, but it sure tastes like it.

Across the hall from the Garlic Garden, you'll find:

⑱ DeLaurenti

This Italian grocery, at 1435 First Ave. (✆ **206/622-0141**), has a great deli case full of Italian cheeses and meats. It also sells imported pastas and has a good selection of wines and beers. Samples of various olive oils are often available.

If you exit DeLaurenti through the door in the wine shop area, you'll be in an atrium, from the ceiling of which hangs a:

⑲ Giant Squid

This life-size copper sculpture was created by a local artist. Although you won't see any squids this size in the nearby Seattle Aquarium (on the waterfront), you can see a live giant octopus there.

⑳ Sasquatch

Beneath the giant squid you'll come face to face with a life-size wooden sculpture of the Northwest's legendary and elusive Sasquatch, also known as Bigfoot.

☕ **WINDING DOWN**
From Sasquatch and the giant squid, head down the hall to The Pike Pub, 1415 First Ave. (✆ **206/622-6044**), where you can enjoy a cool microbrewed beer and relax in one of the pub's easy chairs. Alternatively, you can head outside to First Avenue, where you can get a creamy gelato at Bottega Italiana, 1425 First Ave. (✆ **206/343-0200**).

WALKING TOUR 2   **THE PIONEER SQUARE AREA**

Start:	Pioneer Place at the corner of Yesler Way and First Avenue.
Finish:	Elliott Bay Book Company.
Time:	Approximately 5 hours, including shopping, dining, and museum stops.
Best Times:	Weekdays, when the neighborhood and the Underground Tour are not so crowded.
Worst Times:	Weekends, when the area is very crowded, and Mondays, when galleries are closed.

In the late 19th century, Pioneer Square was the heart of downtown Seattle, so when a fire raged through these blocks in 1889, the city was devastated. Residents and merchants quickly began rebuilding and set about to remedy many of the infrastructure problems that had faced Seattle in the years before the fire. Unfortunately, rebuilding outpaced the city's plans to raise the level of city streets, and by the time streets were raised, many of the Pioneer Square area's buildings had already been constructed. Consequently, the street-level of today was originally the second story for many of the neighborhood's buildings. You can learn all about this area's history on one of the tours operated by Underground Tour (p. 138).

Today this small section of the city is all that remains of old Seattle. Because one architect, Elmer Fisher, was responsible for the design of many of the buildings constructed after the fire, the neighborhood has a distinctly uniform architectural style.

While wandering these streets, don't bother looking for a specific site called Pioneer Square; you won't find it. The name actually applies to the whole neighborhood, not a plaza surrounded by four streets, as you would surmise. Do keep your eye out for interesting manhole covers, many of which were cast with maps of Seattle or Northwest Coast Indian designs. Also be aware that this neighborhood, the original Skid Row, still has several missions and homeless shelters—consequently, expect to see a lot of street people in the area.

To get the most out of downtown Seattle's only historic neighborhood, I've outlined a walking tour that takes in shops, art galleries, and historic buildings.

Start your tour of this historic neighborhood at the corner of Yesler Way and First Avenue on:

❶ Pioneer Place

The triangular plaza at the heart of Pioneer Square is the site of both a bust of Chief Seattle and a Tlingit totem pole. For information on the history of this totem pole, see "Pole to Pole" in chapter 7. Also on this plaza is a 1905 cast-iron pergola that was reconstructed after a truck crashed into it in 2001.

Facing the square are several historic buildings, including the gabled Lowman Building and three buildings noteworthy for their terra-cotta facades. In one of these buildings, at 608 First Ave., you'll find the ticket counter for Seattle's:

❷ Underground Tour

This tour takes a look at the Pioneer Square area from beneath the sidewalks. The tour (☎ **206/682-4646** for information) is a great introduction to the history of the area (if you don't mind off-color jokes) and actually spends quite a bit of time aboveground, duplicating much of the walking tour outlined here.

In the basement of the Pioneer Building, 602 First Ave., one of the architectural standouts on Pioneer Place, you'll find the:

❸ Pioneer Square Antique Mall

This store (☎ **206/624-1164**) is home to dozens of antiques and collectibles dealers.

Running along the south side of Pioneer Place is:

❹ Yesler Way

This was the original Skid Row. In Seattle's early years, logs were skidded down this road to a lumber mill on the waterfront, and the road came to be known as Skid Road. These days, Yesler Way is trying hard to live down its reputation, but because of the number of missions in this neighborhood, a lot of street people are still in the area (and they'll most certainly be asking you for change as you wander the streets).

TAKE A BREAK

If you skipped the Underground Tour, then cross Yesler Way to the Starbucks at Yesler and First Avenue, where you can pick up a latte to help fuel you through this walking tour. Right next door to Starbucks is Cow Chip Cookies, 102A First Ave. S. (☎ **206/292-9808**), where you can get one of the best (though messiest) chocolate-chip cookies you'll ever eat.

With cookie and coffee in hand, glance up Yesler Way, past a triangular parking deck (a monstrosity that prompted the movement to preserve the rest of this neighborhood), to:

❺ Smith Tower

This building, at 506 Second Ave. (☎ **206/622-4004**), was the tallest building west of the Mississippi when it was completed in 1914. The observation floor, near the top of this early skyscraper, is open to the public and provides a very different perspective of Seattle than does the Space Needle. The ornate lobby and elevator doors are also worth checking out.

Now walk back down to First Avenue and turn left, away from Pioneer Place. At the next corner, Washington Street, look across First Avenue and admire the:

❻ Maynard Building

This ornate building, which was named for Seattle founding father David "Doc" Maynard, was the site of Seattle's first bank.

Heading up Washington Street away from the water for half a block will bring you to:

❼ Laguna

This vintage pottery shop, at 116 S. Washington St. (☎ **206/682-6162**), specializes in mid-20th-century pottery, primarily from California. Fiesta, Bauer, and Weller are all well represented.

From here, head back to First Avenue and turn left. On this block, you'll find:

❽ Fireworks Fine Crafts Gallery

This gallery, at 210 First Ave. S. (☎ **206/682-9697**), sells colorful and unusual crafts by Northwest artisans.

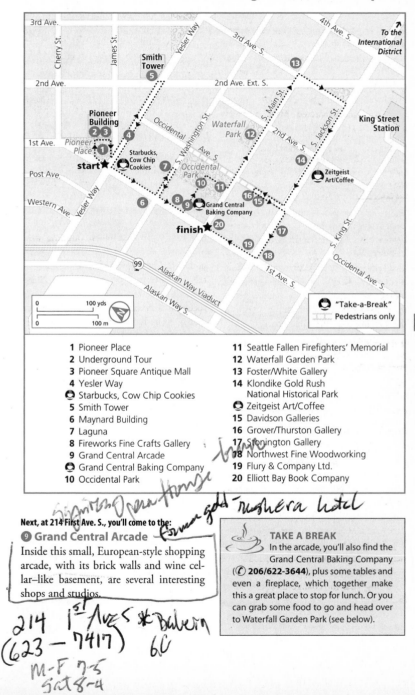

3rd Ave.

Cherry St.

James St.

Yesler Way

3rd Ave. S.

4th Ave. S.

↗
To the
International
District

Smith
Tower
5

2nd Ave.

2nd Ave. Ext. S.

13

Pioneer
Building
2 3

4

Occidental

S. Washington St.

Waterfall
Park **12**

S. Main St.

2nd Ave. S

S. Jackson St.

King Street
Station

1st Ave.

Pioneer
Place **1**

start ★

Starbucks,
Cow Chip
Cookies **7**

Ave. S.

Occidental
Park

10 11

14

Zeitgeist
Art/Coffee

Post Ave.

6

8 9

16 15

Western Ave.

Yesler Way

Grand Central
Baking Company

finish ★ 20

17

S. King St.

19

Occidental Ave. S.

18

99

Alaskan Way Viaduct

Alaskan Way S.

1st Ave. S.

| 0 | 100 yds |
| 0 | 100 m |

"Take-a-Break"

Pedestrians only

CITY STROLLS

8

THE PIONEER SQUARE AREA

1 Pioneer Place	**11** Seattle Fallen Firefighters' Memorial
2 Underground Tour	**12** Waterfall Garden Park
3 Pioneer Square Antique Mall	**13** Foster/White Gallery
4 Yesler Way	**14** Klondike Gold Rush
☕ Starbucks, Cow Chip Cookies	National Historical Park
5 Smith Tower	☕ Zeitgeist Art/Coffee
6 Maynard Building	**15** Davidson Galleries
7 Laguna	**16** Grover/Thurston Gallery
8 Fireworks Fine Crafts Gallery	**17** Stonington Gallery
9 Grand Central Arcade	**18** Northwest Fine Woodworking
☕ Grand Central Baking Company	**19** Flury & Company Ltd.
10 Occidental Park	**20** Elliott Bay Book Company

Signature Opera House [handwritten] *former gold rush era hotel [handwritten]*

Next, at 214 First Ave. S., you'll come to the:

❾ Grand Central Arcade — *former [handwritten]*

Inside this small, European-style shopping
arcade, with its brick walls and wine cellar–like basement, are several interesting
shops and studios.

*214 1ˢᵗ Aves * Bakery [handwritten]*
(623 – 7417) 6U [handwritten]
M–F 7–5 [handwritten]
Sat 8–4 [handwritten]

☕ **TAKE A BREAK**
In the arcade, you'll also find the
Grand Central Baking Company
(📞 **206/622-3644**), plus some tables and
even a fireplace, which together make
this a great place to stop for lunch. Or you
can grab some food to go and head over
to Waterfall Garden Park (see below).

Leaving Grand Central Arcade through the door opposite where you entered will bring you to:

⑩ Occidental Park

On this shady, cobblestone plaza stand four totem poles carved by Northwest artist Duane Pasco. The tallest is the 35-foothigh *The Sun and Raven,* which tells the story of how Raven brought light into the world. Next to this pole is *Man Riding a Whale.* This type of totem pole was traditionally carved to help villagers during their whale hunts. The other two figures that face each other are symbols of the Bear Clan and the Welcoming Figure.

This shady park serves as a gathering spot for homeless people, so you may not want to linger. However, before leaving the park, be sure to notice the grouping of bronze statues, the:

⑪ Seattle Fallen Firefighters' Memorial

This memorial is a tribute to four firefighters who died in a 1995 warehouse fire in Chinatown.

The statues are adjacent to South Main Street, and if you walk up this street to the corner of Second Avenue, you will come to:

⑫ Waterfall Garden Park

The roaring waterfall here looks as if it were transported straight from the Cascade Range. The park is built on the site of the original United Parcel Service (UPS) offices and makes a wonderful place for a rest or a picnic lunch.

Continue up Main Street to the corner of Third Avenue South, where you'll find, at 220 Third Ave. S., another of my favorite Seattle galleries, the:

⑬ Foster/White Gallery

This gallery (℡ 206/622-2833), one of the largest galleries in the West, is best known for its art glass. It's the Seattle gallery for famed glass artist Dale Chihuly and always has several of his works on display.

Now walk south on Third Avenue South to South Jackson Street and turn right. Continue to the corner of Second Avenue South, where, at 319 Second Ave. S., you'll find the:

⑭ Klondike Gold Rush National Historical Park

Not really a park, this small museum (℡ 206/220-4240) is dedicated to the history of the 1897–98 Klondike gold rush, which helped Seattle grow from an obscure town into a booming metropolis.

> ☕ **TAKE A BREAK**
> If it's time for another latte, cross South Jackson Street to Zeitgeist Art/Coffee, 171 S. Jackson St. (℡ 206/583-0497), which serves good coffee in a sort of vintage bookstore setting.

One block west is Occidental Mall, where you'll find a couple of art galleries, including:

⑮ Davidson Galleries

You never know what to expect when you walk through the front door here at 313 Occidental Ave. S. (℡ 206/624-7684). The gallery sells everything from 16th-century prints to contemporary prints and drawings by Northwest artists.

⑯ Grover/Thurston Gallery

Colorful, cartoonish, whimsical art—often with an edginess to it—is frequently featured at this gallery at 309 Occidental Ave. S. (℡ 206/223-0816). Lots of abstract art also makes it onto the walls here.

Around the corner from these two galleries, at 119 S. Jackson St., you'll find the:

⑰ Stonington Gallery

This gallery (℡ 206/405-4040) is one of Seattle's top showcases for contemporary Native American art and crafts. It displays a good selection of Northwest Coast Indian masks, woodcarvings, prints, and jewelry.

Continue to the corner of First Avenue, where you'll find:

⑱ Northwest Fine Woodworking

This large store, at 101 S. Jackson St. (℡ 206/625-0542), sells exquisite hand-crafted wooden furniture, as well as some smaller pieces. It's definitely worth a visit.

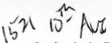

From here, cross South Jackson Street, where you'll see:

⑲ Flury & Company Ltd.

This gallery, at 322 First Ave. S. (✆ **206/587-0260**), specializes in prints by famed early-20th-century Seattle photographer Edward S. Curtis, who is known for his portraits of Native Americans. There's also an excellent selection of antique Native American artifacts.

From here, head up First Avenue to the corner of Main Street, where you'll find the:

⑳ Elliott Bay Book Company

One of the city's most popular bookstores, the Elliott Bay Book Company stands at 101 S. Main St. (✆ **206/624-6600**). It boasts an extensive selection of titles on Seattle and the Northwest. With so much great browsing to be done, this bookstore makes a great place to end your walking tour of the Pioneer Square area.

WALKING TOUR 3	FUN, FUNKY FREMONT

Start:	South end of Fremont Bridge, near Ponti restaurant.
Finish:	North end of Fremont Bridge.
Time:	Approximately 2 hours, not including time spent dining.
Best Times:	Sunday, during the Fremont Sunday Market.
Worst Times:	Early morning or evening, when shops are closed.

The Fremont District definitely marches to the beat of a different drummer. Styling itself the Republic of Fremont and the center of the universe, this small, tightknit community is the most eclectic neighborhood in the city. It has taken as its motto De Libertas Quirkas, which, roughly translated, means "free to be peculiar." Fremont residents have focused on art as a way to draw the community together, and in so doing, they've created a corner of the city where silliness reigns. At this crossroads business district, you find unusual outdoor art, the Fremont Sunday Market (a European-style flea market), several vintage-clothing and furniture stores, a couple of pubs, and many other unexpected and unusual shops, galleries, and cafes. During the summer, outdoor movies are shown on Saturday nights, and in June there's the wacky Solstice Parade, a countercultural promenade of giant puppets, wizards, fairies, naked bicyclists, and hippies of all ages.

Start your tour by finding a parking spot around the corner from Ponti restaurant, at the south end of the:

❶ Fremont Bridge

This is one of the busiest drawbridges in the United States and spans the Lake Washington Ship Canal.

As you approach the north side of the bridge, glance up; in the window of the bridge-tender's tower (on the west side of the bridge) you'll see:

❷ Rapunzel

This is a neon sculpture of the famous fairy-tale maiden with the prodigious mane. Her neon tresses cascade down the wall of the tower.

As you finally land in the Republic of Fremont, you will see, at the end of the bridge on the opposite side of the street from *Rapunzel,* Seattle's most beloved public sculpture:

❸ Waiting for the Interurban

This piece features several people waiting for the trolley that no longer runs between Fremont and downtown Seattle. These statues are frequently dressed up by local residents, with costumes changing regularly.

Cross to the far side of 34th Street and walk east along this street past some of Fremont's interesting shops, to the:

④ History House of Greater Seattle

This neighborhood museum of history, at 790 N. 34th St. (© **206/675-8875**), is complete with modern interactive exhibits and a beautiful artistic fence out front.

Turn left at History House and head uphill underneath the Aurora Bridge, which towers high above. At the top of the hill, you will see, lurking in the shadows beneath the bridge, the:

⑤ Fremont Troll

This massive monster is in the process of crushing a real Volkswagen Beetle. No need to run in fear, though, as a wizard seems to have put a spell on the troll and turned it into cement.

Turn left at the troll and walk a block down North 36th Street; then turn left on Fremont Avenue North, and continue another block to the corner of Fremont Avenue North and North 35th Street, where, a few doors from the corner, is:

⑥ Frank & Dunya

This shop, at 3418 Fremont Ave. N. (© **206/547-6760**), sells colorful household decor, including switch plates, cups and saucers, mirrors, jewelry, art, rustic furniture, and little shrines. It's all very playful.

And a little farther on is:

⑦ Dusty Strings

This basement music shop, at 3406 Fremont Ave. N. (© **206/634-1662**), specializes in acoustic music and instruments. Need a new ukulele, autoharp, or hammered dulcimer? You'll have plenty of choices here; in fact, the shop manufactures harps and hammered dulcimers.

Go back up to the corner and cross Fremont Avenue North to the traffic island, where you'll find both the center of the universe and Fremont's:

⑧ Directional Marker

This old-fashioned signpost has arrows that point to such important locations as the center of the universe (straight down), the *Fremont Troll, Rapunzel,* Atlantis, and the North Pole.

TAKE A BREAK
For a sinfully rich slice of cake, cross Fremont Avenue to Simply Desserts, 3421 Fremont Ave. N. (© **206/633-2671**), a tiny cake shop on the corner across from Frank & Dunya.

From the directional marker, continue west (away from the intersection) on Fremont Place, and in 1 block (at the corner of N. 36th St.) you'll come across a larger-than-life statue of:

⑨ Lenin

This 20-foot-tall statue in no way reflects the attitudes of the many very capitalistic merchants in the neighborhood.

After communing with Comrade Lenin, cross North 36th Street, where you'll find:

⑩ Bitters Co.

This unusual little import shop, at 513 N. 36th St. (© **206/632-0886**), has some of the coolest ethnic arts and crafts you'll ever see. This is a great place to shop for gifts.

From here, walk a block down Evanston Avenue to:

⑪ Les Amis

This boutique, at 3420 Evanston Ave. N. (© **206/632-2877**), is done up to look like a little potting shed; it stocks fun and trendy women's fashions from European and American designers.

Right outside this shop is the launching pad for the:

⑫ Fremont Rocket

Although there is speculation that this rocket was used by the aliens who founded Fremont, the truth is far stranger. You can read the entire history of the rocket on the accompanying map board. (If you haven't already figured it out, the locals don't want you getting lost in their neighborhood, so they've put up maps all over to help you find your way from one famous Fremont locale to the next.)

From here, head down North 35th Street for 1 long block, and then turn left on Phinney Avenue North, where you'll find:

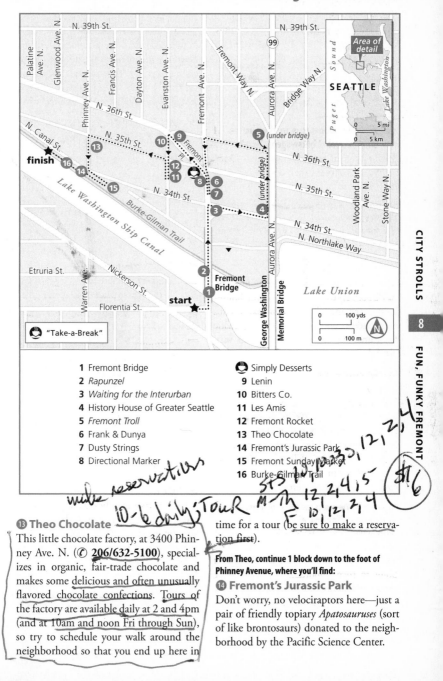

1 Fremont Bridge	Simply Desserts
2 *Rapunzel*	9 Lenin
3 *Waiting for the Interurban*	10 Bitters Co.
4 History House of Greater Seattle	11 Les Amis
5 *Fremont Troll*	12 Fremont Rocket
6 Frank & Dunya	13 Theo Chocolate
7 Dusty Strings	14 Fremont's Jurassic Park
8 Directional Marker	15 Fremont Sunday Market
	16 Burke-Gilman Trail

(handwritten annotations: "make reservations", "10-6 daily", "TOUR M-Th 12, 2, 4", "F 10, 12, 2, 4", "S-S 10, 12, 2, 4", "$16")

⑬ Theo Chocolate *(handwritten: 10-6 daily)* *(handwritten: make reservations)*
This little chocolate factory, at 3400 Phinney Ave. N. (© **206/632-5100**), specializes in organic, fair-trade chocolate and makes some delicious and often unusually flavored chocolate confections. Tours of the factory are available daily at 2 and 4pm (and at 10am and noon Fri through Sun), so try to schedule your walk around the neighborhood so that you end up here in

time for a tour (be sure to make a reservation first).

From Theo, continue 1 block down to the foot of Phinney Avenue, where you'll find:

⑭ Fremont's Jurassic Park
Don't worry, no velociraptors here—just a pair of friendly topiary *Apatosauruses* (sort of like brontosaurs) donated to the neighborhood by the Pacific Science Center.

CITY STROLLS

8

FUN, FUNKY FREMONT

If it happens to be Sunday, you'll see crowds of people and vendors' stalls stretching back toward the Fremont Bridge from Jurassic Park. This is the:

⑮ Fremont Sunday Market

You never know what you might find at this European-style flea market—perhaps some locally made kilts or a rack of vintage Hawaiian shirts. Continue along this street and you'll return to the Fremont Bridge.

Any day of the week, you can head west from the dinosaurs along one of the more scenic stretches of the:

⑯ Burke-Gilman Trail

This section of the popular walking, biking, and skating trail follows the north bank of the Lake Washington Ship Canal. You might see a big commercial fishing boat or a rowing team in the canal as you walk along. Turn around when you're tired or when you reach the industrial area that is one of the trail's less scenic stretches.

Cool Commercial Strips

If you're looking to do some one-stop shopping, but can't stand the soul-killing atmosphere of a mall, there are a number of funky and/or chic commercial strips in Seattle. Get yourself to: the **Pike/Pine Corridor (Map 4)**, **Broadway on Capitol Hill (Map 17)**, **Ballard Avenue (Map 23)**, **36th Street & Fremont Avenue (Map 24)**, **University Way ("The Ave")** in the U District (Map 26), and pretty much anywhere in **Belltown (Map 1)**.

Seattle Shopping

Nordstrom, Eddie Bauer, REI—these names are familiar to shoppers all across the country. They're also the names of stores that got their start here in Seattle. Throw in such regional favorites as Pendleton, Nike, and Filson, and you'll find that Seattle is a great place to shop, especially if you're in the market for recreational and outdoor gear and clothing.

As the Northwest's largest city, Seattle has also become home to all the national retail chains you would expect to find in a major metropolitan area. These chains have opened flashy stores and taken over many of the downtown storefronts. They include Banana Republic, Old Navy, Levi Strauss, Ann Taylor, Coach, St. John, Louis Vuitton, Tiffany, and Barneys New York. If you forgot to pick up that dress in Chicago or those running shoes in New York, have no fear—you can find them here.

Seattle does, however, have one last bastion of local merchandising: **Pike Place Market.** Whether shopping is your passion or just an occasional indulgence, you

shouldn't miss this historic market, which is one of Seattle's top attractions. Once the city's main produce market (and quite a few produce stalls remain), this sprawling collection of buildings is today filled with hundreds of unusual shops, including the **Market Magic Shop,** for magicians and aspiring magicians (© **206/624-4271;** www.generalrubric.com); **Tenzing Momo,** which sells body oils, incense, herbs, and the like (© **206/623-9837;** www.tenzing momo.com); and **Left Bank Books,** a bookstore for anarchists and their kin (© **206/622-0195;** www.leftbankbooks. com). See also the listing for Pike Place Market on p. 126.

After tasting the bounties of the Northwest, it's hard to go back to Safeway, Sanka, and Chicken of the Sea. Sure you can get wine, coffee, and seafood where you live, but do a little food shopping in Seattle and you'll be tapping the source. Washington State wines, coffee from the original Starbucks, and fish that fly—these are just a few of the culinary treats that await you here.

1 THE SHOPPING SCENE

Although Seattle is a city of neighborhoods, many of which have great little shops, the nexus of the Seattle shopping scene is the corner of **Pine Street and Fifth Avenue.** Within 2 blocks of this intersection are two major department stores (**Nordstrom** and **Macy's**) and two upscale urban shopping malls (**Westlake Center** and **Pacific Place**). A sky bridge between Nordstrom and Pacific Place makes shopping that much easier. Fanning out east and south from this intersection are blocks of upscale stores that have started to look more and more familiar as small, local shops have been replaced by national and international boutiques and megastores. Here in this neighborhood, you can now find Ann Taylor, Banana Republic, Barneys New York, Coach, Gap, and Niketown. Among these, a few local independents remain.

Within this downtown shopping district, you also find the loosely affiliated shops of **Rainier Square** (www.rainier-square.com). Although not actually a shopping mall,

Rainier Square, which is bordered by University and Union streets and Fourth and Sixth avenues, is packed with great upscale shops and boutiques, including Brooks Brothers, Louis Vuitton, Northwest Pendleton, and St. John.

The city's main tourist shopping district is the **Pike Place Market** neighborhood, with dozens of T-shirt and souvenir shops, as well as import shops and stores appealing to teenagers and 20-somethings. Pike Place Market is a fascinating warren of cubbyholes that pass for shops. While produce isn't usually something you stock up on during a vacation, several market shops sell ethnic cooking supplies that are less perishable than a dozen oysters or a king salmon. You may not find anything here you really need, but it's fun to look.

Just west of and downhill from Pike Place Market is the Seattle **waterfront,** site of many more gift and souvenir shops. This is the city's tackiest and most touristy neighborhood—save your money for somewhere else.

South of downtown, in the historic **Pioneer Square** area, you'll find numerous art galleries, some of which specialize in Native American art. This neighborhood has several antiques stores, but is also home to a dozen or more bars and attracts a lot of homeless people. It's fun to explore by day but strictly for young partiers by night.

As the center of both the gay community and the city's youth culture, **Capitol Hill** has the most eclectic selection of shops in Seattle. Beads, imports, CDs, vintage clothing, politically correct merchandise, and gay-oriented goods fill the shops along Broadway. Capitol Hill's main shopping plaza is the Broadway Market, which has lots of small shops. The Pike-Pine District, a pair of streets connecting downtown with Capitol Hill, is my favorite shopping neighborhood in this area. Lots of small, independently owned shops offer a very eclectic variety of gifts and other goods.

The **Fremont** neighborhood, just north of Lake Union, is filled with retro stores selling vintage clothing, curious crafts, and mid-20th-century furniture and collectibles. However, in the past decade, the neighborhood has become somewhat gentrified, forcing many of the smaller and more unusual shops out of the neighborhood. Keep looking; you'll still find some of the holdouts.

Just east of Fremont is the **Wallingford** neighborhood, which is anchored by an old school building that has been converted into a shopping arcade full of boutiques selling interesting crafts, fashions, and gifts. This area seems to be most popular with young moms and their kids.

To the west of Fremont, you'll find **Ballard,** a former Scandinavian neighborhood that is currently my favorite shopping district in Seattle. Tree-shaded Ballard Avenue NW is lined with historic brick buildings, most of which now are home to great little shops operated by highly creative individuals. You never know what you'll find in these shops, which is why it's so fun to shop here.

The **University District,** also in North Seattle, has everything necessary to support a student population—and also goes upscale at the University Village shopping center.

2 SHOPPING A TO Z

ANTIQUES & COLLECTIBLES

If antiques are your passion, don't miss the opportunity to spend a day browsing the many antiques stores in the historic farm town of **Snohomish,** located roughly 30 miles north of Seattle. The town has hundreds of antiques dealers and is without a doubt the antiques capital of the Northwest.

Chidori This little Pioneer Square shop is jampacked with exotic antiques from China, Japan, Korea, India, and Southeast Asia. Chidori has been in business for 25 years and always has lots of fascinating pieces for sale. 108 S. Jackson St. © **206/343-7736.** www. chidoriantiques.com.

Pioneer Square Antique Mall   This underground antiques mall is in the heart of Pioneer Square, right beside the ticket booth for the Seattle Underground tour. It contains 60 dealers' stalls selling all manner of antiques and collectibles. Look for glass, old jewelry, and small collectibles. 602 First Ave. ℂ 206/624-1164. www.pioneersquareantiques. com.

Seattle Antique Market   Down in a big, dark warehouse space under the Alaskan Way Viaduct, you can shop for old Japanese fishing floats, Victorian furniture, old pocket knives, whatever. This place reminds me of the big antiques stores my parents used to drag me to as a child, and I almost always find something here that I just have to have. The store is just a few doors south of the Pike Hill Climb. 1400 Alaskan Way. ℂ 206/623-6115. www.seattleantiquesmarket.com.

ART GALLERIES

The **Pioneer Square** area is Seattle's main gallery district, and anyone interested in art should be sure to wander south of Yesler Way. Some galleries are closed on Monday.

General Art Galleries

Davidson Galleries ★★   In the heart of the Pioneer Square neighborhood, this gallery focuses on both contemporary prints by American and European artists and antique prints, some of which date from the 1500s. The gallery also features contemporary paintings and sculptures, with an emphasis on Northwest artists. 313 Occidental Ave. S. ℂ 206/624-7684. www.davidsongalleries.com.

Greg Kucera Gallery   Established in 1983, this space in the Pioneer Square area serves as one of Seattle's most reliably cutting-edge galleries. The shows here often address political or social issues or movements within the art world. 212 Third Ave. S. ℂ 206/624-0770. www.gregkucera.com.

Grover/Thurston Gallery   This Pioneer Square gallery features works by numerous Northwest artists, including Fay Jones, whose colorful, playful works have long graced public spaces around Seattle. Works on display often tend toward bright colors and almost cartoonish imagery. Fun and worth a visit. 309 Occidental Ave. S. ℂ 206/223-0816. www.groverthurston.com.

Lisa Harris Gallery ★   Landscapes and figurative works, by both expressionist and realist Northwest and West Coast artists, are specialties of this gallery, which is located on the second floor of a building in Pike Place Market. 1922 Pike Place. ℂ 206/443-3315. www.lisaharrisgallery.com.

Patricia Rovzar Gallery   Bold, colorful, often whimsical art can be seen at this gallery adjacent to the Seattle Art Museum. Look for the dreamy Northwest landscapes of Z.Z. Wei and the circus-inspired surrealist works of Tyson Grumm. 1225 Second Ave. ℂ 206/223-0273. www.rovzargallery.com.

Art Glass

Canlis Glass   If you've seen the glass bamboo sculptures at Seattle's Hotel 1000 and Boka Kitchen restaurant, you've seen the work of this gallery's co-owner, Jean-Pierre Canlis. Large, abstract glass forms predominate, many inspired by ocean waves. 3131 Western Ave., Ste. 329. ℂ 206/282-4428. www.canlisglass.com.

Foster/White Gallery ★★   If you are enamored of art glass, be sure to stop by one or both of the Foster/White galleries in Seattle. These galleries represent Dale Chihuly and always have works by this master glass artist. Some of Chihuly's pieces even sell for less than $5,000! Foster/White also represents top-notch Northwest artists in the disciplines of painting, ceramics, and sculpture. 220 Third Ave. S. © 206/622-2833. www.foster white.com.

Glasshouse Studio   In the Pioneer Square area and founded in 1972, Glasshouse claims to be the oldest glassblowing studio in the Northwest. In the studio, you can watch hand-blown art glass being made, and then, in the gallery, you can check out the works of numerous local glass artists. 311 Occidental Ave. S. © 206/682-9939. www.glasshouse-studio.com.

Seattle Glassblowing Studio   With a gallery out front and glass-blowing studio in back, this is another great place to get a feel for the Seattle art-glass scene. The gallery/shop has lots of small glass-art pieces that you can take home in your luggage (or have shipped). 2227 Fifth Ave. © 206/448-2181. www.seattleglassblowing.com.

Traver Gallery ★★   This is one of the nation's top art-glass galleries and showcases the work of dozens of glass artists. The pieces displayed are on the cutting edge of glass art, so to speak, and illustrate the broad spectrum of contemporary work by artists in this medium. The gallery is on the second floor. 110 Union St., #200. © 206/587-6501. www.travergallery.com.

Vetri ★   Affiliated with the prestigious Traver Gallery, Vetri showcases innovative work primarily from emerging glass artists and local area studios, but also sells pieces by artists from other countries. It's all high-quality and riotously colorful. Prices are relatively affordable. 1404 First Ave. © 206/667-9608. www.vetriglass.com.

Native American Art

Ancient Grounds ★   This eclectic downtown antiques shop and natural-history gallery sells not only quality Northwest Coast Indian masks, but also Japanese masks, rare mineral specimens, and a wide variety of other rare and unusual pieces from all over the world. An espresso bar is on the premises. 1220 First Ave. © 206/749-0747.

Flury & Company Ltd. ★   This Pioneer Square gallery specializes in prints by famed Seattle photographer Edward S. Curtis, known for his late-19th- and early-20th-century portraits of Native Americans. The gallery also has an excellent selection of antique Native American art and artifacts. 322 First Ave. S. © 206/587-0260. www.fluryco.com.

The Legacy Ltd. ★★   In business since 1933, this is Seattle's oldest and finest gallery of contemporary and historic Northwest Coast Indian and Alaskan Eskimo art and artifacts. You'll find a large selection of masks, boxes, bowls, baskets, ivory artifacts, jewelry, prints, and books for the serious collector. Prints from this shop are used in *Grey's Anatomy*. 1003 First Ave. © 800/729-1562 or 206/624-6350. www.thelegacyltd.com.

Steinbrueck Native Gallery   With art and crafts by both emerging and established Native American artists, this gallery near Pike Place Market is a good place to shop for deals. 2030 Western Ave. © 206/441-3821. www.steinbruecknativegallery.com.

Stonington Gallery   This is another of Seattle's top galleries specializing in contemporary Native American arts and crafts. It offers a good selection of Northwest Coast Indian masks, totem poles, mixed-media pieces, prints, carvings, and Northwest Coast–style jewelry. 119 S. Jackson St. © 866/405-4485 or 206/405-4040. www.stoningtongallery.com.

[handwritten: 1521 10ᵗʰ Ave (Cap. Hill)   M-Th 10-10 / Vast D.I.Y section   F+S 10-11 / backbone of Seattle's literary crowd   Sun 11-9]

In addition to the stores listed below, you'll find more than a half-dozen locations of **Barnes & Noble** around the metro area, including one downtown at 600 Pine St. (📞 206/264-0156). A **Borders** is downtown at 1501 Fourth Ave. (📞 206/622-4599).

Elliott Bay Book Company ★★   With battered wooden floors, a maze of rooms full of books, and frequent readings and in-store appearances by authors, this Pioneer Square bookstore feels as if it has been around forever. It has an excellent selection of titles on Seattle and the Northwest, so if you want to learn more about the region or are planning further excursions, stop by. There's a good little cafe down in the basement. 101 S. Main St. 📞 800/962-5311 or 206/624-6600. www.elliottbaybook.com.

Flora & Fauna Books ★ (Finds)   Gardeners, bird-watchers, and other naturephiles should be sure to search out this fascinating little specialty bookstore near the entrance to Discovery Park in the Magnolia neighborhood. You'll find shelves packed with books that'll have you wishing you were in your garden or out in the woods identifying birds and flowers. 3212 W. Government Way. 📞 206/623-4727. www.ffbooks.net.

Metsker Maps   If you're already thinking about your next vacation and want to peruse some travel guidebooks, or if you simply need a good map of Seattle, drop by this map-filled shop in Pike Place Market. 1511 First Ave. 📞 800/727-4430 or 206/623-8747. www.metskers.com.

Peter Miller   Looking for a picture book of Frank Gehry's architectural follies? How about a retrospective on the work of Alvar Aalto? You'll find these and loads of other beautiful and educational books on architecture and design at this specialty bookstore at the edge of trendy Belltown. 1930 First Ave. 📞 206/441-4114. www.petermiller.com.

Seattle Mystery Bookshop   If whodunits are your passion, don't miss an opportunity to peruse the shelves of this specialty bookstore in the Pioneer Square area. You'll find all your favorite mystery authors, lots of signed copies, and regularly scheduled book signings. 117 Cherry St. 📞 206/587-5737. www.seattlemystery.com.

Wessel & Lieberman Booksellers   *[handwritten: Pioneer Sq]*   Offering new, used, rare, and out-of-print books, Wessel & Lieberman is a good place to look for hard-to-find books on the Northwest, art, architecture, and poetry. The shop often has art exhibits and displays on the book arts. 208 First Ave. S. 📞 206/682-3545. www.wlbooks.com.   *[handwritten: M-Sat 11-6]*

COFFEE & TEA   *[handwritten: gorgeous bldg & lots interesting stores]*

All over the city, on almost every corner, you'll find espresso bars, cafes, and coffeehouses. And even though you can get coffee back home, you might want to stock up on whichever local coffee turns out to be your favorite. If you're a latte junkie, you can even make a pilgrimage to the shop that started it all: the Pike Place Market Starbucks, listed below, that was once the only Starbucks in the world.

Ten Ren/Seattle Best Tea ★ (Finds)   Ever wondered what $150-a-pound Chinese tea tastes like? At this International District tea shop, you can find out. You'll discover not only dozens of different teas here, but also tables where you can sit down, sample the varieties, and experience the traditional Chinese tea ceremony. 506 S. King St. 📞 206/749-9855.

Starbucks   Seattle is well known as a city of coffeeholics, and Starbucks is the main reason. This company has coffeehouses all over town (and all over the world), but this was once the only Starbucks. Although you won't find any tables or chairs here, Starbucks

[handwritten: Univ. Bookstore - 4326 Univ. Way NE (634-3400) / M-F 9-8, Sat 10-7, Sun 12-5]

fans shouldn't miss an opportunity to get their coffee at the source. Pike Place Market, 1912 Pike Place. *206/448-8762.* www.starbucks.com.

Vital T-Leaf   Down at the south end of Pike Place Market, across from the entrance to the luxurious Four Seasons Hotel Seattle, you'll almost always find people sitting at a long counter sipping tea from exotic-looking teapots. This is Vital T-Leaf, a great place to sample and purchase teas you've never tried before. There are also lots of Chinese tea pots and tea cups for sale. 1401 First Ave. *206/262-1628.* www.vitaltleaf.com.

CRAFTS

The Northwest is a magnet for skilled craftspeople, and shops all around town sell a wide range of high-quality and imaginative pieces. At **Pike Place Market** (p. 126), you can see what area craftspeople are creating and meet the artisans themselves.

Fireworks Fine Crafts Gallery   Playful, outrageous, bizarre, beautiful—these are just some of the adjectives that can be used to describe the eclectic collection of Northwest crafts on sale at this Pioneer Square gallery. Cosmic clocks, wildly creative jewelry, artistic picture frames, and creative works of Judaica are among the fine and unusual items found here. 210 First Ave. S. *206/682-9697.* www.fireworksgallery.net. Also at Westlake Center, 400 Pine St. (*206/682-6462*); University Village, 2617 NE Village Lane (*206/527-2858*); and Bellevue Square, 196 Bellevue Sq., Bellevue (*425/688-0933*).

Frank & Dunya   Located in the Fremont neighborhood, this store epitomizes the fun-and-funky Fremont aesthetic. The art, jewelry, and crafts tend toward the colorful and the humorous, and just about everything is made by Northwest artists and artisans. 3418 Fremont Ave. N. *206/547-6760.* www.frankanddunya.com.

Northwest Craft Center ★ (Finds   This large gallery at Seattle Center is the city's premier ceramics showcase. In the main gallery, you'll find art ceramics that push the envelope of what can be made from clay. There's also a gift shop selling less expensive pieces. Seattle Center, 305 Harrison St. *206/728-1555.* www.northwestcraftcenter.com.

Northwest Fine Woodworking ★★   This store has some of the most amazing woodwork you'll ever see. Be sure to stroll through while you're in the Pioneer Square area, even if you aren't in the market for a one-of-a-kind piece of furniture. The warm hues of the exotic woods are soothing, and the designs are beautiful. Furniture, boxes, sculpture, vases, bowls, and much more are created by more than 20 Northwest artisans. 101 S. Jackson St. *206/625-0542.* www.nwfinewoodworking.com.

Twist ★   This store is filled with slightly offbeat yet tasteful objets d'art, including unusual artist-created jewelry pieces, Adirondack chairs made from recycled water skis, twisted glass vases, candlesticks, and ceramics. 600 Pine St., Ste. 130. *206/315-8080.* www. twistonline.com.

DEPARTMENT STORES

Macy's ★   Seattle's "other" department store, formerly the Bon Marché, which was established in 1890, is every bit as well stocked as the neighboring Nordstrom. With such competition nearby, this large department store tries hard to keep its customers happy. 1601 Third Ave. *206/506-6000.* www.macys.com.

Nordstrom ★★★   Known for personal service, Nordstrom has gained a reputation for being among the premier department stores in the United States. The company originated here in Seattle (opening its first store in 1901), and its customers are devotedly loyal. This is a state-of-the-art store, with all sorts of little boutiques, cafes, live piano music, and other features to make your shopping excursion an experience.

Best of all, whether it's your first visit or your 50th, the knowledgeable staff will help you in any way they can. Prices may be a bit higher than those at other department stores, but for your money you get the best service available. You'll also find Nordstrom stores at area shopping malls. 500 Pine St. ✆ **206/628-2111.** www.nordstrom.com.

DISCOUNT SHOPPING

Nordstrom Rack ★ (Value)   This is the Nordstrom overflow shop where you'll find three floors of discontinued lines as well as overstock, all at greatly reduced prices. Women's fashions make up the bulk of the merchandise, but there is also a floor full of men's clothes and shoes, plus plenty of kids' clothes. 1601 Second Ave. ✆ **206/448-8522.** Also at 3920 124th St. SE, Bellevue (✆ **425/746-7200**), and 19500 Alderwood Mall Pkwy., Lynnwood (✆ **425/774-6569**).

FASHION

In addition to the stores listed below, you'll find quite a few familiar names in downtown Seattle, including Ann Taylor, Banana Republic, Barneys New York, Eddie Bauer, Gap, and MaxMara.

Accessories

Byrnie Utz Hats ★ (Finds)   Boasting the largest selection of hats in the Northwest, this cramped hat-wearer's heaven looks as if it hasn't changed in 50 years; in fact, it's been in the same location since 1934. There are Borsalino Panama hats, Kangol caps, and, of course, plenty of Stetsons. 310 Union St. ✆ **206/623-0233.**

Children's Clothing

Boston St.   This Pike Place Market kids' store stocks fun play clothes as well as dressier fashions. You'll see lots of locally made 100% cotton clothing. Prices are moderate to expensive, but there are usually plenty of great deals on the sale racks. 1902 Post Alley. ✆ **206/634-0580.**

Men's Clothing

Utilikilts   If you're man enough to wear a kilt, then you've come to the right town. Seattle has been home to this unique clothing manufacturer since 2000, and the canvas kilts have become a local phenomenon. With a store right in Pioneer Square, you may be seeing even more manly men in skirts around town in the future. 620 First Ave. ✆ **866/666-6985** or 206/282-4226. www.utilikilts.com.

Men's & Women's Clothing

betty lin   This boutique is packed with deeply discounted designer fashions and shoes for both women and men. You'll save up to 75% on such names as Prada, Balenciaga, Miu Miu, and Christian Dior. The catch is that the racks are filled with last season's designs. 608 Second Ave. ✆ **206/442-6888.** www.shopbettyblue.com.

Eddie Bauer   Eddie Bauer got his start here in Seattle back in 1920, and today the chain that bears his name is one of the country's foremost purveyors of outdoor fashions—although these days, outdoor fashion is looking quite a bit more urban. 600 Pine St. ✆ **206/622-2766.** www.eddiebauer.com.

(handwritten: (2nd Ave - 1st Ave) M-F 10-6, Sat 10-5, Sun 11-4)

Ex Officio ★ (**Value**)   If you've already started planning your next trip, be sure to stop **177** by this travel-clothing store up toward the north end of Belltown. It's an outlet for the Seattle-based Ex Officio and is packed full of lightweight, easy-care clothes designed for world travelers. 114 Vine St. ℂ **206/283-4746**. www.exofficio.com.

Northwest Pendleton ★★   For northwesterners, and for many other people across the nation, Pendleton is and always will be _the_ name in classic wool items. This store features tartan plaids and American Indian–pattern separates, accessories, shawls, and blankets. 1313 Fourth Ave. ℂ **800/593-6773** or 206/682-4430. www.nwmuseumstore.com.

Women's Clothing   _(handwritten: M-Sat 10 - 6)_   _(handwritten: Univ - Univ St)_

Alhambra   Alhambra stocks a very eclectic collection of women's clothing and jewelry. There are purses from France, shoes from Italy, and fashions from Turkey and the U.S. These add up to a unique European look that's a little more refined than what you find at Baby & Co. 101 Pine St. ℂ **206/621-9571**. www.alhambranet.com.

Baby & Co. ★★   Claiming to have stores in Seattle and on Mars, Baby & Co. stocks fashions that can be trendy, outrageous, or out of this world. The designs are strictly French, so you aren't likely to find these fashions in too many other places in the U.S. Whether you're into earth tones or bright colors, you'll likely find something you can't live without. 1936 First Ave. ℂ **206/448-4077**.

Endless Knot ★   If you've ever had a thing for funky fashions from Asia, you'll be amazed at how tasteful and upscale such styles can be. The racks of this Belltown boutique are lined with drapey natural-fiber fashions in bold colors—plus, there are lots of accessories to accompany the clothes. 2300 First Ave. ℂ **206/448-0355**.

Les Amis   In the Fremont neighborhood in a funky old wooden building, this little boutique is designed to look a bit like an old cottage or potting shed. The fashions and accessories are fresh and fun and come mostly from France and Italy. 3420 Evanston Ave. N. ℂ **206/632-2877**. www.lesamis-inc.com.

Margaret O'Leary   Classic and classy, the sweaters at this Belltown boutique are hand-knit from cashmere, silk, cotton, and merino wool. Prices are high, but the designs are meant to stand the test of time. 2025 First Ave. ℂ **206/441-6691**. www.margaretoleary.com.

Ragazzi's Flying Shuttle ★★   Fashion becomes art and art becomes fashion at this chic boutique-cum-gallery in the Pioneer Square area. Hand-woven fabrics and hand-painted silks are the specialties, but, of course, such sophisticated fashions require equally unique body decorations in the form of exquisite jewelry creations. Designers and artists from the Northwest and the rest of the nation find an outlet for their creativity at the Flying Shuttle. 607 First Ave. ℂ **206/343-9762**. www.ragazzisflyingshuttle.com.

Synapse 206   Specializing in local, regional, and emerging national designers, this edgy little boutique in the Pioneer Square neighborhood is packed full of distinctive, often one-of-a-kind fashions. Designs are youthful and playful without being trendy. 206 First Ave. S. ℂ **206/447-7731**. www.synapse206.com.

Totally Michael's   If you've got expensive tastes and don't want to look like every other woman at the corporate office or out on the town, check out the luscious offerings at Totally Michael's. Designs display a pronounced sophistication even when cuts and colors are somewhat playful. 521 Union St. ℂ **206/622-4920**. www.totallymichaels.com.

Lutefisk Anyone?

If you're suddenly struck with an insatiable craving for Scandinavian lutefisk, lingonberries, or lefse bread, then head to Ballard, Seattle's Nordic neighborhood, where you can peruse the deli cases and frozen foods at **Olsen's Scandinavian Foods,** 2248 NW Market St. (*ⓒ* **206/783-8288;** www.scandinavianfoods.net). With flatbread and Danish ham in hand, you can head out to the Ballard Locks (Hiram M. Chittenden Locks) for a picnic.

Tuuli This store lends a bit of Scandinavian aesthetic to Pike Place Market. There are imported Finnish fashions, accessories, jewelry, and home decor, plus lots of Marimekko fabrics. 1407 First Ave. *ⓒ* **206/223-1112.**

FOOD

Chukar Cherries ★ Washington is one of the nation's premier cherry-growing regions, and here at the Pike Place Market, you can sample all kinds of candy-coated dried cherries. These little confections are positively addictive. Pike Place Market, Main Arcade, 1529-B Pike Place. *ⓒ* **800/624-9544** or 206/623-8043. www.chukar.com.

La Buona Tavola ★★ Truffle oils are the specialty of this little Pike Place Market shop. In addition to the bottles of olive oil infused with white or black truffles, there's an astonishingly fragrant truffle cream. Yum! Pike Place Market, 1524 Pike Place. *ⓒ* **206/292-5555.** www.trufflecafe.com.

Rose's Chocolate Treasures Hidden away on narrow Post Alley, this dark little shop is filled with all things chocolate. Not only can you get some of Seattle's creamiest and most delicious chocolate confections, but there are also various cocoas, raw cacao beans, toasted cracked cacao nibs, and all sorts of other great gifts for chocoholics. 1906 Post Alley. *ⓒ* **866/315-ROSE.** www.roseschocolatetreasures.com.

The Spanish Table ★ ⓕ**Finds** There are cases full of imported meats and cheeses, as well as all manner of other Spanish ingredients, and, if you've decided your life's goal is to prepare the ultimate paella, this store will set you on the path to perfection. Paella pans and everything you could ever want for cooking Spanish cuisine fill this Pike Place Market shop. 1426 Western Ave. *ⓒ* **206/682-2827.** www.spanishtable.com.

Theo Chocolate Although there's lots of good chocolate to be had in Seattle, Theo is the first roaster of fair-trade cocoa beans. At their Fremont factory, you can sample their chocolates, tour the factory, and, of course, buy yummy chocolate confections. Tours, which cost $6 per person, are offered daily at 2 and 4pm (and at 10am and noon Fri–Sun). Reservations are recommended. 3400 Phinney Ave. N. *ⓒ* **206/632-5100.** www. theochocolate.com.

World Spice Market You probably will never before have seen as many different spices as are on display at this Pike Place Market shop. The shop boasts of having 100 spices from 50 countries, so if you are into ethnic cooking and want to take home some interesting spices, peruse the shelves here. Sample jars let you sniff before you buy. 1509 Western Ave. *ⓒ* **206/682-7274.** www.worldspice.com.

Pike Place Market (p. 126) is the *ne plus ultra* of Seattle souvenirs, with stiff competition from the Seattle Center and Pioneer Square areas.

Bitters Co. ★ This hole-in-the-wall shop in Fremont sums up the neighborhood's design aesthetic. The shop is full of fun and funky imports from Asia, Latin America, and Africa. Even if you're a big fan of ethnic imports, you'll find things here that you've never seen before. Lots of reclaimed materials go into Bitters Co. housewares. 513 N. 36th St. © 866/664-2488 or 206/632-0886. www.bittersco.com.

Lucca, great finds ★ (Finds) Designed to resemble Parisian gift salons of the 1920s and 1930s, this little Ballard shop is an absolute joy to explore. You never know what might turn up amid the vintage classics and chic contemporary items. Perhaps you're in need of some mounted insects for your curiosity cabinet, or maybe you just need some French toothpaste. Whichever you seek, you'll find it here. 5332 Ballard Ave. NW. © 206/782-7337. www.luccastatuary.com.

Made in Washington Whether it's salmon, wine, or Northwest crafts, you'll find a varied selection of Washington State products in this shop. This is an excellent place to pick up gifts for all those friends and family members who didn't get to come to Seattle with you. Pike Place Market, 1530 Post Alley (at Pine St.). © 206/467-0788. www.madein washington.com. Also at Westlake Center, 400 Pine St. (© 206/623-9753).

Pelindaba Lavender If you're as crazy about lavender as I am, be sure to stop in this large store in the City Centre shopping complex. You'll find all manner of lavender products from lotions to teas, and all in beautiful packages. This shop is affiliated with a lavender farm on San Juan Island. Union St. and Sixth Ave. in the city Center Building. © 206/264-0508. www.pelindaba.com.

Watson Kennedy Fine Living This little gift shop, in the courtyard of the Inn at the Market, has a light and airy sort of French country feel. The emphasis is on fine soaps, candles, and small gifts. Owner Ted Kennedy Watson has such an eye for gifts and interior decor that he was called on to help out with Bill and Melinda Gates's wedding. Displays are beautiful. 86 Pine St. © 206/443-6281. www.watsonkennedy.com.

Ye Olde Curiosity Shop (Kids) If you can elbow your way into this waterfront institution, you'll find nearly every inch of space, horizontal and vertical, covered with souvenirs and crafts, both tacky and tasteful (but mostly tacky). Surrounding this merchandise are shrunken heads, a mummy, preserved Siamese twin calves, and many other oddities that have made this one of the most visited shops in Seattle. Pier 54, 1001 Alaskan Way. © 206/682-5844. www.yeoldecuriosityshop.com.

HOUSEWARES, HOME FURNISHINGS & GARDEN ACCESSORIES

Kobo ★★ (Finds) Japanophiles won't want to miss this unusual little Capitol Hill shop and gallery, located in one of the most interesting old buildings in the neighborhood. There are all manner of very tasteful decorative items inspired by the Japanese artistic aesthetic. 814 E. Roy St. © 206/726-0704. www.koboseattle.com. Also at 602–608 S. Jackson St. (© 206/381-3000).

Sur La Table Gourmet cooks should be sure to visit Pike Place Market's Sur La Table, where every imaginable kitchen utensil is available. There are a dozen different kinds of whisks, an equal number of muffin tins, and all manner of cake-decorating tools, tableware, napkins, cookbooks—simply everything a cook would need. By the way, this is the original Sur La Table. 84 Pine St. (*C*) **206/448-2244. www.surlatable.com.**

JEWELRY

Unique artist-crafted jewelry can be found at **Ragazzi's Flying Shuttle** (p. 177) and **Twist** (p. 175).

Facèré Jewelry Art Gallery ★ A big rock on a gold band? How uninspired. At this tiny shop inside the City Centre shopping gallery, rings, earrings, necklaces, and brooches are miniature works of art made from a fascinating range of materials. If you're searching for something unique with which to adorn your body, don't miss this shop. City Centre, 1420 Fifth Ave. (*C*) **206/624-6768. www.facerejewelryart.com.**

Fox's Gem Shop Seattle's premier jeweler, Fox's has been around for nearly a century and always has plenty of a girl's best friends. Colorless or fancy colored diamonds available here are of the finest cut. 1341 Fifth Ave. (*C*) **800/733-2528** or 206/623-2528. **www.foxs gem.com.**

MALLS/SHOPPING CENTERS

Bellevue Square ★ Over in Bellevue, on the east side of Lake Washington, is one of the area's largest shopping malls. Its 200+ stores include Nordstrom, Banana Republic, Eddie Bauer, Coach, and Made in Washington. Bellevue Way and NE Eighth St., Bellevue. (*C*) **425/454-8096. www.bellevuesquare.com.**

Pacific Place ★★ This downtown mall, adjacent to Nordstrom, contains five levels of upscale shop-o-tainment, including Cartier, Tiffany & Co., bebe, Coach, MaxMara, seven restaurants, and a multiplex movie theater. An adjoining garage means you usually have a place to park. 600 Pine St. (*C*) **877/883-2400** or 206/405-2655. **www.pacificplaceseattle. com.**

Westlake Center ★ This upscale urban shopping mall, in the heart of Seattle's main shopping district, has more than 80 specialty stores, including Godiva Chocolatier, Fireworks (a great contemporary crafts shop), and Made in Washington, along with an extensive food court. The mall is also the southern terminus for the monorail to Seattle Center. 400 Pine St. (*C*) **206/467-1600. www.westlakecenter.com.**

MARKETS

Pike Place Market ★★★ Pike Place Market is one of Seattle's most famous landmarks and tourist attractions. Besides produce vendors, fishmongers, and butchers, it shelters artists, craftspeople, and performers. Hundreds of shops and dozens of restaurants (including some of Seattle's best) are tucked away in nooks and crannies on the numerous levels of the market. With so much to see and do, a trip to Pike Place Market can easily become an all-day affair. See also the sightseeing listing on p. 126. Pike St. and First Ave. (*C*) **206/682-7453. www.pikeplacemarket.org.**

Uwajimaya ★★ Typically, your local neighborhood supermarket probably has a section of Chinese cooking ingredients that's about 10 feet long, with half that space taken up by various brands of soy sauce. Now imagine your local supermarket with nothing but Asian foods, housewares, produce, and toys. That's Uwajimaya, Seattle's Asian supermarket in the heart of the International District. A big food court here serves all kinds of Asian food. 600 Fifth Ave. S. (*C*) **206/624-6248. www.uwajimaya.com.**

M-Sat 8-10 & Sun 9-9
From downt take 5th, 3rd @ 2nd Ave (S) to S. Jackson St
(L) onto S. Jackson, (R) onto (6th Ave S; store on (R)

MUSIC

Singles Going Steady   Right in the heart of Belltown, which was the heart of the Seattle grunge scene, this indie record store is one of the best places in town to search out oldies but goodies from Seattle's glory days. Of course, you'll also find the latest in punk, heavy metal, hip-hop, and other alt-rock genres. 2219 Second Ave. ✆ **206/441-7396.** www.singlesgoingsteady.com.

MUSICAL INSTRUMENTS

Dusty Strings   This basement shop in the Fremont neighborhood specializes in hammered dulcimers, ukuleles, harps, and guitars. They also manufacture their own harps and dulcimers. 3406 Fremont Ave. N. ✆ **866/634-1662** or 206/634-1662. www.dustystrings.com.

Lark in the Morning   At Lark in the Morning, you can find just about any kind of instrument from around the world, from Greek bouzoukis and traditional African drums to didgeridoos and bagpipes. Customers are encouraged to try out the instruments in the store. 1401 First Ave. ✆ **206/623-3440.** larkinthemorning.com.

PERFUME

Parfumerie Nasreen ★★   Located just inside the lobby of the luxurious Alexis Hotel, this perfume shop is packed with thousands of bottles of perfume from all over the world. You'll find some of the world's most expensive scents here. 1005 First Ave. ✆ **888/286-1825** or 206/623-9109. www.parfumerienasreen.com.

RECREATIONAL GEAR

Filson ★★   This Seattle company has been outfitting people headed outdoors ever since the Alaskan gold rush at the end of the 1890s. You won't find any high-tech fabrics here—just good old-fashioned wool, and plenty of it. Filson's clothes are meant to last a lifetime (and have the prices to prove it), so if you demand only the best, even when it comes to outdoor gear, be sure to check out this local institution. 1555 Fourth Ave. S. ✆ **866/860-8906** or 206/622-3147. www.filson.com.

KAVU World ★ (**Value**   Rock jocks and rafters, rejoice: Now you can get your favorite rugged outdoor clothes at half-price. KAVU is a Seattle-based clothing manufacturer with a tiny outlet store on a shady street in the Ballard neighborhood. Its durable outdoor clothing is great not just for rafters and rock climbers, but for everyone. 5423 Ballard Ave. NW. ✆ **206/783-0060.** www.kavu.com.

The North Face   The North Face is one of the country's best-known names in the field of outdoor gear, and here in its downtown shop you can choose from a diverse selection of the company's products. 1023 First Ave. ✆ **206/622-4111.** www.thenorthface.com. Also at University Village, 2682 NE Village Lane ✆ **206/525-8500.**

Patagonia   Sure, the prices are high, but this stuff is made to last. Although there are plenty of clothing designs here for playing in the great outdoors, many of the fashions are equally at home on city streets. 2100 First Ave. ✆ **206/622-9700.** www.patagonia.com.

REI ★★★   Recreational Equipment, Inc. (REI) is the nation's largest co-op selling outdoor gear, and the company's impressive flagship is a cross between a high-tech warehouse and a mountain lodge. This massive store sells almost anything you could ever need for pursuing your favorite outdoor sport. It also has a 65-foot climbing pinnacle and a play area for kids. With all this under one roof, who needs to go outside? 222 Yale Ave. N. ✆ **888/873-1938** or 206/223-1944. www.rei.com.

SALMON

If you think that the fish at Pike Place Market looks great but that you could never get it home on the plane, think again. Any of the seafood vendors in Pike Place Market will pack your fresh salmon or Dungeness crab in an airline-approved container that will keep it fresh for up to 48 hours. Alternatively, you can buy vacuum-packed smoked salmon that will keep for years without refrigeration.

Pike Place Fish ★★   Located behind *Rachel*, Pike Place Market's life-size bronze pig, this fishmonger is just about the busiest spot in the market most days. What pulls in the crowds are the antics of the workers here. Order a big silvery salmon and you'll have employees shouting out your order and throwing the fish over the counter. These "flying fish" are a major Seattle attraction, so just step right up and pick your salmon. Pike Place Market, 86 Pike Place. ✆ **800/542-7732** or 206/682-7181. www.pikeplacefish.com.

Portlock Port Chatham Smoked Seafood   If the sight of all the salmon swimming through the fish ladder at the Chittenden Locks has you craving some smoked salmon, just head 2 blocks east from the locks to the retail outlet of this big mail-order smoked-salmon store. They've got all kinds of smoked fish that you can have for a picnic or pack home with you. 2821 NW Market St. ✆ **800/872-5666** or 206/781-7260. www.port chatham.com.

Totem Smokehouse ★   Northwest Coast Indians used alder-wood smoke to pre-serve fish, and the tradition is carried on today with smoked salmon, one of the North-west's delicacies. This store sells vacuum-packed smoked salmon that will keep without refrigeration for several years. Pike Place Market, 1906 Pike Place. ✆ **800/972-5666** or 206/443-1710. www.totemsmokehouse.com.

TOYS

Archie McPhee ★★ (Kids)   You may already be familiar with this temple of the absurd through its mail-order catalog or website. Now imagine the fun of wandering through aisles full of goofy gags and all that other wacky stuff. Give yourself plenty of time and take a friend. Archie's place is in the Ballard neighborhood. 2428 NW Market St. ✆ **206/297-0240.** www.archiemcpheeseattle.com.

Magic Mouse Toys ★ (Kids)   Adults and children alike have a hard time pulling them-selves away from this, the wackiest toy store in downtown Seattle. It's conveniently located in Pioneer Square and has a good selection of European toys. 603 First Ave. ✆ **206/682-8097.**

Market Magic Shop ★★   This little Pike Place Market shop is a must for aspiring magicians. You'll find all kinds of great tricks and all the tools of the trade. There are also juggling supplies and plenty of cool posters. Pike Place Market, 1501 Pike Place, #427. ✆ **206/624-4271.** www.generalrubric.com/magicposters/marketmagic.

Not A Number Cards & Gifts   This shop in the Wallingford neighborhood of north Seattle is packed full of all kinds of wacky toys and gifts and appeals primarily to adults. I love this place, and whenever I take friends by, they always leave with bags in hand and smiles on their faces. 1905 N. 45th St. ✆ **206/784-0965.** www.notanumbergifts.com.

Because the relatively dry summers, with warm days and cool nights, provide an ideal climate for growing grapes, the Northwest has become one of the nation's foremost wine-producing regions. After you've sampled some Washington vintages, you might want to take a few bottles home.

Pike & Western Wine Shop ★★   Visit this shop for an excellent selection of Washington and Oregon wines, as well as bottles from California, Italy, and France. The extremely knowledgeable staff will be happy to send you home with the very best wine available in Seattle. Free tastings are held Friday afternoons between 3 and 6pm. Pike Place Market, 1934 Pike Place. (© 206/441-1307. www.pikeandwestern.com.

Seattle Cellars, Ltd. ★   Wine merchant to the residents of Seattle's Belltown neighborhood, this shop sells wines from all over the world, with a substantial selection from Washington and Oregon. Prices are reasonable, and wine tastings are held Thursday evenings between 5 and 7pm. 2505 Second Ave. (© 206/256-0850. www.seattlecellars.com.

4-6 Weds ($5)

3-6 Fri: free

M-F 9:30-6:30

Sat 9:30-6

Sun 12-5

10

Seattle After Dark

It's true that Seattleites spend much of their free time enjoying the city's natural surroundings, but that doesn't mean they overlook the more cultured evening pursuits. In fact, the winter weather that keeps people indoors, combined with a longtime desire to be the cultural mecca of the Northwest, has fueled a surprisingly active and diverse nightlife scene. Music lovers will find a plethora of classical, jazz, and rock offerings. The Seattle Opera is ranked one of the top companies in the country, and its stagings of Wagner's *Ring* series have achieved near-legendary status. The Seattle Symphony also receives frequent accolades. Likewise, the Seattle Repertory Theatre has won Tony awards for its productions, and a thriving fringe theater scene keeps the city's avant-garde theater buffs contentedly discoursing in cafes and bars about the latest hysterical or thought-provoking performances.

Much of Seattle's entertainment scene is clustered in the **Seattle Center** and **Pioneer Square** areas. The former hosts theater, opera, and classical-music performances; the latter is a bar-and-nightclub district. Other concentrations of nightclubs can be found in **Belltown,** where young and hip crowds flock to the neighborhood's many trendy clubs, and in **Capitol Hill,** with its ultracool gay scene. **Ballard,** formerly a Scandinavian enclave in North Seattle, attracts a primarily middle-class, not-too-hip, not-too-old crowd, including college students and techies. It's not the hip Belltown scene, it's not the PBR-swilling scene of Pioneer Square, and it's not the sleek gay scene of Capitol Hill. It's just comfortable neighborhood nightlife.

While winter is a time to enjoy the performing arts, summer brings an array of outdoor festivals. These take place during daylight hours as much as they do after dark; this chapter lists information on these festivals and performance series.

To find out what's going on when in town, pick up a free copy of *Seattle Weekly* (www.seattleweekly.com), the city's arts-and-entertainment newspaper. You'll find it in bookstores, convenience stores, grocery stores, newsstands, and newspaper boxes downtown and in other neighborhoods. The Friday *Seattle Times* includes "NW Ticket," a guide to the week's arts-and-entertainment offerings.

1 THE PERFORMING ARTS

The Seattle Symphony performs downtown in Benaroya Hall, but the main venues for the performing arts in Seattle are primarily clustered at **Seattle Center,** the special-events complex built for the 1962 world's fair. Here, in the shadow of the Space Needle, are Marion Oliver McCaw Hall, Bagley Wright Theatre, Intiman Playhouse, Seattle Children's Theatre, Seattle Center Coliseum, and Memorial Stadium.

OPERA & CLASSICAL MUSIC
The **Seattle Opera** (© 800/426-1619 or 206/389-7676; www.seattleopera.org), which performs at Seattle Center's Marion Oliver McCaw Hall, is considered one of the finest opera companies in the country and is *the* Wagnerian opera company in the U.S. Wagner's

four-opera *The Ring of the Nibelungen* is a breathtaking spectacle that draws crowds from around the country. Wagner's magnum opus was just staged in 2009, so it will be a few years before you can catch this spectacle again. In addition to such classical operas as *Carmen* and *Parsifal,* the regular season usually includes a more contemporary production. Ticket prices range from around $25 to $175.

The 90-musician **Seattle Symphony** (✆ **866/833-4747** or 206/215-4747; www. seattlesymphony.org), which performs at the acoustically superb Benaroya Hall, offers an exceedingly diverse season that runs from September to July. There is a little something for every type of classical-music fan, including evenings of classical, light classical, and pop music, plus afternoon concerts, children's concerts, guest artists, and more. Ticket prices range from $17 to $97.

THEATER
Mainstream Theaters
The **Seattle Repertory Theatre** (✆ **877/900-9285** or 206/443-2222; www.seattlerep. org), which performs at the Bagley Wright and Leo K. theaters, both at Seattle Center, 155 Mercer St., is Seattle's top professional theater and stages the most consistently entertaining productions in the city. The Rep's season runs from September to May, with eight or nine plays staged in the two theaters. Productions range from classics to world premieres. Tickets go for $15 to $59. When available, rush tickets are distributed half an hour before showtime for $20.

With a season that runs from March to December, the **Intiman Theatre,** Seattle Center, 201 Mercer St. (✆ **206/269-1900;** www.intiman.org), keeps Seattle theatergoers happy during those months that the Seattle Rep's lights are dark. Ticket prices range from $37 to $52.

A Contemporary Theatre (ACT), Kreielsheimer Place, 700 Union St. (✆ **206/292-7676;** www.acttheatre.org), performing in the historic Eagles Building theater adjacent to the Washington State Convention and Trade Center, offers slightly more adventurous productions than the other major theater companies in Seattle, though it's not nearly as avant-garde as some of the smaller companies. The season runs from March to November. Ticket prices usually range from $10 to $55.

Although the **Seattle Shakespeare Company,** Center House Theatre, Seattle Center (✆ **206/733-8222;** www.seattleshakes.org), is neither very large nor very well known even in Seattle, it has been staging productions of the Bard's plays for almost 20 years. The season, which runs from October to June, includes three plays by Shakespeare plus a couple of other productions. Tickets run $18 to $40.

Fringe Theater
Not only does Seattle have a healthy mainstream performing-arts community, but it also has the sort of fringe theater once associated only with such cities as New York, Los Angeles, London, and Edinburgh. The city's more avant-garde performance companies frequently grab their share of the limelight with daring, outrageous, and thought-provoking productions.

Check the listings in *Seattle Weekly* or the Friday *Seattle Times* "NW Ticket" entertainment guide to see what's going on during your visit. The following venues are some of Seattle's more reliable places for way-off-Broadway productions, performance art, and spoken-word performances:

Book-It Repertory Theater, Seattle Center, 305 Harrison St. (✆ **206/216-0833;** www.book-it.org). This theater troupe specializes in adapting literary works for the stage and also performs works by local playwrights. Most performances are held at Seattle Center.

- **Seattle Public Theater at the Bathhouse,** 7312 W. Green Lake Dr. N. (✆ **206/524-1300;** www.seattlepublictheater.org). Seattle Public Theater stages a range of comedies and dramas at the old Green Lake bathhouse. The location right on the lake makes this a great place to catch some live theater.
- **Theater Schmeater,** 1500 Summit Ave. (✆ **206/324-5801;** www.schmeater.org). Lots of weird and sometimes wonderful comedy, including ever-popular live stagings of episodes from *The Twilight Zone* and an annual summertime outdoor performance at the amphitheater in Volunteer Park.

DANCE

Although it has a well-regarded ballet company and a theater dedicated to contemporary dance and performance art, Seattle is not nearly as devoted to dance as it is to theater and classical music. That said, hardly a week goes by without some sort of dance performance being staged somewhere in the city. Touring companies of all types, the University of Washington Dance Department faculty and student performances, the UW World Series (see details below), and the Northwest New Works Festival (see details below) all bring plenty of creative movement to the stages of Seattle. Check *Seattle Weekly* or the *Seattle Times* for a performance calendar.

The **Pacific Northwest Ballet,** The Phelps Center, 301 Mercer St. (✆ **206/441-2424;** www.pnb.org), is Seattle's premier dance company. During the season, which runs from September to June, the company presents a range of classics, new works, and (the company's specialty) pieces choreographed by George Balanchine. Their performance of *The Nutcracker,* with sets designed by children's book author Maurice Sendak, is the highlight every season. The Pacific Northwest Ballet performs at Marion Oliver McCaw Hall at Seattle Center. Tickets range from $25 to $155.

Adventurous choreography is the domain of **On the Boards,** The Behnke Center for Contemporary Performance, 100 W. Roy St. (✆ **206/217-9888;** www.ontheboards. org), which, although it stages a wide variety of performance art, is best known as Seattle's premier modern-dance venue. In addition to dance performances by Northwest artists, there are a variety of productions each year by internationally known performance artists. Most tickets are $18 to $24.

MAJOR PERFORMANCE HALLS

With ticket prices for shows and concerts so high these days, it pays to be choosy about what you see, but sometimes the venue is just as important. Benaroya Hall, the Seattle Symphony's downtown home, has such excellent acoustics that a performance here is worth attending simply for the sake of hearing how a good symphony hall should sound. Seattle also has two restored historic theaters (see below) that are as much a part of a performance as what happens onstage.

Benaroya Hall (✆ **206/215-4747;** www.seattlesymphony.org), on Third Avenue between Union and University streets in downtown Seattle, is the home of the Seattle Symphony. This state-of-the-art performance hall houses two concert halls—the main hall and a smaller recital hall. It's home to the Watjen concert organ, a magnificent pipe organ, as well as a cafe, a symphony store, and a pair of Dale Chihuly chandeliers. Amenities aside, the main hall's excellent acoustics are the big attraction.

The **5th Avenue Theatre,** 1308 Fifth Ave. (© **888/584-4849** or 206/625-1900; www.5thavenuetheatre.org), which opened its doors in 1926 as a vaudeville house, is a loose re-creation of the imperial throne room in Beijing's Forbidden City. Don't miss an opportunity to attend a performance here. Broadway shows are the theater's mainstay; ticket prices usually range from $25 to $93.

The **Paramount Theatre,** 911 Pine St. (© **206/467-5510;** www.theparamount.com), one of Seattle's few historic theaters, shines with all the brilliance it had when it first opened in 1928. The theater hosts everything from rock concerts to Broadway musicals.

Affiliated with the Paramount Theatre, the **Moore Theatre,** 1932 Second Ave. (© **206/ 467-5510;** www.themoore.com), in Belltown, gets lots of national rock acts that aren't likely to draw quite as many people as bands that play at the Paramount. Dating back to 1907, this is the oldest theater in Seattle.

PERFORMING-ARTS SERIES

When Seattle's own resident performing-arts companies aren't taking to the dozens of stages around the city, various touring companies from around the world are. If you're a fan of Broadway shows, check the calendars at the Paramount Theatre and the 5th Avenue Theatre, both of which regularly serve as Seattle stops for touring shows.

The **UW World Series** (© **800/859-5342** or 206/543-4880; www.uwworldseries. org), held at Meany Hall on the University of Washington campus, is actually several different series that include chamber music, classical piano, world dance, and world music and theater. Together these four series keep the Meany Hall stage busy between October and May. Special events are also scheduled. Tickets go for $33 to $46. The box office is at 4001 University Way NE, which is off campus.

New and avant-garde performances are the specialty of the **Northwest New Works Festival** (© **206/217-9888;** www.ontheboards.org), an annual barrage of contemporary dance and performance art staged each spring by On the Boards.

Summer is a time of outdoor festivals and performance series in Seattle, and if you're in town during the sunny months, you'll have a wide variety of alfresco performances from which to choose. The city's biggest summer music festivals are the **Northwest Folklife Festival,** over Memorial Day weekend, and **Bumbershoot,** over Labor Day weekend. See the "Seattle Calendar of Events" (p. 20) for details.

At **Woodland Park Zoo** (© **206/548-2500;** www.zoo.org/zootunes), the **Zoo Tunes** concert series brings in more big-name performers from the world of jazz, easy listening, blues, and rock. Tickets go for $19 to $27; bear in mind that many of these performances sell out almost as soon as tickets go on sale in early May.

North of Seattle, in Woodinville, **Summer Concerts at the Chateau,** 14111 NE 145th St. (© **425/415-3300** for information, or 206/628-0888 for tickets; www.stemichelle.com), is the area's most enjoyable outdoor summer concert series. It's held at Chateau Ste. Michelle's amphitheater, which is surrounded by beautiful estate-like grounds. This is Washington's largest winery, so plenty of wine is available. The lineup is calculated to appeal to the 30- to 50-something crowd (past performers have included Mark Knopfler, James Taylor, B. B. King, and the Gipsy Kings). Ticket prices usually range from $40 to $100. See p. 247 for more on Woodinville and Chateau Ste. Michelle.

At the summertime **Concerts at Marymoor,** 6046 W. Lake Sammamish Pkwy. NE (© **206/628-0888;** www.concertsatmarymoor.com), at Marymoor Park, 20 to 30 minutes east of Seattle at the north end of Lake Sammamish, you can expect the likes of Willie Nelson and Prairie Home Companion. Tickets for most shows are between $30 and $80, although prices sometimes go higher.

Tips   **City Hall Turns Concert Hall**

A few times a month year-round, Seattle's **City Hall,** 600 Fourth Ave. (℃ **206/ 684-7171;** www.seattle.gov/arts), stages free lunchtime concerts from noon to 1pm.

The **White River Amphitheatre,** 40601 Auburn–Enumclaw Rd., Auburn (℃ **360/ 825-6200;** www.whiteriverconcerts.com), is the Seattle area's top amphitheater and pulls in big-name rock bands. Ticket prices can be anywhere from $25 to around $105, with the lowest prices being for space on the lawn. The amphitheater is on the Muckleshoot Indian Reservation, 35 miles southeast of Seattle.

Then, of course, there's Seattle's ever popular Shakespeare-in-the-Park festival, which is staged in July and August in several parks around the city. **GreenStage** (℃ **206/748- 1551;** www.greenstage.org) usually produces two Shakespeare plays per summer and has free performances three to four times each week.

From early July to early September, the **Out to Lunch Concert Series** (http://downtown summer.com/otl) stages 1-hour lunchtime concerts at half a dozen parks around down- town Seattle. Musical styles range from rock to folk to jazz to gospel to Celtic.

---

2 THE CLUB & MUSIC SCENE

Whether you want to hear a live band, hang out in a good old-fashioned bar, or dance all night, **Pioneer Square** is the best place to start. Keep in mind that this neighborhood tends to attract a rowdy crowd and can be pretty rough late at night.

Belltown, north of Pike Place Market, is another good place to club-hop. Clubs here are way more style-conscious than those in Pioneer Square and tend to attract 20- and 30-something trendsetters.

Seattle's other main nightlife district is the formerly Scandinavian neighborhood of **Ballard,** where you'll find more than a half-dozen nightlife establishments, including taverns, bars, and live-music clubs.

Capitol Hill, a few blocks uphill from downtown Seattle, is the city's main gay night- life neighborhood, with much of the action centered on the corner of East Madison Street and 15th Avenue East.

ROCK, FOLK, REGGAE & WORLD BEAT
Downtown

The Triple Door ★★   Popular music for adults? What a concept! This swanky night- club is a total novelty in the Seattle club world. It isn't geared toward the 20-something crowd. The music is diverse—from jazz to world beat, to flamenco, to Maria Muldaur, the Tubes, and Ottmar Liebert. You'll find the club in the basement below the ever- popular Wild Ginger restaurant, across the street from Benaroya Hall. 216 Union St. ℃ **206/ 838-4333.** www.thetripledoor.net. Cover $15–$30 (occasionally more for special shows).

Belltown, Pike Place Market & Environs

The Crocodile   Back in the days when grunge music was sweeping the nation, this was one of Seattle's top live-music venues. After closing down for a while, it has come back again and is as popular as ever, with alternative rock dominating the schedule. 2200 Second Ave. (at Blanchard St.). ℂ 206/441-5611. www.thecrocodile.com. Cover $8–$20.

Showbox at the Market   Located across the street from Pike Place Market, this large club books a wide variety of local and name rock acts. Definitely *the* downtown rock venue for performers with a national following. There's a second club, Showbox Sodo, at 1700 First Ave. S. 1426 First Ave. No phone. www.showboxonline.com. Cover $8–$25 (occasionally higher).

Pioneer Square

Central Saloon   Established in 1892, the Central is the oldest saloon in Seattle. As a local institution, it's a must-stop during a night out in Pioneer Square. You might catch sounds ranging from funk to punk. 207 First Ave. S. ℂ 206/622-0209. www.centralsaloon. com. Cover $5–$10 (Pioneer Square Club Stamp).

Capitol Hill

Chop Suey   Looking like a cross between a down-market Chinese restaurant and a Bruce Lee shrine, this kitschy Capitol Hill club books an eclectic mix of music. Hip-hop and alt-rock styles predominate, and the crowd is a young mix of straights and gays. 1325 E. Madison St. ℂ 206/324-8005. www.chopsuey.com. Cover $5–$18.

Neumo's   Located in a space that has housed numerous clubs over the years, Neumo's is currently Seattle's leading club for indie rock bands that haven't yet developed a big enough following to play the Showbox. 925 E. Pike St. ℂ 206/709-9467. www.neumos.com. Cover $6–$18.

Fremont & Ballard

Nectar Lounge   This little warehouse-like space is just the sort of nightclub you'd expect to find in Fremont. Appealing primarily to the area's neo-hippie types, Nectar puts on an eclectic array of world-beat, reggae, hip-hop, and indie rock shows, both live and DJs. There's a nice patio out front for warm summer nights. 412 N. 36th St. ℂ 206/632-2020. www.nectarlounge.com. Cover $5–$15.

Tractor Tavern   For an ever-eclectic schedule of music for people whose tastes go beyond the latest rap artist, the Tractor Tavern is the place to be. You can catch almost anything from rockabilly to Hawaiian slack-key guitar to singer-songwriters to banjo music to Celtic to folk to zydeco. Sound like your kind of place? 5213 Ballard Ave. NW. ℂ 206/789-3599. www.tractortavern.ypguides.net. Cover $5–$25.

JAZZ & BLUES

Dimitriou's Jazz Alley ★★   Cool and sophisticated, this Belltown establishment is reminiscent of a New York jazz club and has been around for 3 decades now. As Seattle's premier jazz venue (and one of the top jazz clubs on the West Coast), it books only the best performers, including many name acts. 2033 Sixth Ave. ℂ 206/441-9729. www.jazzalley. com. Cover $21–$35 (occasionally more for special shows).

Highway 99 Blues Club   In the basement of an old brick building beneath the waterfront's Alaskan Way Viaduct, this club not far from Pike Place Market is Seattle's

Teatro ZinZanni: Who Needs Cirque du Soleil?

Visiting Seattle without seeing this show would be like going to Las Vegas without seeing Cirque du Soleil. According to **Teatro ZinZanni,** 222 Mercer St. ((📞 **206/802-0015;** www.zinzanni.com), a European-style cabaret of the highest order, circus acts aimed at the upper crust should be accompanied by gourmet cuisine. Staged in an authentic Belgian *spiegeltent* (mirror tent), this evening of comedy, dance, theater, and fine food (catered by celeb chef Tom Douglas) features clowns, acrobats, illusionists, and cabaret singers—more entertainment packed into one night than you'll find anywhere else in Seattle. Tickets are $104 Sunday and Wednesday through Friday, and $125 on Saturday (premium seating $125–$140 Sun and Wed–Fri, and $140–$160 Sat). Rates are slightly higher between Thanksgiving and New Year's. Reserve far in advance!

quintessential blues joint. You can hear the best of local blues bands, as well as touring national acts. 1414 Alaskan Way. 📞 206/382-2171. www.highwayninetynine.com. Cover none–$15.

New Orleans Creole Restaurant If you like your food and your jazz hot, check out the New Orleans in Pioneer Square. Throughout the week, there's Cajun, Dixieland, R&B, jazz, and blues. 114 First Ave. S. 📞 206/622-2563. www.neworleanscreolerestaurant. com. Cover none–$12 (Pioneer Square Club Stamp).

Tula's ★ This jazz club is the real thing: a popular after-hours hangout for musicians and a good place to catch up-and-coming performers. American and Mediterranean food is served. 2214 Second Ave. 📞 206/443-4221. www.tulas.com. Cover $5–$15.

Wasabi Bistro A big, stylish sushi restaurant may not seem like the place to hear live jazz, but that's the odd combo you get at this Belltown restaurant/nightclub. Local bands play everything from Brazilian to New Orleans jazz Sunday through Thursday nights. 2311 Second Ave. 📞 206/441-6044. www.wasabibistro.biz. No cover.

COMEDY, CABARET & DINNER THEATER

Can Can Down below sidewalk level in the same Pike Place Market Building that houses Matt's in the Market (one of my favorite market restaurants), you'll find the latest in urban entertainment. This Moulin Rouge–inspired cabaret stages neoburlesque shows, Django Reinhardt–style jazz performances, and other forms of obscure and imaginative retro entertainment. Yes, the ladies in petticoats really do kick up their heels here! 94 Pike St. 📞 206/652-0832. www.thecancan.com. Cover none–$35.

Julia's on Broadway Several nights each week this restaurant in the heart of Capitol Hill's Broadway commercial strip lets its hair down and stages shows that are designed to appeal to the area's gay population. Currently there is a burlesque and cabaret dinner show at 8pm on Thursday nights, and a female celebrity impersonators show on Friday and Saturday nights. 300 Broadway E. 📞 206/860-1818. www. eatatjulias.com. Cover $20.

Market Theatre Competitive improv comedy at this small back-alley theater in Pike Place Market pits two teams against each other. Suggestions from the audience inspire sketches that can sometimes be hilarious but that just as often fall flat. The young, rowdy crowd never seems to mind one way or the other. 1428 Post Alley. 📞 **206/587-2414.** www. unexpectedproductions.org. Cover $8–$12.

The Pink Door ★★ Better known as Pike Place Market's unmarked restaurant, the Pink Door has a hopping after-work bar scene that tends to attract a 30-something crowd. It also doubles as a cabaret featuring Seattle's most eclectic lineup of performers, including cross-dressing tango dancers, trapeze artists, and the like. Lots of fun and not to be missed. 1919 Post Alley. 📞 **206/443-3241.** www.thepinkdoor.net. No cover Sun–Fri; $15 cover Sat.

DANCE CLUBS

Baltic Room This swanky Capitol Hill hangout for the beautiful people stages a wide range of contemporary dance music (mostly DJs), encompassing everything from electronica to hip-hop and *bhangra* (contemporary Indian disco). 1207 Pine St. 📞 **206/625-4444.** www.thebalticroom.net. Cover none–$10.

Century Ballroom With a beautiful wooden dance floor, this is *the* place in Seattle for a night out if you're into swing, salsa, or tango. Every week, a couple of nights of swing and a couple of nights of salsa include lessons early in the evening. Tuesday night is tango night and Friday nights are often gay nights. The crowd here is very diverse, with patrons of all ages. 915 E. Pine St. 📞 **206/324-7263.** www.centuryballroom.com. Cover $5–$15 (sometimes higher for special shows).

Contour A few blocks up First Avenue from Pioneer Square, this modern dance club attracts a more diverse crowd than most Pioneer Square clubs. The music ranges from deep house to trance to hip-hop, and the partying on Friday and Saturday goes on until 6am the next day. Laser-light shows, fire dancers—this joint is one wild party! 807 First Ave. 📞 **206/447-7704.** www.clubcontour.com. Cover none–$15.

The Last Supper Club Way more stylin' than your average Pioneer Square juke joint, this place may look small from the street, but it actually has three levels of bars and dance floors. DJs and live bands keep the beats pounding several nights each week. 124 S. Washington St. 📞 **206/748-9975.** www.lastsupperclub.com. Cover none–$12 (some higher for special shows).

---

3 THE BAR SCENE

BARS

The Waterfront

Six-Seven Lounge ★ If you got any closer to the water, you'd have wet feet. Inside downtown Seattle's only waterfront hotel, this bar affords what might be the best bar view in town. Watch the ferries come and go, or see the sun set over Puget Sound. In The Edgewater, Pier 67, 2411 Alaskan Way. 📞 **206/269-4575.**

Downtown

The Bookstore—A Bar & Cafe Just off the lobby of the posh Alexis Hotel, this cozy little bar is—surprise—filled with books. There are plenty of interesting magazines on hand as well, so if you want to sip a single malt but don't want to deal with crowds and noise, this is a great option. Very classy. In the Alexis Hotel, 1007 First Ave. 📞 **206/382-1506.**

McCormick & Schmick's   The mahogany paneling and sparkling cut glass lend this restaurant bar a touch of class, but otherwise the place could have been the inspiration for *Cheers*. Very popular as an after-work watering hole of Seattle moneymakers, McCormick & Schmick's is best known for its excellent and inexpensive happy-hour snacks. 1103 First Ave. © **206/623-5500**. www.mccormickandschmicks.com.

Oliver's ★★   Maybe you've been to one too many places that claim to make the best martini and you're feeling dubious. Here at Oliver's, they've repeatedly put their martinis to the test and come out on top. The atmosphere is classy and the happy-hour appetizers are good, but in the end, only you can decide whether these martinis are the best in Seattle. In the Mayflower Park Hotel, 405 Olive Way. © **206/623-8700**. www.mayflowerpark.com.

Sixth Avenue Wine Seller   Up on the third floor of the Pacific Place shopping center, you'll find a well-stocked little wine shop that also has a small bar in the back room. Some nights there's even live piano music. 600 Pine St. © **206/621-2669**.

Vessel ★★   Located next door to the beautiful 5th Avenue Theatre in the 1926 Skinner Building, this stylish bar is my favorite downtown drinking establishment. Not only does it serve classy cocktails that come with long histories, but the bar food is also excellent. Oh, and don't be dissuaded if the place looks full; there's a second floor. 1312 Fifth Ave. © **206/652-0521**. www.vesselseattle.com.

Von's Grand City Café and Martini-Manhattan Memorial ⓥ **Value**   Although best known for its $3.50 house martinis that are basically gin with a spritz of Vermouth from a spray bottle, this popular downtown bar also boasts the largest selection of spirits in Seattle. There's also a fun Wheel of Fortune–style wheel that gets spun every half-hour for a new drink special. 619 Pine St. © **206/621-8667**. www.vonsroasthouse.com.

W Bar ★   Beautiful decor, beautiful people, flavorful cocktails. What more could you ask for, especially if black on black is your favorite fashion statement? The bar here at the W Seattle hotel really is the prettiest bar in the downtown business district. 1112 Fourth Ave. © **206/264-6000**. www.whotels.com/seattle.

Belltown

Del Rey   Sexy, sophisticated, and small, this Belltown bar seems to be where everyone wants to start the evening, so it can be hard to get in or get a drink ordered once you do get in. On the other hand, if you're here to make the scene, be sure to put Del Rey on the schedule. There's good bar food, and on Friday and Saturday nights, there are DJs. 2332 First Ave. © **206/770-3228**. www.delreyseattle.com.

The Local Vine   Up at the north end of Belltown, away from the tourists and the panhandlers, you'll find one of the prettiest and most sophisticated wine bars in the city. With its curved wooden-slat ceiling, the Local Vine is a gorgeous space, perfect for sipping a Washington wine. It also has free Wi-Fi, in case you want to check your e-mail while you drink your wine. 2520 Second Ave. © **206/441-6000**. www.thelocalvine.com.

See Sound Lounge   With walls of colored lights and a front wall that swings open to let in the summer air, this retro-mod bar, on one of the prettiest streets in Belltown, is among the neighborhood's hottest hangouts. The cool scene here is a required stop during a night out in trendy Belltown. 115 Blanchard St. © **206/374-3733**. www.seesoundlounge.com.

Shorty's   Are you a pinball wizard? Want to find out what all the fuss was about back in the days before video games? Either way, check out this retro pinball-parlor bar in

Belltown. It's tiny and funky, but you'll be surrounded by like-minded aficionados of the silver balls. And don't forget to have a hot dog with your beer. 2222A Second Ave. © 206/441-5449. www.shortydog.com.

Virginia Inn Although the Virginia Inn is in *très chic* Belltown, this bar/restaurant has a decidedly Old Seattle feel, due in large part to the fact that it has been around since 1903. Quite surprising for a bar, the Virginia Inn serves decent, inexpensive French food! 1937 First Ave. © 206/728-1937. www.virginiainnseattle.com.

Pike Place Market

Alibi Room If you've been on your feet all day in Pike Place Market and have had it with the crowds of people, duck down the alley under the market clock and slip through the door of this hideaway. The back-alley setting gives this place an atmospheric speak-easy feel. Popular with artists and other creative types. 85 Pike St. (actually in Post Alley). © 206/623-3180. www.seattlealibi.com.

The Tasting Room ★ Located in the Pike Place Market area, this cozy wine bar has the feel of a wine cellar and is cooperatively operated by several small Washington wineries. You can taste the wines of Camaraderie Cellars, Harlequin Wine Cellars, Latitude 46° N Winery, Mountain Dome, Naches Heights Vineyards, Wilridge Winery, and Wineglass Cellars, or buy wine by the glass or bottle. Light snacks are also available. 1924 Post Alley. © 206/770-9463. www.winesofwashington.com.

The Zig Zag Café ★★ You'll have to look hard to find this hidden Pike Place Market bar. It's on one of the landings of the Pike Hill Climb, which is the staircase that links the market with the waterfront. Perfectly crafted cocktails, both classic and contemporary, are the specialty here and are so well made that the bar has garnered national recognition. 1501 Western Ave. © 206/625-1146. www.zigzagcafe.net.

Pioneer Square

FX McRory's Right across the street from the Seattle Seahawks' Qwest Field, and not far from Safeco Field, this bar attracts well-heeled sports fans (with the occasional Mariners and Seahawks player thrown in for good measure). You'll find the city's (and perhaps the country's) largest selection of bourbons here. There's also an oyster bar and good food. 419 Occidental Ave. S. © 206/623-4800. www.fxmcrorys.com.

Ibiza Dinner Club ★ Pioneer Square is mostly all about dive bars, which really makes this swanky dinner club stand out in the crowd. The place is just gorgeous—the type of establishment you might expect to find in Belltown (or Miami), not here in Pioneer Square. The decor and patrons are beautiful, and the food and cocktails are very creative. 528 Second Ave. © 206/381-9090. www.ibizadinnerclub.com.

Marcus' Martini Heaven Seattle's only underground martini bar, Marcus's is hidden down a flight of stairs just off First Avenue in Pioneer Square. Search this place out, and you'll be drinking with the ghosts of the city's past and the lounge lizards of today. There's DJ music a couple of nights each week. This is a much mellower alternative to Pioneer Square's rowdy street-level bars. 88 Yesler Way. © 206/624-3323. www.marcusmartiniheaven.com.

Queen Anne

The Sitting Room With a casual, Euro-bistro vibe, this tucked-away bar in the Lower Queen Anne neighborhood is the perfect spot for a drink before or after a show at On the Boards next door. It's a fun find for anyone exploring this part of town. Fresh herb cocktails are the specialty. 108 W. Roy St. © 206/285-2830. www.the-sitting-room.com.

Tini Bigs   On the border between Lower Queen Anne and Belltown, this bar led the revival of the martini as the cocktail of choice in Seattle. The martinis on the menu feature such an array of ingredients that it's hard to consider most of them to even be martinis. Nevertheless, the drinks are good and the location is convenient to Seattle Center and the Space Needle. 100 Denny Way. (C) 206/284-0931. www.tinibigs.com.

Ballard

Balmar   The name makes it sound like some Miami-inspired tropical-deco place, but that's far from reality. The brick-walled neighborhood bar/restaurant takes its name from the fact that it's at the corner of *Bal*lard and *Mar*ket streets. It's classy yet casual and the most upscale drinking establishment in Ballard. 5449 Ballard Ave. NW. (C) 206/297-0500. www.thebalmar.com.

Fu Kun Wu @ Thaiku ★ (Finds)   You'll find this unforgettable bar at the back of Ballard's Thaiku, one of my favorite Thai restaurants in Seattle. Designed to look like an old Chinese apothecary and filled with Asian wood carvings and artifacts, Fu Kun Wu specializes in various herb-infused cocktails. There's live jazz on Wednesday and Thursday nights. 5410 Ballard Ave. NW. (C) 206/706-7807. www.fukunwu.com.

Portalis   On a shady back street in Ballard, in a dark space in an old brick building, is one of Seattle's best wine bars. It's a great place to nurse a glass of wine. Because it's also a wine shop, you can search the racks for your favorite Washington vintages too. 5205 Ballard Ave. NW. (C) 206/783-2007. www.portaliswines.com.

BREWPUBS

Big Time Brewery & Alehouse   Big Time, Seattle's oldest brewpub, is in the University District and is done up to look like an early-20th-century tavern, complete with a 100-year-old back bar and a wooden refrigerator. The pub serves as many as 12 of its own brews at any given time, and some of these are pretty unusual. 4133 University Way NE. (C) 206/545-4509. www.bigtimebrewery.com.

Elysian Brewing Company ★   This pub is a large place with an industrial feel that sums up the Northwest concept of "local brewpub." The stouts and strong ales are especially good, and the brewers' creativity here just can't be beat. Hands-down, Elysian is the best brewpub in Seattle. You'll find other Elysian pubs at 542 First Ave. S. ((C) 206/382-4498), and 2106 N. 55th St. ((C) 206/547-5929). 1221 E. Pike St. (C) 206/860-1920. www.elysianbrewing.com.

Hale's Ales Brewery & Pub   Located about a mile west of the Fremont Bridge, toward Ballard, this big, lively brewpub produces some of Seattle's favorite beers. In business for more than 25 years, Hale's has long enjoyed a loyal following. This is a good place to stop after a visit to Chittenden Locks to see migrating salmon. 4301 Leary Way NW. (C) 206/706-1544. www.halesales.com.

The Pike Pub& Brewery   In an open, central space inside Pike Place Market, this brewpub makes excellent stout and pale ale, but is best known for its Kilt Lifter Scottish ale. This is a great place to get off your feet after a long day in the market. 1415 First Ave. (C) 206/622-6044. www.pikebrewing.com.

Pyramid Ale House   This pub, south of Pioneer Square in a big old warehouse, is part of the brewery that makes the Northwest's popular Pyramid beers and ales. It's a favorite spot for dinner and drinks before or after baseball games at Safeco Field and

---

Bowled Over in Seattle

A hip bowling alley? Why not? Up on Capitol Hill, you can do a little bowling, shoot some pool, and take in the hipster scene at **Garage,** 1130 Broadway (𝒞 **206/322-2296;** www.garagebilliards.com). When the weather gets warm, the garage doors roll up to let in the fresh air. Definitely not your small-town bowling alley.

---

football games at Qwest Field. There's good pub food, too. 1201 First Ave. S. 𝒞 **206/682-3377.** www.pyramidbrew.com.

IRISH PUBS

Fadó　This Irish pub is part of a national chain but has the feel of an independent pub. Lots of antiques, old signs, and a dark, cozy feel make it a very comfortable place for a pint. There's live Irish music a couple of nights a week, a weekly Wednesday-night pub quiz, and, of course, you can watch soccer and rugby matches on the telly. 801 First Ave. 𝒞 **206/264-2700.** www.fadoirishpub.com. Cover none–$5.

Kells ★　At one time, the space now occupied by this pub was the embalming room of a mortuary. These days, the scene is much livelier and has the feel of a casual Dublin pub. Kells pulls a good pint of Guinness, serves traditional Irish meals, and features live Irish music 7 nights a week. Pike Place Market, 1916 Post Alley. 𝒞 **206/728-1916.** www.kellsirish.com. Cover none–$5.

The Owl & Thistle Pub　Right around the corner from Fadó you'll find this equally authentic pub. The Post Alley entrance gives this place the ambience of a back-street Dublin pub. There's live music most nights, with the house band playing Irish music on most Saturday nights. 808 Post Alley. 𝒞 **206/621-7777.** www.owlnthistle.com. Cover none–$5.

T. S. McHugh's　In the Lower Queen Anne neighborhood adjacent to Seattle Center and many of Seattle's mainstream theaters, T. S. McHugh's has a very authentic feel. It's a good place to relax after an afternoon spent exploring Seattle Center. 21 Mercer St. 𝒞 **206/282-1910.** www.tsmchughs.com.

OTHER PUBS

Brouwer's Café ★　Beer geeks (and I count myself among this tribe) swarm to this friendly, modern Fremont pub for its huge selection of Belgian beers, and while this isn't actually a brewpub, the owner, who also owns Seattle's premier beer store, does have a good IPA custom-brewed for him by a regional brewery. Of the 60 beers on tap and the 300 bottled beers, a preponderance of them are Belgian. 400 N. 35th St. 𝒞 **206/267-BIER.** brouwerscafe.com.

Collins Pub　If you're looking for a place to sip a beer around Pioneer Square without having your nostrils assaulted by the stench of stale beer and industrial cleaners, you don't have a lot of options, which is why the Collins Pub is the only place I'll down a pint in this neighborhood. There's a good selection of regional microbrews and decent food, too. 526 Second Ave. 𝒞 **206/623-1016.** www.thecollinspub.com.

4 THE GAY & LESBIAN SCENE

As Seattle's main gay neighborhood, Capitol Hill has the greatest concentration of gay and lesbian bars and clubs. Look for the readily available *Seattle Gay News* (*C* **206/ 324-4297;** www.sgn.org), where many gay bars and nightclubs advertise.

BARS

Grey Gallery & Lounge This combination art gallery and bar is the most sophisticated little bar in a neighborhood packed with drinking establishments favored by the Seattle GLBT community. A great, quiet spot for a drink with friends. 1512 11th Ave. *C* **206/325-5204.** greygalleryandlounge.com.

Madison Pub This low-key darts-and-pool sports pub on Capitol Hill is popular with guys who have outgrown or just aren't into cruising. So if you just want to hang out with local gays and aren't out to pick someone up, this is a good choice. 1315 E. Madison St. *C* **206/325-6537.** www.madisonpub.com.

Wildrose This friendly restaurant/bar is a longtime favorite of the Capitol Hill lesbian community and claims to be the West Coast's oldest lesbian bar. In spring and summer there is an outdoor seating area. Pool tournaments and karaoke are mainstays here. 1021 E. Pike St. *C* **206/324-9210.** www.thewildrosebar.com. Cover none–$7.

DANCE CLUBS

The Cuff Complex Seattle A virtual multiplex of gay entertainment, this place has three separate bars. There's a quiet bar, a dance club, and a patio for those rain-free nights. It's primarily a leather-and-Levis crowd, but you're still welcome even if you forgot to pack your leather pants. 1533 13th Ave. *C* **206/323-1525.** www.cuffcomplex.com. Cover none–$5.

Neighbours This has been the favorite dance club of Capitol Hill's gay community for years. As at other clubs, different nights of the week feature different styles of music. You'll find this club's entrance down the alley. 1509 Broadway. *C* **206/324-5358.** www. neighboursnightclub.com. Cover none–$10.

Re-Bar Each night there's a different theme, with the DJs spinning everything from funk to punk. This club isn't exclusively gay, but it's still a gay-Seattle favorite. 1114 Howell St. *C* **206/233-9873.** www.rebarseattle.com. Cover $5–$15.

R Place Bar & Grill With three floors of entertainment, including a video bar on the ground floor, pool tables and video games on the second floor, and a dance floor up on the top level, you hardly need to go anywhere else for a night on the town. 619 E. Pine St. *C* **206/322-8828.** www.rplaceseattle.com. Cover none–$7.

5 MOVIES

Summertime in the Fremont neighborhood always means **Fremont Outdoor Movies** (**www.fremontoutdoormovies.com**), a series that features modern classics, B movies (sometimes with live overdubbing by a local improv comedy company), and indie shorts. Films are screened on Saturday nights in the parking lot at North 35th Street and Phinney Avenue North. The parking lot opens at 7:30pm; there is a $5 suggested donation.

Want to sip a martini while you watch the latest indie film hit? Find out what's playing at Belltown's **Big Picture Seattle,** 2505 First Ave. (© **206/256-0566;** www.thebig picture.net). This little basement theater below El Gaucho steakhouse is the coolest little theater in the city and a favorite of fans of indie films.

6 ONLY IN SEATTLE

While Seattle has plenty to offer in the way of performing arts, some of the city's best after-dark offerings have nothing to do with music or theater. There's no better way to start the evening (that is, if the day has been sunny or only partly cloudy) than to catch the **sunset from the waterfront.** The Bell Street Pier and Myrtle Edwards Park are two of the best vantages for taking in nature's light show. Keep in mind that sunset can come as late as 10pm in the middle of summer.

Want the best view of the city lights? Put off your elevator ride to the top of the **Space Needle** until after dark. Or you can hop a ferry and sail off into the night.

Want to learn to dance? On Capitol Hill, the sidewalk along Broadway is inlaid with **brass dance steps.** Spend an evening strolling the strip, and you and your partner can teach yourselves classic dance steps in between noshing on a *piroshky* and savoring a chocolate torte.

11

Side Trips from Seattle

After you've explored Seattle for a few days, consider heading out of town on a day trip. Within a few hours of the city, you can find yourself hiking in a national park, cruising up a fjordlike arm of Puget Sound, gazing into the crater of Mount St. Helens, exploring the San Juan Islands, strolling the streets of a Victorian seaport, or wine tasting at some of Washington's top wineries. With the exception of the San Juan Islands and the Olympic Peninsula, the excursions listed below are all fairly easy day trips that will give you glimpses of the Northwest outside the Emerald City.

For more in-depth coverage of the areas surrounding Seattle, pick up a copy of *Frommer's Washington State* (Wiley Publishing, Inc.).

1 THE SAN JUAN ISLANDS

On a late afternoon on a clear summer day, the sun slants low, suffusing the scene with a golden light. The fresh salt breeze and the low rumble of the ferry's engine lull you into a dream state. All around you, rising from a shimmering sea, are emerald-green islands, the tops of glacier-carved mountains inundated with water at the end of the last ice age. A bald eagle swoops from its perch on a twisted madrona tree. Off the port bow, you spot several fat harbor seals lounging on a rocky islet. As the engine slows, you glide toward a narrow dock with a simple sign above it that reads ORCAS ISLAND. With a sigh of contentment, you step out onto the San Juan Islands and into a slower pace of life.

There's something magical about traveling to the San Juans. Some people say it's the light, some say it's the sea air, some say it's the weather (temperatures are always moderate, and rainfall is roughly half what it is in Seattle). Whatever the answer, the San Juans have become the favorite getaway of urban Washingtonians, and if you make time to visit these idyllic islands, I think you, too, will fall under their spell.

There is, however, one caveat: The San Juans have been discovered. In summer, if you're driving a car, you may encounter waits of several hours to get on the ferries. One solution is to leave your car on the mainland and come over either on foot or by bicycle. If you choose to come over on foot, you can then rent a car, moped, or bike; take the San Juan Island shuttle bus; or use taxis to get around. Then again, you can just stay in one place and relax.

Along with crowded ferries come hotels, inns, and campgrounds booked up months in advance, and restaurants that can't seat you unless you have a reservation. If it's summer, you won't find a place to stay if you don't have a reservation.

In other seasons, it's a different story. Spring and fall are often clear, and in spring, the islands' gardens and hedgerows of wild roses burst into bloom, making this one of the nicest times of year to visit. Perhaps best of all, room rates in spring and fall are much lower than they are in summer.

No one seems to be able to agree on how many islands there actually are in the San Juans; there may be fewer than 200 or almost 800. The lower number represents those

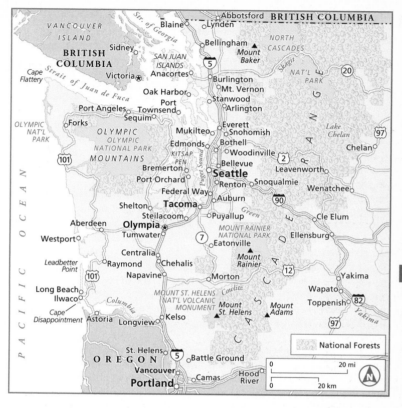

islands large enough to have been named, while the larger number includes all the islands, rocks, and reefs that poke above the water at low tide. Of all these islands, only four (San Juan, Orcas, Lopez, and Shaw) are serviced by the Washington State Ferries, and of these, only three (San Juan, Orcas, and Lopez) have anything in the way of tourist accommodations.

VISITOR INFORMATION

For information on all the islands, contact the **San Juan Islands Visitors Bureau,** P.O. Box 1330, Friday Harbor, WA 98250 (© **888/468-3701;** www.visitsanjuans.com).

For specific information on San Juan, contact the **San Juan Island Chamber of Commerce,** 135 Spring St. (P.O. Box 98), Friday Harbor, WA 98250 (© **360/378-5240;** www.sanjuanisland.org). For Orcas, contact the **Orcas Island Chamber of Commerce,** P.O. Box 252, Eastsound, WA 98245 (© **360/376-2273;** www.orcasislandchamber. com). And for Lopez, contact the **Lopez Island Chamber of Commerce,** 6 Old Post Rd. (P.O. Box 102), Lopez, WA 98261 (© **877/433-2789** or 360/468-4664; www.lopez island.com).

The San Juans As Outdoor Classroom

You can turn a trip to the San Juans into a learning vacation by scheduling a nature workshop with the **San Juan Nature Institute,** 470 Spring St., Ste. 104 (P.O. Box 3110), Friday Harbor, WA 98250 (© **360/378-3646;** www.sjnature.org). One-day workshops cover such topics as the geology of nearby Sucia Island by kayak, wild mushroom identification and cooking, and lichens of Turtleback Mountain.

GETTING THERE

If it's summer and you'd like to visit the San Juans without a car, I recommend booking passage through Victoria Clipper (see below), which operates excursion boats from the Seattle waterfront. If you're traveling by car, you'll need to drive north from Seattle to Anacortes and head out to the islands via **Washington State Ferries** (© **800/843-3779** or 888/808-7977 in Washington, or 206/464-6400; www.wsdot.wa.gov/ferries). Boats run between Anacortes and four of the San Juan Islands (Lopez, Shaw, Orcas, and San Juan) and Sidney, British Columbia (on Vancouver Island near Victoria).

The round-trip fare for a vehicle and driver from Anacortes to Lopez is $24 to $36, to Shaw or Orcas $29 to $43, to San Juan $34 to $51, and to Sidney $43 to $54. The higher fares listed here reflect a summer surcharge, and the lower fares (with the exception of trips to Sidney) are Sunday-through-Tuesday fares.

The round-trip fare for passengers from Anacortes to any of the islands ranges from $10 to $13 ($16 from Anacortes to Sidney). The fare for a vehicle and driver on all westbound Interisland ferries is $17 to $21; walk-on passengers and passengers in cars ride free. Except for service from Sidney, fares are not collected on eastbound ferries, nor are walk-on passengers charged for Interisland ferry service. If you plan to explore the islands by car, you'll save some money by starting your tour on San Juan Island and making your way back east through the islands.

In the summer you may have to wait several hours to get on a ferry, so arrive early.

Note: To cross into Canada and return to the United States by ferry, you will need a passport, passport card, trusted-traveler program card, or an enhanced driver's license. If you are a foreign citizen but a permanent resident of the United States, be sure to carry your passport and your A.R.R. card (green card) or permanent-resident card. Foreign citizens who are only visiting the United States must carry a passport and, if they need one, a visa, when traveling to or from Canada. U.S. children age 15 and under traveling to or from Canada with both parents must have a birth certificate or passport; a child traveling with only one parent should have both a birth certificate and a notarized letter from the other parent giving permission for the child to travel out of the country.

There are also passenger-ferry services from several cities around the region. **Victoria Clipper** (© **800/888-2535,** 206/448-5000, or 250/382-8100; www.victoriaclipper.com) operates excursion boats between Seattle and Friday Harbor on San Juan Island. There are also boats that go to Victoria. For a round-trip to Friday Harbor, expect to pay between $80 and $120 ($40–$60 for children under 12), depending on the time of year. Discounted advance-purchase round-trip fares are often available.

If you're short on time, you can fly to the San Juans. **Kenmore Air** (© **866/435-9524** or 425/486-1257; www.kenmoreair.com) offers floatplane flights that take off from

either Lake Union or the north end of Lake Washington. Round-trip fares to the San Juans are $228 (lower fares available on website). Flights go to Friday Harbor and Roche Harbor on San Juan Island; Rosario Marina, Deer Harbor, and West Sound on Orcas Island; and the Lopez Islander on Lopez Island. There are also flights from Seattle's Boeing Field to the airports in Friday Harbor and Eastsound.

You can also get from Sea-Tac Airport or downtown Seattle to the San Juan Islands ferry terminal in Anacortes on the **Airporter Shuttle** (✆ **866/235-5247** or 360/380-8800; www.airporter.com), which charges $33 one-way and $61 round-trip from the airport. Expect a small additional fuel surcharge.

SAN JUAN ISLAND

Although neither the largest nor the prettiest of the archipelago, San Juan is the most populous and touristy of the San Juan Islands. **Friday Harbor,** where the ferry docks, is the county seat for San Juan County and is the only real town on all the islands. As such, it is home to numerous shops, restaurants, motels, and bed-and-breakfasts that cater to tourists. It's also where you'll find the grocery and hardware stores that provide the necessities of island life. With its large, well-protected marina, it's one of the most popular places in the islands for boaters to drop anchor.

Getting Around

Car rentals are available on San Juan Island from **M&W Auto Sales,** 725 Spring St. (🕻 **800/323-6037** or 360/378-2886; www.interisland.net/mandw), which charges between $50 and $80 per day during the summer.

Cars can also be rented from **Susie's Mopeds,** 125 Nichols St. (🕻 **800/532-0087** or 360/378-5244; www.susiesmopeds.com), which is 1 block from the top of the ferry lanes in Friday Harbor. Susie's rents scooters and mopeds as well, for $30 to $60 per hour or $65 to $130 per day.

For a cab, call **Bob's Taxi** (🕻 **360/378-6777**).

During the summer, **San Juan Transit** (🕻 **800/887-8387** or 360/378-8887; www.sanjuantransit.com) operates a shuttle bus that can be boarded at the ferry terminal. It operates frequently throughout the day, stopping at all the island's major attractions, which makes it a great way to get around for those traveling without a car. Day passes are $15 for adults and $5 for children 5 to 12. Two-day passes ($25 for adults and $10 for children), one-way tickets ($5 adults, $2 children), and round-trip tickets ($10 adults, $3–$4 children) are also available. Children 4 and under always ride free.

Exploring the Island

If you arrive by car, you'll first want to find a parking space, which can be difficult in the summer. Once on foot, take a stroll around **Friday Harbor** to admire the simple wood-frame shop buildings, constructed in the early 20th century. At that time, Friday Harbor was thought of as the southernmost port in Alaska and was a busy little harbor. Schooners and steamships hauled the island's fruit, livestock, and lime (for cement) off to more populous markets. Today such pursuits have all ceased, but reminders of the island's rural roots linger on, and these memories have fueled San Juan's new breadwinner: tourism.

Many of the town's old buildings now house art galleries and interesting shops. At **Waterworks Gallery,** 315 Spring St. (🕻 **360/378-3060;** www.waterworksgallery.com), you'll find fine art and contemporary crafts by local and regional artists. **Arctic Raven Gallery,** 130 S. First St. (🕻 **888/378-3222** or 360/378-3433; www.arcticravengallery. com), specializes in contemporary Native American arts and crafts. Up at the top of Spring Street, behind an amazingly contorted Camperdown elm tree, you can also visit the little **San Juan Islands Museum of Art and Sculpture Park,** 28 First St. (🕻 **360/370-5050;** www.wbay.org), which is affiliated with the Westcott Bay Sculpture Park. The museum, which highlights local and regional artists, is open Thursday through Saturday from noon to 5pm (shorter hours in winter). Admission is by donation.

One of your first stops should be the tasting room at **Island Wine Company,** 2 Cannery Landing (🕻 **800/248-9463** or 360/378-3229; www.sanjuancellars.com), which sells a wide variety of Washington wines and is the only place you can buy wine from the shop's own San Juan Cellars. These latter wines are made from grapes grown in Eastern Washington, not from grapes grown on the islands. You'll find the wine shop on the immediate left as you leave the ferry.

If you walk over to the other side of the ferry landing and then out on the pier that serves as the dock for passenger ferries, you can take a peek at the **Spring Street Landing Aquarium,** a modest tank full of local denizens of the deep. The tank is in a building at the end of the pier. Also keep an eye out for wildlife here; I've seen an otter swimming around by this pier.

Moments   Say Spaaaa!

The San Juan Islands are all about living in the slow lane, and for my money, there's no better way to slow down and relax than by spending time being pampered at a spa. The islands now have several spa options. On San Juan Island, you can get a massage at Friday Harbor's **Lavendera Day Spa,** 440 Spring St. (**© 800/ 349-0337** or 360/378-3637; www.lavenderadayspa.com). Up at the north end of the island, there is the luxurious **Afterglow Roche Harbor Spa** (**© 360/378-9888;** www.rocheharbor.com). On Orcas Island, try the **Orcas Spa & Athletic Center,** 188 A St., Eastsound (**© 888/894-8881;** www.orcasspaandathletics.com).

Continuing along the waterfront toward the marina, you'll come to **Fairweather Park,** where you'll find artist Susan Point's traditional Northwest Coast Indian house-post sculpture, which is similar to a totem pole. The sculpture represents the human–animal relationship and the marine ecosystem. Here in the park, you'll also find some covered picnic tables.

Whale-watching is one of the most popular summer activities in the San Juans, and no one should visit the islands at this time of year without going out to see the area's orca whales. Before you head out, stop by **The Whale Museum** ★, 62 First St. N. (**© 800/ 946-7227,** ext. 30, or 360/378-4710; www.whale-museum.org), where you can see whale skeletons and models of whales and learn all about the area's pods of orcas (also known as killer whales). The museum is open daily from 10am to 5pm; admission is $6 for adults, $5 for seniors, and $3 for students and children 5 to 18. The museum is closed late January through early February and on Thanksgiving, Christmas, and New Year's Day.

If you're interested in learning more about island history, stop by the **San Juan Historical Museum,** 405 Price St. (**© 360/378-3949;** www.sjmuseum.org), which is housed in an 1894 farmhouse and also includes several other historic buildings on its grounds. June to September, the museum is open Wednesday through Saturday from 10am to 4pm and Sunday from 1 to 4pm; October and April, the museum is open Saturday from 10am to 4pm. Open by appointment in other months. Admission is $5 for adults, $4 for seniors, $3 for children ages 6 to 18, and free to children 5 and under.

Most of the island's main attractions can be seen on a long loop drive around the perimeter of San Juan Island. Start the drive by following Roche Harbor signs north out of Friday Harbor (take Spring St. to Second St. to Tucker Ave.).

In about 3 miles, you'll come to **San Juan Vineyards** ★, 3136 Roche Harbor Rd. (**© 360/378-9463;** www.sanjuanvineyards.com), which makes wines both from grapes grown off the island and from its own estate-grown Siegerrebe and Madeleine Angevine grapes. The tasting room is housed in an old schoolhouse built in 1896. It's open daily from 11am to 5pm in summer (call for hours or an appt. in other months).

A little farther north is **Roche Harbor,** once the site of large limestone quarries that supplied lime to much of the West Coast. Many of the quarries' old structures are still visible, giving this area a decaying industrial look, but amid the abandoned machinery stands the historic **Hotel de Haro,** a simple whitewashed wooden building with verandas across its two floors. Stop to admire the old-fashioned marina and colorful gardens, and have a drink or a meal on the deck of the hotel's lounge. In an old pasture on the edge

All About Orcas

Although they are also known as killer whales and were once much maligned as the wolves of the deep, orcas are actually highly intelligent, family-oriented mammals. Orcas can be found in every ocean, but one of their highest concentrations is in the waters stretching north from Puget Sound along the coast of British Columbia. Consequently, this has become one of the most studied and most publicized orca populations in the world.

These whales, which can grow to 30 feet long and weigh almost 9,000 pounds, are the largest members of the porpoise family. In the wild, they can live for up to 80 years, with female orcas commonly living 20 to 30 years longer than males.

Orcas are among the most family-oriented creatures on earth, and related whales will often live together their entire lives, sometimes with three generations present at the same time. Family groups frequently band together with other closely related groups into extended families known as pods. A community of orcas consists of several pods, and in this region the community numbers around 100 individuals. There are three distinct populations of orcas living in the waters off Vancouver Island, British Columbia. They are referred to as the northern and southern resident communities and the transient community. It's the southern resident community that whale-watchers in the San Juan Islands are most likely to encounter.

As predators, orcas do live up to the name "killer whale" and have been known to attack whales much larger than themselves. Some orcas off the coast of Argentina even swim up onto the shore, beaching themselves to attack resting sea lions, and then thrash and twist their way back into the water. But not all orcas feed on other marine mammals. Of the three communities frequenting the waters near Vancouver Island, only the transients feed on mammals. The two resident communities feed primarily on salmon, which are abundant in these waters, especially off the west side of San Juan Island during the summer.

of the resort property, you'll find the **Westcott Bay Sculpture Park** (© 360/370-5050; www.wbay.org), a sculpture park that includes more than 100 works of art set in grassy fields and along the shores of a small pond. Admission to the sculpture park is a suggested $5 donation. Back in the woods near the resort is an unusual **mausoleum,** which was erected by the founder of the quarries and the Hotel de Haro.

South of Roche Harbor, on West Valley Road, you'll come to the **English Camp** unit of **San Juan Island National Historical Park** ★ (© 360/378-2902; www.nps.gov/sajh). This park commemorates the San Juan Island Pig War, one of North America's most unusual and least remembered confrontations. In 1859, San Juan Island nearly became the site of a battle between the British and the Americans. The two countries had not yet agreed upon the border between the United States and Canada when a British pig on San Juan Island decided to have dinner in an American garden. Not taking too kindly to this, the owner of the garden shot the pig. The Brits, instead of welcoming this succulent addition to their evening's repast, demanded redress. In less time than it takes to smoke a ham, both sides were calling in reinforcements. Luckily, this pigheadedness was defused, and a more serious confrontation was avoided.

The English Camp unit of the historical park is set on picturesque Garrison Bay, and, with its huge old shade trees, wide lawns, and white wooden buildings, it's the epitome of British civility. There's even a formal garden surrounded by a white picket fence. You can look inside the reconstructed buildings and imagine the days when this was one of the most far-flung corners of the British Empire. If you're full of energy, hike the 1.25-mile trail to the top of 650-foot **Mount Young** for a beautiful panorama of the island. An easier 1-mile hike hugs the shoreline out to the end of **Bell Point.** The visitor center is open from June through early September daily from 9am to 5pm. Throughout the summer, various living-history programs are held here on weekends.

South of English Camp, watch for the Mitchell Bay Road turnoff. This connects to the Westside Road, which leads down the island's west coast. Along this road you'll find **San Juan County Park,** a great spot for a picnic. A little farther south is **Lime Kiln Point State Park** ★★ (© 360/378-2044; www.parks.wa.gov), the country's first whale-watching park and a great place to spot these gentle giants in summer. This latter park is open daily from 8am to dusk. Flanking the state park are Deadman Bay Preserve and Lime Kiln Preserve, two properties acquired for public use by the San Juan County Land Bank. Together the state park and the two preserves have more than 3 miles of hiking trails, making this the best hiking area on the island. South of Deadman Bay Preserve, you can also access the shore at the Westside Scenic Preserve.

As Westside Road moves inland, a left onto Wold Road will bring you to **Pelindaba Lavender Farms,** 33 Hawthorne Lane (© 866/819-1911 or 360/378-4248; www.pelindaba.com). The farm has 20 acres of lavender plants, including a cutting field where visitors can cut their own lavender stems. Although the farm fields are open year-around, the gift shop is open April through October daily from 9:30am to 5:30pm. The gift shop is packed with lavender-scented products. There's a second gift shop—Pelindaba Friday Harbor—in the Friday Harbor Center shopping plaza, 150 First St. in downtown Friday Harbor. This shop is open daily from 9:30am to 5pm throughout the year. The farm has a **Lavender Harvest Festival** each year in mid-July.

At the far south end of the island is the wind-swept promontory on which **American Camp** stood during the Pig War. Here you'll find two reconstructed buildings and a visitor center (late May–early Sept, daily 8:30am–5pm; early Sept–late May, day and hours vary—call for current information); before American Camp was built here, this

---

(**Moments**)   **Under Sail in the San Juans**

If you leave the San Juan Islands without doing some sort of boating, you've missed the point. The waters surrounding these islands are ideal for exploring by boat, and one of my favorite ways to see the San Juans is from the deck of a sailboat. A good option is **Emerald Isle Sailing Charters** (© **866/714-6611** or 360/376-3472; www.emeraldislesailing.com), which offers 6-hour day sails, as well as overnight and multiday sailboat charters. On a sail through the islands you're likely to see orcas, harbor seals, harbor porpoises, and plenty of bald eagles. A 6-hour tour is $135 per person.

was the site of a Hudson's Bay Company farm. The meadows sweeping down to the sea were once grazed by sheep and cattle, but today you'll see only rabbits browsing amid the high grasses and wildflowers (and the occasional red fox stalking the rabbits). Hiking trails here lead along the bluffs and down to the sea. My favorites are the **Mount Finlayson Trail,** which leads to the top of a grassy hill, and the **Lagoon Trail,** which passes through a dark forest of Douglas fir to **Jackle's Lagoon,** a great spot for bird-watching. Keep your eyes peeled for bald eagles, which are relatively plentiful around here. If you'd just like to picnic at a pleasant and secluded beach, head to the park's **Fourth of July Beach.**

Continuing past American Camp will bring you to Cattle Point, site of a lighthouse and the **Cattle Point Interpretive Area,** one of the best picnic spots on the island. In the 1920s, this was a Navy Radio Compass Station that helped ships navigate the nearby waters. Today there are rock outcrops, two tiny beaches, great views of Lopez Island, interpretive signs, and a few picnic tables. Cattle Point is also a good destination for a bike ride from Friday Harbor.

Sports & Outdoor Pursuits

BIKING ★ Winding country roads are ideal for leisurely trips. If you didn't bring your own wheels, you can rent a bike in Friday Harbor from **Island Bicycles,** 380 Argyle St. (© **360/378-4941;** www.islandbicycles.com), which charges $9 to $18 per hour (2-hr. minimum) or $36 to $72 per day.

HIKING In addition to the hiking trails at English Camp and American Camp, and adjacent to Lime Kiln Point State Park ★★, you'll find a network of almost 20 miles of trails just outside Roche Harbor, on the north end of the island. You can find out more about these and other island trails at the website of the **San Juan Island Trails Committee** (www.sanjuanislandtrails.org), which also has printable trail maps. The trails near Roche Harbor link up with trails in the English Camp unit of San Juan Island National Historical Park.

SEA KAYAKING ★★ Between early April and early November, sea-kayak tours are offered by **San Juan Outfitters** (© **866/810-1483** or 360/378-1962; www.sanjuan islandoutfitters.com), which operates out of Roche Harbor, at the north end of the island. You'll pay $75 for a 3-hour tour and $89 for a 5-hour tour. This company also operates out of Friday Harbor. **Crystal Seas Kayaking** (© **877/732-7877** or 360/378-4223; www.crystalseas.com), which paddles the waters off the west side of San Juan, does anything from 3-hour tours ($75) and sunset tours ($75) to all-day tours ($95) and multiday trips. Three- and 4-day trips are offered by **San Juan Kayak Expeditions** (© **360/378-4436;** www.sanjuankayak.com), which charges $480 and $580, respectively, for its outings.

WHALE-WATCHING ★★ When it's time to spot some whales, you have three choices. You can take a whale-watching cruise, go out in a sea kayak, or head over to **Lime Kiln Point State Park ★★,** where a short trail leads down to a rocky coastline from which orca whales, minke whales, Dall's porpoises, and sea lions can sometimes be seen. The best months to see orcas are June through September, but it's possible to see them throughout the year.

April through October, 3- to 3½-hour whale-watching cruises from Friday Harbor are offered by **San Juan Safaris** (© **800/450-6858** or 360/378-1323; www.sanjuansafaris. com), which charges $75 for adults and $49 for children 2 to 12. Similar cruises are offered

(**Moments**)   **Thar She Blows!**

While summer visitors to San Juan have a few ways to go whale-watching, as far as I'm concerned, the best way to search for orcas is from a sea kayak, and the best kayaking company for such an outing is **Outdoor Odysseys** (℡ **800/647-4621,** 360/378-3533 in summer, or 206/361-0717 in winter; www.outdoor odysseys.com), which has been operating in the San Juans for more than 20 years. This company's trips start from San Juan County Park and head out through the local orca pods' favorite feeding grounds near Lime Kiln Point State Park. In the summer, you stand a good chance of seeing orcas, and any time of year, you're likely to see harbor seals and bald eagles. Day tours, offered mid-May through September, cost $91 and include lunch.

by **San Juan Excursions** (℡ **800/809-4253** or 360/378-6636; www.watchwhales.com), which operates out of Friday Harbor. Cruises are $75 for adults and $49 for children 2 to 12. If you're staying up at the north end of the island, you can go out with **San Juan Outfitters** (℡ **866/810-1483** or 360/378-1962; www.sanjuanislandoutfitters.com), which offers 3- to 4-hour whale-watching tours for $75 adults, $49 children ages 2 to 12).

Where to Stay

Earthbox Motel & Spa ★ (**Kids**)   This lodging 4 blocks uphill from the ferry dock is one of the hippest hotels on the island. That said, with its complimentary bikes and indoor pool and Jacuzzi, it is also a great choice for families. With an associated day spa, this is also a good place for a hedonistic couple's retreat. There are a number of different equally stylish room types from which to choose, but most have hardwood floors and black platform beds with plush mattresses and linens, definitely not what you would expect from the well-maintained but dated architecture of this place. This hotel also operates the nearby Bird Rock Hotel, where rooms have a similar contemporary, urban feel.

410 Spring St. (P.O. Box 1729), Friday Harbor, WA 98250. ℡ **800/793-4756** or 360/378-4000. Fax 360/378-4351. www.earthboxmotel.com. 72 units. Mid-June to early Sept $207–$227 double, $257–$407 suite/house; May to mid-June and early Sept to late Sept $177–$197 double, $217–$357 suite/house; Oct–Apr $147–$167 double, $187–$257 suite/house. Children 11 and under stay free in parent's room. AE, MC, V. Pets accepted ($15 per night). **Amenities:** Bikes; concierge; exercise room and access to nearby health club; Jacuzzi; indoor pool; room service; sauna; day spa. *In room:* TV, fridge, hair dryer, Wi-Fi.

Friday Harbor House ★★   With its contemporary yet distinctly Northwest architecture, this luxurious little boutique hotel brings urban sophistication to Friday Harbor. From the hotel's bluff-top location, you have excellent views of the ferry landing, the Friday Harbor marina, and, in the distance, Orcas Island. Guest rooms have fireplaces and oversized whirlpool tubs, making this place a great choice for a romantic getaway. In some rooms, you can relax in your tub and gaze at both the view out the window and your own crackling fire. Many units have small balconies. Rooms and suites here are some of the best in the San Juan Islands, and if you enjoy contemporary styling, you'll love this place.

130 West St. (P.O. Box 1385), Friday Harbor, WA 98250. ℡ **866/722-7356** or 360/378-8455. Fax 360/378-8453. www.fridayharborhouse.com. 23 units. Memorial Day weekend to Sept $205–$325 double, $360 suite; Oct to Memorial Day weekend $135–$200 double, $265 suite. Lower midweek rates in winter. Rates

include continental breakfast. Children 15 and under stay free in parent's room. AE, DISC, MC, V. **Amenities:** Restaurant (Northwest), lounge; access to nearby health club. *In room:* TV/VCR/DVD, fridge, hair dryer, minibar, Wi-Fi.

Juniper Lane Guest House ★ (Value)

This cedar-shingled house, with its colorful trim, sits on the outskirts of Friday Harbor and has views of pastures just over the back fence. Constructed primarily from salvaged wood, this eco-friendly guesthouse is a labor of love for young owner Juniper Maas, who patterned her lodging after places she's visited in her world travels. The interior is a bold blend of burnished wood and bright colors, with eclectic artwork on display throughout. Some guest rooms have shared bathrooms, while others have private bathrooms. My personal favorite is the Regal room, with its clawfoot tub. Although breakfast is not included in the rates, guests have use of the kitchen. Young travelers, and the young at heart, should like this place as much as I do.

1312 Beaverton Valley Rd., Friday Harbor, WA 98250. ℂ **888/397-2597** or 360/378-7761. www.juniper laneguesthouse.com. 6 units. $65–$85 double with shared bathroom; $89–$135 double with private bathroom; $100–$185 family room; $150–$199 cabin. Children 7 and under allowed only in cabin. MC, V. *In room:* Hair dryer, no phone, Wi-Fi.

Lakedale Resort at Three Lakes ★★ (Kids)

Although best known as the island's favorite private campground, Lakedale Resort at Three Lakes also has six very attractive modern log cabins, a 10-room lodge that is a luxurious rendition of a classic log mountain lodge, and 14 canvas-walled, tentlike cabins. The cabins are attractively and individually decorated, with large cedar porches that overlook the forest and lake. All have two bedrooms, two bathrooms, a full kitchen, and a gas fireplace. There's a hot tub in a gazebo, and guests have access to the resort's 82 acres, which include trails and several lakes that are good for trout fishing, swimming, and canoeing (boat rentals are available). Think of this as a sort of summer camp for the entire family. Lots of fun and very woodsy. Guests staying in the lodge get a continental breakfast, and those staying in a canvas tent get breakfast in a canvas "mess tent."

4313 Roche Harbor Rd., Friday Harbor, WA 98250. ℂ **800/617-2267** or 360/378-2350. Fax 360/378-0944. www.lakedale.com. 20 units. $139 canvas cabin double (available May–Oct); $179–$249 lodge double; $249–$349 cabin; $419–$489 house. Children 15 and under not allowed in lodge; children 15 and under stay free in parent's cabin. AE, DC, DISC, MC, V. Pets accepted in cabins ($25 per night). **Amenities:** Canoe rentals. *In room (lodge):* TV/DVD, fridge, hair dryer, Internet. *In room (cabin and house):* TV/DVD, fridge, kitchen.

Olympic Lights Bed & Breakfast ★★

Located at San Juan's dry southwestern tip, the Olympic Lights is a Victorian farmhouse surrounded by wind-swept meadows, and if it weren't for the sight of Puget Sound out the window, you could easily mistake the setting for the prairies of the Midwest. There are colorful flower gardens, an old barn, even some hens to lay the eggs for your breakfast. The ocean breezes, nearby beach, and friendliness of innkeepers Christian and Lea Andrade lend a special feel to this American classic. My favorite room here is the Ra Room, which is named for the Egyptian sun god and features a big bay window. The view is enough to soothe the most stressed-out soul.

146 Starlight Way, Friday Harbor, WA 98250. ℂ **888/211-6195** or 360/378-3186. Fax 360/378-2097. www. olympiclights.com. 4 units. Mid-May to mid-Oct $150–$160 double; mid-Oct to mid-May $105 double. Rates include full breakfast. 2-night minimum July–Sept. No credit cards. *In room:* Hair dryer, no phone.

Roche Harbor ★★ (Kids)

At the north end of San Juan, Roche Harbor is steeped in island history and makes a fascinating getaway. The centerpiece of this resort is the historic Hotel de Haro, which was built in 1886 and overlooks the resort's marina and a

gorgeous formal garden. Because the old hotel has not been renovated in recent years, its
rooms are the most basic here. To fully appreciate Roche Harbor's setting, you should
stay in a suite (the Quarryman Hall suites are among the finest rooms on the island), a
Company Town cottage, or one of the carriage houses or cottages on the green. The
condominiums, although dated, are good bets for families. The waterfront dining room
has a view of the marina, and the deck makes a great spot for a sunset cocktail. In addition to the amenities listed below, there are moped rentals, whale-watching cruises, and
sea-kayak tours.

248 Reuben Memorial Dr. (P.O. Box 4001), Roche Harbor, WA 98250. (C) **800/451-8910** or 360/378-2155.
Fax 360/378-6809. www.rocheharbor.com. 78 units,16 with shared bathroom. Summer $139 double with
shared bathroom, $229–$449 suite, $269–$379 condo, $339–$799 cottage or town house; other months
$79 double with shared bathroom, $139–$239 suite, $179–$279 condo, $199–$429 cottage or town
house. AE, MC, V. **Amenities:** 3 restaurants, lounge; outdoor pool; full-service spa; 2 tennis courts.
In room: Hair dryer.

Tucker House ★   This collection of 1898 Victorian houses, just 2 blocks from the
ferry landing, is a convenient choice, especially if you came to the islands without a car.
Most rooms and suites have their own two-person whirlpool tubs, and some also have
balconies. If you enjoy a luxurious bathroom, ask for the Dove in the Window or
Patience Corner room. A four-course breakfast is served each morning in the inn's garden
cafe. The inn's owners also operate the adjacent Harrison House Suites Bed & Breakfast
and Coho Restaurant.

260 B St., Friday Harbor, WA 98250. (C) **800/965-0123** or 360/378-2783. www.tuckerhouse.com. 10 units.
$175–$260 double; $275–$385 suite; $150–$260 cottage (lower rates Oct–May). Rates include full breakfast. Children 6 and under stay free in parent's room. AE, MC, V. Pets accepted ($25 per night). **Amenities:**
Restaurant; bikes; concierge; access to nearby health club. *In room:* TV/VCR, hair dryer, no phone, Wi-Fi.

Where to Dine

In addition to the restaurants listed below, Friday Harbor has several other places where
you can get a quick, simple meal. About a block from the top of the ferry lanes is **The
Market Chef,** 225 A St. (C) **360/378-4546**), a combination espresso bar and gourmet
takeout restaurant that also bakes outrageously good chocolate-chip cookies. This place
is open Monday through Friday from 10am to 6pm. If you're staying someplace with a
kitchen and want fresh seafood for dinner, stop by **Friday Harbor Seafood** (C) **360/
378-5779**), on the main dock in the Friday Harbor marina. This seafood market also
sells smoked fish (including succulent smoked scallops), which makes great picnic fare.

For a decent latte, head to **San Juan Coffee Roasting Company,** 18 Cannery Landing
((C) **360/378-4443;** www.rockisland.com/~sjcoffee), on the dock at the ferry landing, or

---

(**Moments**   **Striking Colors at Roche Harbor**

As the summer sun sets over the San Juans, strains of the *Colonel Bogie March*
drift over the boats docked at the Roche Harbor marina. The music signals the
nightly lowering of the four flags that fly over the marina. With plenty of pomp
and circumstance, the flags of Washington state, the United States, Canada, and
Great Britain are lowered by Roche Harbor employees. Appropriate music accom-
panies the lowering of each flag, and a cannon is fired as the U.S. flag is lowered.
There's no better way to end a summer day on San Juan Island.

the **Doctor's Office,** 85 Front St. (© 360/378-8865), just across the street from the ferry landing. When it's time for beer, heft a pint of locally brewed ale at the **Front Street Ale House,** 1 Front St. (© 360/378-2337; www.sanjuanbrewing.com).

If you're up near the north end of the island at mealtime, you've got several good options at the Roche Harbor resort, marina, and historic hotel. **McMillin's Dining Room** (© 360/378-5757; www.rocheharbor.com) is the most formal option and serves the best food. For a more casual setting and a waterside deck, try the **Madrona Grill** (© 360/378-5757), which is popular with the boating crowd that ties up in the marina. For lunch or a light dinner, try the **Lime Kiln Cafe** (© 360/378-5757), on the dock at Roche Harbor. This lively little cafe serves good chowder and fish and chips. Big windows let you gaze out at the boats in the marina. If you're an early riser, you can also drop by here for a hearty breakfast or some fresh cinnamon-and-sugar donuts.

Backdoor Kitchen ★★ ECLECTIC/INTERNATIONAL   This is the sort of gem that travelers dream of discovering. Hidden at the back of a warehouse-like building in Friday Harbor, the Backdoor Kitchen is a back-alley find serving some of the best food in the islands. The clientele seems to be primarily locals, many of whom come to sip creative cocktails and hang out in the restaurant's little bar. The menu ranges all over the globe for inspiration and changes seasonally. I once had a delicious and unusual spiced-duck cake appetizer here, but there are also plenty of well-prepared salads and mussel and clam appetizers from which to choose. Entrees are as diverse as pan-seared scallops with ginger-sake beurre blanc and a classic Mediterranean lamb sirloin. Don't miss this place.

400b A St. © **360/378-9540.** www.backdoorkitchen.com. Reservations recommended. Main courses $24–$31 dinner. MC, V. Wed–Mon 5–9pm.

Coho Restaurant ★★ NORTHWEST   Coho, housed in a little Craftsman bungalow a block from the ferry lanes, serves the best food in Friday Harbor. Small and sophisticated (there are only eight tables), this restaurant features a short menu that changes with the season. The hazelnut-encrusted lavender chicken I once had here ranked right up there with some of the best chicken I've ever had, and the Asian-inspired, sesame-seed-encrusted salmon is another good bet. The owners, Anna Maria de Freitas and David Pass, also own the nearby Tucker House and Harrison House B&Bs. Coho gets much of its produce locally and participates in the Island's Certified Local Program.

120 Nichols St. © **360/378-6330.** www.cohorestaurant.com. Reservations recommended. Main courses $18–$30; 3-course dinner $30. AE, MC, V. June–Sept Mon–Sat 5–9pm; call for days and hours in other months.

Duck Soup Inn ★★ NORTHWEST/INTERNATIONAL   This restaurant, located 4½ miles north of Friday Harbor, perfectly sums up the San Juan Islands experience. It's rustic and casual, set in tranquil rural surroundings beside a small pond, and yet it serves superb multicourse dinners. Inside the quintessentially Northwest building, you'll find lots of exposed wood and a fieldstone fireplace. The menu changes frequently, depending on the availability of fresh produce, but is always very creative (the chef has a penchant for the flavors of Asia and the Mediterranean). You might find chicken braised in pomegranate sauce or grilled coriander-crusted scallops.

50 Duck Soup Lane. © **360/378-4878.** www.ducksoupinn.com. Reservations highly recommended. Main courses $17–$35. MC, V. July to mid-Sept Tues–Sun 5–10pm; call for days and hours in other months. Closed Nov–Mar.

The Place Bar & Grill ★★ NORTHWEST/INTERNATIONAL   Just to the right as you get off the ferry, and housed in a small wooden building that was once part of a U.S. Coast Guard station, the Place is the island's finest waterfront restaurant. The menu

Did You Know?

- With 375 miles of saltwater shoreline, San Juan County, which encompasses the San Juan Islands, has more shoreline than any other county in the United States.
- Channels between the San Juan Islands range from 600 to 1,000 feet deep.
- Water temperatures off the San Juan Islands range from 45°F (7°C) in winter to 52°F (11°C) in summer.
- Lt. Henry Martyn Robert, author of *Robert's Rules of Order*, was stationed on San Juan Island during the Pig War.
- All Washington State Ferries have Native American names, except those of the Evergreen class.
- Puget Sound's first ferry went into operation on January 1, 1889, and car ferries were added in 1915. The first ferry cost 5¢.

changes regularly, but one of my favorite dishes—baked oysters with hazelnut-garlic butter—is almost always available. No matter what you order for your entree, I recommend starting your meal with the mushroom sauté, which was featured in *Bon Appétit* magazine. I like to accompany my dessert with a glass of Lopez Island Vineyards raspberry wine.

1 Spring St. © **360/378-8707.** www.theplacesanjuan.com. Reservations highly recommended. Main courses $18–$34. MC, V. Daily 5–9pm (winter hours may vary).

Steps Wine Bar and Cafe ★★ NEW AMERICAN   The menu at this stylish restaurant is short and changes frequently to take advantage of whatever is fresh, while the wine list is long, featuring excellent wines from all over the world. Whether you just need a few light snacks to go with a glass of wine or a filling dinner, you'll be happy. Small plates and starters make up the bulk of the offerings, so you can piece together a dinner that fits your appetite. Just don't order too much before you get to dessert. I like to eat downstairs, which has a view of the open kitchen, but the quieter loft level is a good place for a romantic dinner.

In Friday Harbor Center, First Street (btw. Spring and East sts.). © **360/370-5959.** www.stepswine barandcafe.com. Reservations recommended. Main dishes $16–$36. MC, V. Summer Mon–Sat 5–9pm (shorter hours other months).

ORCAS ISLAND

Shaped like a horseshoe, and named for an 18th-century Mexican viceroy (not for the area's orca whales, as is commonly assumed), Orcas Island has long been a popular summer vacation spot and is the most beautiful of the San Juan Islands. Orcas is a particular favorite of nature lovers, who come to enjoy the views of green rolling pastures, forested mountains, and fjordlike bays.

Getting Around

For car rentals on Orcas Island, **M&W Auto Sales** (© **800/323-6037** or 360/376-5266; www.sanjuanauto.com) charges $60 and is open only from mid-May through mid-October.

From the end of June to the middle of September, the **Orcas Island Shuttle** (© 360/ 376-7433; www.orcasislandshuttle.com) can transport you around the island. The fare is $6 per person between any two points on the island or $12 for a day pass. This same company also rents cars.

Exploring the Island

Eastsound, the largest town on the island, has several interesting shops and good restaurants. Other villages on Orcas include Deer Harbor, West Sound, and Olga.

In Eastsound, be sure to stop in at **Darvill's Bookstore,** 296 Main St. (© 360/376-2135; www.darvillsbookstore.com), which specializes in Northwest fiction, history, and guidebooks. Chocoholics won't want to miss **Kathryn Taylor Chocolates,** 109 N Beach Rd. (© 360/376-1030; www.ktchocolates.com), where you can get hand-dipped chocolates made with local fruits and nuts. If you're a gardener, don't miss the fascinating **Smith & Speed Mercantile,** 294 A St. (© 360/376-1006; www.smithandspeed.com), which sells homestead supplies and tools. You've never seen so many different spades and garden forks in one place. To learn more about Orcas Island, stop by the interesting little **Orcas Historical Museum,** 181 North Beach Rd. (© 360/376-4849; www.orcas museum.org), which is housed in a collection of six interconnected historic buildings that were moved to the center of Eastsound from locations around the island. The museum is open late May through late September, Tuesday through Sunday from 11am to 4pm. Admission is $5 for adults, $4 for seniors, $3 for students, and children 12 and under are free.

Just outside Eastsound, off Horseshoe Highway, you'll find **Howe Art,** 236 Double Hill Rd. (© 360/376-2945; www.howeart.net), a studio and gallery run by sculptor Anthony Howe, who fashions fascinating hanging kinetic sculptures from stainless steel.

Several interesting pottery shops are located around the island. A few miles west of Eastsound off Enchanted Forest Road is **Orcas Island Pottery,** 338 Old Pottery Rd. (© 360/376-2813; www.orcasislandpottery.com), the oldest pottery studio in the Northwest. Between Eastsound and Orcas, on Horseshoe Highway, is **Crow Valley Pottery,** 2274 Orcas Rd. (© 877/512-8184 or 360/376-4260; www.crowvalley.com), housed in an 1866 log cabin. There's also a second Crow Valley Pottery shop in Eastsound at 296 Main Street. And on the east side of the island in the community of Olga, you'll find **Orcas Island Artworks,** 11 Point Lawrence Rd. (© 360/376-4408; www.orcasartworks.com), which is full of beautiful works by island artists. Just a couple of blocks from this gallery, you'll find the much smaller **Olga Pottery,** 6928 Olga Road (© 360/376-4648; www.olgapottery.com), which showcases the work of potter Jerry Weatherman.

Sports, Outdoor Pursuits & Tours

Moran State Park ★★ (© 360/902-8844; www.parks.wa.gov) covers 5,252 acres of the island. This is the largest park in the San Juans and the main destination for most island visitors. If the weather is clear, you'll enjoy great views from the summit of Mount Constitution, which rises 2,409 feet above Puget Sound. Also here are five lakes, 33 miles of hiking trails, and an environmental learning center. Popular park activities include fishing, hiking, boating, mountain biking, and camping (for campsite reservations, contact **Washington State Parks** at © 888/226-7688, or go to www.parks.wa.gov/ reservations). The park is off Horseshoe Highway, approximately 13 miles from the ferry landing.

BIKING ★ Although Orcas is considered the most challenging of the San Juan Islands for biking, plenty of cyclists pedal the island's roads. **Dolphin Bay Bicycles** (© 360/376-4157 or 360/317-6734; www.rockisland.com/~dolphin), located just to the right as you get off the ferry, has long been my favorite place in the islands to rent a bike. It's so close to the ferry dock that you can come to Orcas without a car, walk up the street to the shop, and hop on a bike. From here you can explore Orcas Island or take a free ferry to Lopez Island or Shaw Island. Bikes rent for $30 per day, $70 for 3 days, and $100 per week.

If you're already on the island and staying up near Eastsound, try **Wildlife Cycles,** 350 North Beach Rd., Eastsound (© **360/376-4708;** www.wildlifecycles.com), where bikes rent for $30 to $45 per day, $75 to $110 for 3 days, and $105 to $160 for a week. Hourly rentals are also available.

BOAT RENTALS & CHARTERS For a much slower and more relaxing excursion, take a sailboat ride with **Northwest Classic Day Sailing** (© **360/376-5581;** www.classicday sails.com). Tours are aboard the 1940s vintage sloop *Aura,* which is skippered by Ward Fay. Three-hour afternoon and evening tours operate out of Deer Harbor and cost $70 for adults and $55 for children under 13. The season runs from mid-May through September.

If you're an experienced sailor or powerboater, you can rent a boat from **Orcas Boat Rentals** (© **360/376-7616;** www.orcasboats.com), which rents 16- to 19-foot run-abouts ($225–$250 for 4 hr., $300–$325 for 8 hr.). They also rent 24-foot sailboats ($225 for 4 hr., $300 for 8 hr.).

Outer Island Expeditions (© **360/376-3711;** www.outerislandx.com), based at Brandt's Landing Marina near the Smuggler's Villa Resort on the north shore of Orcas Island, operates a ferry to Sucia Island, a state park and one of the prettiest islands in the San Juans. Round-trip service costs $45, with a two-person minimum. Mountain bikes (there are trails on the island) and sea kayaks can also be transported.

HIKING **Moran State Park** ★★, with its 33 miles of trails, is the best known and most popular place on Orcas to hike. The park offers hikes ranging from short, easy strolls alongside lakes to strenuous, all-day outings. However, the very best hiking destination on the island is in the 1,576-acre **Turtleback Mountain Preserve** (© **360/378-4402;** www.sjclandbank.org/turtle_back.html), which is on the west side of the island. A trail runs north–south through the preserve, and the hike up from the southern trail head is the best hike in the entire Puget Sound region. In 1 hour's strenuous uphill walking, you'll climb nearly 1,000 feet and reach a rocky knoll from which you can look east to the pastures and hedgerows of Crow Valley and west across West Sound to dozens of islands scattered across shimmering waters. In the distance rise the Olympic Mountains

Ⓜ**Moments** **Winging It on Orcas**

While the view from the top of Mount Constitution, in Moran State Park, is pretty impressive, you can get an even more memorable view of Orcas and the rest of the San Juan Islands from the cockpit of a Travelair biplane operated by **Magic Air Tours** (© **800/376-1929** or 360/376-2733; www.magicair.com). Plane rides for one person cost $249 and rides for two people cost $299. Flights are offered April through October and occasionally in other months.

and the hazy blue ridges of Canada's Vancouver Island. Come in June and you'll likely see wildflowers on Turtleback Mountain's open slopes. To reach the southern trail head, drive about a mile west from the community of West Sound on Deer Harbor Road and turn right on Wild Rose Lane. The parking area is about 100 yards up this gravel road.

Another good hiking spot can be found south of the community of Olga, on the east arm of the island, where you'll find a .5-mile trail through **Obstruction Pass State Park** ★★. This trail leads to a quiet little cove that has a few walk-in/paddle-in campsites. The park is at the end of Obstruction Pass Road.

If you'd like to have a knowledgeable local guide to take you out on the trails at Moran State Park or, better yet, on one of the outer islands of the San Juans, contact **Gnat's Nature Hikes** (© 360/376-6629; www.orcasislandhikes.com). Half-day hikes in Moran State Park cost $30 per person; outer-island hike prices vary.

SEA KAYAKING ★★   The best way to see the Orcas Island coast is by sea kayak. My favorite local kayaking company is **Shearwater Adventures** (© 360/376-4699; www.shearwaterkayaks.com), which offers guided 3-hour tours ($60), as well as sunset and moonlight paddles ($60), wildflower trips ($70), and trips around nearby Sucia Island ($125). These tours go out from several locations around the island, but I think those departing from Deer Harbor are the most scenic.

If you're on the island without a car, it's possible to go out from right at the ferry landing with **Orcas Outdoors** (© 360/376-4611; www.orcasoutdoors.com), which offers guided sea-kayak tours lasting from 1 hour ($30) to 3 hours ($60). All-day and multiday tours are also offered.

Two-hour paddle tours ($30) are offered by **Spring Bay** (© 360/376-5531; www.springbayinn.com), which is on the east side of the island near the village of Olga. These trips are in an area where bald eagles nest in summer.

WHALE-WATCHING ★★   If you want to see some of the orca whales for which the San Juans are famous, you can take a whale-watching excursion with **Deer Harbor Charters** (© **800/544-5758** or 360/376-5989; www.deerharborcharters.com), which operates out of both Deer Harbor and Rosario Marina and charges $49 to $69 for adults and $35 to $44 for children under 14 (lower rates are for off season, when orcas are rarely seen); or with **Orcas Island Eclipse Charters** (© **800/376-6566** or 360/376-6566; www.orcasislandwhales.com), which operates out of the Orcas Island ferry dock and charges $72 for adults and $48 for children.

Where to Stay

The Inn at Ship Bay ★★   Set on a high bluff just outside the village of Eastsound, this inn boasts a tranquil setting and rooms that are both luxurious and comfortable. Pillow-top king beds and gas fireplaces make it easy to spend way too much of your visit just cozying up in the rooms here. If you sit back in the Adirondack chairs on your balcony and gaze out over the water, you may never leave. Although guest rooms are in modern buildings that have been designed to look old, the inn's centerpiece is an 1869 home that serves as the restaurant.

326 Olga Rd., Orcas Island, WA 98245. © **877/276-7296** or 360/376-5886. www.innatshipbay.com. 11 units. Summer $175–$195 double, $275–$295 suite; other months $125–$150 double, $250 suite. Rates include continental breakfast. MC, V. **Amenities:** Restaurant. *In room:* TV, fridge, Wi-Fi.

Inn on Orcas Island ★★   Looking as if it were transplanted from Cape Cod or Martha's Vineyard, this inn blends traditional styling with contemporary lines to create a classically inspired beauty. Situated on a meadow overlooking a small bay just off Deer

Harbor, this elegant inn has luxurious rooms in the main house plus a cottage and a more casually decorated carriage house. Some rooms have balconies; suites have jetted tubs. All of the accommodations feature water views, impeccable decor, and the plushest beds in the San Juans. Innkeepers Jeremy Trumble and John Gibbs once owned a frame shop and spent years collecting and framing all the art that now hangs in the inn. A sunroom in the main house is a wonderful place to while away the morning. Breakfasts are lavish affairs that will leave you full until dinner. If you'd like to get out on the water, there's a rowboat you can borrow.

114 Channel Rd. (P.O. Box 309), Deer Harbor, WA 98243. ℂ 888/886-1661 or 360/376-5227. Fax 360/376-5228. www.theinnonorcasisland.com. 8 units. July–Aug $205 double, $235–$305 suite, cottage, or carriage house; June and Sept $185 double, $215–$285 suite, cottage, or carriage house; Oct–May $145 double, $185–$245 suite, cottage, or carriage house. Rates include full breakfast. 2-night minimum May–Oct, holidays, and all weekends. AE, MC, V. No children 15 or under. **Amenities:** Bikes. *In room:* Fridge, hair dryer, Wi-Fi.

The Kingfish Inn ★ (Finds)   Housed in the old West Sound general store, this inn is about as quaint as they come. Downstairs, the old general store has been converted into a cozy little cafe, while upstairs, there are three rooms with views over West Sound. These views are among the best on the island. The fourth room is just off the cafe's deck. However, the upstairs rooms are much more attractively furnished, with a sort of Tuscan feel, and you should try to get one of these rooms. These rooms have rustic armoires and beautiful beds with fluffy duvets. One of the rooms has a woodstove and one has a picture-perfect porch. Bathrooms, however, are very basic and have showers only.

Deer Harbor and Crow Valley rds., West Sound (mailing address 4362 Crow Valley Rd., Eastsound, WA 98245). ℂ 360/376-4440. www.kingfishinn.com. 4 units. May–Oct $160–$170 double; Nov–Apr $140 double. Rates include breakfast. MC, V. **Amenities:** Restaurant. *In room:* TV/VCR, hair dryer.

Turtleback Farm Inn ★★   Nowhere on Orcas will you find a more idyllic setting than at this bright-green restored farmhouse, which overlooks 80 acres of farmland at the foot of Turtleback Mountain. Simply furnished with antiques, the guest rooms range from cozy to spacious, and each has its own special view. My favorite unit in the main house is the Meadow View Room, which has a private deck and a clawfoot tub. The four rooms in the Orchard House are among the biggest and most luxurious on the island (with gas fireplaces, clawfoot tubs, balconies, wood floors, and refrigerators). Days here start with a big farm breakfast served at valley-view tables that are set with bone china, silver, and linen, or, if you're staying in the Orchard House, with a breakfast delivered to your room.

1981 Crow Valley Rd., Eastsound, WA 98245. ℂ 800/376-4914 or 360/376-4914. Fax 360/376-5329. www.turtlebackinn.com. 11 units. Main house: June–Oct $115–$195 double; Orchard House: June–Sept $260 double. Lower rates other months. Rates include full breakfast. 2-night minimum June–Sept, weekends, and holidays. DISC, MC, V. Children 4 and under stay free in parent's room in Orchard House; no children 8 or under in farmhouse. Pets accepted ($50 fee). **Amenities:** Concierge. *In room:* CD player, hair dryer, Wi-Fi.

Where to Dine

Housed in a little cottage in Eastsound, **The Kitchen,** 249 Prune Alley (ℂ 360/376-6958), is my favorite spot on the island for healthy light meals. This place isn't strictly vegetarian, but it does lots of great Asian-inspired wraps and rice-and-noodle dishes. In summer, the Kitchen is open Monday through Saturday from 11am to 7pm; hours are shorter in other months. If you just need some wine for a picnic, head to **Country Corner Cellars,** 837 Crescent Beach Dr. (ℂ 360/376-6907; www.countrycornercellars.com), which is behind the gas station just east of Eastsound.

Tips Good Food at the Odd Fellows Hall

Eastsound's **Odd Fellows Hall,** 112 Haven Rd. (© **360/376-5640;** www.oddshall. org), a block off Main Street on the road to picturesque Madrona Point, has for many years been a starting point for creative Orcas Island cooks. From year to year, you never know what sort of restaurant you'll find here in this historic building, but it's almost always good and a well-guarded local secret.

You really shouldn't leave the island without having a picnic somewhere. My favorite spots include Eastsound Waterfront Park, right on the water in the village of Eastsound, Deer Harbor Waterfront Park, just before the marina in the village of Deer Harbor, and, if you don't mind a 30-minute uphill hike to your picnic spot, Turtleback Mountain Preserve.

Cafe Olga ★ (Finds) INTERNATIONAL   Housed in an old strawberry-packing plant that dates from the days when these islands were known for their fruit, Cafe Olga is a good spot for reasonably priced breakfasts and lunches. Everything is homemade, using fresh local produce whenever possible. The blackberry pie is a special treat, especially when accompanied by Lopez Island Creamery ice cream. This building also houses Orcas Island Artworks, a gallery representing more than 60 Orcas Island artists.

11 Point Lawrence Rd. (Horseshoe Hwy.), Olga. © **360/376-5098.** Main courses $11–$19 lunch, $22–$25 dinner. MC, V. June–Sept Sun–Wed 9am–4pm and 5–8pm, Thurs–Sat 9am–6pm; shorter hours other months. Closed Jan to mid-Feb.

Inn at Ship Bay ★★ NORTHWEST   About midway between Eastsound and Moran State Park, you'll spot the Inn at Ship Bay, a cluster of yellow farmhouse-style buildings set behind an old orchard in a field high above the water. The restaurant kitchen relies heavily on fresh local seafood, and there are always great local oysters on the half-shell for a starter. The clam chowder (if it's on the menu) is also excellent. If the mussels in shallot-saffron broth are available, don't miss them, either. Try to get a window table so you can enjoy the views of the water.

326 Olga Rd., Eastsound. © **877/276-7296** or 360/376-5886. www.innatshipbay.com. Reservations recommended. Main courses $22–$32. MC, V. Tues–Sat 5:30–9 or 9:30pm. Closed late-Dec to early Feb.

Kingfish Inn Dining Room (Westsound Café) ★ (Finds) AMERICAN   Want to eat where the locals go to get away from the tourists? Check out this casual spot on the west side of the island at the junction of Crow Valley and Deer Harbor roads. I always go for the fish and chips, which are the best on the island, but you can get plenty of more creative fare as well. There are halibut-and-shrimp cakes with spicy avocado sauce, fish tacos, and Thai curry halibut. In summer, try to get a table on the deck.

4362 Crow Valley Road, West Sound. © **360/376-4440.** www.kingfishinn.com. Reservations recommended. Main courses $9.50–$18. MC, V. Wed–Sat 5–8pm.

Rose's ★ ECLECTIC   This is one of my favorite island eateries. With its Tuscan-influenced decor, big patio, and stone pizza oven, Rose's is a casual, yet stylish, place for inexpensive lunches and decent dinners. The menu features creative sandwiches, flavorful soups, designer pizzas, and a few more substantial entree specials. Be sure to keep an eye out for the rose-scented ice cream. The restaurant also has an associated gourmet-food shop where you can pick up imported cheeses, baked goods, wine, and other foodstuffs. As much as possible, Rose's uses local and organic produce and free-range chicken and eggs.

382 Prune Alley, Eastsound. (C) **360/376-4292.** Reservations recommended. Main courses $8–$18 lunch. MC, V. Mon–Sat 10am–4pm. Closed Jan.

Thai Sisters Café This casual Thai restaurant just up the hill from Eastsound's main intersection is a favorite of locals who don't want to pay exorbitant tourist prices. I like the *larb,* a spicy, tangy salad made with either ground pork or ground chicken. Since you are in the islands, you might also want to try the stir-fried mussels. Locals tend to get their Thai food to go, and, if the weather is good, I suggest you do the same. There are waterfront picnic tables in the little park 2 blocks away. If you want to stay put, try to get a table on the restaurant's deck.

18 Urner St., Eastsound. (C) **360/376-3993.** Reservations not accepted. Main courses $10–$14. MC, V. Apr–Sept Tues–Sat 11:30am–3pm and 4–9pm; Oct–Mar Tues–Sat 11:30am–3pm and 4–8pm.

LOPEZ ISLAND

Of the three islands with accommodations, Lopez is the least developed, and although it is less spectacular than Orcas or San Juan, it is flatter, which makes it popular with bicyclists who prefer easy grades to stunning panoramas. Lopez maintains more of its agricultural roots than either Orcas or San Juan, and likewise has fewer activities for tourists. If you just want to get away from it all and hole up with a good book for a few days, this may be the place for you.

Exploring The Island

Lopez Village is the closest this island has to a town, and it's where you'll find almost all the island's restaurants and shops. Be sure to check out the **Chimera Gallery,** Lopez Village Plaza, Lopez Road ((C) **360/468-3265;** www.chimeragallery.com), which is full of art by Lopez Island artists.

At the **Lopez Island Historical Museum,** Weeks Road ((C) **360/468-2049;** www. lopezmuseum.org), in Lopez Village, you can learn about the island's history and pick up a map of historic buildings. The museum is open May through September, Wednesday to Sunday from noon to 4pm.

Lopez Island Vineyards ★, 724 Fisherman Bay Rd. ((C) **360/468-3644;** www.lopez islandvineyards.com), between the ferry landing and Lopez Village, was the first winery to make wine from grapes grown in the San Juans. Both its Siegerrebe and Madeleine Angevine are from local grapes, and its organic fruit wines are made with local fruit. Lopez Island Vineyards also makes wines from grapes grown in the Yakima Valley. In July and August, the winery tasting room is open Wednesday through Saturday from noon to 5pm; in May, June, and September it's open on Friday and Saturday from noon to 5pm; and in April and October it's open on Saturday from noon to 5pm.

(**Fun Facts**)   **The Lopez Wave**

Lopez Islanders are particularly friendly—they wave to everyone they pass on the road. The custom has come to be known as the "Lopez Wave."

From June to Labor Day, you can pick organic strawberries a couple of days a week (usually Tues and Fri from 9am to 3pm) at **Crowfoot Farm,** 3759 Port Stanley Rd. (© **360/468-4748**). You'll find this "U-pick" farm a mile or so east of Lopez Village at the corner of Port Stanley and Hummel Lake roads. Be sure to call first to find out if there are berries and which days the farm will be open. They also have raspberries.

Sports & Outdoor Pursuits

Eight county parks, one state park, and numerous preserves provide plenty of access to the woods and water on Lopez Island. The first park off the ferry is **Odlin County Park** (© **360/378-8420;** www.sanjuanco.com/parks/lopez.aspx), which has a long beach, picnic tables, and a campground. Athletic fields make this more a community sports center than a natural area, so this should be a last-resort camping choice. Between April and October, campsites are $15 to $22 per night; other months you'll pay $12 to $16 per night.

A more natural setting for a short, easy hike is **Upright Channel Park,** on Military Road (about a mile north of Lopez Village in the northwest corner of the island). Right in Lopez Village, you can walk out into the marshes at the 22-acre **Weeks Wetland Preserve.** The trail through the wetlands begins on Weeks Point Way just behind the little shopping complex that houses Holly B's Bakery. There are a few interpretive plaques along the trail.

A little farther south and over on the east side of the island on Bakerview Road, you'll find **Spencer Spit State Park** ★ (© **360/468-2251;** www.parks.wa.gov), which has a campground. Here, the forest meets the sea on a rocky beach that looks across a narrow channel to Frost Island. You can hike the trails through the forest or explore the beach.

South of Lopez Village on Bay Shore Road is the small **Otis Perkins Park,** which is between Fisherman Bay and the open water. It has one of the longest beaches on the island. Continuing to the end of this road (it turns to gravel) will bring you to the **Fisherman Bay Spit Preserve** at the end of the spit that forms the mouth of Fisherman Bay. This preserve has trails and access to the beach along the sandy spit. It's one of the prettiest and most serene spots on the island; don't miss it.

Down at the south end of Lopez, you'll find the tiny **Shark Reef Sanctuary** ★★, where a short trail leads through the forest to a rocky stretch of coast that is among the prettiest on any of the ferry-accessible islands. Small offshore islands create strong currents that swirl past the rocks here. Seals and the occasional whale can be seen just offshore as well. It's a great spot for a picnic. To reach this natural area, drive south from Lopez Village on Fisherman Bay Road, turn right on Airport Road, and then turn left onto Shark Reef Road.

Also down toward the south end of the island, you'll find the **Watmough Bay Preserve,** which protects a beautiful little cove that is a well-guarded local secret. The cove has a 100-yard-long gravel beach and is bordered on one side by cliffs and on the other by forest. The beach is a short, easy walk on a wide path. To reach the trail head parking area, drive Fisherman Bay Road south from Lopez Village, turn right on Center Road and right again on Mud Bay Road, and follow this road through twists and turns to a right onto Aleck Bay Road. When this latter road makes a 90-degree curve to the right, go straight onto a gravel road and quickly fork left onto Watmough Head Road and take a left at the signed Watmough Bay Preserve.

BIKING ★★   Because of its size, lack of traffic, numerous parks, and relatively flat terrain, Lopez is a favorite of cyclists. You can rent bikes for $5 to $20 an hour or $25 to $65 a day from **Lopez Bicycle Works,** 2847 Fisherman Bay Rd. (© **360/468-2847;** www.lopezbicycleworks.com), at the marina on Fisherman Bay Road.

Saving the San Juans

The San Juans are so beautiful that they have for some time been on the verge of being loved to death. However, one local organization is doing what it can to preserve the character of the islands. The **San Juan County Land Bank** (*C* **360/ 378-4402;** www.sjclandbank.org) has been responsible for the acquisition of some of my favorite public open spaces here in the islands. Almost every year the land bank opens new parcels of land to the public, so be sure to check with them to see what new and as-yet-undiscovered green spaces are there to be discovered.

SEA KAYAKING ★★ If you want to explore the island's coastline by kayak, contact **Cascadia Kayak Tours** (*C* **360/468-3008;** www.cascadiakayaktours.com), which offers trips of varying lengths along some of the most picturesque stretches of the Lopez coastline. A half-day trip costs $65, full-day trips are $90, and sunset paddles are $45. Alternatively, May through October, you can rent a kayak from **Lopez Island Sea Kayak** (*C* **360/468-2847;** www.lopezkayaks.com) at the marina on Fisherman Bay Road. Single kayaks rent for $15 to $25 per hour, $30 to $50 per half-day. Double kayaks rent for $25 to $35 per hour, $50 to $70 per half-day.

Where to Stay

Edenwild Inn ★★ This modern Victorian country inn, located right in Lopez Village, is a good choice if you've come here to bike or want to use your car as little as possible. Within a block of the inn are all of the island's best restaurants and cafes. Most of the guest rooms here are quite large and have views of the water. All rooms have interesting antique furnishings; several have fireplaces as well. In summer, colorful gardens surround the inn, and guests can breakfast on a large brick patio. The front veranda, overlooking distant Fisherman Bay, is a great place to relax in the afternoon.

132 Lopez Rd. (P.O. Box 271), Lopez Island, WA 98261. *C* **800/606-0662** or 360/468-3238. www.edenwild inn.com. 8 units. $170–$195 double. Rates include full breakfast. MC, V. No children 11 or under. **Amenities:** Bikes. *In room:* Hair dryer, no phone, Wi-Fi.

Lopez Farm Cottages and Tent Camping ★★ (**Value**) Set on 30 acres of pastures, old orchards, and forest between the ferry landing and Lopez Village, these modern cottages are tucked into a grove of cedar trees on the edge of a 2-acre meadow. From the outside, the board-and-batten cottages look like old farm buildings, but inside you'll find a combination of Eddie Bauer and Scandinavian design. There are kitchenettes, plush beds with lots of pillows, and, in the bathrooms of four of the cottages, showers with double showerheads. If showering together isn't romantic enough for you, a hot tub is tucked down a garden path. Also on the property is a deluxe tents-only campground.

555 Fisherman Bay Rd. (P.O. Box 610), Lopez Island, WA 98261. *C* **800/440-3556.** www.lopezfarmcottages. com. 5 units. June–Sept $170–$205 double; Oct–May $145–$170 double. Tent sites $39 double. Cottage rates include continental breakfast. DISC, MC, V. No children 13 or under. **Amenities:** Jacuzzi. *In room:* TV, hair dryer, kitchenette.

Lopez Islander Bay Resort ★ (**Kids**) About a mile south of Lopez Village, the Lopez Islander may not look too impressive from the outside, but it's actually a very comfortable lodging. All the rooms have great views of Fisherman Bay; most have balconies as well. The more expensive rooms have coffeemakers, wet bars, microwaves, and refrigerators. In addition to the amenities listed below, the Islander has a full-service marina, and kayak rentals are available.

2864 Fisherman Bay Rd. (P.O. Box 459), Lopez Island, WA 98261. (C) **800/736-3434** or 360/468-2233. Fax 360/468-3382. www.lopezislander.com. 31 units. July–Aug $119–$189 double, $259–$299 suite; lower rates Sept–June. Children 17 and under stay free in parent's room. AE, DISC, MC, V. Pets accepted ($20 1st night, $5 each night thereafter). **Amenities:** Restaurant, lounge; bikes; exercise room; Jacuzzi; outdoor pool. *In room:* TV, fridge (in some), hair dryer.

MacKaye Harbor Inn ★   This former sea captain's home at the south end of the island was built in 1904 and was the first home on the island to have electric lights. Since that time this old house has gone through many incarnations, and is today a very comfortable B&B with a mix of classic beach-cottage styling and plenty of modern creature comforts. The big white farmhouse is set on a pretty little stretch of flat beach, and, with kayaks for rent and the calm water of MacKaye Harbor right across the road, this is a good place to give sea kayaking a try. Bikes are also available for guests, and the innkeepers can direct you to good hikes in the area.

949 MacKaye Harbor Rd., Lopez Island, WA 98261. (C) **888/314-6140** or 360/468-2253. www.mackaye harborinn.com. 4 units. July–Aug $175–$195 double, $235 suite; May–June and Sept $155–$185 double, $215 suite; Oct–Apr $135–$155 double, $165 suite. 2-night minimum weekends and holidays. Rates include breakfast. No children 11 or under. MC, V. **Amenities:** Bikes; concierge; watersports rentals. *In room:* CD player, hair dryer, Wi-Fi.

Where to Dine

When it's time for espresso, head to Lopez Village and drop by **Isabel's Espresso** ((C) **360/ 468-4114**), a local hangout in the Village House Building on the corner of Lopez Road North, Lopez Road South, and Old Post Road. Across the street, you'll find divinely decadent pastries and other baked goods at **Holly B's Bakery** ((C) **360/468-2133;** www. hollybsbakery.com). Note that this bakery is closed from late November to early April. For fresh-squeezed juices and healthy light meals, try **Vortex Juice Bar & Good Food,** Lopez Road South ((C) **360/468-4740**), which is located in Lopez Village in the Old Homestead. Next door to the juice bar, you can shop for natural foods at **Blossom Natural Grocery,** 135B Lopez Rd. ((C) **360/468-2204**).

Turn up Village Road North and you'll find **Vita's** ((C) **360/468-4268**), which sells wines and tasty gourmet takeout food from a colorfully painted Victorian house. In summer, this place is open Monday through Friday from 10am to 5pm and Saturday from 10am to 3pm. A little farther along this same street is the **Lopez Island Old-Fashioned Soda Fountain,** 157 Village Rd. ((C) **360/468-4511;** www.lopezislandpharmacy.com), in the Lopez Island Pharmacy. For local produce (and handicrafts), check out the **Lopez Farmers Market,** which is held on summer Saturday mornings in a park on Village Road in Lopez Village. Down at the south end of the island, you can get good sandwiches, burgers, and fish and chips at the **South End Deli,** 3024 Mud Bay Rd. ((C) **360/468- 3982**), which is located in the back of the Islandale Store.

Bay Café ★★ NORTHWEST/INTERNATIONAL   This is the sort of place where diners animatedly discuss what that other flavor is in the *mole* sauce on the pork tenderloin, and where people walk through the door and exclaim, "I want whatever it is that smells so good." The Bay Café, housed in an eclectically decorated old waterfront commercial building with a deck that overlooks Fisherman Bay, serves some of the best food in the state. The menu, though short, spans the globe and changes frequently. Come with a hearty appetite; meals include soup and salad, and the desserts are absolutely to die for.

For the quintessential Lopez dinner, accompany your meal with a bottle of wine from **221** Lopez Island Vineyards.

In Village Center, 9 Old Post Rd., Lopez Village. (C) **360/468-3700**. www.bay-cafe.com. Reservations highly recommended. Main courses $19–$36; tasting menu $30–$35. AE, DISC, MC, V. Summer daily 5:30–8pm; other months Wed–Sun 5:30–8pm.

Love Dog Café ★ AMERICAN/ITALIAN   With its sunny dining room and big deck looking out to the waters of Fisherman Bay, the Love Dog is a casual, friendly place serving a mix of comfort foods and more creative dishes. You'll find everything from burgers to tamales and lasagna, but I tend to opt for the pasta dishes and such hearty entree specials as halibut with blackberry-wine reduction sauce and steak with cabernet reduction sauce. Unfortunately, service here can be a bit lackadaisical.

1 Village Center, Lopez and Village rds., Lopez Village. (C) **360/468-2150**. Reservations recommended. Main courses $10–$27. MC, V. Summer Thurs–Mon noon–8:30pm; call for hours other months.

---

2 PORT TOWNSEND: A RESTORED VICTORIAN SEAPORT

Named by English explorer Capt. George Vancouver in 1792, Port Townsend did not attract its first settlers until 1851. By the 1880s, however, the town had become a major shipping port and was expected to grow into one of the most important cities on the West Coast. Port Townsend residents felt that their city was the logical end of the line for the transcontinental railroad that was pushing westward in the 1880s, and based on the certainty of a railroad connection, real-estate speculation and development boomed. Merchants and investors erected mercantile palaces along Water Street and elaborate Victorian homes on the bluff above the wharf district. Unfortunately, the railroad never arrived. Tacoma got the rails, and Port Townsend got the shaft.

With its importance as a shipping port usurped by Seattle and Tacoma, Port Townsend slipped into quiet obscurity. Progress passed it by, and its elegant homes and commercial buildings were left to slowly fade away. In 1976, the waterfront district and bluff-top residential neighborhood were declared a National Historic District, and the town began a slow revival. Today, the streets of Port Townsend are once again crowded with people; the waterfront district is filled with boutiques, galleries, and other interesting shops; and many of the Victorian homes atop the bluff have become bed-and-breakfasts.

ESSENTIALS

VISITOR INFORMATION   Contact the **Port Townsend Chamber of Commerce Visitor Information Center,** 2437 E. Sims Way, Port Townsend, WA 98368 ((C) **888/365-6978** or 360/385-2722; www.ptguide.com).

GETTING THERE   Port Townsend is on Wash. 20, off U.S. 101 in the northeast corner of the Olympic Peninsula. The Hood Canal Bridge, which connects the Kitsap Peninsula with the Olympic Peninsula and is on the route from Seattle to Port Townsend, sometimes closes due to high winds; if you want to be certain that it's open, call (C) **800/419-9085.**

Washington State Ferries ((C) **800/843-3779** or 888/808-7977 within Washington, or 206/464-6400; www.wsdot.wa.gov/ferries) operates a ferry between Port Townsend and Keystone (on Whidbey Island). The crossing takes 30 minutes and costs $9 to $11 for a vehicle and driver, $2.60 per passenger (discounted fares for seniors and youths).

From late March to early October, passenger-boat service between Port Townsend and Friday Harbor (in the San Juan Islands) is offered by **P.S. Express** (© **360/385-5288;** www.pugetsoundexpress.com), which also carries bicycles and sea kayaks. One-way fares are $50 to $53 for adults and $35 to $43 for children; round-trip fares are $69 to $79 for adults and $49 to $54 for children.

GETTING AROUND   Because parking spaces in downtown Port Townsend are hard to come by on weekends and anytime in summer, **Jefferson Transit** (© **800/371-0497** or 360/385-4777; www.jeffersontransit.com), the local public bus service, operates a shuttle into downtown Port Townsend from a park-and-ride lot on the south side of town. Jefferson Transit also operates other buses around Port Townsend. The fare is $1.25.

FESTIVALS   As a tourist town, Port Townsend schedules quite a few festivals throughout the year. In late March, the town celebrates its Victorian heritage with the **Victorian Festival** (© **360/379-2847;** www.victorianfestival.org). The end of July brings the Centrum's **Jazz Port Townsend** (© **360/385-3102;** www.centrum.org). The **Wooden Boat Festival** (© **360/385-3628;** www.woodenboat.org), the largest of its kind in the United States, is on the first weekend after Labor Day. To see inside some of the town's many restored homes, schedule a visit during the **Homes Tour** (© **888/365-6978** or 360/385-2722; www.ptguide.com/homestour), on the third weekend in September. During the **Kinetic Sculpture Race** (www.ptkineticrace.org), held the first weekend in October, outrageous human-powered vehicles race on land, on water, and through a mud bog. The **Olympic Music Festival** (© **360/732-4800;** www.olympicmusicfestival.org), held nearby in an old barn near the town of Quilcene, is the area's most important music festival. This series of weekend concerts takes place between late June and early September. Also in September, there's the **Port Townsend Film Festival** (© **360/379-1333;** www.ptfilmfest.com).

EXPLORING THE TOWN

Port Townsend abounds with restored Victorian homes and commercial buildings, and is a great place for a walking or driving tour of historic districts. The town is divided into the waterfront commercial district and the residential uptown area. This latter neighborhood is atop a bluff that rises precipitously only 2 blocks from the water. Uptown Port Townsend developed in part so that proper Victorian ladies would not have to associate with the riffraff that frequented the waterfront. At the Port Townsend Visitor Information Center, you can pick up a guide that lists the town's many historic homes and commercial buildings.

Water Street is the town's main commercial district. It is lined for several blocks with restored 100-year-old brick buildings, many of which have ornate facades. Within these buildings are dozens of interesting shops and boutiques, several restaurants, and a handful of hotels and inns. To learn a little more about the history of this part of town and to gain a different perspective, walk out on **Union Wharf,** at the foot of Taylor Street. Here you'll find interpretive plaques covering topics ranging from sea grass to waterfront history.

Make one of your first stops in town the **Jefferson County Historical Society Museum,** 540 Water St. (© **360/385-1003;** www.jchsmuseum.org), where you can learn about the history of the area. Among the collections here are regional Native American artifacts and antiques from the Victorian era. The museum is open daily from 11am to 4pm. Admission is $4 for adults and $1 for children ages 3 to 12. May through September, the museum sponsors guided history walks on Saturday and Sunday at 2pm. These tours cost $10 for adults and $5 for children ages 3 to 12.

The town's noted Victorian homes are in uptown Port Townsend, atop the bluff that rises behind the waterfront's commercial buildings. This is where you find stately homes, views, and the city's favorite park. To reach the uptown area, either drive up Washington Street (1 block over from Water St.) or walk up the stairs at the end of Taylor Street, which start behind the Haller Fountain.

At the top of the stairs, you'll see both an 1890 bell tower, which once summoned volunteer firemen, and the **Rothschild House,** at Taylor and Franklin streets (℃ **360/385-1003;** www.jchsmuseum.org). Built in 1868, this Greek Revival house is one of the oldest buildings in town and displays a sober architecture compared to other area homes. The gardens contain a wide variety of roses, peonies, and lilacs. It's open May through September daily from 11am to 4pm. Admission is $4 for adults and $1 for children 3 to 12. A $6 pass gets you into both this historic house and the Jefferson County Historical Society Museum.

Also here in the uptown neighborhood, at the corner of Garfield and Jackson streets, is **Chetzemoka Park,** established in 1904 and named for a local S'Klallam Indian chief. The park is perched on a bluff overlooking Admiralty Inlet and has access to a pleasant little beach. However, most visitors head straight for the rose garden, arbor, and waterfall garden.

Shopping is just about the most popular activity in Port Townsend's old town, and of the many stores in the historic district, several stand out. **Earthenworks Gallery,** 702 Water St. (℃ **360/385-0328;** www.earthenworksgallery.com), showcases colorful ceramics, glass, jewelry, and other American-made crafts. **Ancestral Spirits Gallery,** 701 Water St. (℃ **360/385-0078;** www.ancestralspirits.com), is a large space with a great selection of Northwest Native American prints, masks, and carvings.

FORT WORDEN STATE PARK

Fort Worden State Park (℃ 360/344-4400; www.fortworden.org), once a military installation that guarded the mouth of Puget Sound, is north of the historic district and can be reached by turning onto Kearney Street at the south end of town, or onto Monroe Street at the north end of town, and following the signs. Built at the turn of the 20th century, the fort is now a 434-acre state park where a wide array of attractions and activities ensure that it's busy for much of the year. Many of the fort's old wooden buildings have been restored and put to new uses.

At the **Commanding Officer's Quarters** (℃ 360/385-1003; www.jchsmuseum.org/coq.html), you can see what life was like for a Victorian-era officer and his family. The home has been fully restored and is filled with period antiques. June through August, it's open daily from 11am to 5pm (mid-Apr through May, Sat–Sun noon–4pm; closed other months). Admission is $4 for adults and $1 for children 3 to 12. Within the park, you'll also find the **Coast Artillery Museum** (℃ 360/385-0373), which is open daily from 11am to 4pm between Memorial Day and Labor Day (Sat–Sun noon–4pm in May). Admission is $2 for adults and $1 for children ages 6 to 12.

Here at the park you can also learn about life below the waters of Puget Sound at the **Port Townsend Marine Science Center,** 532 Battery Way (℃ **800/566-3932** or 360/385-5582; www.ptmsc.org). The center has great tide-pool touch tanks filled with crabs, starfish, anemones, and other marine life. A fascinating exhibit on the area's terrestrial natural history includes fossils from around the peninsula. Don't miss the exhibit on the glaciers that once covered this region. Mid-June through Labor Day, the center is open Wednesday through Monday from 11am to 5pm; fall through spring hours are Friday through Sunday from noon to 4pm. Between November and March, only the natural history exhibit is open, and in January, the center is closed. Admission is $5 for adults and $3 for youths 6 to 17.

For many people, however, the main reason to visit the park is to hang out on the beach or at one of the picnic areas. Scuba divers also frequent Fort Worden, which has an underwater park just offshore. In spring the Rhododendron Garden puts on a colorful floral display. Throughout the year there is a wide variety of concerts and other performances at the **Centrum** (© 360/385-3102; www.centrum.org). Also on the premises are campgrounds, a restaurant, and restored officers' quarters that can be rented as vacation homes.

PORT TOWNSEND FROM THE WATER

If you'd like to explore this area from the water, you've got several options. Three-hour sailboat tours ($75) are offered by **Brisa Charters** (© 877/412-7472 or 360/385-2309; www.olympus.net/brisa_charters). Several times a year, the **Port Townsend Marine Science Center** (© 800/566-3932 or 360/385-5582; www.ptmsc.org) operates boat tours ($55) to nearby Protection Island, a wildlife refuge that is home to puffins, rhinoceros auklets, and other nesting seabirds. One trip a year is done on a 101-foot historic schooner ($75).

From late May to early September, whale-watching cruises ($75 for adults, $59 for children 2–10) through the San Juan Islands are offered by **P.S. Express,** Point Hudson Marina, 227 Jackson St. (© 360/385-5288; www.pugetsoundexpress.com), which also operates passenger-ferry service to Friday Harbor.

You can paddle a kayak out at Fort Worden State Park, where **PT Outdoors,** 1017-B Water St. (© 888/754-8598 or 360/379-3608; www.ptoutdoors.com), rents kayaks for between $20 and $40 for the first hour and $10 and $15 for subsequent hours. This company also offers guided kayak tours ($55–$120).

AREA WINERIES

While you're visiting the area, you might want to check out Port Townsend's two wineries, both of which are south of town. **Sorensen Cellars,** 274 S. Otto St. (© 360/379-6416; www.sorensencellars.com), is open March through May and mid-September through mid-November, Friday through Sunday from noon to 5pm; June through mid-September, it's open daily noon to 5pm. To find this winery, turn east off Wash. 20 onto Frederick Street and then south on Otto Street.

Fair Winds Winery, 1984 Hastings Ave. W. (© 360/385-6899; www.fairwindswinery.com), is the only winery in the state producing Aligote, a French-style white wine. Memorial Day to Labor Day the winery is open daily from noon to 5pm; other months it's open Friday to Monday from noon to 5pm. To get here, drive south from Port Townsend on Wash. 20, turn west on Jacob Miller Road, and continue 2 miles to Hastings Avenue.

WHERE TO STAY

Ann Starrett Mansion Boutique Hotel ★ Built in 1889 for $6,000 as a wedding present for Ann Starrett, this Victorian jewel box is by far the most elegant and ornate historic hotel in Port Townsend (or the entire state, for that matter). The rose-and-teal-green mansion is a museum of the Victorian era: A three-story turret towers over the front door, and every room is exquisitely furnished with period antiques. Note that although this hotel seems as though it would be a bed-and-breakfast inn, it does not serve breakfast. However, you'll find plenty of good breakfast places in the area.

F. W. Hastings House/Old Consulate Inn ★★   The Old Consulate Inn is another example of the Victorian excess so wonderfully appealing today. The attention to detail and quality craftsmanship, in both the construction and the restoration of this elegant mansion, are evident wherever you look. Despite its heritage, however, the Old Consulate avoids being a museum; it's a comfortable yet elegant place to stay. If you're here for a special occasion, consider splurging on one of the turret rooms. Of the other units, my favorite is the Parkside. For entertainment, you'll find a grand piano, a billiards table, and a VCR, as well as stunning views out most of the windows. A multicourse breakfast is meant to be lingered over, so don't make any early-morning appointments. Afternoon refreshments and a hot tub add to the experience.

313 Walker St., Port Townsend, WA 98368. ℭ **800/300-6753** or 360/385-6753. Fax 360/385-2097. www. oldconsulateinn.com. 8 units. June–Oct $110–$210 double; Nov–May $99–$189 double. Rates include full breakfast. MC, V. No children 11 or under. **Amenities:** Jacuzzi. *In room:* Hair dryer, no phone.

James House ★★   With an eclectic blend of antique and new furnishings, this grand 1889 Victorian sits atop the bluff overlooking Admiralty Inlet. The entry hall features a parquet floor and a big staircase climbing straight up to the second floor. In the two parlors are fireplaces that make the perfect gathering spots on cool evenings. The views from the upper front bedrooms are some of the best in town (ask for the Master Suite, which has a balcony, or the Chintz Room, which has a deck). You can even see Mount Rainier on a clear day. If you don't like climbing stairs, opt for one of the ground-floor suites or the Gardener's Cottage. An additional private bungalow, adjacent to the James House, is done in a contemporary style and has a water and mountain view.

1238 Washington St., Port Townsend, WA 98368. ℭ **800/385-1238.** www.jameshouse.com. 12 units. June–Sept $145–$165 double, $150–$250 suite or cottage; Oct–Apr $125–$150 double, $135–$195 suite or cottage. Rates include full breakfast. MC, V. Children 13 and over welcome. *In room:* Hair dryer, Wi-Fi.

Manresa Castle ★ ⟨Value⟩   Built in 1892 by the first mayor of Port Townsend, this reproduction of a medieval castle later became a Jesuit retreat and school. Today, traditional elegance pervades Manresa Castle, and of all the hotels and B&Bs in Port Townsend, this place offers the most historic elegance for the money. The guest rooms have a genuine vintage appeal that manages to avoid the contrived feeling that so often sneaks into the room decor of B&Bs. The tower suite is my favorite room in the hotel and is worth a splurge. In this huge room, you get sweeping views from a circular seating area. An elegant lounge and dining room further add to the Grand Hotel feel of this unusual accommodation. Oh, and by the way, the hotel is haunted.

651 Cleveland St. (P.O. Box 564), Port Townsend, WA 98368. ℭ **800/732-1281** or 360/385-5750. www. manresacastle.com. 40 units. $109–$119 double; $169–$229 suite. Rates include continental breakfast. DISC, MC, V. **Amenities:** Restaurant, lounge. *In room:* TV, Wi-Fi.

WHERE TO DINE

One place on nearly everyone's itinerary is **Elevated Ice Cream,** 627 Water St. (ℭ **360/385-1156;** www.elevatedicecream.com), which scoops up the best ice cream in town. For pastries, light meals, and coffee, try the **Courtyard Cafe,** 230 Quincy St. (ℭ **360/379-3355**). If you're a tea drinker, check out **Wild Sage,** 924 Washington St. (ℭ **360/379-1222;** www.wildsageteas.com).

If you're heading out to Fort Worden State Park for a picnic, you can pick up supplies at the **Port Townsend Food Co-Op,** 414 Kearney St. (© **360/385-2883;** www.food coop.coop), which is at the south end of town at the turn-off for Fort Worden. Also try **Aldrich's Market,** 940 Lawrence St. (© **360/385-0500;** www.aldrichs.com), a wonderful little upscale market in the uptown neighborhood. If you happen to be in town on a Saturday between early May and mid-November, be sure to stop by the **Port Townsend Farmers Market** (© **360/379-9098;** www.ptfarmersmarket.org), held on the corner of Lawrence and Tyler streets. The market is open from 9:30am to 1:30pm. Between mid-June and late September, at the corner of Polk and Lawrence streets, there is also a Wednesday farmers market from 3:30 to 6:30pm.

If you're looking for someplace interesting to have a drink at the end of the day, check out **Water Street Brewing,** 639 Water St. (© **360/379-6438;** www.waterstreetbrewing. com), right in downtown Port Townsend. There's also the **Port Townsend Brewing Company,** 330 Tenth St. (© **360/385-9967;** www.porttownsendbrewing.com), which has a tasting room and beer garden south of downtown in the Port Townsend Boat Haven marina. For good beer and occasional live music, check out **The Public House,** 1038 Water St. (© **360/385-9708;** www.thepublichouse.com), which has the feel of a 19th-century tavern.

Fountain Cafe ★ ⏣**Finds** ECLECTIC   Housed in a narrow clapboard building, this funky little place has long been a favorite of Port Townsend locals and counterculture types on a tight budget. Eclectic furnishings decorate the room, which has a few stools at the counter. The menu changes seasonally, but you can rest assured that the simple fare will be utterly fresh and that the offerings will include plenty of shellfish and pasta. The Greek pasta is a mainstay that's hard to beat, and the clam chowder is excellent. The wide range of flavors here assures that everyone will find something to his or her liking.

920 Washington St. © **360/385-1364.** Reservations accepted only for parties of 6 or more. Main courses $9.50–$11 lunch, $14–$26 dinner. MC, V. Daily 11:30am–3pm and 5–9pm (Fri–Sat until 9:30pm).

Khu Larb Thai ★ THAI   Located half a block off busy Water Street, Khu Larb seems a world removed from Port Townsend's sometimes-overdone Victorian decor. Thai easy-listening music plays on the stereo, while the pungent fragrance of Thai spices wafts through the dining room. One taste of any dish on the menu and you'll be convinced that this is great Thai food. The *tom kha gai,* a sour-and-spicy soup with a coconut-milk base, is particularly memorable. The curry dishes made with mussels are also good bets.

225 Adams St. © **360/385-5023.** www.khularbthai.com. Reservations only for parties of 8 or more. Main courses $10–$15. AE, MC, V. Tues–Sun 11am–9pm.

Silverwater Cafe ★★ ⏣**Value** NORTHWEST   Works by local artists, lots of plants, and New Age music on the stereo set the tone for this casual restaurant. Though the menu focuses on Northwest dishes, it includes preparations from around the world. You can start your meal with an artichoke-and-parmesan pâté, and then move on to ahi tuna with lavender pepper, prawns with cilantro-ginger-lime butter, or smoked chicken with brandy and apples. The oysters in a blue-cheese sauce are a favorite of mine. If you're a vegetarian, you'll find several options.

237 Taylor St. © **360/385-6448.** www.silverwatercafe.com. Reservations recommended. Main courses $8–$20 at lunch, $13–$25 at dinner. MC, V. Mon–Thurs 11:30am–2:30pm and 5–8:30pm, Fri–Sat 11:30am–9:30pm, Sun 11:30am–8:30pm; bar until later.

T's Restaurant ★★ ITALIAN   In the Point Hudson Marina at the north end of downtown Port Townsend, this romantic, low-key place has long been my favorite restaurant in town. The menu usually features plenty of daily specials; local oysters, mussels, and clams show up frequently and are hard to resist. I always start with the creamy oyster stew, which is made with pancetta and fennel. You'll find a wide variety of interesting pasta dishes from which to choose, but the rigatoni gorgonzola is my favorite.

141 Hudson St. ℂ **360/385-0700.** www.ts-restaurant.com. Reservations recommended. Main courses $17–$31. AE, MC, V. Wed–Mon 4–9pm.

3 SEQUIM: LAVENDER FIELDS FOREVER

If the economy and the exchange rate have combined to keep you from that long-dreamed-of vacation in Provence, then perhaps you need to spend a day in sunny Sequim. In the rain shadow of the Olympic Mountains, Sequim (pronounced *Skwim*) is the state's driest region west of the Cascade Range—and, consequently, it is an almost perfect place to grow lavender plants. Every summer, beginning in mid-June and extending through July, parts of Sequim take on the look of Provence. Lavender fields paint the landscape with billowy rows of purple, and visitors descend on Sequim to immerse themselves in purple. Throughout the area, there are "U-pick" farms where you can cut your own lavender, shops selling lavender products, and, of course, an annual lavender festival.

The lack of rainfall and the temperate climate have also made Sequim a very popular retirement community. Sodden Northwesterners have taken to retiring here in droves. While the rains descend on the rest of the region, the fortunate few who call Sequim home bask in their own personal microclimate of sunshine and warmth.

Before lavender and retirement homes lured people to the area, there were the crabs. To the north of Sequim lies the Dungeness Spit, a long narrow sand spit tipped by a historic lighthouse. This spit lends its name to the Dungeness crab, the most popular crab in the Northwest. Dungeness crab is as much a staple of Washington waters as the blue crab is in the Chesapeake Bay region. At more than 6 miles in length, Dungeness Spit is the longest sand spit in the world.

ESSENTIALS

VISITOR INFORMATION   For information, contact the **Sequim–Dungeness Chamber of Commerce,** 1192 E. Washington St. (P.O. Box 907), Sequim, WA 98382 (ℂ **800/737-8462** or 360/683-6197; www.visitsun.com).

GETTING THERE   From Seattle, take the Bainbridge Island ferry; once on the west side of Puget Sound, follow Wash. 305 to Wash. 3 to Wash. 104 to U.S. 101. Sequim and the Dungeness Valley lie to the north of U.S. 101, between Port Townsend and Port Angeles. It's about an hour's drive from Bainbridge Island to Sequim.

LAVENDER, WINE & WILDLIFE

Sequim has become well known around the Northwest for its many lavender farms, which paint the landscape with their colorful blooms each summer from late June through August. Sequim's climate is ideal for growing lavender, and you'll likely pass numerous large fields of this fragrant Mediterranean plant as you tour the area.

To find your way around the area's lavender farms, stop by the Sequim-Dungeness Valley Chamber of Commerce visitor center (see above) or check out **www.lavender growers.org**. In mid-July, when the lavender fields are in full bloom, the town observes the season with its **Sequim Lavender Festival** (© **877/681-3035** or 360/681-3035; www.lavenderfestival.com).

If you'd like to wander through fragrant fields of lavender, you've got plenty of options. **Purple Haze Lavender Farm,** 180 Bell Bottom Rd. (© **888/852-6560** or 360/683-1714; www.purplehazelavender.com), an organic "U-pick" farm east of downtown Sequim off West Sequim Bay Road, is one of my favorites. From June to early September the farm is open daily from 10am to 5pm, and in April and May, it's open Friday through Sunday from 10am to 5pm. The farm has a seasonal gift shop in a small barn as well as the year-round **Purple Haze Lavender Downtown Store,** 127 W. Washington St., in downtown Sequim. This latter shop is open Monday through Friday from 9am to 5pm and Saturday from 10am to 5pm. North of here, don't miss **Graysmarsh Farm,** 6187 Woodcock Rd. (© **800/683-4367** or 360/683-0624; www.graysmarsh.com), which has both beautiful lavender fields and "U-pick" berry fields, where, in season, you can pick strawberries, raspberries, blueberries, and loganberries.

Up near the Dungeness Spit, you'll find a very pretty organic lavender farm, **Jardin du Soleil,** 3932 Sequim-Dungeness Way (© **877/527-3461** or 360/582-1185; www.jardindusoleil.com), which surrounds an old farmhouse and its Victorian gardens. From April to September the farm is open daily from 10am to 5pm; in October, November, December, February, and March, it's open Friday through Sunday from 10am to 4pm. In the same area, you can visit the **Olympic Lavender Farm,** 1432 Marine Dr. (© **360/683-4475;** www.olympiclavender.com), which is open from mid-June through mid-August daily from noon to 5pm.

Cedarbrook Lavender & Herb Farm, 1345 S. Sequim Ave. (© **800/470-8423** or 360/683-7733; www.cedarbrooklavender.com), is more than just a lavender farm. Here you can buy herb plants as well as herb vinegars, potpourris, dried flowers, lavender wands, garlic braids, and the like. You'll find this farm south of downtown Sequim at the top of a hill overlooking the town. It's open Tuesday through Thursday from 10am to 4pm and Friday and Saturday from 10am to 8pm.

Off to the southwest of Sequim is **Lost Mountain Lavender,** 1541 Taylor Cutoff Rd. (© **888/507-7481** or 360/681-2782; www.lostmountainlavender.com). June through August, this farm is open daily from 10am to 6pm; September through May, it's open Thursday through Monday from 10am to 5pm.

If you're interested in tasting some locally produced wine, you can also stop at **Olympic Cellars,** 255410 U.S. 101 (© **360/452-0160;** www.olympiccellars.com), which is housed in a large barn on the west side of Sequim. April through October the tasting room is open daily from 11am to 6pm; November to March, it's open daily 11am to 5pm.

If you've got the kids with you, Sequim's **Olympic Game Farm ★**, 1423 Ward Rd. (© **800/778-4295** or 360/683-4295; www.olygamefarm.com), is a must. You'll get up close and personal with bison, Kodiak bears, zebras, wolves, elk, deer, and many other species of wild animals that have appeared in over 100 movies and TV shows. There are drive-through tours (admission is $10 for adults, $9 for seniors and children 6 to 14, and free for children 5 and under) and a petting farm. The farm is open daily from 9am (call for seasonal closing times).

⌒ Fun Facts   K-E-L-K Radio

Sequim is home to a herd of around 100 Roosevelt elk, which have a habit of wandering back and forth across U.S. 101. To reduce the number of automobile-elk collisions, several members of the herd have had radio collars put on them. When these elk approach the highway, the signals emitted by their collars trigger yellow ELK CROSSING warning lights to start flashing.

The biggest local attraction is Dungeness Spit, which is protected as the **Dungeness National Wildlife Refuge** ★★ (© 360/457-8451; www.fws.gov/washingtonmaritime/ dungeness). Within the refuge, there's a .5-mile trail to a bluff-top overlook, but the best reason to visit is to hike the spit, which extends for more than 5 miles to the historic New Dungeness Lighthouse. Along the way, you're likely to see numerous species of birds as well as harbor seals. There's a fee of $3 per family to visit the spit.

Near the base of the Dungeness Spit, you'll also find the **Dungeness Recreation Area,** 554 Voice of America Rd. (© 360/683-5847; www.clallam.net/CountyParks/html/ parks_dungeness.htm), which has a campground, picnic area, and trail leading out to the spit. If you're not up for a 10-mile round-trip hike to the lighthouse, you can paddle out with **Dungeness Kayaking,** 5021 Sequim-Dungeness Way (© 360/681-4190; www.dungenesskayaking.com), which charges $100 per person for a 4-hour tour to the lighthouse.

WHERE TO STAY

Dungeness Bay Cottages ★   This pretty little collection of cottages is set on a bluff overlooking the Strait of Juan de Fuca and is located across the street from the waters of Dungeness Bay. Great views and economical accommodations make this an outstanding getaway. Most units actually have views of both the water and the Olympic Mountains. My favorite is the large San Juan Suite, which comes complete with a fireplace. The summer sunsets here simply cannot be beat.

140 Marine Dr., Sequim, WA 98382. © **888/683-3013** or 360/683-3013. www.dungenessbay.com. 6 units. Apr 16–Oct 14 $110–$170 double; Oct 15–Apr 15 $95–$155 double. 2- to 3-night minimum. DISC, MC, V. *In room:* TV/DVD, hair dryer, kitchen, Wi-Fi.

Juan de Fuca Cottages ★   Right across the street from the water and surrounded by wide green lawns, these well-tended cottages have excellent views. While most face the water, the best views are actually from the one cottage that faces the Olympic Mountains to the south. This cabin has skylights and a long wall of windows. Other units have skylights as well, and all have whirlpool tubs and kitchenettes. The cottages also have their own private beach. Each cottage sleeps at least four people. Kayaks can be rented here and massages can be arranged.

182 Marine Dr., Sequim, WA 98382. © **866/683-4433** or 360/683-4433. www.juandefuca.com. 13 units. July–Sept $165–$260 double; Oct–June $99–$230 double. 2-night minimum July–Aug. Children 1 and under stay free in parent's room. DISC, MC, V. Pets accepted ($20 per night). **Amenities:** Bike rentals; concierge; access to nearby health club; watersports rentals. *In room:* TV/VCR/DVD, CD player, fridge, hair dryer, kitchenette, Wi-Fi.

If you're in need of a light lunch, don't miss **Jean's Deli** ★, 134 S. Second St. (© 360/683-6727). This sandwich shop is located in a historic church building a block off Sequim's main street. For a retro diner experience, try **Hiway 101 Diner,** 392 W. Washington St. (© **360/683-3388**). My brother says his family won't let him drive through Sequim without stopping here for burgers and milkshakes.

For a caffeine fix, head to **Hurricane Coffee,** 104 W. Washington St. (© **360/681-6008;** www.hurricanecoffee.com), or **The Buzz,** 128 N. Sequim Ave. (© **360/683-2503;** www.thebuzzbeedazzled.com), which is right across the street and serves coffee from my favorite Seattle roaster—Caffé Vita. If you need a pastry or artisan bread for a picnic, stop by **Bell Street Bakery,** 175 W. Bell St. (© **360/681-6262**), which is affiliated with nearby Cedar Creek restaurant.

Alder Wood Bistro ★ NEW AMERICAN With a menu that changes seasonally and incorporates lots of local, organic, and sustainably produced ingredients, the casual little Alder Wood Bistro is a local's favorite here in Sequim. The wood-fired oven turns out great pizzas as well as various other dishes. At lunch, don't miss the savory tart, which is made with a delicious butter crust. At dinner, you'll find the likes of polenta lasagna, duck confit pizza. Lunch or dinner, you might want to get a side of the truffled french fries. For dessert? Try the apple pie warmed in the wood oven.

139 W. Alder St. © 360/683-4321. www.alderwoodbistro.com. Reservations recommended. Main courses $10–$25. DISC, MC, V. Tues–Sat 11am–2pm and 5–9pm.

The 3 Crabs ★ SEAFOOD The 3 Crabs is an Olympic Peninsula institution—folks drive from miles around to enjoy the fresh seafood and sunset views at this friendly waterfront restaurant overlooking the Strait of Juan de Fuca and the New Dungeness Lighthouse. For almost 50 years, this place has been serving up Dungeness crabs in a wide variety of styles. You can order your crabs as a cocktail, in a sandwich, cracked, or as crab Louie salad. Clams and oysters also come from the local waters and are equally good. There's great bird-watching here, too, especially in winter.

11 Three Crabs Rd. © 360/683-4264. www.the3crabs.com. Reservations recommended. Main courses $8–$26. DISC, MC, V. Sun–Thurs 11:30am–8pm; Fri–Sat 11:30am–9pm.

4 OLYMPIC NATIONAL PARK & ENVIRONS

Snow-capped peaks, rainforests, miles and miles of deserted beaches—Olympic National Park has all this and more. Preserving more than 900,000 acres of wilderness, this national park, because of its amazing diversity, is recognized as one of the world's most important wild ecosystems. The park is unique in the contiguous United States for its temperate rainforests, which are found in the west-facing valleys of the Hoh, Queets, Bogachiel, Clearwater, and Quinault rivers. In these valleys, rainfall can exceed 150 inches per year, trees (such as Sitka spruce, western red cedar, Douglas fir, and western hemlock) grow nearly 300 feet tall, and mosses enshroud the limbs of big-leaf maples.

Within a few miles of the park's rainforests, the Olympic Mountains rise to the 7,965-foot peak of Mount Olympus and an alpine zone where no trees grow at all. Together, elevation and heavy snowfall (the rain of lower elevations is replaced by snow at higher elevations) combine to form dozens of glaciers. It is these glaciers that have carved the Olympic Mountains into the jagged peaks that mesmerize visitors and beckon hikers and climbers. Rugged and spectacular sections of the coast have also been preserved as part of the national park, and the offshore waters are designated the Olympic Coast National Marine Sanctuary.

With fewer than a dozen roads, none of which leads more than a few miles into the park, Olympic National Park is for the most part inaccessible to the casual visitor. Only two roads penetrate the high country, and only one of these is paved. Likewise, only two paved roads lead into the park's famed rainforests. Although a long stretch of beach within the national park is paralleled by U.S. 101, the park's most spectacular beaches can only be reached on foot.

The park may be inaccessible to cars, but it is a wonderland for hikers and backpackers. Its rugged beaches, rainforest valleys, alpine meadows, and mountaintop glaciers offer an amazing variety of hiking and backpacking opportunities. For alpine hikes, there are the trail heads at Hurricane Ridge and Deer Park. To experience the rainforest in all its drippy glory, you can take to the trails of the Bogachiel, Hoh, Queets, and Quinault valleys. Of these rainforest trails, the Hoh Valley has the most accessible (and consequently most popular) trails, including the trail head for a multiday backpack trip to the summit of Mount Olympus. Favorite coastal hikes include the stretch of coast between La Push and Oil City and from Rialto Beach north to Lake Ozette and onward to Shi Shi Beach.

VISITOR INFORMATION

For more information on the national park, contact **Olympic National Park,** 600 E. Park Ave., Port Angeles, WA 98362 (© **360/565-3130** or 360/565-3131; www.nps.gov/olym). For information on Port Angeles and the rest of the northern Olympic Peninsula, contact the **Olympic Peninsula Visitor Bureau,** 338 W. First St., Ste. 104 (P.O. Box 670), Port Angeles, WA 98362 (© **800/942-4042** or 360/452-8552; www.olympic peninsula.org), or the **Port Angeles Regional Chamber of Commerce Visitor Center,** 121 E. Railroad Ave., Port Angeles, WA 98362 (© **360/452-2363;** www.portangeles. org). The park entry fee is $15 per vehicle.

GETTING THERE

U.S. 101 circles Olympic National Park, with main park entrances south of Port Angeles, at Lake Crescent, and at the Hoh River south of Forks.

Kenmore Air Express (© **866/435-9524** or 425/486-1257; www.kenmoreair.com) flies between Seattle's Boeing Field and Port Angeles's William Fairchild Airport (with a free shuttle from Seattle–Tacoma International Airport to Boeing Field). Rental cars are available in Port Angeles from **Budget** (© **800/527-0700;** www.budget.com).

EXPLORING THE PARK'S NORTH SIDE

The northern portions of Olympic National Park are the most accessible and heavily visited areas of the park. It is here, south of Port Angeles, that you will find the only two roads leading into the national park's high country. Of these two roads, only the one to Hurricane Ridge is paved, and thus Hurricane Ridge is the most popular alpine region of the park. Because the route to the Deer Park area is a harrowing one-lane gravel road, this latter area is little visited. However, if you have nerves of steel and want to escape the crowds, it's the place to go. West of Port Angeles and within the national park lie two large lakes, Lake Crescent and Lake Ozette, which attract boaters and anglers. Also in this region are two hot springs—the developed Sol Duc Resort and the natural Olympic Hot Springs.

Outside the park boundaries, along the northern coast of the peninsula, are several campgrounds and a couple of small sport-fishing ports, Sekiu and Neah Bay, which are also popular with scuba divers. Neah Bay, which is on the Makah Indian Reservation, is the site of one of the most interesting culture-and-history museums in the state. This reservation also encompasses the dramatic cliffs of Cape Flattery, the northwestern-most point in the contiguous United States. Along the coastline between Port Angeles and Neah Bay are several spots popular with sea kayakers.

Port Angeles, primarily a lumber-shipping port, is the largest town on the north Olympic Peninsula and serves both as a base for people exploring the national park and as a port for ferries crossing the Strait of Juan de Fuca to Victoria, British Columbia. It is here that you'll find the region's greatest concentration of lodgings and restaurants.

Port Angeles is also home to the national-park headquarters and the **Olympic National Park Visitor Center,** 3002 Mount Angeles Rd. (© **360/565-3130**), on the south edge of town. In addition to offering lots of information, maps, and books about the park, the center has exhibits on the park's flora and fauna. It's open daily throughout the year, with hours varying with the seasons.

Hurricane Ridge

From the main visitor center, continue another 17 miles up Mount Angeles Road to Hurricane Ridge, which on clear days offers the most breathtaking views in the park. In summer the surrounding subalpine meadows are carpeted with wildflowers, and you're likely to see deer grazing and Olympic marmots lounging on rocks or nibbling flowers. (Marmots are a large member of the squirrel family; if you get too close to one, it's likely to let out a piercing whistle.)

Several trails lead into the park from here, and several day hikes are possible. The 3-mile **Hurricane Hill Trail** and the 1-mile **Meadow Loop Trail** are the most scenic. Stop by the **Hurricane Ridge Visitor Center** to see its exhibits on plants and wildlife; this is a good place to learn about the fragile nature of this beautiful alpine landscape.

In winter Hurricane Ridge is a popular cross-country skiing area and also has two rope tows and a Poma lift for downhill skiing. However, because the ski area is so small and the conditions so unpredictable, it is used almost exclusively by local families. For more information, contact the **Hurricane Ridge Winter Sports Club** (© **360/457-2879** or 360/565-3131 for road conditions; www.hurricaneridge.net).

Lake Crescent

West of Port Angeles on U.S. 101 lies **Lake Crescent,** which is one of the most beautiful lakes in the state. This glacier-carved body of water is surrounded by steep forested mountains that give the lake the feel of a fjord. Near the east end of the lake, you'll find the 1-mile trail to 90-foot-high **Marymere Falls** and the **Storm King Ranger Station** (© **360/928-3380**), which is usually open in the summer (and in other seasons when a ranger is in the station). From the Marymere Falls Trail, you can hike the steep 1.7 miles up **Mount Storm King** to a viewpoint overlooking Lake Crescent (climbing above the viewpoint is not recommended).

On the north side of the lake, the **Spruce Railroad Trail** parallels the shore, crosses a picturesque little bridge, and is one of the only trails in the park open to mountain bikes. As the name implies, this was once the route of the railroad built to haul spruce out of these forests during World War I. Spruce was the ideal wood for building biplanes because of its strength and light weight. By the time the railroad was completed, however, the war was over and the demand for spruce had dwindled.

You can rent various types of small boats during the warmer months at several places on the lake. **Lake Crescent Lodge** has rowboats for rent ($9 per hour), while the **Fairholm General Store** (© 360/928-3020), at the lake's west end, has kayaks ($9 per hour) available.

Sol Duc Hot Springs

Continuing west from Lake Crescent, watch for the turnoff to **Sol Duc Hot Springs** (© 866/476-5382; www.visitsolduc.com). For 14 miles the road follows the Soleduck River, passing the Salmon Cascades along the way. Sol Duc Hot Springs were for centuries considered healing waters by local Native Americans, and after white settlers arrived in the area, the springs became a popular resort. In addition to the hot swimming pool and soaking tubs, you'll find cabins, a campground, a restaurant, and a snack bar. The springs are open daily from late March through late October; admission is $12 for adults, and $8.50 for seniors and children ages 4 to 12. A 4.5-mile loop trail leads from the hot springs to **Sol Duc Falls,** which are among the most photographed falls in the park. Alternatively, you can drive to the end of the Sol Duc Road and make this an easy 1.5-mile hike. Along this same road, you can hike the .5-mile **Ancient Groves Nature Trail.** *Note:* Sol Duc Road is one of the roads on which you have to pay an Olympic National Park entry fee.

RAINFORESTS & WILD BEACHES: EXPLORING OLYMPIC NATIONAL PARK WEST

The western regions of Olympic National Park can be roughly divided into two sections—the rugged coastal strip and the famous rainforest valleys. Of course, these are the rainiest areas within the park, and many a visitor has cut short a vacation here because of rain. Well, what do you expect? It is, after all, a *rainforest.* Come prepared to get wet.

The coastal strip can be divided into three segments. North of La Push, which is on the Quileute Indian Reservation, the 20 miles of shoreline from Rialto Beach to Cape Alava are accessible only on foot. The northern end of this stretch of coast is accessed from Lake Ozette off Wash. 112 in the northwest corner of the peninsula. South of La Push, the park's coastline stretches for 17 miles from Third Beach to the Hoh River mouth and is also accessible only on foot. The third segment of Olympic Park coastline begins at Ruby Beach, just south of the Hoh River mouth and the Hoh Indian Reservation, and stretches south to South Beach. This segment of coastline is paralleled by U.S. 101.

Inland of these coastal areas, which are not contiguous with the rest of the park, lie the four rainforest valleys of the Bogachiel, Hoh, Queets, and Quinault rivers. Of these valleys, only the Hoh and Quinault are penetrated by roads, and it is in the Hoh Valley that the rainforests are the primary attraction.

Forks is the largest community in the northwest corner of the Olympic Peninsula and is on U.S. 101, which continues south along the west side of the peninsula to the town of Hoquiam. For more information on the Forks area, contact the **Forks Chamber of Commerce,** 1411 S. Forks Ave. (P.O. Box 1249), Forks, WA 98331 (© 800/443-6757 or 360/374-2531; www.forkswa.com).

West of Forks lie miles of pristine beaches and a narrow strip of forest (called the Olympic Coastal Strip) that are part of the national park but that are not connected to the inland mountainous section. The first place where you can actually drive right to the Pacific Ocean is just west of Forks. At the end of a spur road, you come to the Quileute Indian Reservation and the community of **La Push.** Right in town there's a beach at the

Twilight Time in Forks

If the names Bella and Edward mean anything to you, then you or your children must be fans of the *Twilight* teen vampire novels. Set on the Olympic Peninsula, the young-adult romance novels feature real locales in Forks and Port Angeles, and promoting *Twilight* has become big business on the peninsula.

In Port Angeles, you can dine at **Bella Italia** (see p. 238), where characters Bella and Edward went on their first date; you can even order the same thing they ordered. Luckily, Bella Italia also happens to be one of my favorite restaurants on the peninsula.

In Forks, you'll likely spot an old red pickup truck just like the one Bella drives in the books. You can stop by the high school the characters attend, see the reserved hospital parking space of a doctor in the books, and see the police station where another character works. More settings from the book can be found west of Forks in the Native American community of La Push. In Forks, there are vampire-themed *Twilight* rooms at the **Dew Drop Inn Motel,** 100 Fern Hill Rd. (© **888/433-9376** or 360/374-4055; www.dewdropinnmotel. com) and at the **Pacific Inn Motel,** 352 Forks Ave. S. (© **800/235-7344;** www. pacificinnmotel.com). Of course, shops around town are full of *Twilight* and vampire souvenirs. There are even vampire kiss lattes at one coffee shop, and a local winery had plans to produce a *Twilight* wine. If you want to be sure you see it all, book a tour with **Dazzled by Twilight Tour Company,** 61 N. Forks Ave., Forks (© **360/374-8687;** www.dazzledbytwilight.com), which is affiliated with the Dazzled by Twilight gift shop.

mouth of the Quillayute River; before you reach La Push, however, you'll see signs for **Third Beach** ★★ and **Second Beach** ★★, which are two of the prettiest beaches on the peninsula. Third Beach is a 1.5-mile walk and Second Beach is just over half a mile from the trail head. If you do hike out to these beaches, do not leave any valuables in your car; break-ins are commonplace at the Second and Third Beach trail heads. **Rialto Beach** ★★, just north of La Push, is another beautiful and rugged beach; it's reached from a turnoff east of La Push. This is a good place for a day-hike along the beach. **Hole in the Wall,** where ceaseless wave action has bored a large tunnel through solid rock, is a favorite hiking destination. It's 1 mile up the beach from the Rialto Beach parking lot. It is also possible to backpack north for 24 miles from Rialto Beach to Cape Alava. On any of these beaches, keep an eye out for bald eagles, seals, and sea lions.

Hoh River Valley

Roughly 8 miles south of Forks is the turnoff for the Hoh River Valley. It's 17 miles up this side road to the **Hoh Rain Forest Visitor Center** (© **360/374-6925**), campground, and trail heads. This valley receives an average of 140 inches of rain per year—and sometimes as much as 190 inches—making it the wettest region in the continental United States. At the visitor center, you can learn all about the natural forces that cause this tremendous rainfall.

To see the effect of so much rain on the landscape, walk the .8-mile **Hall of Mosses**
Trail, where the trees (primarily Sitka spruce, western red cedar, and western hemlock)
tower 200 feet tall. Here you'll also see big-leaf maple trees with limbs draped in thick
carpets of mosses. If you're up for a longer walk, try the **Spruce Nature Trail.** If you've
come with a backpack, there's no better way to see the park and its habitats than by hiking the **Hoh River Trail,** which is 17 miles long and leads to Glacier Meadows and Blue
Glacier on the flanks of Mount Olympus. A herd of elk live in the Hoh Valley and can
sometimes be seen along these trails.

Continuing south on U.S. 101, but before crossing the Hoh River, you'll come to a
secondary road (Oil City Rd.) that heads west from the Hoh Oxbow campground. From
the end of the road, it's a hike of less than a mile to a rocky beach at the **mouth of the
Hoh River.** You're likely to see sea lions or harbor seals feeding just offshore here, and to
the north are several haystack rocks that are nesting sites for numerous seabirds. Primitive
camping is permitted on this beach, and from here backpackers can continue hiking for
17 miles north along a pristine wilderness of rugged headlands and secluded beaches.

Ruby Beach, Kalaloch & Queets

U.S. 101 finally reaches the coast at **Ruby Beach.** This beach gets its name from its pink
sand, which is composed of tiny grains of garnet. With its colorful sands, tide pools, sea
stacks, and driftwood logs, Ruby Beach is the prettiest of the beaches along this stretch
of coast.

For another 17 miles or so south of Ruby Beach, the highway parallels the wave-swept
coastline. Along this stretch of highway are turnoffs for five beaches that have only numbers for names. Beach 6 is a good place to look for whales and sea lions and also to see
the effects of erosion on this coast (the trail that used to lead down to the beach has been
washed away). At low tide the northern beaches offer lots of tide pools to explore. Near
the south end of this stretch of road, you'll find Kalaloch Lodge, which has a gas station,
and the adjacent **Kalaloch Ranger Station** (✆ **360/962-2283**), which is usually open
from late May to late September, daily from 9am to 5pm.

Quinault Lake

From Kalaloch, you'll drive through a long stretch of clear-cuts and tree farms, mostly on
the Quinault Indian Reservation, to scenic **Quinault Lake.** Surrounded by forested
mountains, this deep lake is the site of the rustic Lake Quinault Lodge and offers boating
and freshwater fishing opportunities, as well as more rainforests to explore on a couple
of short trails (a total of about 10 miles of trails are on the south side of the lake). On
the north shore of the lake, you'll find the world's largest western red cedar tree. This is
a good area in which to spot Roosevelt elk.

Art in the Outback

Also in the Forks area are quite a few artists' studios and galleries. You can pick up
an **Olympic West Arttrek** guide and map to these studios and galleries at the
Forks Chamber of Commerce, 1411 S. Forks Ave. (✆ **800/443-6757** or 360/374-
2531; www.forkswa.com/arttrek).

BIKING   If you're interested in exploring the region on a bike, you can rent one at **Sound Bikes & Kayaks,** 120 E. Front St., Port Angeles (✆ **360/457-1240;** www.sound bikeskayaks.com), which can recommend good rides in the area. Bikes are $30 per day or $9 per hour. The Olympic Discovery Trail, a paved bike path, is right outside the shop's front door and stretches all the way east to Sequim.

FISHING   The rivers of the Olympic Peninsula are well known for their fighting salmon, steelhead, and trout, and in Lake Crescent and Lake Ozette, you can fish for such elusive species as Beardslee and Crescenti trout. No fishing license is necessary to fish for trout on national-park rivers and streams or in Lake Crescent or Lake Ozette. However, you will need a state punch card—available wherever fishing licenses are sold—to fish for salmon or steelhead. For more information on freshwater fishing in the park, contact Olympic National Park (see "Visitor Information," above). Boat rentals are available on Lake Crescent at Fairholm General Store, the Log Cabin Resort, and Lake Crescent Lodge.

If you're more interested in heading out on open water to do a bit of salmon or deep-sea fishing, numerous charter boats operate out of Sekiu and Neah Bay. In Neah Bay, try **King Fisher Charters** (✆ **888/622-8216;** www.kingfisherenterprises.com). Expect to pay from $180 to $220 per person for a day of fishing.

LLAMA TREKKING   If you want to do an overnight trip into the backcountry of the national park but don't want to deal with all the gear, consider letting a llama carry your stuff. **Deli Llama,** 17045 Llama Lane, Bow, WA 98232 (✆ **360/757-4212;** www.deli llama.com), offers trips through Olympic National Park lasting 4 to 7 days ($155–$195 per person per day).

SEA KAYAKING & WHITE-WATER RAFTING   Sea-kayaking trips on nearby Lake Aldwell, at Freshwater Bay, and at Dungeness National Wildlife Refuge are offered by **Olympic Raft & Kayak** (✆ **888/452-1443** or 360/452-1443; www.raftandkayak.com), which charges between $42 and $99 per person. The steep mountains and plentiful rains of the Olympic Peninsula are the source of some great white-water rafting on the Elwha and Hoh rivers. This same company can take you out for some white-water rafting. Rates start at $54 ($44 for children 5–11) for a 2- to 2½-hour rafting trip.

WHERE TO STAY

In addition to the lodgings listed here, there are numerous campgrounds in or near Olympic National Park. For general information on national-park campgrounds, contact **Olympic National Park** (✆ **360/565-3130**). Make reservations at the national park's Kalaloch Campground by contacting the **National Recreation Reservation Service** (✆ **877/444-6777** or 518/885-3639; www.recreation.gov).

The national park's **Heart o' the Hills Campground** (105 campsites), on Hurricane Ridge Road 5 miles south of the Olympic National Park Visitor Center, is the most convenient campground for exploring the Hurricane Ridge area. On Olympic Hot Springs Road up the Elwha River, you'll find both **Elwha Campground** (40 campsites) and **Altair Campground** (30 campsites). The only campground on Lake Crescent is **Fairholme** (88 campsites), at the west end of the lake. The nearby **Sol Duc Campground** (82 campsites), set amid impressive stands of old-growth trees, is adjacent to Sol Duc Hot Springs. The national park's remote **Ozette Campground** (15 campsites), on the north shore of Lake Ozette, is a good choice for people wanting to day-hike out to the beaches on either side of Cape Alava.

The national park's **Mora Campground** (94 campsites) is near beautiful Rialto Beach at the mouth of the Quillayute River west of Forks. If you want to say you've camped at the wettest campground in the contiguous United States, head for the park's **Hoh Campground** (88 campsites), in the Hoh River Valley. South of the Hoh River, along the only stretch of U.S. 101 right on the beach, you'll find **Kalaloch Campground** (170 campsites), the national park's largest campground and the only one that takes reservations.

In Port Angeles

Domaine Madeleine ★★ Seven miles east of Port Angeles, this contemporary B&B is set on 5 wooded acres and has a very secluded feel. Big windows take in the views, while inside you'll find lots of Asian antiques and other interesting touches. Combine this with the waterfront setting and you have a fabulous hideaway—you may not even bother exploring the park. The guest rooms are in several different buildings surrounded by colorful gardens. All rooms have fireplaces and views of the Strait of Juan de Fuca and of the mountains beyond. Some have whirlpool tubs; some have kitchens or air-conditioning. For added privacy, there is a separate cottage.

146 Wildflower Lane, Port Angeles, WA 98362. (*C*) **888/811-8376** or 360/457-4174. www.domaine madeleine.com. 5 units. $140–$310 double. Rates for rooms in main house include full breakfast. 2-night minimum mid-Apr to mid-Oct, holidays, and weekends throughout the year. AE, DISC, MC, V. No children 11 or under. **Amenities:** Access to nearby health club. *In room:* TV/VCR/DVD, hair dryer, Wi-Fi.

West of Port Angeles

Beyond Port Angeles, accommodations are few and far between, and those places worth recommending tend to be very popular. Try to have room reservations before heading west from Port Angeles.

Lake Crescent Lodge ★ This historic property, 20 miles west of Port Angeles on the shore of Lake Crescent, is the lodging of choice for national-park visitors wishing to stay on the north side of the park. Wood paneling, hardwood floors, a stone fireplace, and a sunroom make the lobby a popular spot for just sitting and relaxing. The guest rooms in this main lodge building have the most historic character but have shared bathrooms. Other rooms are mostly aging motel-style rooms that lack the character of the lodge rooms. The Roosevelt cabins, which have fireplaces, are the most comfortable accommodations here. However, a couple of the Singer cabins (nos. 20 and 21) do have great views. All but the main lodge rooms have views of either the lake or the mountains. From mid-October to early May, Roosevelt cottages can be rented on weekends, but no other services are offered.

416 Lake Crescent Rd., Port Angeles, WA 98363. (*C*) **360/928-3211.** www.lakecrescentlodge.com. 52 units, 5 with shared bathroom. $105 double without bathroom; $154–$169 double with bathroom; $186–$239 cottage. Children 5 and under stay free in parent's room. AE, DC, DISC, MC, V. Pets accepted in cottages ($25). **Amenities:** Restaurant, lounge; watersports rentals; Wi-Fi. *In room:* No phone.

Sol Duc Hot Springs Resort The Sol Duc Hot Springs have for decades been a popular family vacation spot, with campers, day-trippers, and resort guests spending their days soaking and playing in the hot-water swimming pool. The grounds of the resort are grassy and open, and the forest is kept just at arm's reach. Unfortunately, the cabins have very little character and are basically free-standing motel rooms. Don't come expecting a classic mountain cabin experience. There's a restaurant here, as well as a poolside deli and grocery store. Three hot-spring-fed soaking pools and a large swimming pool are the focal point and are open to the public.

12076 Sol Duc Hot Springs Rd. (P.O. Box 2169), Port Angeles, WA 98362. *©* **866/476-5382.** Fax 360/327-3593. www.visitsolduc.com. 32 units. $147–$179 cabin for 2; $311 suite. Rates include full breakfast. Children 3 and under stay free in parent's room. AE, DISC, MC, V. 2-night minimum on holiday weekends. Closed late Oct to early Mar. Pets accepted ($15 per night). **Amenities:** 2 restaurants; outdoor pool; 3 hot-spring-fed soaking pools. *In room:* Hair dryer, no phone.

In the Forks Area

The town of Forks has several inexpensive motels and is a good place to look for cheap lodgings if you happen to be out this way without a reservation.

Along the Park's West Side, South of Forks

Kalaloch Lodge ★★   These are the national park's only oceanfront accommodations, comprising a rustic, cedar-shingled lodge and a cluster of cabins perched on a grassy bluff above the thundering Pacific Ocean. Wide sand beaches stretch north and south from the lodge, and huge driftwood logs are scattered at the base of the bluff. The rooms in the old lodge are the least expensive, and the oceanview bluff cabins, some of which have been renovated, are the most popular. The log cabins across the street from the bluff cabins don't have the knockout views, but some of these have been renovated. For modern comforts, the Sea Crest House has renovated motel-style rooms. The lodge also has a general store and a gas station. Because this place is popular throughout the year, you should make reservations 4 to 11 months in advance.

157151 U.S. 101, Forks, WA 98331. *©* **866/525-2562.** Fax 360/962-3391. www.visitkalaloch.com. 57 units. Late May to early Oct $159–$172 double, $182–$308 suite, $213–$309 bluff cabin, $169–$210 log cabin; lower rates other months. Children 5 and under stay free in parent's room. AE, DISC, MC, V. Pets accepted in cabins ($15). **Amenities:** Restaurant, lounge. *In room:* Hair dryer, no phone.

Lake Quinault Lodge ★★   On the shore of Lake Quinault in the southwest corner of the park, this imposing grande dame of the Olympic Peninsula wears an ageless tranquillity. A recent renovation has given the lobby a classic, old-time feel that makes it an even more enjoyable place to hang out than ever before. Huge old firs and cedars shade the rustic lodge, and Adirondack chairs on the deck command a view of the lawn. The accommodations include recently renovated small rooms in the historic main lodge, modern rooms with TVs and small balconies, and rooms with fireplaces. The fireplace rooms and the Lakeside rooms are the most appealing. The annex rooms are the least attractive, but they do have large bathtubs. The dining room serves creative Northwest cuisine. For diversion, the lodge offers lawn games and rainforest tours.

345 S. Shore Rd., Quinault, WA 98575. *©* **800/562-6672** or 360/288-2900. Fax 360/288-2901. www.visit lakequinault.com. 91 units. Mid-June to late Sept and winter holidays $130–$228 double, $256 suite; late Sept to mid-June $90–$175 double, $200 suite. Children 11 and under stay free in parent's room. AE, DISC, MC, V. Pets accepted ($15 per night). **Amenities:** Restaurant, lounge; indoor pool; sauna; watersports rentals; Wi-Fi. *In room:* Hair dryer, no phone.

WHERE TO DINE

In Port Angeles

For great espresso and the best pastries on the peninsula, don't miss downtown's **Itty Bitty Buzz,** 110 E. First St. (*©* **360/565-8080;** www.thebuzzbedazzled.com), which is affiliated with The Buzz in Sequim.

Bella Italia ★ ITALIAN   This downtown Port Angeles restaurant is only a couple of blocks from the terminal for ferries to and from Victoria, which makes it very convenient for many travelers. Dinners start with a basket of delicious bread accompanied by a garlic-and-herb dipping sauce. Local seafood makes it onto the menu in the form of smoked-salmon ravioli, smoked-salmon fettuccine, steamed mussels and clams, and other dishes, and these are among your best choices on the menu. There are also some interesting individual pizzas and a good selection of wines, as well as a wine bar, an espresso bar, and plenty of excellent Italian desserts.

118 E. First St. ℂ **360/457-5442.** www.bellaitaliapa.com. Reservations recommended. Main courses $9–$30. AE, DC, DISC, MC, V. Sun–Thurs 4–9pm; Fri–Sat 4–10pm.

C'est Si Bon ★★FRENCH   Four miles south of town just off U.S. 101, C'est Si Bon is a brightly painted roadside building that, from the exterior, you might not think would be serving delicious traditional French food. Inside, the building's colorful exterior paint job gives way to more classic decor: reproductions of European works of art, crystal chandeliers, and old musical instruments used as wall decorations. The restaurant serves deftly prepared Gallic standards such as French onion soup or escargot for starters. Follow that with *coquille Saint Jacques* or a Dungeness crab soufflé, finish with a rich and creamy *mousse au chocolat,* and *voilà!* You have the perfect French meal. Specials feature whatever is fresh.

23 Cedar Park Rd. ℂ **360/452-8888.** www.cestsibon-frenchcuisine.com. Reservations recommended. Main courses $24–$36. AE, DISC, MC, V. Tues–Sun 5–11pm.

West of Port Angeles

Outside of Port Angeles, the restaurant choices become exceedingly slim. Your best options are the dining rooms at **Lake Crescent Lodge** (see above), which is open from early May to mid-October, and the **Log Cabin Resort**, 3183 E. Beach Rd. (ℂ **360/928-3325;** www.logcabinresort.net), which is open from late May through September. Both are on the shores of Lake Crescent. Continuing west, you'll find food at the dining room of **Sol Duc Hot Springs Resort,** open late March through late October.

In the town of Forks, you'll find several basic diners and family restaurants, but nothing really worth recommending. South of Forks, your best bets are the dining rooms at **Kalaloch Lodge** and **Lake Quinault Lodge.** If you happen to be hungry up the Hoh River, don't miss the juicy burgers at the **Hard Rain Cafe,** 5763 Upper Hoh Rd. (ℂ **360/ 374-9288;** www.hardraincafe.com).

---

5 MOUNT RAINIER

Weather forecasting for Seattleites is a simple matter: Either the Mountain is out and the weather is good, or it isn't (out or good). "The Mountain" is, of course, Mount Rainier, the 14,410-foot-tall dormant volcano that looms over Seattle on clear days; and though it looks as if it's on the edge of town, it's actually 90 miles southeast of the city.

The mountain and more than 200,000 acres surrounding it are part of **Mount Rainier National Park,** which was established in 1899 as the fifth U.S. national park. From downtown Seattle, the preferred route to the mountain is via I-5 south to exit 142A. Then take Wash. 18 east to Wash. 164 to Enumclaw, continuing east on Wash. 410, which will take you to the northeast corner of the park. The route is well marked. Allow yourself 2½ hours to reach the park's Sunrise area. *Note:* This is a summer-only routing. During the winter Sunrise is closed by snow, as are the roads to Ohanapecosh and from Ohanapecosh to Paradise. In winter, you can, however, visit Paradise from the southwest (Nisqually) entrance to the park.

It's advisable to leave as early in the day as possible, especially if you're heading to the mountain on a summer weekend. Traffic along the route and crowds at the park can be daunting.

Before you go, get information by contacting **Mount Rainier National Park,** 55210 238th Ave. E., Ashford, WA 98304 (© **360/569-2211;** www.nps.gov/mora). Keep in mind that during the winter, only the Longmire and Paradise areas of the park are open. Park entrances other than the Nisqually entrance are closed by snow throughout the winter.

The entry fee to Mount Rainier National Park is $15 per motor vehicle.

Follow signs for **Sunrise,** which, at 6,400 feet in elevation, is the highest spot in the park accessible by car. A beautiful old log lodge here serves as the visitor center. From here you can see not only Mount Rainier, seemingly at arm's length, but also Mount Baker and Mount Adams. During July and August, the alpine meadows here are ablaze with wildflowers. Some of the park's most scenic trails begin at Sunrise. Because this area is usually less crowded than Paradise, it is my favorite spot for an alpine hike.

Drive back down from Sunrise to Wash. 410 and continue south to Cayuse Pass, where you can make a short detour east to scenic Chinook Pass. From Cayuse Pass, continue south on Wash. 123 to the **Ohanapecosh Visitor Center** (© **360/569-6046**), where you can walk through a forest of old-growth trees, some more than 1,000 years old. This visitor center is usually open from late May to early September. From here, follow signs west to Paradise. On the way to Paradise, be sure to stop at the aptly named **Reflection Lakes** for the best photo op in the park.

Paradise (elevation 5,400 ft.), an aptly named mountainside aerie, affords a breathtaking close-up view of Mount Rainier. However, Paradise is the park's most popular destination, so expect crowds. As at Sunrise, July and August bring spectacular displays of wildflowers, which makes this another great place for day hikes. A short walk from the new **Henry M. Jackson Memorial Visitor Center,** you can view Nisqually Glacier. Many miles of other trails lead out from Paradise, looping through meadows and up onto snowfields above the timberline. It's not unusual to find plenty of snow at Paradise as late as July. In 1972 the area set a world record for snowfall in 1 year: 93½ feet! This record held until the 1998–99 winter season, when La Niña climatic conditions produced record-breaking conditions on Mount Baker, which is north of Mount Rainier. More than 94 feet of snow fell on Mount Baker that season.

Continuing west and downhill from Paradise will bring you to Longmire, site of the National Park Inn and the **Longmire Museum** (© **360/569-2211,** ext. 3314), which has exhibits on the park's natural and human history. You'll also find a hiker information center that issues backcountry permits. In winter, when this is one of the only areas of the park open to vehicles, a ski-touring center in Longmire rents cross-country skis and snowshoes.

At both Paradise and Sunrise, hikers can choose from a good variety of outings, from short, flat nature walks to moderately difficult loops to long, steep, out-and-back hikes.

If you don't have a car but still want to visit Mount Rainier National Park, book an all-day tour through **Seattle Tours** (© **888/293-1404** or 206/768-1234; www.seattle citytours.com), which charges $97 for adults and $69 for children 3 to 12 for a 10-hour tour. These tours spend most of that time in transit, but you get to see the mountain up close and even get in a couple of hours of hiking at Paradise.

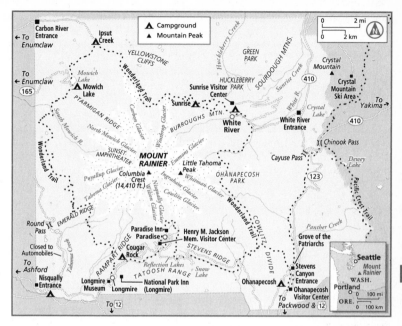

WHERE TO STAY

In addition to the two lodges listed below, there are several campgrounds within the national park. Two of these—Cougar Rock and Ohanapecosh—take reservations, which should be made several months in advance for summer weekends. To make reservations, contact the **National Recreation Reservation Service** (✆ **877/444-6777** or 518/885-3639; www.recreation.gov).

National Park Inn ★ Located in Longmire, in the southwest corner of the park, this rustic lodge opened in 1920 and is set in the dense forests that blanket the lower slopes of Mount Rainier. The inn's front veranda has a good view of the mountain, and it is here that guests often gather at sunset on clear days. The lounge, with its river-rock fireplace, is the perfect place to relax on a winter's night. Guest rooms vary in size and contain rustic furnishings but are definitely not the most memorable part of a stay here. The inn's restaurant serves familiar American fare and manages to have something for everyone. The National Park Inn is popular in winter with cross-country skiers and snowshoers, and equipment can be rented at the gift shop here.

Mount Rainier National Park, 55106 Kernahan Rd. E., Ashford, WA 98304. ✆ **360/569-2275.** Fax 360/569-2770. www.mtrainierguestservices.com. 25 units, 7 with shared bathroom. $111 double with shared bathroom; $148–$205 double with private bathroom. Rates from Nov to late Apr include full breakfast. Children 2 and under stay free in parent's room. AE, DC, DISC, MC, V. **Amenities:** Restaurant (American). In room: Hair dryer, no phone.

Paradise Inn ★★ Built in 1916 high on the flanks of Mount Rainier in the area aptly known as Paradise, this rustic lodge should be your first choice of accommodations in the park, so book early. Cedar-shake siding, huge exposed beams, cathedral ceilings, and a gigantic stone fireplace make this the quintessential mountain retreat. Offering breathtaking views of the mountain, the inn is also the starting point for miles of trails that in summer wander through flower-filled meadows. Guest rooms vary in size. The inn reopened in May 2008 after a major 2-year rehabilitation.

Mount Rainier National Park, 55106 Kernahan Rd., Ashford, WA 98304. © **360/569-2275.** Fax 360/569-2770. www.rainier.guestservices.com. 121 units,33 with shared bathroom. $104 double with shared bathroom; $155–$235 double with private bathroom; $255 suite. Children 2 and under stay free in parent's room. AE, DC, DISC, MC, V. Closed early Oct to mid-May. **Amenities:** 2 restaurants (American). *In room:* No phone.

6 FERRY EXCURSIONS FROM SEATTLE

Among Seattle's most popular excursions are ferry trips across Puget Sound to Bainbridge Island (Seattle's quintessential bedroom community) and Bremerton (home of the Naval Shipyards). If your interests run to shopping, small towns, wineries, parks, and gardens, you'll want to head over to Bainbridge Island. If, on the other hand, you're more interested in naval history and antiques and collectibles, visit Bremerton. It's also possible to link these two excursions by taking one ferry out and the other ferry back. It's not a long drive between Bainbridge Island and Bremerton (less than 1 hr.), but if you stop often to enjoy the sights, you can certainly have a long day's outing.

BAINBRIDGE ISLAND & POULSBO

Start the trip by taking the **Bainbridge Island ferry** from the Colman Dock ferry terminal at Pier 52 on the Seattle waterfront. For a current sailing schedule, contact **Washington State Ferries** (© 800/843-3779 or 888/808-7977 in Washington, or 206/464-6400; www.wsdot.wa.gov/ferries). Onboard you can see the Seattle skyline and, on a clear day, Mount Rainier to the southeast and the Olympic Mountains to the west. One-way fares for the 35-minute crossing from Seattle to Bainbridge Island are $11.55 ($14.45 May to second Sat in Oct) for a car and driver, $6.70 for adult car passengers or walk-ons, $3.35 for seniors, and $5.40 for children 6 to 18. Car passengers and walk-ons pay fares only on westbound ferries.

Just up the hill from the Bainbridge Island ferry terminal is the island's main shopping district, where you'll find lots of interesting shops and restaurants. A stroll around town will give you a good idea of what island life is all about and will probably leave you wondering how you can live here, too. Start a tour of town by dropping by **Blackbird Bakery,** 210 Winslow Way E. (© **206/780-1322**), for a pastry and a coffee. If it's a hot day, you can get some of the Puget Sound region's best ice cream at **Mora Ice Creamery,** 139 Madrone Lane (© **206/855-8822;** moraicecream.com), which is just off Winslow Way East in the middle of the shopping district. Here amid the many interesting shops and boutiques, you'll also find the tasting room of **Eleven Winery,** 278 Winslow Way E. (© **206/842-4669;** www.elevenwinery.com), which makes a wide range of wines, including a couple of different port-style wines. February through December, the tasting room is open Wednesday through Sunday from noon to 5pm; in January, it's open Thursday through Sunday from noon to 5pm.

After you've explored the shops along Winslow Way, wander down to Waterfront Park, where you'll find kayaks, canoes, and swan boats for rent at **Back of Beyond Outdoors,** 181 Winslow Way (© **206/842-9229;** www.tothebackofbeyond.com), which is located on a barge tied up to the city dock. Sea kayaks and canoes rent for $15 to $20 per hour, depending on the type of boat you select. The unusual swan boats (patterned after those in Boston) go for $15 per half-hour. You can also wander along the town's Waterfront Trail, which for part of its short length is a boardwalk that skirts a marina. This trail will lead you to the **Pegasus Coffee House and Gallery,** 131 Parfitt Way SW (© **206/842-6725;** www. pegasuscoffeehouse.com), which is my favorite espresso bar in town. A little farther on the Waterfront Trail will bring you to the **Harbour Public House,** 231 Parfitt Way SW (© **206/842-0969;** www.harbourpub.com), a tavern with a nice view of the marina.

If you want to learn more about Bainbridge Island history, stop in at the **Bainbridge Island Historical Society and Museum,** 215 Ericksen Ave. NE (© **206/842-2773;** www.bainbridgehistory.org). This little museum, housed partly in a red 1908 schoolhouse, is open Wednesday through Monday from 10am to 4pm in the summer and from 1 to 4pm in other months. Admission is $2.50 for adults and $1.50 for students and seniors (children under 5 are free). If you have the family along, you may also want to spend some time at the **Kids Discovery Museum,** 305 Madison Ave. N. (© **206/855-4650;** www.kidimu.org), which is open Tuesday through Saturday from 10am to 4pm and Sunday from noon to 4pm. Admission is $5 per person. Between mid-April and late October, on Saturdays from 9am to 1pm, the **Bainbridge Island Farmers' Market** (© **206/855-1500;** www.bainbridgefarmersmarket.com) is held in the center of town at City Hall Park, which is accessible from Winslow Way midway between Ericksen Avenue and Madison Avenue.

Down at the south end of the island is **Fort Ward State Park** (© **360/902-8844;** www.parks.wa.gov), on the quiet shore of Rich Passage. The park offers picnicking, good bird-watching, and a 2-mile hiking trail.

If you'd like to sample some more local wines, drop by **Bainbridge Island Vineyards and Winery,** 8989 Day Rd. E. (© **206/842-9463;** www.bainbridgevineyards.com), which is 4½ miles from the ferry landing (take Wash. 305 for 4 miles to the stoplight and turn right on Day Rd. E.). The winery specializes in European-style white wines made from estate-grown grapes. These wines are quite good and are only available here and at a few select restaurants. The winery is open Friday through Sunday from 11am to 5pm.

Garden enthusiasts will want to visit the **Bloedel Reserve** ★, 7571 NE Dolphin Dr. (© **206/842-7631;** www.bloedelreserve.org), 6 miles north of the ferry terminal off Wash. 305 (turn right on Agate Point Rd.). The expansive and elegant grounds are the ideal place for a quiet stroll amid plants from around the world. Admission is $12 for adults, $8 for seniors, and $6 for children 5 to 12. The gardens are open Wednesday through Sunday from 10am to 4pm. Reservations are required to visit the gardens, so be sure to call in advance. Nearby, at the northern tip of the island, you'll find **Fay Bainbridge State Park** (© **206/842-3931;** www.parks.wa.gov), which offers camping and great views across the sound to the Seattle skyline.

After crossing the Agate Pass Bridge to the mainland of the Kitsap Peninsula, take your first right, and at the gas station on the edge of the village of **Suquamish,** turn left to reach the grave of Chief Sealth, for whom Seattle was named. Nearby is **Old Man House Park,** which preserves the site of a large Native American longhouse. The Old Man House itself is long gone, but you'll find an informative sign and a small park with picnic tables. To find this park, go back to the gas station and go straight across the main road.

From Suquamish, head back to Wash. 305, continue a little farther west, and watch for signs to the **Suquamish Museum,** 15838 Sandy Hook Rd. (© **360/598-3311,** ext. 422; www.suquamish.nsn.us/museum), on the Port Madison Indian Reservation. The museum houses a compelling history of Puget Sound's native people, with lots of historic photos and quotes from tribal elders about growing up in the area. From May through September, the museum is open daily from 10am to 5pm; October through April it's open Friday through Sunday from 11am to 4pm. Admission is $4 for adults, $3 for seniors, and $2 for children 12 and under. A new museum is currently under construction and should be open some time in 2010, so be sure to call first before planning a visit to this museum.

Continuing north on Wash. 305, you'll come to the small town of **Poulsbo,** which overlooks fjordlike Liberty Bay. Settled in the late 1880s by Scandinavians, Poulsbo was primarily a fishing, logging, and farming town until it decided to play up its Scandinavian heritage. Today, shops in the Scandinavian-inspired downtown sell all manner of Viking and Scandinavian souvenirs, but there are also several good art galleries, fashion boutiques, and other interesting stores. Throughout the year numerous Scandinavian-themed celebrations are held. For more information, contact the **Greater Poulsbo Chamber of Commerce,** 19351 Eighth Ave. (P.O. Box 1063), Poulsbo, WA 98370 (✆ **877/768-5726** or 360/779-4848; www.poulsbochamber.com).

If you have a sweet tooth, don't miss **Sluys Poulsbo Bakery,** 18924 Front St. NE (✆ **360/697-2253**), which bakes mounds of Scandinavian-inspired goodies (very sweet), as well as stick-to-your-ribs breads. When you need a cup of espresso, head to the **Poulsbohemian Coffeehouse,** 19003 Front St. (✆ **360/779-9199;** http://poulsbohemian. com), which has an excellent view of Liberty Bay from atop the bluff on the edge of downtown.

If you're interested in seeing Poulsbo from the water, you can rent a sea kayak from **Olympic Outdoor Center,** 18971 Front St. (✆ **800/592-5983** or 360/697-6095; www. olympicoutdoorcenter.com), which charges $14 to $19 per hour or $50 to $70 by the day.

If you have time and enjoy visiting historic towns, continue north from Poulsbo on Wash. 3 to **Port Gamble** (www.portgamble.com). This community was established in 1853 as a company town for the Pope and Talbot lumber mill and looks like a New England village dropped down in the middle of the Northwest woods. Along the town's shady streets are Victorian homes that were restored by Pope and Talbot. Stop by the **Port Gamble General Store and Cafe,** 32400 Rainier Ave. NE (✆ **360/297-7636**), a classic general store that is home to the **Of Sea and Shore Museum** (www.ofseaandshore.com). This little museum houses an exhibit of seashells from around the world and is open daily from 9am to 5pm; admission is free. Around the back of the building that houses the general store, you'll find the **Port Gamble Historical Museum** (✆ **360/297-8074**), a collection of local memorabilia. Admission is $4 for adults and $3 for seniors and students (free for children 6 and under). From May through October the museum is open daily from 9:30am to 5pm; the rest of the year it's open Friday through Sunday, and major holiday Mondays, from 9:30am to 5pm.

BREMERTON & ITS NAVAL HISTORY

If you are interested in big ships and naval history, ride the ferry from Seattle to Bremerton (see above for information on Washington State Ferries). Bremerton is home to the Puget Sound Naval Shipyard, and there are always plenty of navy ships in the harbor. Over the years, mothballed U.S. Navy ships have included the aircraft carriers USS *Nimitz* and USS *Midway* and the battleships USS *Missouri* and USS *New Jersey.*

One mothballed destroyer, the USS *Turner Joy,* is open to the public as a memorial to those who have served in the U.S. Navy and who helped build the navy's ships. Operated

by the **Bremerton Historic Ships Association** (© 360/792-2457; www.ussturnerjoy.
org), the *Turner Joy* is docked about 150 yards east of the Washington State Ferries terminal. From May through September, the ship is open daily from 10am to 5pm; October through April, it's open Friday through Sunday from 10am to 4pm. Admission is $10 for adults, $8 for seniors, and $6 for children 5 to 12.

Nearby is the **Puget Sound Navy Museum,** 251 First St. (© 360/479-4774; www. history.navy.mil/museums/psnm/psnm.htm), an official U.S. Navy museum that showcases naval history and the historic contributions of the Puget Sound Naval Shipyard. The museum is open Monday through Saturday from 10am to 4pm and Sunday from 1 to 4pm (closed on Tues Oct–May). Admission is free.

Heading north from Bremerton on Wash. 3, you'll soon see signs for the **Naval Undersea Museum,** 1103 Hunley Rd. (© 360/396-4148; www.history.navy.mil/museums/ keyport/index1.htm), located 3 miles east of Wash. 3 on Wash. 308 near the town of Keyport. The museum examines all aspects of undersea exploration, with interactive exhibits, models, and displays that include a deep-sea exploration-and-research craft, a Japanese kamikaze torpedo, and a deep-sea rescue vehicle. The museum is open daily from 10am to 4pm (closed on Tues Oct–May); admission is free. The reason this museum is here: The **Bangor Navy Base,** home port for a fleet of Trident nuclear submarines, is nearby. The base is on Hood Canal, a long, narrow arm of Puget Sound.

Bremerton isn't just about naval history; it's also home to the **Aurora Valentinetti Puppet Museum,** 257 Fourth St. (© 360/373-2992; www.ectandpuppets.com), which has a large collection of puppets and marionettes and is sure to be a hit with your younger children. The museum is open Wednesday through Saturday from 11am to 4pm. Admission is by donation.

7 SNOQUALMIE FALLS & THE SNOQUALMIE VALLEY

One of the reasons so many people put up with Seattle's drawbacks—urban sprawl, congested highways, and high housing prices—is that less than an hour east lie mountains so vast and rugged you can hike for a week without crossing a road. Between the city and this wilderness lie the farmlands of the **Snoqualmie Valley,** the Seattle region's last bit of bucolic countryside. Here you'll find small towns, pastures full of spotted cows, "U-pick" farms, and a few unexpected attractions, including an impressive waterfall and a reproduction of a medieval village. While driving the back roads of the Snoqualmie Valley, keep an eye out for historic markers that include old photos and details of the valley's past.

Snoqualmie Falls ★★, the valley's biggest attraction, plummets 270 feet into a pool of deep blue water. The falls are surrounded by a park owned by Puget Power, which operates a hydroelectric plant inside the rock wall behind the falls. The plant, built in 1898, was the world's first underground electricity-generating facility. Within the park you'll find two overlooks near the lip of the falls and a .5-mile trail down to the base of the cascade. The river below the waterfall is popular both for fishing and white-water kayaking. To reach the falls, take I-90 east from Seattle for 35 to 45 minutes and get off at exit 27. If you're hungry for lunch, try the restaurant at **Salish Lodge,** the hotel at the top of the falls.

Snoqualmie Falls is located just outside the town of **Snoqualmie,** which is where you'll find the restored 1890 railroad depot that houses the **Northwest Railway Museum,** 38625 SE King St. (☏ **425/888-3030;** www.trainmuseum.org). The museum, an absolute must for anyone with a child who is a fan of Thomas the Tank Engine or *The Polar Express,* operates the **Snoqualmie Valley Railroad** on weekends from April through October. The 70-minute railway excursions run between here and the town of **North Bend.** Fares are $10 for adults, $9 for seniors, and $7 for children 2 to 12. Be sure to check the current schedule. The museum displays railroad memorabilia and has a large display of rolling stock.

Outside of North Bend rises **Mount Si,** one of the most hiked mountains in the state. Carved by glaciers long ago, this mountain presents a dramatic face to the valley, and if you're the least bit athletic, it is hard to resist the temptation to hike to the top. For more information, see p. 152.

Between North Bend and the town of **Carnation,** you'll pass several "U-pick" farms, where, throughout the summer, you can pick your own berries.

The Snoqualmie Valley is also the site of **Camlann Medieval Village,** 10320 Kelly Rd. NE (☏ **425/788-8624;** www.camlann.org), located north of Carnation off Wash. 203. On weekends between mid-July and late August, this reproduction medieval village stages numerous medieval festivals and becomes home to knights and squires and assorted other costumed merrymakers. There are crafts stalls and food booths, and medieval clothing is available for rent if you forgot to pack yours. Throughout the year, the village stages a wide variety of banquets, seasonal festivals, and weekend living-history demonstrations. Ye Bors Hede Inne restaurant is open Tuesday through Sunday for traditional dinners ($19 per person). Fair admission is $10 for adults and $6 for seniors and children 6 to 12. Admission to both the fair and a banquet is $45.

On the way to or from Snoqualmie Falls, you may want to pull off I-90 in the town of **Issaquah** (15 miles east of Seattle) for a bit of shopping and candy sampling. Take exit 17 and, at the bottom of the exit ramp, turn right and then immediately left onto NE Gilman Boulevard. Just a short distance up the road, you'll come to **Boehms Candies,** 255 NE Gilman Blvd. (☏ **425/392-6652;** www.boehmscandies.com), which specializes in chocolate confections such as truffles, turtles, and pecan rolls. From Boehms, drive back the way you came (staying on Gilman Blvd. through the intersection that leads to the freeway), and you will come to **Gilman Village,** 317 NW Gilman Blvd. (☏ **425/392-6802;** www.gilmanvillage.com), an unusual collection of historic buildings that were moved to this site and turned into a shopping center full of interesting little shops.

Also here in Issaquah is the **Issaquah Salmon Hatchery,** 125 W. Sunset Way (☏ **425/391-9094** or 425/427-0259), where throughout the year you can see the different stages of rearing salmon from egg to adult. In October adult salmon can be seen returning to the hatchery; each year on the first weekend in October, the city holds the Salmon Days Festival to celebrate the return of the natives.

WHERE TO STAY

Salish Lodge & Spa ★★★   Set at the top of 270-foot Snoqualmie Falls and only 30 minutes east of Seattle on I-90, the Salish Lodge & Spa is a popular weekend getaway spot for Seattle-area residents. With its country-lodge atmosphere, the Salish aims for casual comfort and hits the mark, though the emphasis is clearly on luxury. Guest rooms, which are designed for romantic escapes, have wood-burning fireplaces, oversize whirlpool tubs, feather beds, and down comforters. A full-service spa makes this getaway even

more attractive. The lodge's country breakfast is a legendary feast that will likely keep you **247**
full right through to dinner, and at night you can choose from one of the most extensive
lists of Washington wines in the state. The lounge has a great view of the falls.

6501 Railroad Ave. (P.O. Box 1109), Snoqualmie, WA 98065-1109. © **800/272-5474** or 425/888-2556. Fax
425/888-2420. www.salishlodge.com. 89 units. $219–$449 double; $569–$908 suite. All rates plus $15
resort fee. Children 17 and under stay free in parent's room. AE, DC, DISC, MC, V. **Amenities:** 3 restaurants
(Northwest), lounge; bikes; exercise room; full-service spa. *In room:* A/C, TV, hair dryer, minibar, Wi-Fi.

8 THE WOODINVILLE WINE COUNTRY

Washington produces more wine than any other state except California, and although
the main wine country lies more than 200 miles to the east, in Central and Eastern
Washington, there is a concentration of wineries a 30-minute drive north of Seattle,
outside the town of Woodinville. More than two dozen wineries in the Woodinville area
are open to the public on a regular basis (although often only on Sat afternoons), and
their proximity to Seattle makes this an excellent day's outing. Woodinville is also home
to the Northwest's top restaurant and a gorgeous contemporary lodge, which, with the
wineries, add up to a great place for a romantic getaway.

To reach this miniature wine country from Seattle, head east on Wash. 520 or I-90 to
I-405, drive north on I-405 and take the NE 124th Street exit, and drive east to 132nd
Avenue NE. Turn left here and continue north to NE 143rd Place/NE 145th Street. Turn
right and drive down the hill. At the bottom of the hill, you will be facing the first of the
area's wineries.

Most of the wineries in the area charge a $5 to $8 tasting fee, but your fee is usually
refunded if you buy any wine. For more information and a map to area wineries, contact
Woodinville Wine Country (© **425/205-4394;** www.woodinvillewinecountry.com) or
look for this organization's wineries brochure at any area winery. If you'd prefer to let
someone else do the driving, book a tour with **Bon Vivant Wine Tours** (© **206/524-
8687;** www.bonvivanttours.com), which charges $79 per person for a day tour of the
wineries.

The **Columbia Winery,** 14030 NE 145th St. (© **800/488-2347** or 425/482-7490;
www.columbiawinery.com), has one of Washington's largest tasting bars and produces a
wide range of good wines. It's open daily from 10am to 6pm. This winery tends to be
crowded on weekends, so try to arrive early.

Directly across NE 145th Street from the Columbia Winery, you'll find the largest and
most famous of the wineries in the area, **Chateau Ste. Michelle** ★, 14111 NE 145th St.
(© **800/267-6793** or 425/415-3633; www.ste-michelle.com). In a grand mansion on a
historic 1912 estate, this is by far the most beautiful winery in the Northwest. It's also the
largest winery in the state and is known for its consistent quality. Hours are daily from
10am to 5pm; if you take the free tour, you can sample several of the less expensive wines.
For a $10 tasting fee, you can try some older reserve wines. For $15, you can have a private
tasting of older wines (reservations required). Because this winery is so big and produces so
many different wines, you never know what you might find in the tasting room. An amphitheater on the grounds stages big-name music performances throughout the summer.

If you drive north from Chateau Ste. Michelle, NE 145th Street becomes Woodinville-Redmond Road (Wash. 202) and you soon come to **Januik Winery,** 14710
Woodinville-Redmond Rd. NE (© **425/481-5502;** www.januikwinery.com), which

SIDE TRIPS FROM SEATTLE

11

THE WOODINVILLE WINE COUNTRY

shares its tasting room with **Novelty Hill Winery** (www.noveltyhillwines.com). With its concrete walls and intersecting geometric shapes and patterns, this large winery is the most architecturally unusual wine facility in the area. A variety of tastings, costing $5 to $10, are offered daily from 11am to 5pm. Along this stretch of road, you'll also find **Silver Lake Winery,** 15029 Woodinville-Redmond Rd. NE (© **425/485-2437,** ext. 109; www.silverlakewinery.com). This winery sometimes crafts good reds but can be hit-or-miss. This is, however, a good place to look for wine bargains. The tasting room is open Monday through Saturday from 11am to 5pm and Sunday from noon to 5pm.

Next up the road heading north is a hidden gem, the small **Facelli Winery,** 16120 Woodinville-Redmond Rd. NE (© **425/488-1020;** www.facelliwinery.com), which is open Saturday and Sunday from noon to 4pm and produces some good red wines.

Continue a little farther to get to **DiStefano Winery,** 12280 Woodinville Dr. SE (© **425/487-1648;** www.distefanowinery.com), which is best known for its full-bodied red wines but also produces some memorable whites. The tasting room is open Saturday and Sunday from noon to 5pm.

If you want to visit some of the area's smaller wineries, head east a quarter-mile from Columbia Winery and Chateau Ste. Michelle on Woodinville-Redmond Road to the intersection with 140th Place NE. At this corner, you'll find **Brian Carter Cellars,** 14419 Woodinville-Redmond Rd. NE (© **425/806-9463;** www.briancartercellars.com), which is open daily from noon to 5pm during the summer (closed Tues–Wed in other months).

From Brian Carter Cellars, drive north on 140th Place NE to downtown Woodinville, turn right on NE Woodinville-Duvall Road, left on NE North Woodinville Road, and right on 144th Avenue NE. Here, in a warehouse industrial complex, you'll find a dozen or more small wineries. Between May and September, many of these wineries are open from 4 to 8pm on the third Thursday of the month for the **Woodinville Warehouse Wineries Thursday Wine Walk** (www.woodwarewine.com). Admission to this monthly event costs $20 per person (cash only), which gets you tastings at all the participating wineries. The following wineries are some of my favorites among these warehouse wineries.

For the most bang for your buck, head to 19495 144th Ave. NE, Suite 240, a single tasting room that is home to **Smasne Cellars** (© **509/305-1007;** www.smasnecellars.com), **Almaterra Wines** (© **509/592-0756;** www.almaterrawines.com), and **Gård Vintners** (© **509/346-8726;** www.gardvintners.com). What ties these three little wineries together is winemaker Robert Smasne, who has worked at numerous wineries across the state. There are often particularly good deals to be had here. The tasting room is open Friday from 1 to 6pm and Saturday and Sunday from noon to 6pm.

At **Anton Ville Winery,** 19501 144th Ave. NE, Ste. D-300 (© **206/683-3393;** www.antonvillewinery.com), you can sample a variety of good Bordeaux-style reds in the $30 price range. May through October, the tasting room here is open Friday through Sunday from 1 to 5pm; November through April, it's open Saturday from 1 to 5pm.

Want really BIG red wines? Head to **Sparkman Cellars,** 19501 144th Ave., Ste. D-700 (© **425/398-1045;** www.sparkmancellars.com), where Bordeaux blends are in the $40 to $50 range. Grapes for many of the Sparkman wines are sourced from Washington's top vineyards. The tasting room is open Saturday from 1 to 5pm.

Cuillin Hills Winery, 19495 144th Ave. NE, Ste. A-110 (© **425/402-1907;** www.cuillinhills.com), makes delicious New World-style red wines. The tasting room is open Saturday from noon to 4pm.

If you're a jazz fan and your tastes run to sangiovese and zinfandel, be sure to stop by **Des Voigne Cellars,** 19501 144th Ave. NE, Ste. B-500 (② **425/415-8466;** www. desvoignecellars.com), which features jazz musicians on its labels. This winery also does a good viognier-roussanne blend. The tasting room is open Saturday from noon to 4pm.

Page Cellars, 19495 NE 144th Ave. NE, Ste. B-205 (② **253/232-9463;** www. pagecellars.com), focuses on cabernet sauvignon and sauvignon blanc but also does syrah and a rosé. The tasting room is open Saturday from noon to 4pm and Sunday from 1 to 5pm.

Red Sky Winery, 19495 144th Ave. NE, Ste. B-220 (② **425/481-9864;** www.redsky winery.com), does a variety of Bordeaux blends as well as Semillon, syrah, and merlot. The tasting room is open Saturday from noon to 4pm.

Just because this is wine country doesn't mean you can't get a good pint of beer. The large **Redhook Ale Brewery,** 14300 NE 145th St. (② **425/483-3232;** www.redhook. com), next door to Columbia Winery, is one of Washington's top breweries. Tours are available; there's a pub here as well.

If you're up this way on a Saturday between early May and mid-October, be sure to stop by the **Woodinville Farmers Market,** NE 175th Street and 133rd Avenue NE (② **425/485-1042;** www.woodinvillefarmersmarket.com), which is at the intersection with Woodinville-Redmond Road just east of Chateau Ste. Michelle and Columbia Winery. The market is open from 9am to 3pm.

WHERE TO STAY

Willows Lodge ★★★ ⓕFinds In the heart of the Woodinville wine country, about 30 minutes north of Seattle, and adjacent to the much-celebrated Herbfarm Restaurant (see below), this lodge is a beautiful blend of rustic and contemporary. From the moment you turn into the lodge's parking lot, you'll recognize it as someplace special. A huge fire-darkened tree stump is set like a sculpture outside the front door, and the landscaping has a distinctly Northwest feel. Inside, the abundance of polished woods (some salvaged from a Portland, OR port facility) gives the place something of a Japanese aesthetic. It's all very soothing and tranquil, an ideal retreat from which to visit the nearby wineries. In the guest rooms, you'll find beds with down duvets; slate tables made from salvaged pool tables; and all kinds of high-tech amenities.

14580 NE 145th St., Woodinville, WA 98072. ② **877/424-3930** or 425/424-3900. Fax 425/424-2585. www. willowslodge.com. 84 units. $199–$379 double; $449–$699 suite. Children 17 and under stay free in parent's room. AE, DC, DISC, MC, V. Valet parking $5. Pets accepted ($25 fee). **Amenities:** 2 restaurants (Northwest), 2 lounges; bikes; concierge; exercise room; Jacuzzi; room service; sauna; full-service spa. *In room:* A/C, TV, hair dryer, minibar, Wi-Fi.

WHERE TO DINE

If you aren't out this way specifically to have dinner at The Herbfarm and just want a decent meal while you tour the area, try the **Forecaster's Public House** at the Redhook Ale Brewery, 14300 NE 145th St. (② **425/483-3232**). Another excellent choice is the Barking Frog restaurant at the **Willows Lodge** (see above).

The Herbfarm Restaurant ★★★ NORTHWEST The Herbfarm, the most highly acclaimed restaurant in the Northwest, is known for its extraordinarily lavish themed meals that change with the seasons. Wild gathered vegetables, Northwest seafood and meats, organic produce, wild mushrooms, and, of course, fresh herbs from The Herbfarm gardens are the ingredients from which the restaurant creates its culinary extravaganzas. Dinners are paired with complementary Northwest wines.

The restaurant is housed in a reproduction country inn beside a contemporary Northwest-style lodge. Highlights of a dinner might include a paddlefish caviar on crisp salmon skin; rosemary-mussel skewers with cucumber kimchi; oysters with sorrel sauce; Dungeness crab and wild mushroom "handkerchiefs"; salmon in a squash blossom with lemon thyme; perch on salsify puree with parsley-lovage sauce; lamb served three ways; truffled cheese; and, for dessert, muscat-poached peaches with anise hyssop ice. Sure, it's expensive, but if you're a foodie, you need to have a dinner like this at least once in your life.

14590 NE 145th St., Woodinville. ℂ **425/485-5300.** www.theherbfarm.com. Reservations required. Fixed-price 9-course dinner $175–$195 per person with five matched wines. AE, MC, V. Seatings Thurs–Sat at 7pm; Sun at 4:30pm.

Purple Café and Wine Bar ★ NEW AMERICAN   This stylish wine bar is convenient to all the wineries in the area and is my favorite lunch spot in Woodinville. It also makes a great place for an early dinner at the end of an afternoon of wine tasting. The menu is long, and, as you would expect in a wine bar, features lots of great appetizers (including delicious grilled asparagus). Other dishes worth trying include the chopped salad and the penne pasta with gorgonzola and pancetta. However, when I eat here, I usually opt for one of Purple's perfect pizzas.

14459 Woodinville–Redmond Rd. NE. ℂ **425/483-7129.** www.thepurplecafe.com. Reservations recommended. Main courses $10–$33. AE, DISC, MC, V. Tues–Thurs 11am–9pm; Fri–Sat 11am–10pm; Sun 11am–9pm.

9 SNOHOMISH: ANTIQUES CAPITAL OF THE NORTHWEST

If antiques are your passion, you won't want to miss the opportunity to spend a day shopping the many antiques stores in the historic farm town of Snohomish. Located roughly 30 miles north of Seattle, off I-5, Snohomish was established in 1859 on the banks of the Snohomish River and was the county seat until 1897. When the county government was moved to Everett, Snohomish lost its regional importance and development slowed considerably. But an abundance of turn-of-the-20th-century buildings remained as the legacy of the town's early economic growth. By the 1960s, these old homes had begun attracting people interested in restoring the structures to their original condition, and soon antiques shops began proliferating in the historic downtown area.

Today the town has hundreds of antiques dealers and is without a doubt the antiques capital of the Northwest. Surrounding Snohomish's commercial core are neighborhoods full of restored Victorian homes. Each year on the third Sunday in September, you can get a peek inside some of the town's most elegant homes on the annual **Snohomish Historical Society Tour of Homes.** To find out more, and to pick up a guide to the town's antiques stores and historic homes, contact the **Snohomish Visitor Information Center,** 1301 First St., Snohomish (ℂ **360/862-9609;** www.cityofsnohomish.com). It's open daily from 10am to 5pm.

While in town, you should visit the **Blackman House Museum,** 118 Ave. B (ℂ **360/ 568-5235;** www.blackmanhouse.net), an 1878 Queen Anne Victorian that has been restored and filled with period furnishings. The museum is open Saturday and Sunday from 1 to 4pm; admission is by suggested $5 donation.

10 TACOMA'S MUSEUMS & GARDENS

The cities of Seattle and Tacoma have long had an intense rivalry, and though Seattle long ago claimed the title of cultural capital of Washington, Tacoma has not given up the fight. Tacoma has two world-class art museums, and for anyone with an interest in art glass and famed Northwest glass artist Dale Chihuly, these two museums are a must. If it is Dale Chihuly's work in particular that brings you to Tacoma, be sure to stop in at **Union Station,** which is just up the street from the Tacoma Art Museum and contains a large Chihuly installation.

If you're in town on the third Thursday of the month, be sure to stick around for the evening **Artwalk** (© **253/272-4327;** www.artwalktacoma.com), which runs from 5 to 8pm. Participants include more than a dozen galleries and museums.

The Tacoma area is also home to some of the most outstanding public gardens in the state. Within a 20-mile radius, you can visit two world-class bonsai collections, check out the orchids in a Victorian-era conservatory, tour an estate garden, and marvel at myriad species of rhododendrons.

To get to Tacoma from Seattle, take I-5 south for about 45 minutes. For more information on this area, contact the **Tacoma Regional Convention & Visitor Bureau,** 1119 Pacific Ave., Ste. 500, Tacoma, WA 98402 (© **800/272-2662** or 253/627-2836; www.traveltacoma.com), which has an information desk inside the Courtyard by Marriott Tacoma Downtown, 1516 Pacific St.

MUSEUMS

Museum of Glass ★★   Chihuly's work inspired the construction of this museum, which travels far and wide to bring the very best art glass to Tacoma. A vast variety of glass artworks is featured in the galleries of this high-style building on the waterfront: Whether it's stained glass in the style of Tiffany, a traveling exhibit from a European museum, or the latest thought-provoking installation by a cutting-edge glass artist, you'll find it here. The highlight is the hot shop, a huge cone-shaped studio space where visitors can watch glass artists work at several kilns. Connecting the museum to the rest of the city is the 500-foot-long Chihuly Bridge of Glass, which spans the I-705 freeway. Adjacent to this museum at 1821 E. Dock St. are the **Traver Gallery** (© **253/383-3685;** www.travergallery.com) and **Vetri International Glass** (© **253/383-3692;** www.vetri glass.com), which are outposts of Seattle's Traver Gallery, the most highly respected art-glass gallery in the region.

SIDE TRIPS FROM SEATTLE

11

TACOMA'S MUSEUMS & GARDENS

Tips   Hello Dale, Is That You?

If you're in Tacoma on a Chihuly pilgrimage, be sure to bring your cellphone and dial the **Ear for Art: Chihuly Glass Cell Phone Tour** (© **888/411-4220**). This self-guided walking tour of Chihuly art works has 12 stops. At each stop, just dial the toll-free number and punch in that stop number to learn more about the art you're seeing. You can also get a podcast of this tour by going to the Tacoma Art Museum website (www.tacomaartmuseum.org).

1801 Dock St. (C) **866/468-7386** or 253/284-4750. www.museumofglass.org. Admission $10 adults, $8 seniors, $4 children 6–12, free for children 5 and under. Free to all on 3rd Thurs of each month from 5–8pm. Memorial Day to Labor Day Mon–Sat 10am–5pm (until 8pm on 3rd Thurs of each month), Sun noon–5pm; other months closed Mon–Tues. Closed Thanksgiving, Christmas, and New Year's Day.

Tacoma Art Museum ★★   Housed in a building designed by noted contemporary architect Antoine Predock, the Tacoma Art Museum may not have as big a reputation as the Seattle Art Museum, but it mounts some impressive shows. The building is filled with beautiful galleries in which to display both the museum's own collections and traveling exhibitions. The museum is best known for its large collection of art by native son Dale Chihuly, and fans of the glass artist can sign up for a walking tour of many of his works both here in the museum and around downtown. Tours are offered a couple of days each week, cost $15, and include museum admission. The museum also has respectable collections of European Impressionism, Japanese woodblock prints, and American graphic art, and regularly brings in large traveling shows.

1701 Pacific Ave. (C) **253/272-4258.** www.tacomaartmuseum.org. Admission $7.50 adults, $6.50 seniors and students, free for children 5 and under. Free to all on 3rd Thurs of each month. Tues–Sat 10am–5pm (until 8pm on 3rd Thurs of each month), Sun noon–5pm. Closed New Year's Day, Martin Luther King, Jr. Day, Thanksgiving, and Christmas.

Washington State History Museum ★ (**Kids**)   A massive archive of Washington state history, this impressive museum is like no other history museum in the Northwest. A full barrage of high-tech displays make history both fun and interesting. From a covered wagon to a sprawling HO-scale (3.5mm: 1 ft.) model railroad layout, a Coast Salish longhouse to a Hooverville shack, the state's history comes alive through the use of life-size mannequins, recorded narration, and "overheard" conversations. With loads of interactive exhibits and several films screened daily, it's obvious this museum is trying to appeal to the video-game generation, but older visitors will have fun, too.

1911 Pacific Ave. (C) **888/238-4373** or 253/272-3500. www.wshs.org/wshm. Admission $8 adults, $7 seniors, $6 students 6–17, free for children 5 and under (free admission 3rd Thurs of each month from 2–8pm). Wed–Fri 10am–4pm; Sat–Sun 10am–5pm (open until 8pm 3rd Thurs). Closed Memorial Day, July 4, Labor Day, Thanksgiving, and Christmas.

GARDENS

You'll find more public gardens at the sprawling **Point Defiance Park,** on the north side of town at the end of Pearl Street. This is one of the largest urban parks in the country and, in addition to a rose garden, a Japanese garden, a rhododendron garden, a dahlia test garden, and a native-plant garden, is home to the Point Defiance Zoo & Aquarium, Fort Nisqually Historic Site, and the Camp 6 Logging Museum. Founded in 1888, this

---

(**Tips**)   **Wednesday Bargains**

With the **Museum of Glass,** the **Tacoma Art Museum,** and the **Washington State History Museum** all within three blocks of one another, Tacoma is an even better museum town than Seattle. You can save a little on the cost of visiting these three museums by visiting on a Wednesday when you can get into all three museums for $22 ($20 for seniors and $18 for students). For adults, this is a savings of $5.50.

(Finds) Bonsai by the Bay

Driving west from Tacoma on Wash. 16, just past the town of Port Orchard, you can't help but be curious about the odd collection of stunted trees and sculptures wedged between the highway and the waters of Sinclair Inlet. **Elandan Gardens,** 3050 W. Wash. 16 at milepost 28, Gorst (© **360/373-8260;** www. elandangardens.com), is the result of one man's passion for bonsai. The collection includes trees that are more than 1,000 years old and have been trained for decades. There are also Japanese-style gardens to wander. April through October, the gardens are open Tuesday through Sunday from 10am to 5pm; November through March, the gardens are open Friday through Sunday from 10am to 5pm. Admission is $8 for adults and $1 for children under 12. The gardens are closed in January.

park preserved one of the region's most scenic points of land. Winding through the wooded park is **Five Mile Drive,** which connects all the park's main attractions, as well as picnic areas, and hiking and biking trails. You can reach the park by following Ruston Way or Pearl Street north.

Lakewold Gardens ★   Formerly a private estate, this 10-acre garden 10 miles south of Tacoma was designed in the late 1950s by noted landscape architect Thomas Church. The gardens here include extensive collections of Japanese maples and rhododendrons. There are also rose, fern, and alpine gardens that include numerous rare and unusual plants.

12317 Gravelly Lake Dr. SW, Lakewood. © **888/858-4106** or 253/584-4106. www.lakewoldgardens.org. Admission $7 adults, $5 seniors and students, free for children 12 and under. Apr–Sept Wed–Sun 10am–4pm; Oct–Nov and Feb–Mar Fri–Sun 10am–3pm; Dec–Jan Fri 10am–3pm. Take exit 124 off I-5.

Rhododendron Species Foundation and Botanical Garden ★★   Covering 22 acres, this garden 8 miles north of Tacoma has one of the most extensive collections of species (unhybridized) rhododendrons and azaleas in the world. More than 10,000 plants put on an amazing floral display from March through May. Also included in these gardens are collections of ferns, maples, heathers, and bamboos. For serious gardeners, this is one of the Northwest's garden musts.

2525 S. 336th St., Weyerhaeuser corporate campus, Federal Way. © **253/838-4646.** www.rhodygarden. org. Admission $5 adults, $3 seniors and students, free for children 11 and under. Free admission Nov–Feb. Mar–Sept Fri–Wed 10am–4pm; Oct–Feb Sat–Wed 11am–4pm. Take exit 143 off I-5.

W. W. Seymour Botanical Conservatory ★   Constructed in 1908, this elegant Victorian conservatory is one of only three of this type on the West Coast and is listed on the National Register of Historic Places. More than 250 species of exotic plants (including more than 200 orchids) are housed in the huge greenhouse, which is built of more than 3,000 panes of glass. The conservatory stands in downtown Tacoma's Wright Park, which is a shady retreat from downtown's pavement.

Wright Park, 316 S. G St. © **253/591-5330.** www.metroparkstacoma.org. Free admission. Tues–Sun 10am–4:30pm. Closed Thanksgiving, first 4 days of Dec, Christmas, and New Year's Day.

If you're just looking for someplace interesting to have a drink or an inexpensive meal, check out **The Swiss,** 1904 S. Jefferson Ave. (📞 **253/572-2821;** www.theswisspub. com), just uphill from the Washington State History Museum at the top of a long flight of stairs that links the museum with the University of Washington Tacoma campus. The pub has not only a great beer selection and decent food, but also a collection of Dale Chihuly glass sculptures. *Note:* Because this is a pub, you must be 21 or older to eat here.

Harmon Pub & Brewery ★ AMERICAN   In a renovated old commercial building across from the Washington State History Museum, this large pub is Tacoma's favorite downtown after-work hangout and business-lunch spot. The menu features primarily burgers and pizza, plus some interesting specials and, of course, plenty of good micro-brews. The pub has an outdoors theme.

1938 Pacific Ave. 📞 **253/383-2739.** www.harmonbrewing.com. Reservations not accepted. Main courses $9.50–$17. AE, DISC, MC, V. Mon–Thurs 11am–11pm; Fri–Sat 11am–midnight; Sun 11am–9:30pm.

11 MOUNT ST. HELENS NATIONAL VOLCANIC MONUMENT

Once it was regarded as the most perfect of the Cascade peaks, a snow-covered cone rising above lush forests—but on May 18, 1980, all that changed. On that day a massive volcanic eruption blew out the entire north side of Mount St. Helens, laying waste to a vast area and darkening the skies of the Northwest with billowing clouds of ash. In the quarter-century since the eruption, life has slowly returned to the blast zone, and today, both the massive destruction and the slow process of regeneration can be witnessed at the Mount St. Helens National Volcanic Monument.

In the fall of 2004, the volcano awoke from many years of relative quiet, and the lava dome inside the volcano's crater began growing again. Plumes of ash were once again seen billowing from the volcano on an irregular basis, and this increased activity attracted lots of curious visitors. In response to the volcanic activity, summit climbs were sometimes halted and parts of the monument were occasionally closed to the public. By 2009, the volcano was once again quiet, but officials continue to closely monitor the volcano's activity. If things heat up again, you can count on more closures.

The monument is roughly 160 miles south of Seattle, off I-5 (take the Castle Rock exit). Admission to the monument's two main visitor centers is $8 for adults and free for children 15 and under. If you just want to park at one of the monument's trail heads and go for a hike, all you need is a valid Northwest Forest Pass, which costs $5 per day. In winter you'll need a Sno-Park permit, which costs $10 to $11 per day. For more information, contact **Mount St. Helens National Volcanic Monument** (📞 **360/449-7800;** www.fs.fed.us/gpnf/mshnvm).

The best place to start an exploration of the monument is the **Mount St. Helens Visitor Center at Silver Lake** (📞 **360/274-0962;** www.parks.wa.gov/mountsthelens. asp), which is operated by Washington State Parks and is located at Silver Lake, 5 miles east of Castle Rock on Wash. 504. The visitor center houses extensive exhibits on the eruption and its effects on the region. Mid-May through September, it's open daily from

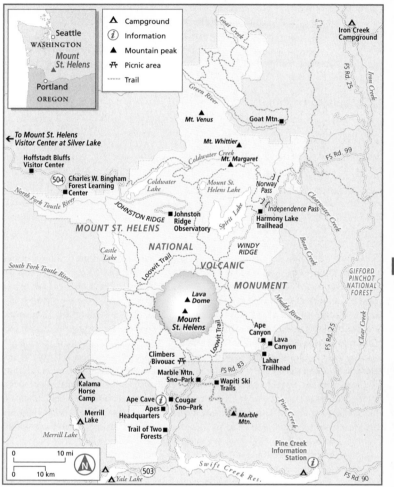

9am to 5pm (until 4pm in other months; Jan–Mar closed Tues–Wed). Admission is $3 for adults, $1 for children 7 to 17, and free for children 6 and under. A family pass is $8.

Continuing east from the visitor center, at milepost 27, you'll come to the **Hoffstadt Bluffs Visitor Center,** 15000 Spirit Lake Hwy. (© **360/274-5200;** www.hoffstadtbluffs. com). This is primarily a snack bar and takeoff site for 30-minute helicopter flights over Mount St. Helens ($169 per person), but it also has great views. In summer, this visitor center is open daily from 9am to 7pm; other months, it's open Thursday through Monday from 9am to 7pm.

A few miles farther, just past milepost 33, is the **Charles W. Bingham Forest Learning Center at Mount St. Helens** (✆ 360/274-7750; www.mountsthelens.com/Forest-Learning-Center.html), open mid-May through mid-October daily from 10am to 6pm (until 5pm in Oct). This is primarily a promotional center for the timber industry, but, in a theater designed to resemble an ash-covered landscape, you can watch a short, fascinating video about the eruption. Outside both the Hoffstadt Bluffs Visitor Center and the Forest Learning Center, you can usually see numerous elk on the floor of the Toutle River Valley far below.

Of the many visitor centers, none offers a more awe-inspiring view than that from the **Johnston Ridge Observatory**, 24000 Spirit Lake Hwy. (✆ 360/274-2140). Built into the mountainside and designed to blend into the landscape, this observatory houses the equipment that is still used to monitor activity within Mount St. Helens. The observatory is open from mid-May to October, daily from 10am to 6pm. If you're up for a bit of hiking, the best choice on this side of the monument is the **Boundary Trail,** which heads east from the Johnston Ridge Observatory, with a jaw-dropping view of the blast zone the entire way. This trail leads for many miles across the monument, so you can hike as much or as little as you want, although it does lead along a very precipitous mountainside that for many hikers is just too steep and scary to cross. There is a good turnaround point about 1 mile out from the observatory.

For a different perspective on the devastation wrought by Mount St. Helens's eruption, drive around to the mountain's east side and take the road up to Windy Ridge. Although it takes a couple of hours longer to get to this side of the mountain, you will be rewarded with equally amazing views, better hiking opportunities, and smaller crowds. To reach the east side of the mountain, take U.S. 12 east from exit 68 off I-5. In Randle, head south on Forest Road 25 and watch for Forest Road 99, the road to the Windy Ridge Viewpoint. This road crosses many miles of blown-down trees that were felled by a single blast, a reminder of the awesome power of nature. More than a quarter-century after the eruption, life is slowly returning to the devastated forest. At the **Windy Ridge Viewpoint,** visitors get one of the best close-up views of the crater. A long staircase climbs more than 200 feet up the hill above the parking area for even better views. Below Windy Ridge lies Spirit Lake, once one of the most popular summer vacation spots in the Washington Cascades. Today the lake is desolate and lifeless. The 1-mile **Harmony Trail** leads down to the shore of Spirit Lake and is a very worthwhile hike; just keep in mind that it's a 600-foot climb back up to the trail head parking lot.

If you're an experienced hiker in good physical condition, the climb to the summit of Mount St. Helens is a must. From the trail head on the south side of the mountain, the hike takes 8 to 10 hours and can require an ice ax. Climbing permits, which cost $22 between April and October and are free other months, are required and are only available through the **Mount St. Helens Institute**, 42218 NE Yale Bridge Rd., Amboy, WA 98601 (✆ 360/449-7887; www.mshinstitute.org). Because the climb is very popular, you'll need to make a reservation. Reservations are taken beginning in early February, and summer weekends book up fast. Between November 1 and March 31, no reservation is necessary—but expect lots of snow. Due to volcanic activity in recent years, the rim is sometimes closed to hikers, so be sure to check the current status before planning this climb.

On the south side of the monument, you can explore the **Ape Cave,** a lava tube that was formed 1,900 years ago when lava poured from the volcano. When the lava finally stopped flowing, it left a 2-mile-long cave that is the longest continuous lava tube in the

June and Labor Day, you can join a regular ranger-led exploration of the cave or rent a lantern ($5) to explore on your own.

If you'd like to turn a visit to Mount St. Helens into a learning vacation, check the schedule of seminars being offered by the **Mount St. Helens Institute,** 42218 NE Yale Bridge Rd., Amboy, WA 98601 (℃ **360/449-7887;** www.mshinstitute.org).

Fast Facts

1 FAST FACTS: SEATTLE

AREA CODES The area code is **206** in Seattle, **425** for the Eastside (including Kirkland and Bellevue), and **253** for south King County (near the airport).

ATM NETWORKS See "Money & Costs," p. 31.

AUTOMOBILE ORGANIZATIONS Motor clubs will supply maps, suggested routes, guidebooks, accident and bail-bond insurance, and emergency road service. The **American Automobile Association (AAA)** is the major auto club in the United States. If you belong to a motor club in your home country, inquire about AAA reciprocity before you leave. You may be able to join AAA even if you're not a member of a reciprocal club; to inquire, call AAA (✆ **800/ 222-4357; www.aaa.com**). AAA is actually an organization of regional motor clubs, so look under "AAA Automobile Club" in the White Pages of the telephone directory. AAA has a nationwide emergency road service telephone number (✆ 800/AAA-HELP).

BUSINESS HOURS The following are general hours; specific establishments' hours may vary. Banks are open Monday through Friday from 9am to 5pm (some also Sat 9am–noon). Stores are open Monday through Saturday from 10am to 6pm, and Sunday from noon to 5pm (malls usually stay open Mon–Sat until 9pm). Bars are legally allowed to be open until 2am.

DRINKING LAWS The legal age for purchase and consumption of alcoholic beverages is 21; proof of age is often required at bars, nightclubs, and restaurants, so it's always a good idea to bring ID when you go out. Do not carry open containers of alcohol in your car or any public area that isn't zoned for alcohol consumption. The police can fine you on the spot. And nothing will ruin your trip faster than getting a citation for DUI (driving under the influence), so don't even think about driving while intoxicated.

DRIVING RULES See "Getting There & Getting Around," p. 24.

ELECTRICITY Like Canada, the United States uses 110 to 120 volts AC (60 cycles), compared to 220 to 240 volts AC (50 cycles) in most of Europe, Australia, and New Zealand. Downward converters that change 220–240 volts to 110–120 volts are difficult to find in the United States, so bring one with you.

EMBASSIES & CONSULATES All embassies are located in the nation's capital, Washington, D.C. Some consulates are located in major U.S. cities, and most nations have a mission to the United Nations in New York City. If your country isn't listed below, call for directory information in Washington, D.C. (✆ **202/ 555-1212**) or check **www.embassy.org/ embassies**.

The embassy of **Australia** is at 1601 Massachusetts Ave. NW, Washington, DC 20036 (✆ **202/797-3000; www.austemb. org**). There are consulates in New York, Honolulu, Houston, Los Angeles, and San Francisco.

The embassy of **Canada** is at 501 Pennsylvania Ave. NW, Washington, DC 20001 (© **202/682-1740;** www.canadian emb.org). Other Canadian consulates are in Buffalo (New York), Detroit, Los Angeles, New York, and Seattle.

The embassy of **Ireland** is at 2234 Massachusetts Ave. NW, Washington, DC 20008 (© **202/462-3939;** www.ireland emb.org). Irish consulates are in Boston, Chicago, New York, San Francisco, and other cities. See website for complete listing.

The embassy of **New Zealand** is at 37 Observatory Circle NW, Washington, DC 20008 (© **202/328-4800;** www.nzemb. org). New Zealand consulates are in Los Angeles, Salt Lake City, San Francisco, and Seattle.

The embassy of the **United Kingdom** is at 3100 Massachusetts Ave. NW, Washington, DC 20008 (© **202/588-7800;** www.britainusa.com). Other British consulates are in Atlanta, Boston, Chicago, Cleveland, Houston, Los Angeles, New York, San Francisco, and Seattle.

EMERGENCIES   Call © **911** to report a fire, call the police, or get an ambulance anywhere in the U.S. This is a toll-free call. (No coins are required at public telephones.)

GASOLINE (PETROL)   At press time, in the U.S., the cost of gasoline (also known as gas, but never petrol) is running close to $3 per gallon in most places. Taxes are already included in the printed price. One U.S. gallon equals 3.8 liters or .85 imperial gallons. Fill-up locations are primarily known as gas stations.

HOLIDAYS   Banks, government offices, post offices, and many stores, restaurants, and museums are closed on the following legal national holidays: January 1 (New Year's Day), the third Monday in January (Martin Luther King, Jr., Day), the third Monday in February (Presidents' Day), the last Monday in May (Memorial Day), July 4 (Independence Day), the first Monday in September (Labor Day), the second Monday in October (Columbus Day), November 11 (Veterans' Day/Armistice Day), the fourth Thursday in November (Thanksgiving Day), and December 25 (Christmas). The Tuesday after the first Monday in November is Election Day, a federal government holiday in presidential-election years (held every 4 years, and next in 2012).

For more information on holidays, see "Seattle Calendar of Events," in chapter 3.

LEGAL AID   If you are "pulled over" for a minor infraction (such as speeding), never attempt to pay the fine directly to a police officer; this could be construed as attempted bribery, a much more serious crime. Pay fines by mail or directly into the hands of the clerk of the court. If accused of a more serious offense, say and do nothing before consulting a lawyer. Here the burden is on the state to prove a person's guilt beyond a reasonable doubt, and everyone has the right to remain silent, whether he or she is suspected of a crime or actually arrested. Once arrested, a person can make one telephone call to a party of his or her choice. International visitors should call their embassy or consulate.

LOST & FOUND   Be sure to tell all your credit card companies the minute you discover your wallet has been lost or stolen and file a report at the nearest police precinct. Your credit card company or insurer may require a police report number or record of the loss. Most credit card companies have an emergency toll-free number to call if your card is lost or stolen; they may be able to wire you a cash advance immediately or deliver an emergency credit card in a day or two. Visa's U.S. emergency number is © **800/847-2911** or 410/581-9994. American Express cardholders and traveler's check holders should call © **800/221-7282.** MasterCard holders should call ✆ **800/307-7309** or 636/722-7111. For other credit cards, call the toll-free number directory at ✆ **800/ 555-1212.**

If you need emergency cash over the weekend when all banks and American Express offices are closed, you can have money wired to you via **Western Union** (✆ **800/325-6000;** www.westernunion. com).

MAIL At press time, domestic postage rates are 28¢ for a postcard and 44¢ for a letter. For international mail, a first-class letter of up to 1 ounce costs 98¢ (75¢ to Canada and 79¢ to Mexico); a first-class postcard costs the same as a letter. For more information, go to **www.usps.com** and click on "Calculate Postage."

If you aren't sure what your address will be in the United States, mail can be sent to you, in your name, c/o General Delivery at the main post office of the city or region where you expect to be. (Call ✆ **800/275-8777** for information on the nearest post office.) The addressee must pick up mail in person and must produce proof of identity (driver's license, passport, and so forth). Most post offices will hold your mail for up to 1 month, and are open Monday to Friday from 8am to 6pm, and Saturday from 9am to 3pm.

Always include zip codes when mailing items in the U.S. If you don't know your zip code, visit www.usps.com/zip4.

MEDICAL CONDITIONS If you have a medical condition that requires **syringe-administered medications,** carry a valid signed prescription from your physician; syringes in carry-on baggage will be inspected. Insulin in any form should have the proper pharmaceutical documentation. If you have a disease that requires treatment with **narcotics,** you should also carry documented proof with you—smuggling narcotics aboard a plane carries severe penalties in the U.S.

For **HIV-positive visitors,** requirements for entering the United States are somewhat vague and change frequently. For up-to-the-minute information, contact **AIDSinfo** (✆ **800/448-0440** or 301/ 519-6616 outside the U.S.; www.aidsinfo. nih.gov) or the **Gay Men's Health Crisis** (✆ **212/367-1000;** www.gmhc.org).

MEDICAL INSURANCE Although it's not required of travelers, health insurance is highly recommended. Most health insurance policies cover you if you get sick away from home—but check your coverage before you leave.

International visitors to the U.S. should note that unlike many European countries, the United States does not usually offer free or low-cost medical care to its citizens or visitors. Doctors and hospitals are expensive, and in most cases will require advance payment or proof of coverage before they render their services. Good policies will cover the costs of an accident, repatriation, or death. Packages such as **Europ Assistance's Worldwide Healthcare Plan** are sold by European automobile clubs and travel agencies at attractive rates. **Worldwide Assistance Services, Inc.** (✆ **800/777-8710;** www. worldwideassistance.com) is the agent for Europ Assistance in the United States.

Though lack of health insurance may prevent you from being admitted to a hospital in non-emergencies, don't worry about being left on a street corner to die: The American way is to fix you now and bill the daylights out of you later.

If you're ever hospitalized more than 150 miles from home, **MedjetAssist** (✆ **800/527-7478;** www.medjetassistance. com) will pick you up and fly you to the hospital of your choice in a medically equipped and staffed aircraft 24 hours a day, 7 days a week. Annual memberships are $225 individual, $350 family; you can also purchase short-term memberships.

Canadians should check with their provincial health plan offices or call **Health Canada** (📞 866/225-0709; www. hc-sc.gc.ca) to find out the extent of their coverage and what documentation and receipts they must take home in case they are treated in the United States.

Travelers from the U.K. should carry their European Health Insurance Card (EHIC), which replaced the E111 form as proof of entitlement to free/reduced cost medical treatment abroad (📞 **0845/606-2030;** www.ehic.org.uk). Note, however, that the EHIC only covers "necessary medical treatment," and for repatriation costs, lost money, baggage, or cancellation, travel insurance from a reputable company should always be sought (www.travelinsuranceweb. com).

NEWSPAPERS & MAGAZINES The *Seattle Times* is Seattle's daily newspaper. *Seattle Weekly* is the city's free arts-and-entertainment weekly.

PASSPORTS The websites listed provide downloadable passport applications as well as the current fees for processing applications. For an up-to-date, country-by-country listing of passport requirements around the world, go to the "International Travel" tab of the U.S. State Department at **http://travel.state.gov**. International visitors to the U.S. can obtain a visa application at the same website. *Note:* Children are required to present a passport when entering the United States at airports. More information on obtaining a passport for a minor can be found at www.travel.state.gov. Allow plenty of time before your trip to apply for a passport; processing normally takes 4 to 6 weeks (3 weeks for expedited service) but can take longer during busy periods (especially spring). And keep in mind that if you need a passport in a hurry, you'll pay a higher processing fee.

For Residents of Australia You can pick up an application from your local post office or any branch of Passports Australia, but you must schedule an interview at the passport office to present your application materials. Call the **Australian Passport Information Service** at 📞 **131-232,** or visit the government website at www. passports.gov.au.

For Residents of Canada Passport applications are available at travel agencies throughout Canada or from the central **Passport Office,** Department of Foreign Affairs and International Trade, Ottawa, ON K1A 0G3 (📞 **800/567-6868;** www. ppt.gc.ca). *Note:* Canadian children who travel must have their own passport. However, if you hold a valid Canadian passport issued before December 11, 2001, that bears the name of your child, the passport remains valid for you and your child until it expires.

For Residents of Ireland You can apply for a 10-year passport at the **Passport Office,** Setanta Centre, Molesworth Street, Dublin 2 (📞 **01/671-1633;** www. irlgov.ie/iveagh). Those under age 18 and over 65 must apply for a 3-year passport. You can also apply at 1A South Mall, Cork (📞 **21/494-4700**) or at most main post offices.

For Residents of New Zealand You can pick up a passport application at any New Zealand Passports Office or download one from the website. Contact the **Passports Office** at 📞 **0800/225-050** in New Zealand or 04/474-8100, or log on to www. passports.govt.nz.

For Residents of the United Kingdom To pick up an application for a standard 10-year passport (5-yr. passport for children under 16), visit your nearest passport office, major post office, or travel agency, or contact the **United Kingdom Passport Service** at 📞 **0870/521-0410** or search its website at www.ukpa.gov.uk.

POLICE For police emergencies, phone 📞 **911.**

TAXES The U.S. has no value-added tax (VAT) or other indirect tax at the national level. Every state, county, and city may levy its own local tax on all purchases, including hotel and restaurant checks and airline tickets. These taxes will not appear on price tags.

Seattle has a 9.5% sales tax. In restaurants, there's an additional .5% food-and-beverage tax. The hotel-room tax in Seattle is 15.6%. On rental cars, you pay an 19.2% tax, plus, if you rent at the airport, an 11.1% airport concession fee (plus several other fees for a total of around 40%!).

TELEGRAPH, TELEX & FAX **Telegraph and telex services** are provided primarily by **Western Union** (✆ **800/325-6000;** www.westernunion.com). You can telegraph (wire) money, or have it telegraphed to you, very quickly over the Western Union system, but this service can cost as much as 15% to 20% of the amount sent.

Most hotels have **fax machines** available for guest use (be sure to ask about the charge to use it). Many hotel rooms are wired for guests' fax machines. A less expensive way to send and receive faxes may be at stores such as **The UPS Store.**

TIME The continental United States is divided into **four time zones:** Eastern Standard Time (EST), Central Standard Time (CST), Mountain Standard Time (MST), and Pacific Standard Time (PST). Alaska and Hawaii have their own zones. For example, when it's 9am in Los Angeles (PST), it's 7am in Honolulu (HST), 10am in Denver (MST), 11am in Chicago (CST), noon in New York City (EST), 5pm in London (GMT), and 2am the next day in Sydney.

Daylight saving time is in effect from 1am on the second Sunday in March to 1am on the first Sunday in November, except in Arizona, Hawaii, the U.S. Virgin Islands, and Puerto Rico. Daylight saving time moves the clock 1 hour ahead of

standard time. Seattle is in the Pacific Standard Time zone.

TIPPING Tips are a very important part of certain workers' income, and gratuities are the standard way of showing appreciation for services provided. (Tipping is certainly not compulsory if the service is poor!) In hotels, tip **bellhops** at least $1 per bag ($2–$3 if you have a lot of luggage) and tip the **chamber staff** $1 to $2 per day (more if you've left a disaster area for him or her to clean up). Tip the **doorman** or **concierge** only if he or she has provided you with some specific service (for example, calling a cab for you or obtaining difficult-to-get theater tickets). Tip the **valet-parking attendant** $1 every time you get your car.

In restaurants, bars, and nightclubs, tip **service staff** 15% to 20% of the check, tip **bartenders** 15% to 20%, tip **checkroom attendants** $1 per garment, and tip **valet-parking attendants** $1 per vehicle.

As for other service personnel, tip **cab drivers** 15% of the fare; tip **skycaps** at airports at least $1 per bag ($2–$3 if you have a lot of luggage); and tip **hairdressers** and **barbers** 15% to 20%.

TOILETS You won't find public toilets or "restrooms" on the streets in most U.S. cities, but they can be found in hotel lobbies, bars, restaurants, museums, department stores, railway and bus stations, and service stations. Large hotels and fast-food restaurants are often the best bet for clean facilities. Restaurants and bars in resorts or heavily visited areas may reserve their restrooms for patrons.

VISAS For information about U.S. visas, go to **http://travel.state.gov** and click on "Visas." Or go to one of the following websites:

Australian citizens can obtain up-to-date visa information from the **U.S. Embassy Canberra,** Moonah Place, Yarralumla, ACT 2600 (✆ **02/6214-5600**), or by checking the U.S. Diplomatic

Mission's website at **http://usembassy-australia.state.gov/consular.**

British subjects can obtain up-to-date visa information by calling the **U.S. Embassy Visa Information Line** (✆ **0891/ 200-290**) or by visiting the "Visas to the U.S." section of the American Embassy London's website at **www.usembassy.org.uk.**

Irish citizens can obtain up-to-date visa information through the **Embassy of the USA Dublin,** 42 Elgin Rd., Dublin 4,

Ireland (✆ **353/1-668-8777**), or by checking the "Consular Services" section of the website at **http://dublin.us embassy.gov.**

Citizens of **New Zealand** can obtain up-to-date visa information by contacting the **U.S. Embassy New Zealand,** 29 Fitzherbert Terrace, Thorndon, Wellington (✆ **644/472-2068**), or get the information directly from the website at **http:// wellington.usembassy.gov.**

2 AIRLINE, HOTEL & CAR RENTAL WEBSITES

MAJOR AIRLINES

Aeroméxico
www.aeromexico.com

Air Canada
www.aircanada.ca

Air France
www.airfrance.com

Alaska Airlines/Horizon Air
www.alaskaair.com

American Airlines
www.aa.com

Asiana Airlines
http://us.flyasiana.com

British Airways
www.british-airways.com

Continental Airlines
www.continental.com

Delta Air Lines
www.delta.com

EVA Air
www.evaair.com

Hawaiian Airlines
www.hawaiianair.com

Icelandair
www.icelandair.com

Korean Air
www.koreanair.com

Lufthansa
www.lufthansa.com

Midwest Airlines
www.midwestairlines.com

Scandinavian Airlines
www.scandinavian.net

Sun Country Airlines
www.suncountry.com

United Airlines
www.united.com

US Airways
www.usairways.com

Virgin America
www.virginamerica.com

BUDGET AIRLINES

AirTran Airways
www.airtran.com

Frontier Airlines
www.frontierairlines.com

JetBlue Airways
www.jetblue.com

Southwest Airlines
www.southwest.com

Best Western International
www.bestwestern.com

Clarion Hotels
www.choicehotels.com

Comfort Inns
www.ComfortInn.com

Courtyard by Marriott
www.marriott.com/courtyard

Crowne Plaza Hotels
www.ichotelsgroup.com/crowneplaza

Days Inn
www.daysinn.com

Doubletree Hotels
www.doubletree.com

Econo Lodges
www.choicehotels.com

Embassy Suites
www.embassysuites.com

ExtendedStay America
www.extendedstayamerica.com

Farfield Inn by Marriott
www.farfieldinn.com

Four Seasons
www.fourseasons.com

Hampton Inn
www.hamptoninn1.hilton.com

Hilton Hotels
www.hilton.com

Holiday Inn
www.holidayinn.com

Howard Johnson
www.hojo.com

Hyatt
www.hyatt.com

La Quinta Inns and Suites
www.lq.com

Loews Hotels
www.loewshotels.com

Marriott
www.marriott.com

Motel 6
www.motel6.com

Quality
www.QualityInn.ChoiceHotels.com

Radisson Hotels & Resorts
www.radisson.com

Ramada Worldwide
www.ramada.com

Red Lion Hotels
www.redlion.rdln.com

Red Roof Inns
www.redroof.com

Renaissance
www.renaissancehotels.com

Residence Inn by Marriott
www.marriott.com/residenceinn

Rodeway Inns
www.RodewayInn.com

Sheraton Hotels & Resorts
www.starwoodhotels.com/sheraton

Super 8 Motels
www.super8.com

Travelodge
www.travelodge.com

Westin Hotels & Resorts
www.starwoodhotels.com/westin

Wyndham Hotels & Resorts
www.wyndham.com

CAR RENTAL AGENCIES

Advantage
www.advantage.com

Alamo
www.alamo.com

Avis
www.avis.com

Budget
www.budget.com

Dollar
www.dollar.com

Enterprise
www.enterprise.com

Hertz
www.hertz.com

National
www.nationalcar.com

Thrifty
www.thrifty.com

FAST FACTS

12

AIRLINE, HOTEL & CAR RENTAL WEBSITES

INDEX

See also Accommodations and Restaurant indexes, below.

Visitor Ctr pg-126 ———— NOTES ————